American

Ethical

Thought

Guy W. Stroh

Nelson-Hall nh Chicago

Library of Congress Cataloging in Publication Data

Stroh, Guy W
 American ethical thought.

 Bibliography: p.
 Includes index.
 1. Ethics—United States—History. I. Title.
BJ352.S87   170'.973   79-891
ISBN 0-88229-356-7

Manufactured in the United States of America

10 9 8 7 6 5 4 3 2 1

To my wife, Marion

Contents

To be an American is of itself almost a moral condition, an education, and a career.

George Santayana:
Character and Opinion in the United States

Preface

At no point in our history more than at present has the subject of American ethics been of greater significance and concern. After the 200th anniversary of our nation's birth, in the wake of the moral crises and public agony over the Vietnam War, Watergate, racial tensions, and a burgeoning crime rate, Americans are today facing and asking a series of real and perplexing ethical questions. Some of the questions have been asked before; some are largely rhetorical; but some indeed are new and all too urgent. We want to know about the ethics of our public officials, large corporations, law enforcement agencies, and political contributors. We want to know how to reduce the alarming crime rate; what can be done about traffic in drugs and the problem of addiction; what to do about rape, abortion, and pornography. In short, today we are concerned with the most difficult questions of personal and social ethics.

Correspondingly, after a period of relative detachment from substantive ethical questions, many American philosophers are turning from the exclusively epistemological and linguistic analysis of ethics to some of the same issues that so greatly concern the public.

These present interests and issues demand a careful examination of our ethical traditions, one which focuses attention on the central ideas, issues, and thinkers which have been and continue to be most influential. By careful study and evaluation of the main traditions of our ethical past, we will be in a better position to face and understand our present ethical situations. This book seeks to provide the reader with an understanding of the most important moral ideas and issues that the American experience has produced. While not pretending to discuss all the ideas, issues, and thinkers included in the American tradition, it does claim to examine those of greatest prominence and significance.

This book should prove interesting to the concerned American citizen who reads about these moral issues in his daily newspaper as well as to the college student who also faces these problems and studies them from various points of view in his regular course work. Many current college courses in sociology, economics, political science, and philosophy, as well as those in departments of education, business, and interdisciplinary studies, definitely concern themselves with ethical questions. Both instructors and students demonstrate the need to come to grips with the central moral problems of our time in their attempts to make courses more relevant.

This book is designed to help the intelligent layman and the student understand the key questions and issues that appear in American ethics. It intentionally focuses attention on the most important issues, ideas, and thinkers in order to develop a coherent and meaningful context for the reader to understand and appreciate the moral issues of today.

Each central issue is placed in its historical context. Ideas and arguments are presented in a way that tries to be faithful to the individuals who created or advocated them. Also included is a critical assessment of each major period or thinker which should encourage the reader to judge and evaluate these issues in the light of his own interests and ideas. Ethics, after all, is not a neutral subject; it flourishes in controversy and prompts all of us to take some stand.

American ethics is important to us because we are Americans, and because we can neither escape from judging our own values and lives, nor from having our values and lives constantly judged by others. Nor can we accept any simple answers or opinions as truth in something as important as morals. Unable to evade these issues and to accept or adopt any facile answers or resolutions, we must make our own responsible choices and decisions. If this book encourages the reader to clarify his own ethical beliefs and to increase his own ethical insight by studying some of the best ideas that this country has produced, its aim will have been amply fulfilled.

Introduction

From the very beginning ethical concerns and issues have been an integral part of American life and culture. At every major turning point in American history—in times of war, economic crisis, rapid social change, and prosperity—we can find a number of important ethical concerns and issues engaging the minds and lives of people. These ethical issues are, to be sure, invariably bound up with religious, political, legal, economic, and other concerns. Moral issues involve complex, many-sided questions with important implications for religion, government, and law as well as for the ethics or morality of individuals. And it is this very interconnection between ethical and political, religious, economic and other endeavors that makes ethics so important.

Basically, ethics signifies a code of conduct or set of principles that is used to guide and explain one's moral life. We speak of medical ethics or business ethics as a set of ideas that clarify, approve, and disapprove of certain forms of conduct for doctors or businessmen. We say it is unethical for a doctor to betray the confidence of a patient or for a businessman to cheat a client. While it is rather obvious that one's ethics has practical implications or consequences, not so obvious is that one's ethics has a philosophy behind it, implicitly at least. Since any code of conduct is inextricably bound to the rest of life, such a code must rest on philosophical assumptions that express a view of man's place in the universe. What has traditionally been called moral philosophy is in reality the attempt of various thinkers to clarify, criticize, and explain the ethical concerns of man. Of course man practiced a morality long before he theorized about it. In fact it is difficult for us to imagine what we should identify as human life as being without moral or ethical concerns of some sort. Indifference to or ignorance of all differences of moral right or wrong would indicate something less or other than what we call human. Equally significant, however, is the fact that serious differences of opinion over many moral issues have always existed. Controversy and disagreement in ethics has been apparent not only among philosophers but also throughout the general public. American ethics has been no exception to this. From Puritan beginnings to the present, American ethics has been replete with numerous important controversies and issues that have aroused considerable public debate while engaging the minds of some of its greatest thinkers. What are these central issues? What ideas do they involve? And what thinkers have argued them with the greatest force and skill?

To locate these issues in terms of the ideas and men that articulate them, it is instructive to look at the historical development of American ethics by focusing on its main periods: the early period roughly from the early eighteenth century to the Civil War; the modern or classical period from the Civil War to World War II; and the recent or contemporary period. Each of these periods contains its own characteristic ethical problems as well as a number of central thinkers whose writings form the principal resource for understanding the primary ethical concerns of that time.

American ethics begins with the New England Puritans and their attempt to define, live by, and justify a God-centered morality in the strictest possible terms. Consequently the central issues for Puritan Ethics were:

(1) How is true virtue to be defined?

(2) How is true virtue to be attained if man is by his very nature sinful and even depraved?

(3) How is man's predestination to be explained, since common sense tends toward belief in free will or choice but God's preknowl-

edge of all events implies that man is not really free to choose but is predestined in all his choices and actions by what the divine being permits him to do?

(4) How is the ethical goodness of the divine being itself to be explained given the premise that He in fact permits men to sin or creates them in full knowledge that they will sin?

These central issues of Puritan Ethics revolved around the attempt to maintain a highly religious morality or what may be termed a theological ethics.

Jonathan Edwards (1703-1758) was the thinker who gave the most forceful and skillful philosophical formulation of Puritan Ethics. Edwards served most of his career as a clergyman in Massachusetts; in 1757, the year before his death, he was chosen President of the College of New Jersey, now Princeton University. Principally in his two works, *The Nature of True Virtue* and *Freedom of the Will*, Edwards carefully articulated and defended an ethics based on predestination. The doctrines that Edwards defended were based on Christian doctrine as interpreted by John Calvin (1509-1564). What was original and important in Edwards' writings was his subtlety and depth of philosophical insight. In defending the notions of original sin and predestination, Edwards gave American Puritanism its most sophisticated articulation. And although Puritanism eventually lost its hold on American life, its influence has remained. Later developments in American ethics could only come into their own by throwing off the Puritan influence or by incorporating Puritan ideas.

This is certainly the case with respect to Enlightenment Ethics. During the second half of the eighteenth century, the Founding Fathers were not only interested in political independence but were vitally concerned with religious and moral freedom. Such men as Thomas Jefferson, Benjamin Franklin, and Thomas Paine not only led in the cause of freeing America from British domination, but they were also moral leaders seeking to free the mind of man from ignorance, superstition, and all forms of tyranny. In agreement with the Puritans, the thinkers of the American Enlightenment believed that the universe definitely displayed a moral order. But they interpreted this idea as natural rather than supernatural and sought to expound an ethics of the natural rights of man. The central issues of Enlightenment Ethics were the following:

(1) How can moral virtue be explained as natural to man?

(2) To what things does man have a natural right?

(3) How can these natural rights or freedoms be made secure (i.e., how can such vital needs as freedom of speech, freedom of religion, and freedom from all forms of tyranny over the mind be secured and made to work)?

(4) How can a free or democratic society be made to function under a rule of reason?

(5) How can all forms of human slavery be eradicated, especially the importation, buying, and selling of the Negro?

Thomas Jefferson (1743-1826) gave by far the most forceful and skillful formulation of Enlightenment Ethics. In his original draft of the *Declaration of Independence, Notes on the State of Virginia, Autobiography,* and extensive correspondence, Jefferson articulated the philosophical foundations of Enlightenment Ethics better than any other American. Jefferson drew on his vast knowledge of classical and European authors for many of his ideas. But at the same time he managed to fashion his own distinct version of Enlightenment Ethics in simple yet forceful terms. Because Jefferson was in the forefront of America's struggle for independence and self-government, he wielded an immense influence that is clearly felt to the present day. As Minister to France, Secretary of State under Washington, Vice-President under Adams, President for two terms, and founder and first president of the University of Virginia, Jefferson's hand and pen were deeply involved in shaping the destiny of America. Jefferson lived to see the results of his many efforts brought to fruition in the presidencies of Madison and Monroe, and he lived to observe the fiftieth anniversary of the Declaration of Independence in 1826.

By the 1830's, the literary efforts of the New England Transcendentalists had begun to flower. Such writers as Ralph Waldo Emerson (1803-1882) and Henry David Thoreau (1817-1862) were the intellectual leaders in formulating the new romantic outlook on life that has come to be called American Transcendentalism. In such beautifully written essays as *Nature, Self-Reliance, The American Scholar, The Emancipation Proclamation,* and others, Emerson gave a clear and forceful formulation of the Transcendentalist Ethics. Similarly Thoreau, especially in such works as *Walden* and *On The Duty of Civil Disobedience,* articulated the vital concerns of the new romantic ethics in America. The central issues of Transcendentalist Ethics were:

(1) How can man realize the highest moral values within himself in terms of self-reliance?

(2) How can man find true moral value in the beauty of nature, in the discovery that all things are divine?

(3) Why are moral laws superior to political or legal laws?

(4) Under what conditions should man follow his highest impulses and even break the laws of the land to demonstrate his allegiance to the highest spiritual laws?

By speaking out in clear, influential terms on such issues as the Fugitive Slave Law, John Brown, and civil disobedience, Emerson and Thoreau formed an idealistic type of ethics that not only had relevance to their own times but has continued to inspire men to the present day. Transcendentalism as a social movement never gathered much momentum, but people the world over continue to find much inspiration in the finely crafted prose of Emerson and Thoreau.

In 1859 Charles Darwin published his famous *Origin of Species.* Darwin's idea of evolution and Herbert Spencer's philosophical interpretations of this concept produced a great influence and sparked a number of important controversies in the United States. The idea of evolution challenged philosophic, moral, and religious views of long standing. Responding to this challenge, a number of American thinkers sought to understand the new idea of evolution and explain its implications. Charles Peirce (1839-1914), John Fiske (1842-1901), and William James (1842-1910) were perhaps the most prominent American thinkers who sought to incorporate the idea of evolution into their philosophies. Peirce, who was also the founder of American pragmatism, developed a bold, speculative philosophy or metaphysics in which he made use of the concept of evolutionary love. Fiske, who greatly admired Herbert Spencer's evolutionary philosophy, attempted to develop what he termed a cosmic philosophy which would reconcile the idea of evolution with ethics and religion. Some of the central issues of American Evolutionary Ethics were:

(1) Does evolution offer any evidence of a purposeful goal for the universe?

(2) Can human morality be explained as the result of evolution?

(3) Does any inherent conflict exist between the notion of evolution and belief in religion and morality?

Although Charles Peirce originated American pragmatism, credit belongs to William James for first developing the Pragmatist Ethics. Peirce had used the term "pragmatism" to signify an experimental method for finding the meaning of general ideas or concepts in terms of their future, practical consequences. James extended Peirce's idea by claiming that the truth and value of ideas is to be located in their practical consequences. By applying pragmatism to the realms of morals and religion, James essentially turned pragmatism into a humanistic philosophy. In such works as *The Will to Believe, The Moral Philosopher and the Moral Life, The Dilemma of Determinism,* and his famous *Pragmatism,* James succeeded in bringing the idea of pragmatism to the attention of the world. The central issues of Pragmatist Ethics were:

(1) How do moral beliefs have practical consequences, and does the desire to believe something actually influence the outcome?

(2) If the essence of good in pragmatic terms is to satisfy demand, how does one decide which demands to satisfy?

(3) If pragmatic truth and value are found in ideas that are successful, can lies and deceptions be pragmatically true or beneficial if they work or succeed?

(4) Can there be pragmatic justification for the right to believe in such things as free will, religion, and general optimism?

Idealism in America is as old as the Puritans. Jonathan Edwards had developed a form of idealism in claiming that all existence is fundamentally mental or spiritual in quality depending on the spiritual power of the divine being. Emerson also asserted a form of idealism in his pantheistic Transcendentalism, maintaining that all things are divine when viewed with the proper insight. Not until the late nineteenth century, however, did Josiah Royce (1855-

1916), a scholar of the history of philosophy, give American idealism its systematic formulation. During his tenure as professor of philosophy at Harvard, Royce developed his own system of philosophical idealism, including an ethics based on dialectical reason, with such works as *The Philosophy of Loyalty, The World and the Individual,* and *The Hope of the Great Community.* The central issues of his idealistic approach to ethics were:

(1) If loyalty is essential to all moral values, how can conflicts between loyalties be resolved?

(2) How can belief in any objective moral order in the universe be maintained in the light of the existence of evil of all kinds?

(3) How can the seemingly irrational problems of violence, racial prejudice, and war be understood and solved by the use of reason?

By the early twentieth century, American philosophy had clearly arrived at its real maturity. As one of the best indications of this, Harvard University alone could boast of three very different world-famous philosophical talents on its faculty: William James, Josiah Royce, and George Santayana. Santayana (1863-1952) had been a student of James and Royce, but he disagreed with them philosophically. In 1905 he published the first major statement of his naturalism in *The Life of Reason.* Naturalism in ethics is at least as old as Aristotle, and Santayana believed that modern man does not need a new ethics so much as the wisdom to appreciate and live up to the oldest and the best. Naturalism in ethics calls for a delicate balance between the rational and animal sides of human nature, maintaining that every moral ideal has a natural biological basis and that everything natural has a moral idealization possible within it. Consequently Santayana's writings represent an effort to interpret all the major facets of human life, including religion, art, science, and society, in terms of a balanced form of naturalism.

Some of the central issues of naturalistic ethics were:

(1) How can sense be made from the naturalistic view that moral values are relative to human interests, desires, and needs which often vary greatly?

(2) What is the relation between moral values and aesthetic values?

(3) How can religion be conceived to have any moral value in naturalistic terms?

(4) Can naturalism avoid what has been termed "the naturalistic fallacy" of supposing the concept of good can be defined in terms of pleasure, desire, or interest?

Naturalistic Ethics gained a considerable stronghold in the United States during this century. Many thinkers believed that ethical naturalism was the only kind of moral philosophy that could do justice to, and keep pace with, continual progress in the natural sciences. It is understandable in this regard why John Dewey's (1859-1952) progressive experimental view of ethics should have been so influential. Dewey sought to combine the assets of both pragmatism and naturalism into a progressive, scientifically oriented philosophy. Dewey's instrumentalism, as his position was called, asserted that ideas should be looked upon as instruments for solving problems both in theory and practice. Moral ideas therefore must be viewed pragmatically and naturalistically, in terms of the practical consequences toward which they lead and in terms of the natural world where experimental inquiries are the only ones that lead to verifiable, dependable results. With the publication of such works as *Ethics,* in collaboration with James H. Tufts, *Moral Principles in Education, Theory of Valuation, Freedom and Culture,* and *Experience and Nature,* Dewey not only became famous as the father of progressive education; he also became world-renowned for his progressive and experimental views in ethics. Some of the central issues of his ethics were:

(1) If, as Dewey asserts, the solution of any moral problem gives rise to new problems, how can any real moral progress result?

(2) How can individualism be reconciled with social responsibility?

(3) How can an experimental ethics develop any substantial values, and how can it maintain a genuine respect for the dignity of human life?

(4) How can education include moral values? Can moral values be taught or learned in schools?

Recent contemporary developments in American ethics can be dated approximately from the period of World War II to the present. Although a wealth of writings have been produced during this period by many American writers on ethics, certain tendencies and thinkers can be singled out as characteristic of the most important developments. One feature that generally dominates recent moral philosophy in the United States is the stress on careful analytical methods with special attention to the language of morals. This analytical linguistic turn in American ethics has been given the name "metaethics" to indicate that its concern is basically centered on clarifying the meaning of ethical concepts and assertions. Charles L. Stevenson's book *Ethics and Language*, published in 1944, was the first major American work to articulate the way in which our ethical concepts and words function and take on meaning. In developing an emotive theory of the meaning of ethical language, Stevenson has exercised considerable influence. Especially important in Stevenson's work was the problem of the nature of ethical disagreement and the methods by which ethical judgments can be proved or supported.

In 1946 Clarence Irving Lewis (1883-1964) published *An Analysis of Knowledge and Valuation*. This work has had a great influence on the course of American philosophy. Lewis' major work in ethics, *The Ground and Nature of the Right,* was published in 1955. His method in ethics was heavily epistemological as he defended a cognitive approach to values and imperatives in contradistinction to Stevenson's noncognitivist or emotivist position. Lewis' defense of rational imperatives in ethics places him in line with such thinkers as Kant and Royce, but his insistence that value judgments are empirical and intimately related to action also places him in the traditions of naturalism and pragmatism.

In recent years American philosophers have given considerable attention to the Is-Ought question and to the logical status of the relation between facts and values. John Searle's article "How to Derive 'Ought' from 'Is'" (1964) has produced a considerable debate among philosophers over the question whether it is logically possible to derive evaluative conclusions from descriptive premises. By attempting to show how ought-statements can be derived from is-statements, Searle challenges the traditional view of the separation or logical independence of facts and values. Also challenging the separation or opposition of facts and values, James K. Feibleman in his *Moral Strategy* (1967) has developed an entire system of ethics which seeks to integrate values and facts in a naturalistic and also in a cosmic framework.

While religion and ethics have always been intimately related, recent developments in Christian ethics have had considerable impact under the name of "situation ethics." Joseph Fletcher's *Situation Ethics, The New Morality,* published in 1966, has achieved much popularity. Like other theologians, Fletcher emphasizes the need to reinterpret traditional religious ideas and apply them to contemporary situations. Such problems as euthanasia, abortion, artificial insemination, and sexual morality in general have received considerable attention from recent American religious thinkers.

Currently there is a pronounced interest in problems relating to morality and law. Attention has centered on such topics as conscientious objection to serving in the armed forces or fighting in an unjust war, justification of civil disobedience, moral justification of punishment, problems of racial discrimination, and basic human rights. Martin Luther King, Jr., John Rawls, Richard Wasserstrom, and others have written extensively on many of these topics. John Rawls, Professor of Philosophy at Harvard University, has published many important papers dealing with justice and social ethics that have had considerable impact. Rawls' book *A Theory of Justice,* published in 1971, concerns the problem of trying to develop a complete, coherent notion of justice as fairness. By defending and developing a contract theory of justice, Rawls has sought to construct a view of justice which he believes superior to traditional utilitarian accounts. Included in Rawls' theory is an analysis and justification of civil disobedience and conscientious refusal. The problem of one's right to dissent and to refuse obedience to unjust laws has been given considerable attention in recent years. One serious problem concerns whether social protest and civil disobedience must be nonviolent. Rawls and Martin Luther King, Jr., defend a nonviolent approach, while Robert Paul Wolff in a provocative analysis of the concept of violence (*On Violence,* 1969) contends that the idea of nonviolence is inherently confused and that the doctrine of nonviolence contains no logical merit.

A further illustration of the interest of contemporary philosophers in the problems of morality and law involves the question of the moral justification of punishment. On the one hand it seems clear that no adequate system of criminal justice can exist without punishment in some form. Yet the very idea of punishment, especially capital punishment, conveys the idea of cruel and inhuman treatment of human beings. Richard Wasserstrom, for one, has written extensively on the topic of punishment and the interrelation between morality and law. In a provocative essay entitled *Why Punish the Guilty?* (1964), he examines whether it is morally justified to punish the guilty or whether criminal behavior should be regarded as some form of sickness and treated accordingly.

Today moral philosophy in the United States seems to focus attention on both the theoretical and practical problems of ethics. Philosophers consider it important to clarify the meanings of our basic ethical concepts and discourse, as well as to tackle the knotty moral problems of everyday living. The fact that philosophers today return to some of the same problems addressed a century and more ago by Thoreau, Jefferson, and Edwards does not indicate that no progress has been made in American ethics. It indicates rather the continuing importance and complexity of such issues as civil disobedience, natural or human rights, and freedom of the will. Because these and other issues have reappeared throughout American history, it is instructive to examine historically the main lines of American ethics in order to appreciate the importance and intricacy of these problems. Thus, so that he may clarify his own thoughts and opinions on many of the moral issues of today, in the following pages the reader is invited to examine how some of the major issues, ideas, and men involved in American ethics took shape.

Chapter 1

Puritan Ethics

American Puritanism

American ethics began with the Puritans who migrated to New England in the 1630's. Their ideas and way of life not only dominated the life of colonial New England, but their influence persisted and spread throughout the New World. The Puritans received their name from the fact that, as English Protestants, they sought to purify the Church of England of all unnecessary and unessential beliefs and practices. The American Puritans sought to establish a holy commonwealth in the New World, a visible testament of their faith and glorification of the divine being. Essential to their outlook was the idea that everything in the world exists for the sake or glorification of the Creator. Not only do man and nature depend on the Creator for their existence; the whole point and justification of man's existence must be viewed in terms of serving the will or plan of God. Man on his own is nothing. The Puritans held that man is basically depraved or inherently sinful and cannot be saved by good works or his own efforts. This points up the most important feature of the Puritan attitude toward morality or ethics: Man cannot rightly take credit for moral virtues or good conduct; but he must take the blame for immorality or sin. On his own man is incapable of true virtue since the Puritans firmly believed in the notion of original or hereditary sin. Since the fall of Adam, all men come into the world with an inherent tendency to satisfy their own

1

selfish personal interests rather than to obey or follow the will of the divine being. Man has the capacity to love, choose, and reason; but all of these powers are by themselves imperfect and unable to produce lasting happiness and to overcome misery and death. The divine being permits man to sin and justly condemns the unregenerate to eternal damnation. But at the same time, the divine being elects or chooses to help some overcome their worldliness and sin. Some men are elected for salvation, through no merit of their own, to be of service to God, to glorify him, and to spread his message. To be saved one must be born again and receive the supernatural grace of the divine being. Consequently one is saved by faith, not by good works.

The early New England Puritans believed that they had been chosen by the divine being to build a holy commonwealth in the New World. They believed they had a covenant with God which put them under the obligation to follow his laws and do his will; and in return they would be strengthened in their faith and enjoy God's help and deliverance from damnation. Consequently the early Puritans under the leadership of such men as John Cotton, John Winthrop, Increase Mather, and Cotton Mather established very strict and rigorous rules of morality. The unique aspect of this morality involved the difficult attempt of applying lofty Christian ideals to all details of everyday life. The Puritans, in other words, sought to improve their material conditions of life while being careful not to fall in love with the world. They believed in and practiced such virtues as prudence, thrift, cleanliness, enterprise, and justice—not for the final or ultimate purpose of happiness, but for the glorification of God. Good works were the results of divine grace or election, not the causes of salvation or happiness. Their sermons constantly reminded them to expect misery, suffering, and disappointment in this life. Nevertheless they were to persevere in their hard work and enterprise since such works were a sign from heaven that they were chosen to perform the glorious work of the divine being. As the New England scholar Perry Miller asserted, "That every man should have a calling and work hard in it was a first premise of Puritanism."[1] The Puritan Ethic thus amounted to a life of industrious piety. Each act in life took on a moral meaning to the extent that it was done out of a sense of reverence for the Creator. Since everything in existence belonged to God or was the result of his creation, man could not properly claim anything for his own or give anything to the divinity—except reverence and thanksgiving. But the Puritans were well aware that man has an innate pride or tendency to think of himself before anything else. Man's pride or vanity is a sign of depravity even when it is associated with externally good works. Consequently the man who is honest, hardworking, and considerate to others but who takes pride in, or credit for, his virtues is really sinful and immoral. Any act by man that does not exhibit true piety or reverence to God is immoral.

In its fundamentals, Puritan Ethics is simple and straightforward. It equates immorality with sin and morally good behavior with piety. In its applications or consequences, however, it becomes much more complex, harder to identify, and controversial. The Puritans in their moral and religious zeal ruthlessly desired to expose and root out sin. Although keenly practical in many ways, they were also zealots—one might even say fanatics—in their stated mission to build a holy commonwealth in the New World. As a consequence they dealt harshly with heretics or what they saw as deviations from their own and their God's true cause. Although they prized and encouraged learning, set up schools, and founded Harvard College as early as 1636, they also encouraged emotionalism and even persecution that resulted in bitter controversies and loss of life. Not at all tolerant of other religious views, they early faced and decided the important question of the liberty of individual conscience by expelling such people as Roger Williams and Ann Hutchinson from their midst. Roger Williams, as early as 1644, adopted a firm position against religious persecution and enforced conformity. "It is the will and command of God, that (since the coming of his Son the Lord Jesus) a permission of the most Paganish, Jewish, Turkish, or Anti-Christian consciences and worships, be granted to all men in all Nations and Countries."[2] Roger Williams insisted on distinction or separation between religious and civil government, a view at odds with the orthodox Puritan position. "An enforced uniformity of Religion throughout a Nation or civil state, confounds the Civil and Religious, denies the principles of Christianity and civility, and that Jesus Christ is come in the Flesh."[3] These views clearly conflicted with the central Puritan idea of developing a holy commonwealth in the New World. As a result Roger Williams was banished from the Massachusetts colony in 1635 and departed to found a new colony at Providence, Rhode Island. Puritan ethics dealt even more harshly with the Quakers, who were imprisoned, whipped, and even executed for their views.[4] Perhaps the most notorious instance of Puritan fanaticism in rooting out heresy and sin was the case of the Salem Witchcraft Trials of 1691, where nineteen individuals believed to be witches were put to death. Although Puritan Ethics upheld the virtues of charity and kindness, it also upheld a hard line on sin or anything believed to be opposed to the Creator's will. In a similar vein, Puritan Ethics attempted to combine a whole series of elements that, on the surface, at least, appear simply incompatible. On the one hand, Puritanism upheld an other-worldly outlook and set of values; on the other, it upheld a firm sense of making those values work in this world. With its sense of the fallen nature of man and the inevitability of sin, it endorsed the doctrine of man's predestination which would seem to leave no place for human incentives. But here is perhaps the most curious fact about their ethic: By demanding things that were in fact humanly impossible, the Puritans inspired their members with superhuman zeal. The idea that man could not be saved, could not improve himself by his own efforts, did not imply despair or idleness. For idleness and despair were sinful, whereas industry and success were visible signs of divine election or intervention in the lives of men. The Puritan belief that God would help, sustain, and provide for his elect was a motivating or energizing idea, giving cosmic significance to what otherwise was small and insignificant. The Puritans were indeed fond of allegory and saw themselves as participating in a divine drama. Although they regarded good deeds and prosperity as visible signs of God's grace, they also believed in Satan and the devil's subtle influence. Mere good works and material prosperity without saving grace were evil, to be guarded against. Not to believe in the reality of Satan and his influence was tantamount to submitting to the real temptations of sin. The curious logic of Puritan belief in the devil is nowhere better expressed than in the following statement of Cotton Mather: "That there is a *Devil* is a thing Doubted by none but such as are under the influence of the *Devil*."[5]

However, material prosperity along with continued disagreements concerning church government were two important factors in the decline of Puritanism by the end of the seventeenth century.

American Puritanism failed in its original purpose of establishing a lasting holy commonwealth. According to E.S. Morgan, "The Puritan system failed because the Puritans relied upon their children to provide the church with members and the state with citizens,"[6] But although it failed in its central purpose, it succeeded in establishing a pronounced and lasting ethical influence. Puritan Ethics in a sense succeeded in the very way in which the holy commonwealth failed. Certainly Puritan Ethics was transformed to the needs and uses of the eighteenth century and later. Benjamin Franklin is an excellent example, continuing the Puritan virtues of enterprise, thrift, and prudence without the theological underpinnings. "Benjamin Franklin's *Autobiography* is the record of what Puritan habits detached from Puritan beliefs were capable of achieving in the eighteenth-century world of affairs."[7] But the eighteenth-century philosopher-theologian Jonathan Edwards, a contemporary of Franklin, gave American Puritanism its most forceful and brilliant defense. It is ironic, perhaps, that Puritanism had to wait until it lost its hold and vitality before receiving its most articulate philosophical formulation on American shores. Puritan Ethics had been stated and argued by John Cotton, Increase and Cotton Mather, and other seventeenth-century divines; but in theological rather than philosophical terms. Jonathan Edwards was able to state and argue the principles of Calvinism in terms of the philosophical ideas of John Locke which were current in his day. In this way Edwards succeeded in expressing Puritan Ethics in more universal, logical terms. As Perry Miller has stated: "Many definitions of Puritanism have been offered by historians. For the student of American culture, I suspect that the most useful would be simply that Puritanism is what Edwards is . . . he used science and sensation, not to erect a new system of theology, but to bring men face to face with what Puritanism always demands that they face, the divinity of divinity."[8]

Jonathan Edwards:
Principal Figure of Puritan Ethics

Jonathan Edwards (1703-1758) is equally famous for his forceful sermon *Sinners in the Hands of an Angry God,* preached at

Enfield, Connecticut in 1741, and his essay "Freedom of the Will," published in 1754. These two works vividly display the relentless logic of the tough-minded moral standpoint found throughout Edwards' life and writings. They state in clear, uncompromising terms the very essence of Puritan Ethics. The ideas contained in Edwards' message were not new in substance. They were clearly restatements of Scripture and John Calvin.

> Natural men are held in the hand of God, over the pit of hell; they have deserved the fiery pit, and are already sentenced to it; and God is dreadfully provoked, his anger is as great towards them as to those that are actually suffering the executions of the fierceness of his wrath in hell, and they have done nothing in the least to appease or abate that anger, neither is God in the least bound by any promise to hold them up one moment; the devil is waiting for them, hell is gaping for them, the flames gather and flash about them, and would fain lay hold on them, and swallow them up; the fire pent up in their own hearts is struggling to break out: and they have no interest in any Mediator, there are no means within reach that can be any security to them. In short, they have no refuge, nothing to take hold of; all that preserves them every moment is the mere arbitrary will, and uncovenanted, unobliged forbearance of an incensed God.[9]
>
> The God that holds you over the pit of hell, much as one holds a spider, or some loathesome insect over the fire, abhors you, and is dreadfully provoked.[10]
>
> The bow of God's wrath is bent, and the arrow made ready on the string, and justice bends the arrow at your heart, and strains the bow, and it is nothing but the mere pleasure of God, and that of an angry God, without any promise or obligation at all, that keeps the arrow one moment from being made drunk with your blood.[11]

Edwards' restatement of Calvinism was unflinching in its adherence to the ideas of (1) the supremacy and authority of the divine being, (2) the depravity and helplessness of man, and (3) the predestination and dependence of all creation on the sovereign will of God. Thus, instead of stating and arguing a new moral outlook, he skillfully delineated and defended a very old tradition. There was, at the time, a falling away from the strictures of Puritan or Calvinistic doctrine, and this falling away was to continue despite the efforts of Edwards and others at revivals, including those of The Great Awakening around 1740.

It is clear that Edwards made use of careful, intricate, logical arguments in his treatises defending the Calvinist position. His sermons tracing out the inevitable implications and applications of his premises are tightly argued. Nevertheless Edwards firmly maintained that both true religion and true virtue or morality are based on feeling, not reason; on the heart, rather than the head. Emotion enables man ultimately to judge the difference between virtue and vice, piety and impiety. Although reason is not excluded from matters of morality and religion, it does not form their basis or incentive. Edwards in his own early religious experiences had developed an attachment to empiricism in his basic philosophic outlook. As a student at Yale College, which he entered in 1716 at the age of thirteen, Edwards became acquainted with the writings of the British empiricist John Locke.

Edwards' reflections on Locke and his own religious experiences are recorded in his early essay "Notes on the Mind" and in his *Diary*. He argued that all existence is mental or spiritual in character. "How impossible is it, that the world should exist from Eternity, without a Mind."[12] He asserted that "we learn the necessity of the Eternal Existence of an All-comprehending Mind; and that it is the complication of all contradictions to deny such a mind."[13] Further, he claimed that "the human body, and the brain itself, exist only mentally, in the sense that other things do."[14] To be or exist is to be perceived by an idea in the mind; and since the divine mind is omniscient and omnipresent, all being or existence is fundamentally an idea or series of ideas contained in God. What can a thing be, apart from some idea that the mind forms of what it looks like, sounds like, feels like? To talk of anything existing independently of ideas or outside of any mind's perception is to talk of sheer nonentity, of which we have no idea at all. In this manner Edwards made use of rational argument to show the necessity of direct experience by the mind as a prerequisite for both knowledge and existence.

Edwards strongly opposed any form of materialism as a source of knowledge and existence. We know that matter exists only because of the ideas we have of it. To talk of material bodies existing apart from any mind and its ideas is to talk of something unreasonable or contradictory. Thus reason was used by Edwards to support his empirical view that all knowledge and existence depend upon experience.

Reason was also used by Edwards to show that empiricism implies idealism or spiritualism, the view that all existence is mental or spiritual in its basic character. By use of rational argument Edwards tried to show the need for extending empiricism beyond the ordinary confines of the senses to the supposition of a divine and supernatural sense. He argued that true religion and morality depend upon man's reception of holy or gracious affections that are supplied supernaturally by the divine being. To be converted to true religion or virtue, man cannot rely upon his own limited natural powers or abilities. These natural powers present man with nothing absolutely perfect or infinitely good. Man's natural powers and perceptions only reveal relative, finite objects and values.

Edwards admits the existence of man's natural conscience or moral sense, but not as the source of true virtue or morality. "This natural conscience, if well-informed, will approve of true virtue, and will disapprove and condemn the want of it, and opposition to it; and yet without seeing the true beauty of it."[15] The same principle is involved when Edwards argued that natural affection of any kind, such as love of parents for their children, is at best consistent with true virtue but not identical with it.

> If any being or beings have by natural instinct, or any other means, a determination of mind to benevolence, extending only to some particular persons or private system, however large that system may be—or however great a number of individuals it may contain, so long as it contains but an infinitely small part of universal existence, and so bears no proportion to this great and universal system—such limited private benevolence, not arising from, not being subordinate to benevolence to being in general, cannot have the nature of true virtue.[16]

True virtue must be based on love or benevolence, but the only kind of love that is perfect is the love of God, or love for what Edwards termed "being in general." Perfect love is total, infinite, beyond the reach of natural man. Any person's act of true virtue must thus result from the grace of the divine being working supernaturally through that person. This is consistent with the Calvinistic notion of divine election, that man cannot earn his salvation by good works, that the divine being chooses to infuse certain mortals with saving grace.

In 1755, three years before he died, Edwards wrote the definitive statement of Puritan Ethics, *The Nature of True Virtue*. The conclusion at which he arrived is simple and orthodox: that true virtue is benevolence to being in general; it is the love of God. But the analysis and argumentation he used to reach this conclusion is extremely intricate and subtle. Edwards drew a number of important and subtle distinctions to show how true virtue is to be distinguished from apparent virtue. "I use the phrase true virtue, and speak of things truly beautiful, because I suppose it will generally be allowed, that there is a distinction to be made between some things which are truly virtuous, and others which only seem to be so, through a partial and imperfect view of things."[17] After stating that virtue is a form of beauty or excellence, he argued that:

> Not all excellence or beauty can be called virtue, only that which pertains to creatures with understanding and will. Moral virtue cannot exist without the mind and its power of choosing or deciding. The beauty of flowers or the singing of birds, for example, cannot be called moral excellence or beauty. But not all operations of the mind or decisions of men can be characterized as moral in quality either. Only those decisions of the mind that are based on the heart, that is, affections and choices that deserve praise or blame, can be called moral.[18]

Edwards argued that "when a form or quality appears lovely, pleasing and delightful in itself, then it is called beautiful; and this agreeableness or gratefulness of the idea is *beauty*."[19] Consequently if moral virtue is a kind of beauty or excellence, it must depend on direct experience or feeling, not on reasoning or argumentation. We do not reason or infer that something is beautiful; we immediately feel it. Similarly we do not reason or infer that kindness or benevolence is morally excellent or beautiful; we directly feel or experience it. Not all love or beauty is on the same level, however. Sensual love or beauty is inferior to spiritual love or beauty. Love of family, friends, even love of mankind is inferior to that love which has being in general for its object. Edwards maintained that degrees of being exist which correspond to degrees of excellence. Man has more being than an animal or plant because man has more positive qualities and understanding. Since all existence is mental in quality, a thing has more existence as it has more perception, sensitivity, or awareness. Thus God has more being or existence than anything else since the divine being is aware of all ideas and comprehends being in general. Divine love and excellence are, as a consequence, completely universal and eternal, whereas man's own love is partial and temporal.

It is interesting to note that Edwards was so taken with the idea of God's spatial extensiveness that he identified space with God. After finding that space is infinite, necessary, and omnipresent, he argued that:

> We can with ease Conceive how all other beings should not be, we Can remove them out of our Minds and Place some Other in the Room of them, but Space is the very thing that we Can never Remove, and Conceive of its not being. If a man would imagine space any where to be Divided So as there should be Nothing between the Divided parts, there Remains Space between notwithstanding and so the man Contradicts himself, and it is self evident I believe to every man that space is necessary, eternal, infinite, and Omnipresent. But I had as Good speak Plain, I have already said as much as that Space is God.[20]

Man's sinfulness, therefore, is a function of weakness, smallness, or deformity of affection or love: "All sin has its source from selfishness, or from self-love not subordinate to a regard to being in general."[21] Man's moral ability is imperfect, as it rests on self-interest rather than on universal benevolence. But man's moral duty or responsibility is perfect or absolute. While recognizing that he should be honest, benevolent, and just, he is unable to attain these ideals by himself. How is this disparity explained: that man has the freedom or power to sin and do what he selfishly chooses, but is unable by himself to choose what is absolutely good?

In order to explain man's moral predicament, his infirmity of will in the face of what he recognizes he ought to choose, Edwards launched a classic defense of the Calvinist notion of predestination. True virtue depends on making the right choices or having what is termed "good will." But although virtuous choices must clearly be conscious or voluntary, they cannot be spoken of as free. Consistent with the Calvinist notion of predestination, Edwards staunchly defended the position that man has no free will. In what is perhaps his most famous and skillfully argued philosophical work, *A Careful and Strict Enquiry into the Modern Prevailing Notions of that Freedom of the Will. . .* published in 1754, Edwards attempted to demolish the popular belief in man's freedom of will. That common belief in man's freedom of the will is thought to be necessary in order to be able to blame or praise any man for his actions. For it is assumed that if a man is unable to make free choices he cannot be blamed or held responsible for them. Also unless man's will is self-determined or free, he can have no dignity or moral character of any worth. If man's will is not free then it is fated or determined, and man cannot control his own actions.

Edwards maintained it reasonable to hold that nothing happens without a cause. Although we may not always know the cause of a particular effect or event, it is nevertheless rational and sensible for us to hold that a cause for every event exists. This also applies to human actions and decisions. If a man behaves in a certain way, there must be cause or causes for his behavior. But questions arise: Are any causes necessary rather than contingent? And is man's will self-caused or fixed by necessity? "Necessity" to Edwards meant an infallible connection or certainty that effects will follow their causes. He offered examples of necessity operating in the natural sphere: that men feel pain when their bodies are wounded, that men's bodies move downward when nothing supports them, and so on. He argued that "Moral Necessity may be as absolute, as natural Necessity. That is, the effect may be as perfectly connected with its moral cause, as a natural necessary effect is with its natural cause."[22] By "moral cause" he meant a conscious choice, motive, or inclination. "When motives or previous biases are very strong, all will allow that there is some *difficulty* in going against them. And if they were yet stronger, the difficulty would be still greater. And therefore, if more were still added to their strength, to a certain degree, it would make the difficulty so great, that it would be wholly *impossible* to surmount it."[23] Edwards claimed that men never choose or will anything contrary to their desires. A sufficiently strong or intense desire necessarily leads to a choice or volition in favor of that desire. Man's will is therefore necessarily determined by his strongest desire or motive. Also, man never makes conscious or voluntary choices without the power of understanding what he is choosing. Hence every man's will is determined by his understanding or what he perceives and knows. Thus it follows, according to Edwards, that men never make undetermined, self-determined, or free choices. Every choice a man makes is determined by his level of understanding and by his strongest motive. A free will in the strict sense, a will that determines itself, is an impossibility.

Another way that Edwards argued the same conclusion was to observe that men make choices according to their nature or makeup. A man with a violent temper or volatile nature will act in accordance with that temper and nature. Another man who is peaceful and meek will act accordingly. To make this point, Edwards used the phrase "moral inability," and distinguished this from physical inability. A child with sufficiently strong love of his parents cannot choose to murder them, though presumably he is physically capable of killing them. A drunkard with sufficiently strong motivation to drink cannot choose to abstain. Moral inability signifies an inability to will or choose a certain thing and is to be distinguished from physical inability. People may be forced to do things contrary to their wills, of course, but since they did not choose those actions they cannot be held responsible for them.

To be held morally responsible for a certain action, the agent must have voluntarily or consciously chosen that action; it is not necessary that the choice be free. Choice implies assent; when we choose a thing we necessarily give our assent to that thing. Thus Edwards concluded that, although men are often able to do what they choose, they are never able to choose with "free will." Free will is impossible since it signifies a totally independent choice—one that is not in any way governed by the person's strongest motive.

When it is said that men make choices in accordance with their basic nature or makeup, it must also be recalled that, for Edwards and the Puritans, this meant that man makes choices in accordance with his fallen or depraved condition. Man is prone to sin, prone to disregard or disobey the Creator's will as revealed in Scripture. Since the fall of the first man, Adam's disobedience to God, men no longer have any supernatural principle in their basic makeup. Edwards held that when Adam was expelled from paradise, he and all his progeny were left without any saving grace which would enable them infallibly to choose the proper course. Edwards argued that man is predestined for damnation and can only be saved from that terrible fate by intervention of the divine being. No surer sign of election or conversion exists, in fact, than man's realization through true humility that he is nothing by himself and that he must place himself entirely in the hands of God. Man takes pride in himself and his own accomplishments and hence inherently resists the adoption of true humility. God, while permitting man to sin and do as he chooses, at the same time elects a few for saintliness. Those who are saved are equally predestined, and according to Edwards the saintly person is exactly the one who gives the divine being credit for conversion or salvation.

Man's will is not self-determined or free, and his illusory belief in his own free will is an illustration of his depravity and false pride. Man considers himself to have free will because he overestimates himself and believes that he has more control of his destiny than he really does. But belief in free will goes against reason, according to Edwards, and illustrates how unreasonable man actually is. To believe that the will determines itself is to fly in the face of rational evidence that one's strongest desire or motive, along with one's level of understanding, determines the will. Man's choices are not autonomous or free, but are determined by antecedent causes from all eternity. As Edwards remarked, to suggest that the will is self-determined or free is like saying that a bird's power of flight has the power to fly. A bird has the power to fly, but this power is not self-caused; it was given or provided through an external cause by its Creator. Likewise man has the power to choose, but this power is not self-caused; man's power to choose does not have the power to choose. Man's power to choose was given to him by his Creator. That man tends to deny or forget this fact only demonstrates his own imperfection and original depravity.

Free Will, Original Sin, and Predestination

It is a curious fact that although the early Puritans braved New England's rocky soil and long winters in order to practice their religion freely, they neither believed in real religious freedom nor practiced tolerance of other religious convictions. They believed that each individual should be educated in order to be able to read and understand Scripture for himself, but this did not imply a liberal or free thinking view of Biblical interpretation. In their initial attempts to establish a holy commonwealth in the New World, they exercised great vigilance, as already noted, against heresy and unorthodox views. As time passed, however, serious disagreements about church government and various theological matters arose. The Puritans were compelled to face the problem of the liberty of individual conscience as well as the independence of individual congregations.

Central to Puritan Ethics was a strong conception of authority. God's authority was, of course, primary. But equally important to the Puritan way of life was the authority of parents over their children, husband over wife, clergyman over congregation, and magistrates over the people. The Puritans strongly believed in order and regimentation. Man must submit to authority and laws for his own good. In submitting to the authority of laws, he is better able to serve the divine being. Regarding the Puritan attitude toward government, Perry Miller wrote as follows:

> The government of Massachusetts, and of Connecticut as well, was a dictatorship . . . not of a single tyrant, or of an economic class, or of a political faction, but of the holy and regenerate. Those who did not hold with the ideals entertained by the righteous, or who believed God had preached other principles, or who desired that in religious belief, morality, and ecclesiastical preferences all men should be left at liberty to do as they wished—such persons had every liberty, as Nathaniel Ward said, to stay away from New England. If they did come, they were expected to keep their opinions to themselves; if they discussed them in public or attempted to act upon them, they were exiled; if they persisted in returning, they were cast out again; if they still came back, as did four Quakers, they were hanged on Boston Common.[24]

The idea that religion and government (church and state) were separate entities was foreign to the Puritan outlook. They did, of course, distinguish between spirit and flesh, between God and the world. But this only signified that authority was vested in the divine being and Biblical revelations and that the government and morality of men were to be steered by divine rather than by man-made or secular laws. The idea that religion would control society and government was central to building a holy commonwealth in the New World. As time passed and men became more prosperous, this original idea faded and was replaced by other ideas. When Jonathan Edwards preached and wrote, New England had in effect lost its overriding sense of sin as well as its original mission to build a holy commonwealth. By Edwards' time, Puritan beliefs had already been compromised in practice, and Puritan theology was threatened by such ideas as deism or natural religion and Arminianism, which held that man's will is self-determined or free.

One of the most controversial ideas in Christian theology is the notion of original sin. If man is born with an innate tendency to sin, how can he be held responsible for his sinful actions? Further, if mankind inherits sin from the fall of Adam, does this not make the divine being the author of sin and depravity? In 1757 Edwards wrote his elaborately argued treatise, *The Great Christian Doctrine of Original Sin Defended.* Basically, this work was a response to objections by John Taylor and others to this doctrine. Edwards saw that the belief in original sin was central to the whole Puritan or Calvinistic outlook on rebirth or divine election. Any compromise in that belief would imply a loss of the real sense of man's sin as well as the absolute need of man's redemption by God. Taylor and others had argued that the notions of original sin and total depravity are exaggerations; that it is reasonable to consider that many more men are honest and law-abiding than not. In other words, the doctrine of original sin is too negative and unfair to the positive, virtuous accomplishments of man. Worse, this doctrine is fatalistic and attributes the cause of man's sin to the Creator who supposedly made man a sinful creature through no choice of man. In replying to these charges, Edwards sought to bring men back to the original Puritan doctrines founded squarely on Scripture. Edwards argued that the nature of man's sin cannot be understood in exclusively human terms, but must be viewed as a violation against the infinite goodness of God. "There is an infinite demerit in all sin against God, which must therefore immensely outweigh all the merit which can be supposed to be in our virtue."[25] Man forgets that all sin is against a God of absolute or infinite perfection, hence that all sin is infinitely evil or depraved. Man is under an absolute obligation to a being of pure love, and the smallest sin in man's eyes is infinitely great in the view of the Creator. Evidence of man's utter depravity is, in fact, that he tends to make light of his sin and view it as less serious than it really is. In a similar fashion, a man overestimates his own virtuous capacity and performance by comparing his own virtue with another's rather than by comparing all men's efforts at virtue with the infinite goodness of God. To Edwards, man's total depravity is confirmed by experience and is convincingly portrayed in Scripture. "The great depravity of man's nature appears, not only in that they universally commit sin, who spend any long time in the world, but in that men are naturally so prone to sin, that none ever fail of *immediately* transgressing God's law, and so of bringing infinite guilt on themselves, and exposing themselves to eternal perdition, as soon as they are capable of it."[26] What makes sin so evil is that it lies in every man's heart or will to assent to, or side with, selfish and worldly impulses rather than universal, spiritually exalted goals. For Edwards, it is because true virtue is so very pure and beautiful that any single transgression, by contrast, is so ugly and depraved. Edwards admitted that God permits men to sin, but such permission is not to be interpreted that the Creator is the author or cause of man's transgressions. What makes sin original with man is the fact that man has intelligence and choice which he invariably uses for his private benefit rather than for the glory of God. That even the best of men feel a strong sense of guilt and are subject to misery and death is ample evidence that the ground of sin lies in the original human condition, not some extraneous cause. For Edwards, it was not at all flattering to man that his uniqueness among all other creatures of the earth is simply his strong tendency and capacity to sin. Finally, evidence of man's original proneness to sin is involved in the leading idea of Scripture, that man must be born again in order to be redeemed. Man if not originally born in sin and depravity would be subject to improvement, however slow or long the process. But it is not the lesson of Scripture that man *can* help himself and gradually improve. Man needs to be completely turned around and experience a new birth.

Edwards clearly saw that the free will question was of central importance to the whole fabric of true religion and morality. "The grand question about the freedom of the will, is the main point that belongs to the science of the will. Therefore I say, the importance of this subject greatly *demands* the attention of Christians, and especially of divines."[27] In Edwards' time, this issue presented a serious threat to Christian unity and teachings about morality. Calvinism was under heavy attack, being essentially accused of teaching a doctrine of fatalism that said man had no free choice of whether to sin or not to sin. The name "Arminianism" came to be associated with the main opposition to the Calvinist denial of man's free will.

> The Arminians began as a Dutch religious sect who took their name from Jacobus Arminius (1560-1609). Their influence spread to England, and by 1734 they were gaining many converts in America. Edwards, in fact, viewed them as a serious threat to Calvinism, since the Arminians believed in the freedom or self-determining power of man's will. This implied that man could freely choose to sin or not to sin which in turn implied a denial of man's predestination or absolute dependence on God.[28]

Edwards quoted Church of England theologian Daniel Whitby (1638-1726) as presenting the typical Arminian or anti-Calvinist viewpoint as follows: " 'If all human actions are necessary, virtue and vice must be empty names; we being capable of nothing that is blameworthy, or deserveth praise; for who can blame a person for doing only what he could not help, or judge that he deserveth praise only for what he could not avoid?' "[29] Edwards entered the controversy as both a theologian and philosopher. He sought to defend the strict Calvinistic notions of man's predestination and God's absolute foreknowledge of all future events; but he endeavored at the same time to present purely rational, philosophical arguments against the notion of free will and in favor of determinism of the will. This double purpose marks the first serious, profound attempt in America to face and examine the free will question as it pertains to moral or ethical philosophy.

Edwards argued that if universal causality is accepted as a principle of reason and good sense, every event must be caused. Further, if every event has a cause or reason for happening, there is no escaping the conclusion that a necessary connection exists between an event and its cause. As he wrote, "To suppose that there are some events which have a cause and ground of their existence, that yet are not necessarily connected with their cause, is to suppose that they have a cause which is not their cause."[30] Contingency or accidental happenings merely signify a lack of knowledge on our part. We do not in fact know the actual causes of every event, but that ignorance does not mean that events have no causes or that they are contingent in themselves. Contingency only applies to our not knowing or seeing a necessary connection between a given cause and effect. Necessary connection equally applies to will or choice. There is no such thing as a contingent or accidental choice in itself. If a choice has been made, it must have a cause which was necessary to produce that choice. "Acts of the will are never contingent, or without necessity."[31] Consequently if free will signifies either uncaused or unnecessary choice (i.e., choice that, once made, did not have to be made) the notion of free will is unreasonable and impossible. Edwards argued that whatever has already happened has now become necessary and cannot be otherwise. Imagination may lead us to suppose that a thing which has happened need not have happened or could have happened otherwise. But imagination is not knowledge; it is not based on evidence. To know or understand an event is to apprehend the evidence upon which it is based. To know with certainty can only mean to apprehend a connection that is certain or fixed in things themselves. All contingency or hesitancy regarding past or future events only signifies the lack of certain knowledge of the connection that is in things themselves. Our knowledge of future events is largely contingent, which means that we do not see what will necessarily come to pass. But we cannot infer the contingency of future events themselves from our lack of knowledge of what will exactly or necessarily come to pass. Man's future choices and decisions may be unknown to him in the present moment, but this signifies neither that they will not occur nor that they are not now fixed by necessity. There can, of course, be no moral actions without choice or will; all parties in the dispute over the free will question are agreed on this. Edwards' point, however, was that no moral actions can exist without causes for them and that these causes must be necessary and cannot be contingent.

Moral causes, as already noted, pertain to voluntary choices or volitions. No one can be held morally responsible for involuntary actions or for actions done against one's will. An individual can be held morally responsible for his action only if the action is voluntary. This means that the connection between moral choice and moral action must be causally necessary and can never be accidental or contingent. To blame a man for murder, the case must be made that he did not accidentally kill another person but that the killing was willful or intended. This shows, according to Edwards, that moral causes are logically and necessarily connected with their moral effects. But we must remember that all causes are logically connected with their effects. Therefore a moral choice itself must be necessarily caused; it cannot be produced by accident. If a man willfully chooses to murder another, logically that choice must be necessarily determined by its cause. For Edwards, men always choose according to their strongest motive and according to what seems most agreeable to them.[32] Consequently men's choices are always determined, never free in the sense of being uninfluenced or undetermined. A man's choices are always determined by those things in *his own* character or makeup that have the greatest force and constancy. To have any moral significance, however, these causes must be conscious; the person must be aware of them, even though his understanding of them may be imperfect. Men are blamed because they have bad motives or intentions which in turn are caused by bad or evil desires. Therefore Edwards can say *both* that men are free to do what they choose and that men are to be held responsible for what they choose—not only because they caused the action which they chose to do, but because their own desires or inclinations, no one else's, caused them to choose in the first place.

Edwards thus turned the Arminian belief in free will around and argued that, without determined or unfree choices, no one could be held accountable for his actions. The Arminian denial of necessarily determined choice or will results in making moral choice and action a mere matter of caprice. Edwards further noted that the will cannot be regarded as free in the sense of being self-determined. Will signifies an actual commitment or assent to something. It may and does determine a consequent action, but it does not determine itself. Will or actual choice is also determined by prior desires or inclinations, not by itself. In other words, man's will is not autonomous, not free to choose or not choose, since the will is not a person or agent but simply an aspect or part of a person or agent. The will alone does not have the power to choose; it is the person or agent who has the power of will which enables him to choose. Free or self-determined will is thus like a power without an agent or, as Edwards declares, like the power of flight without a bird. Powers cannot operate without agents. Hence willpower or free will without an agent is a complete misnomer or nonentity.

Regarding his dispute with the Arminians, Edwards had to explain how it makes sense to blame a person for doing what he could not help but do. Edwards first pointed out that moral blame makes sense only toward actions which are morally wrong. Whether the person could or could not have acted otherwise does not signify that he should be blamed if no misdeed was committed in the first place. If helplessness in committing a certain deed means that the action was done not by the person's choice or done against his will, Edwards agreed that blame would be improper. But if a person willfully chooses to perform a certain action which is wrong, he must be blamed simply because he chose or caused it to happen. If a person's desires for performing morally wrong actions are sufficiently strong and persistent, they will inevitably produce evil choices. Equally if a person's desires for performing morally good actions are the most powerful, those desires will inevitably produce good choices. But in either case the person is worthy of blame or praise not because his choice was free or undetermined but because of the *quality* of his choice. It is reasonable to praise good choices and blame corrupt ones. The more constant and strong a good choice is, in fact, the more it deserves praise; likewise the more constant and strong a bad choice is, the more it deserves blame. The worst actions, those that are most morally evil, are those that are most determined by evil intentions or desires.

The full force of Edwards' reply to the Arminians on the free will controversy, however, cannot be understood without reference to Edwards' theological principles. While it is true that he attempted to refute the Arminian belief in free will by appeals to reason and rational argument, he also used religious arguments and evidence based on Scripture. Consistent with his view that man's will is necessarily determined and not free, he argued that God's will is also determined. The divine being acts, and can only act, from holy or excellent motives. He insisted that even the Arminians must believe that God is all good, and that this can only mean that the divine being always operates from benevolent motives or intentions. God's goodness is completely necessary, yet deserving of praise. All Christians, Edwards observed, must believe that the divine being is certainly praiseworthy, yet is completely determined or destined to perform only the best, most holy of actions. This view signifies that the will of the divine being is to be praised because of its quality, not because it is undetermined, indifferent, or free. God's omniscience, including his foreknowledge of future events, is inconsistent with the Arminian view or any view of indeterminacy. If the divine being knows the future course of events before they happen, this can only be true if his divine knowledge comprehends the nature and connection of these events themselves. Otherwise, this knowledge has no subject matter or is simply fortuitous. Predestination must exist if God is omniscient and has true foreknowledge. The divine being must know what is, and what will be, in the hearts or intentions of men. Also, the divine being must know who will be redeemed and who will be lost. Although no one is lost and condemned to damnation who does not deserve this fate, the majesty and omnipotence of God demand that men are helpless to save or redeem themselves. Edwards argued that, according to Scripture, God has not only predestined the course of events but has in fact ordered certain events that men have carried out. The Crucifixion is a case in point. "'Tis certain, that God thus, for excellent, holy, gracious and glorious ends, ordered the fact which they committed, who were concerned in Christ's death; and that therein they did but fulfill God's designs.'"[33] This suggests that men's actions are not only predestined from all eternity but that even men's transgressions can be and are put to a glorious, morally excellent purpose by the divine being. Man's sin, although it represents a violation of divine law, is permitted by God—since, in some way that man fails to comprehend, it serves a greater divine purpose. For Edwards, sin was metaphysically necessary to God's plan. God is perfectly entitled to use men and their sins for his greater glory. That this is not congenial to man's natural or ordinary desires is perfectly consistent with man's original sin or depravity. To rebel against predestination is as naturally expectable as it is fruitless or vain. In this sense Edwards never pretended that the strict doctrine of Puritanism which he argued and preached would be a favorite one with mankind. But he forcefully and relentlessly argued that it is the one true and certain doctrine.

Assessment

Though Puritanism has long since vanished from the American scene, its moral influence and significance persist. Measured in terms of the time it actually lasted or in terms of the number of its ardent advocates, Puritanism must be counted as rather short-lived and diminutive. It must, in terms of realizing its stated goal, count as an actual failure. Despite these shortcomings, it has nevertheless exercised an enormous moral influence on American life. Its importance derives in some measure simply because it came first. Its real significance, however, resides in the peculiar kind of tough-minded, practical idealism that it managed to transmit to later generations. Puritan Ethics survived because it could be transformed and suited to the needs and aspirations of later times. In the process of this transformation and survival, its original meaning and theological structure were lost. But its moral purpose, seriousness, and tenacity remained remarkably intact.

Puritanism bequeathed a sense of mission and high moral expectations that became ingrained in the American mind and way of life. This legacy is primarily the result of what Samuel Eliot Morison observed as the three institutions of lasting significance which we owe to the Puritans: "the college, the public-school system, and the Congregational Church."[34] Through these institutions the moral values of Puritanism were articulated, taught, and passed on to succeeding generations. But the influence of Puritanism in American life is equally observable in its distinct influence on and through outstanding individuals. Though such men as Jefferson, Franklin, Emerson, Lincoln, and Wilson were certainly not Puritans in the religious sense, they may nevertheless be described as Puritans in the moral sense of the term. Each definitely exhibited the high moral seriousness and sense of mission in life found in the Puritan sense of virtue. In fact what has been variously termed the Protestant or Puritan ethic—a conscientious dedication to hard work, frugality, and achievement of success in "the business of life"—has become so ingrained in American life that it is taken for granted and not always recognized as an offshoot of much earlier religious beliefs and practices.

Any fair appraisal of Puritan Ethics must consider the high intellectual level of articulateness it achieved so early in our history. As Perry Miller has observed, the "Puritans considered religion a very complex, subtle, and highly intellectualized affair, and they trained their experts in theology with all the care we would lavish upon preparing men to be engineers or chemists."[35] Without doubt Jonathan Edwards stands far above all Puritan thinkers in the astuteness and brilliance of his theological works. But more than this, Edwards stands above many if not most later American thinkers in the ability of his philosophical argumentation, which is indeed no small accomplishment. In the form in which Edwards presented the nature and analysis of true virtue, we see not only the essence of Puritan Ethics but the real beginning of philosophical thinking and reflection on moral ideas in America. That Edwards' works on ethics were largely polemical and controversial served as a real stimulus to further thought. Edwards was not a dogmatist, however, in the true sense of the term. He never advocated belief without evidence or against rational argument. In this sense, to interpret either him or the best ideas in Puritan Ethics as fanatical or irrational is completely mistaken. It is true that Puritanism displayed excesses and irrational moments as in the slaughter of the Pequot Indians, the persecution of the Quakers, and the Salem Witchcraft Trials of 1691. However fanatical and irrational these episodes may have been, they cannot be considered representative of Puritanism as a whole or of its best principles.

The most important idea in Puritan Ethics is the distinction between true and apparent (or natural) virtue. True virtue is total or complete moral excellence while natural virtue, no matter how good, is always incomplete—good in some respects but not in all. This notion goes to the center of both the practice and theory of this ethics because it simultaneously contains the greatest insight and the most important difficulty in the whole Puritan moral outlook. It is this distinction that Edwards sought to articulate with the greatest clarity; and the whole validity or cogency of Puritan Ethics may well stand or fall on whether this distinction can be sustained. Through this distinction, the difference between the elect or regenerate and the damned or lost is maintained.

The Puritans, as we have seen, insisted that good works alone and man's natural moral sense or conscience are not sufficient for true virtue. Yet there is a connection between them. True virtue in the spiritual sense implies the divinely given ability and propensity to do good works; and man's natural moral sense or conscience must agree with the purely spiritual or supernatural moral sense. As Edwards asserted: "Thus has God established and ordered that this principle of natural conscience, which, though it implies no such thing as actual benevolence to being in general, nor any delight in such a principle, simply considered, and so implies no truly spiritual sense or virtuous taste, yet should approve and condemn the same things that are approved and condemned by a spiritual sense or virtuous taste."[36] In other words, man is at least able to bring himself into agreement with what is to be judged as virtuous and what is not. Man does, then, in some sense possess a correct sense of moral right and wrong. Yet in another sense man 'does not really have a correct sense of virtue since his sense of virtue is incomplete, human, and not divine. There is, of course, a serious dilemma here. How can natural conscience and a purely supernatural sense agree on the question of virtue if the very existence of virtue depends upon its motive or the manner in which it is performed? Virtue as a kind of beauty or love depends upon the operations of understanding and will. Creatures with no understanding and will have no idea of, nor participation in, moral virtue. But it should equally follow that creatures with no true sense of virtue would not, by any natural faculty or power, be able to approve and disapprove the same things that a sensitivity to true virtue would choose. The same problem emerges in a different light when we look at actions. If truly virtuous actions require a truly benevolent heart or will, actions performed on a principle of natural conscience cannot, in fact, be truly virtuous. Yet if by use of their natural moral sense or conscience, men are, as Edwards stated, able to approve or disapprove the same things as would a truly spiritual sense, they should be able to do what true virtue demands.

This points up a serious problem in both the theory and

practice of Puritan Ethics. It is necessary in the moral sphere for one to assume that "ought" implies "can." In other words, if an agent or person is unable to do what ought to be done, the whole idea of moral responsibility vanishes. An agent may be physically unable to perform a certain deed, but this implies no moral wrong or defect. If an agent is morally unable to do any actions required by either natural conscience or a supernatural sense, *ipso facto* that creature is not a moral agent. It is not enough that an agent be able to do what it chooses to do; an agent must be able to do what it morally *ought* to do. But Edwards could only allow that freedom or power which enables man to do what he chooses. Man is not free or able to do in any truly moral sense what ought to be done.

This points up another serious flaw in Puritan ethics. Because morality is made to depend upon religion, man's moral obligations are intrinsically beyond his ability. But if this is so, in what sense is man morally responsible? This point may be pressed if we ask whether man is morally good enough to realize how bad he supposedly is. It is exactly at this point that the notion of man's total depravity seems to destroy the entire Puritan Ethic. If man is totally or inherently depraved, he should have no such thing as a natural moral sense or conscience—certainly not one that can agree with a supernatural or spiritual sense of true virtue. If man is totally depraved, one might reasonably ask, exactly what is Satan? If man is morally depraved, he is unworthy of redemption since moral depravity would seem to signify not the idea of trying to be good and failing, but the idea of not even trying.

Concerning the Puritan belief in man's depravity, one might suggest that the Puritans did not always practice what was clearly faulty in their theory. They, as much or more than others, operated on the premise that man indeed has genuine moral concerns and is not morally indifferent. The positive or constructive side of their ethics, in fact, augmented and greatly encouraged man's existing moral interests and concerns. To their credit, they emphatically taught man not to overestimate or exaggerate his own importance and powers. But in their constant endeavor to remind man of his sin, they seriously underestimated or ignored some of his most important potentialities and sensitivities. In this respect Puritan Ethics can be charged not only with narrowness but with outright callousness, especially in regard to the whole matter of human suffering. Like the ancient Stoic philosophers, the Puritans taught man to accept, even to expect, suffering and death as the condition or penalty for existence. But suffering is not always deserved, and death is not simply a form of cosmic punishment. This gloomy, depressing side of Puritan Ethics has been frequently criticized and rejected by later times.

The character and rationality of Edwards' defense of Puritanism has been praised for its fine reasoning and subtle distinctions. But one should not fail to notice its heavy reliance on purely *a priori* arguments. Edwards' elucidation of determinism regarding the will of man is flawed by its reliance on such closed arguments. To suppose, as Edwards did,[37] that a contingent causal connection is not really a causal connection at all because it lacks necessity is simply to decide the whole issue by stipulation or definition. One might just as well argue that probable evidence or accumulated probabilities are not evidence at all since they are not necessary or certain. For Edwards, all contingency rested not on empirical evidence but on the lack of true evidence or knowledge. This makes contingency subjective by definition. Chance or accidental happenings are thus not features of the way things are, but are simply reflections of the imperfect way we know or apprehend them. But from the idea that every event has a cause, it does not at all follow that every event has a *necessary* cause. When Edwards argued that "if there be in a cause sufficient power exerted, and in circumstances sufficient to produce an effect, and so the effect be actually produced at *one time*; these things all concurring, will produce the effect at *all times*,"[38] he presented a conclusion about the empirical world that is not at all based on empirical evidence but is simply *a priori*. The point that effects have causes is not the same as saying that a particular effect has a particular cause. That heat causes metal to expand or ice to melt is an empirical or contingent fact about the world. Logically such facts are not necessary, as we can easily conceive or imagine other alternatives. Any causal law that purports to describe and predict features of the empirical world may not only be falsified but must actually be falsifiable in principle in order that it not beg the question.

In order to claim that men's choices or acts of will are never contingent or without necessity,[39] Edwards had to ignore empirical evidence. Edwards' view that men are not morally free to choose, but are only free to do what they choose, must in some sense be based on what can be observed or learned from experience. The only way we know that men are not always able to do what they choose is from experience. To argue that men are able to do what they choose must mean that men are able to control their behavior, and this conclusion must be based on empirical evidence. To argue that men are *never* able to choose freely what they do choose must mean that men are never able to control their choices. But this result is not based on empirical evidence and quite clearly flaunts the evidence we do have. Men *are* able in some measure to control their choices or will. If they were totally incapable of this, they would in fact be unable to make moral choices, choices for which they can be held responsible.

It is one thing to allege that man is deficient in moral virtue and quite another to suggest that he is innately or inherently incapable of it. The former view can allow that empirical evidence is always relevant, though never decisive, to any moral problem or decision. The latter view can always discount whatever empirical evidence does not suit its design; and even allow empirical facts to count as long as they fall into the proper place. But this is exactly the weakness of Puritan Ethics.

In its penchant for moral certainty and rectitude, it saw the facts according to its closed preconceptions of them. In this sense Puritan Ethics not only cannot lead to any improvements within itself, but it can never answer the charge that its reading of the facts is simply arbitrary and irrelevant. For all its rational arguments and subtle distinctions, it can only leave the essential facts of man's moral life shrouded in mystery. It can even say, along with Edwards, that the divine being has so ordered men's lives that they must necessarily commit the worst of sins; yet such sinfulness is alleged to be nothing less than sordid means to a more glorious moral end.

In the final analysis, everything in Puritan Ethics comes back to its conception of the divine being. The deity is not only ascribed with all perfection and credit, but these attributes are inevitably bestowed at the expense of man. The Puritans could not venture to give man any credit or true virtue for fear of detracting from those very qualities of the Creator. If one wondered finally why this must be so, the answer could not be rendered in terms of either reason or experience; it must always seem a mystery to man. No wonder that, to succeeding generations, this theology seemed increasingly unintelligible and irrelevant. But although the gloomy theological underpinnings of this ethics were discarded, its energy and sense of high moral purpose and seriousness in life survived—and have, in fact, become undeniable features of the American experience.

Chapter 2

Enlightenment Ethics

The American Enlightenment

No period in American history better illustrates the vital connection between moral aspirations or ideals and their practical applications than the period of the Revolution and the Enlightenment. During the last half of the eighteenth century the American people not only fought for, won, and defended their political independence, they defined, elaborated, and skillfully justified a system of moral and political principles that has managed to withstand the tests of time. Largely through the talents and wisdom of the Founding Fathers, American democracy was built on the foundations of common sense and aspirations within the bounds of reason. Such men as Benjamin Franklin, Thomas Jefferson, Thomas Paine, James Madison, and others were gifted, practical intellectuals who possessed the rare ability to codify or put into working order a set of ideals that earned the respect of Americans and, eventually, of the whole civilized world.

Although Puritan Ethics had encouraged learning and enlightenment, the Puritan outlook was much too dominated by a sense of man's innate sinfulness and helplessness to provide a lasting, workable set of aspirations for the American people. Puritan Ethics had emphasized predestination rather than freedom, hope of the world to come rather than real faith in the possibilities latent within the natural world. In contrast to the Puritan leaders, who were all

29

clergymen, the leaders of the American Enlightenment were inventors, statesmen, and men of the world who believed in the innate goodness and perfectability of man.

The American Enlightenment signified a broad spectrum of interests and projects centered on a staunch moral confidence in the value of human freedom and progress. Underlying this faith in freedom and progress was the belief that all of nature and all affairs of men work, or are governed, by reason and natural law. Human reason and experiment are the only oracles needed by man to understand the world about him and to control his affairs with other men. Neither the authority of kings nor scriptural revelations can be counted upon to serve man's best interests. Moral confidence in the reasonableness of common sense and the tangibility of scientific experiment was, for Enlightenment thought, far superior to reliance on the divine right of kings or the performance of miracles. Franklin's experiments with electricity and Jefferson's experiments with new farming techniques and machinery, as well as the Declaration of Independence and the Constitution, are perfect illustrations of the Enlightenment's concern with practical knowledge for the advancement of mankind.

In contrast to Puritanism, moral virtue during the Enlightenment was not to be identified with religion but was viewed in humanistic or secular terms. True, the Enlightenment endorsed many of the same virtues or values important to the Puritans, but for rather different reasons. Justice, honesty, thrift, hard work, and prudence were valued for their utility in this world rather than for their supernatural value or as a penance for man's sin. But none of these virtues would be worth very much without the presence of freedom. A man has rights as well as obligations. Puritan Ethics had certainly emphasized man's duties to his fellow man and to the divine being, but had neglected his own natural rights. In this idea we can note the single most important contribution of Enlightenment Ethics: its concept of the natural rights of man.

The notion of natural or inalienable rights forms the cornerstone of Enlightenment views on religion, government, and education. Essentially this idea signifies that each person is born free and equal and that each man has an innate moral right to live his life, exercise his freedom, and pursue his happiness so long as these do not infringe upon the equal rights of others. The classic statement of this view is found in Jefferson's formulation of the Declaration of Independence. Thomas Paine also gave emphatic expression of the natural rights doctrine in his *Rights of Man,* published in 1791-92. Paine asserted that:

> Natural rights are those which appertain to man in right of his existence. Of this kind are all the intellectual rights, or rights of the mind, and also all those rights of acting as an individual for his own comfort and happiness which are not injurious to the natural rights of others. Civil rights are those which appertain to man in right of his being a member of society. Every civil right has for its foundation some natural right preexisting in the individual.[1]

On the negative side, this doctrine asserts that all forms of oppression or tyranny over the minds and lives of people are morally wrong and intolerable—even to the extent that man has an innate right to revolt and overthrow such oppression.

In matters of religion, this means that governments have no authority to impose religious beliefs and practices. Each man is free to believe what his conscience indicates. In respecting the rights of each man's conscience, the Enlightenment encouraged religious pluralism, maintaining that religion itself must be judged on moral grounds. The leading thinkers of this time identified themselves with deism or natural religion. Franklin, Jefferson, Paine, and others endorsed a religion based on reason and observation. Man's natural powers of reason and perception reveal a universe of order, design, and law. Such a world could not have resulted from mere chance, but indicates the superintending power of a divine architect who fashioned the world according to law and purpose.

Governments are needed to secure the natural rights of man. Without the protection of government, man's life, liberty, and pursuit of happiness must remain undeveloped and insecure. But just as nature itself is governed by natural laws of motion and rest, so governments must be based on, and judged in terms of, reason. Thus the only rational form of government is democracy wherein all laws of the land are based on, or derived from, consent of the governed. According to Jefferson, the land belongs to the living, and the only way to implement the natural rights of man is to build a system of government containing checks and balances with final authority vested in the will of the people themselves. This idea admits that governments are fallible and need revision or change from time to time. What was unique about American democracy, Jefferson saw, was the very attempt to make the will of all the people effective on a large scale. Representative democracy would have its difficulties, as is true with any human experiment. But with enlightenment and education, its errors could be corrected, its shortcomings remedied.

For this reason the leaders of the Enlightenment saw education and science as essential to American democracy. Jefferson stated this very clearly when he wrote, "If a nation expects to be ignorant and free in a state of civilization, it expects what never was and never will be."[2] He further asserts, "I look to the diffusion of light and education as the resource most to be relied on for ameliorating the condition, promoting the virtue, and advancing the happiness of man."[3] This implies that one of man's inborn natural rights is the right to learn and develop his mind and talents in order to make the most of his life, liberty, and manner of pursuing happiness. Education is to be placed among the articles of public trust since the improvement and even preservation of the country depends upon the acquisition of knowledge and technical skill which private enterprise cannot completely or adequately supply.

Enlightenment Ethics stands for the view that man can be counted on to make his own moral judgments and to make his own way in this world. Man is unique in his sense and need of justice and virtue. But his need to improve himself, to perfect his virtues and talents, is just as great. In other words, enlightenment is not only natural to man; it is the whole key to his progress.

Thomas Jefferson:
Principal Figure of Enlightenment Ethics

If Benjamin Franklin was the first great figure of the American Enlightenment and James Madison the last, Thomas Jefferson was its central, most influential, and brilliant mind. Historian Henry Steele Commager says of Jefferson, "No other Enlightenment figure on either side of the Atlantic was as consistent, as active, or as effective . . . Jefferson alone of the great galaxy of the *philosphes* embraced the whole of Enlightenment philosophy, interpreted it with matchless eloquence, added to it from his own well-stored mind, and translated it into law and practice on one of the great theaters of history."[4]

Unlike Jonathan Edwards who composed elaborate arguments and treatises on the subjects of free will and true virtue, Jefferson never wrote any books or treatises on moral philosophy—or on any branch of philosophy, for that matter. Jefferson complained, in fact, that his many activities and duties in public service left too little time for philosophical reflection and study. It is therefore quite remarkable that, amid all the activities of Jefferson's busy life in politics, he was able to organize his ideas into a coherent philosophy at all. We find his philosophy stated principally in his voluminous correspondence.

Philosophically, Jefferson was a materialist and a realist who was extremely well read in the ancient classics as well as in the modern European thinkers. As a materialist, Jefferson held the view that matter and its motions are fundamental in the universe and that mind and life depend upon them. He dismissed all skeptical arguments against the existence of matter or against the possibility of knowing its essential nature as inconsistent with experimental science as well as the practicality of common sense. The best evidence for the existence of matter and our dependence on it is to be found in the success of the physical sciences and in all the practical facts of technology and action. Matter and its manifold effects can be measured, counted, and also controlled. Jefferson admired Sir Isaac Newton and other scientists for their discovery of laws and properties of matter, because such discovery served to free man from superstition and ignorance—and contained numerous practical advantages and applications as well. Jefferson aligned himself with the ancient Greek Epicureans, who were also materialists. For them and for Jefferson, human happiness or well-being is the whole aim and purpose of life; and this is to be advanced by prudent pursuit of the right pleasures and avoidance of unnecessary pains. Moral virtue itself is to be valued for its utility in giving man tranquility, peace of mind, health, and general well-being. Ignorance and fear are two major obstacles to man's happiness. But for Jefferson, the more knowledgeable or enlightened that man becomes toward his material and social environment, the better he will be able to pursue his genuine happiness.

As a philosophical realist, Jefferson admired the Scottish commonsense philosophy of his own time. This philosophy declared that men's perceptions and ideas are not imprisoned behind a screen of subjectivity, but reveal objective, hard facts about an external, independently existing world. Man's perceptions, feelings, and ideas are not merely private fantasies or dreamlike appearances; rather they are real and true encounters with objective facts. Truth itself is not enclosed within the mind but indicates a real correspondence between the mind's ideas or perceptions and outside facts or realities. Some of our ideas or senses can be mistaken, of course; but according to Jefferson, not all of them are. We see the sides of a road apparently converge at a distance, but we easily correct this impression by other ideas—by traveling down the road or by remembering having done so. This realism also applies to man's moral ideas which, instead of revealing merely personal preferences or imagined opinions, reveal real moral facts or important, objective moral values. The commonsense position which Jefferson endorsed declared that man has an inborn moral sense as natural to him as his arm or leg. This sensitivity enables each person to judge for himself the moral rightness or justness of actions. Man is gifted with a basic sense of what is honest or fair and needs no elaborate reasoning or external authority to determine this for him. Morality is essentially social in its postulation of a basic interest that all men share in common—in contrast, for example, to taste or fashion. But Jefferson admits that the applications of man's moral sense may vary in different circumstances. He claims that the test of virtue is utility and that the same action may prove useful in certain circumstances and not in others. That circumstances may vary the uses or outcomes of man's basic moral sense is no reason, according to Jefferson, for one to doubt or deny the existence of this moral instinct common to mankind. It is clear to Jefferson that men have an innate sense of justice or moral rightness, since the only alternatives would make morality contrived, artificial, and hence arbitrary.

Jefferson considers a number of other views concerning the basis of morality and tries to show their inadequacy. To the suggestion that the basis of morality is religious and therefore depends upon the love of the divine being, Jefferson claims that the true situation is in fact the reverse. He asks, "If we did a good act merely from the love of God and a belief that it is pleasing to Him, whence arises the morality of the Atheist? It is idle to say, as some do, that no such being exists."[5] Religion must be based on the moral sense and must be subject to moral tests. Similarly self-love or self-interest cannot be the basis of morality either, since one's own interest can be selfishly gained at the expense of others. "Egoism, in a broader sense, has been thus presented as the source of moral action. It has been said that we feed the hungry, clothe the naked, bind up the wounds of the man beaten by thieves, pour oil and wine into them, set him on our own beast and bring him to the inn, because we receive ourselves pleasure from these acts."[6] But how is it, Jefferson asks, that we take pleasure in helping others? He answers, "Because nature hath implanted in our breasts a love of others, a sense of duty to them, a moral instinct, in short, which prompts us irresistibly to feel and to succor their distresses."[7] There would be no morality if man had no social feelings for the well-being of his fellow man. There would, in fact, be no natural rights either. If morality were artificially contrived or based simply on self-interest, a man's right to his life, liberty, and pursuit of happiness would also be contrived or a matter of contract.

Consequently Jefferson's view that morality is inherent or natural to man is essential to the view that man is entitled to certain rights as a human birthright. All men are entitled to be treated with equal respect as human beings. Natural rights are moral, not political, rights. They depend on man's sense of, and need for, justice and do not derive their authority from any government. Rather, governments derive their authority from the natural rights of man. As a consequence, every government has a moral responsibility which it neither creates nor can abolish. No government, for example, has the right to impose religious beliefs and practices on its citizens or to enforce any beliefs and practices without the consent of the people themselves. No government has the right to buy and sell human beings and impose involuntary slavery on man. All of these natural rights have, of course, been violated at one time or another. They were, in fact, significant issues during Jefferson's own time. The questions of religious freedom, the right to self-government, and the institution of slavery were three principal areas wherein Jefferson's moral belief in man's inalienable rights was brought to its severest test.

In his moral philosophy, Jefferson simultaneously held that man is governed by reason, that he has definite, inalienable rights, and that utility is the test of moral virtue. Fundamentally Jefferson believed that these three ideas were in harmony with one another. He had confidence not only that democracy or the will of the people would be able to work on a large scale, but that the reasonableness of the people could be trusted to support and respect the natural rights of all men. He further believed that the moral and natural rights of man could prove themselves by their utility in promoting human happiness and progress. Consequently some of Jefferson's greatest efforts were directed toward implementing and convincing others to accept (1) the separation of church and state, (2) the ideas that government belongs to the people themselves and that the earth belongs to the living, (3) the abolition of slavery, and (4) the idea that education is a public trust.

That Jefferson dedicated himself to applying his moral philosophy to the most criticial issues of his day, and that he achieved such great success in so doing, is perhaps the most important fact about his ethics. Not content merely to entertain and debate his moral ideas, Jefferson attempted the more difficult, far-reaching task of attempting enactment of these ideas into law. The difficulties and failures he encountered, as we shall see, became as important as his successes for later history.

Religious Freedom, Self-government, and the Problem of Slavery

In Jefferson's day, some persons believed that a common faith should be imposed on all the people in order to assure national unity. As many as five of the American states had, in fact, inherited Anglican religious establishments. It was against this background that Jefferson led in Enlightenment attempts to free the mind from coercion, especially in matters of religion. He asserted that "the legitimate powers of government extend to such acts only as are injurious to others. But it does me no injury for my neighbor to say there are twenty gods, or no God."[8] He regarded the Statute of the State of Virginia for Religious Freedom (1786) as one of his most important accomplishments. Quoted in part, it reads,

> We, the General Assembly of Virginia, do enact that no man shall be compelled to frequent or support any religious worship, place, or ministry whatsoever, nor shall be enforced, restrained, molested, or burdened in his body

or goods, nor shall otherwise suffer on account of his religious opinions or belief; but that all men shall be free to profess, and by argument to maintain, their opinions in matters of religion, and that the same shall in no wise diminish, enlarge, or affect their civil capacities.[9]

Jefferson considered this act a triumph of reason because he regarded the freedom of religious belief as part of that larger freedom that must be granted to the mind of man. As a deist, Jefferson was primarily interested in the moral side of religion, and he sought to locate those ideas that contribute to the genuine well-being of man in various religions and philosophies of the past. Jefferson dismissed as idle and irrelevant the theological side of religion, with its long history of divisive disputes over doctrines and dogmas. His admiration for the old Epicurean philosophers was primarily based on the wisdom of their teachings concerning tranquility and freedom from superstition and fear concerning the gods. This admiration, however, did not prevent him from criticizing their moral philosophy. He found their social ethics defective in developing man's duties and responsibilities to others. The specific concern with our duties to others was what Jefferson admired in the ethics of Christianity and the morality of Jesus. Of the latter he asserts, "A system of morals is presented to us, which, if filled up in the style and spirit of the rich fragments he left us, would be the most perfect and sublime that has ever been taught by man."[10]

Perhaps the most important moral implication of the whole notion of natural rights is the right to self-government. "Every man, and every body of men on earth, possesses the right of self-government. They receive it with their being from the hand of nature. Individuals exercise it by their single will—collections of men by that of their majority; for the law of the *majority* is the natural law of every society of men."[11] Men by their nature are entitled to the government of their own choosing. Consequently they have a moral right to abolish all forms of government that seek to impose themselves without the consent of the governed. This right to the government of one's own choosing, in Jefferson's view, implied that a truly democratic or free society must be willing to undergo a little rebellion now and then for its own good.[12] For Jefferson, the very idea of self-government or a free society implied its willingness and ability to tolerate strong differences of opinion and rebellion within its ranks. "If there be any among us who would wish to dissolve this Union or to change its republican form, let them stand undisturbed as monuments of the safety with which error of opinion may be tolerated where reason is left free to combat it."[13]

Jefferson's view that the earth belongs to the living implied that no generation of men has a right to bind another by its laws or constitution. Consequently there can be no perpetual law or perpetual constitution. Each generation has the moral or natural right to adopt or reject whatever laws and system of government it chooses.

As previously stated, Jefferson believed that enlightenment and education were essential to the successful working of self-government or a free society. He meant education not just for the few or for an elite aristocracy, however, but for the general populace. Jefferson wrote, "Enlighten the people generally . . . . No other sure foundation can be devised for the preservation of freedom and happiness . . . . Preach a crusade against ignorance; establish and improve the law for educating the common people. Let our countrymen know that the people can protect us against the evils of misgovernment."[14] As historian Henry Steele Commager observes, "All the founding fathers were educators . . . . Greatest of them all was Jefferson, who planned a complete educational system for Virginia, wrote educational provisions into the ordinances governing the West, and built the University of Virginia."[15] This statement points out a rather important difference between the European and American Enlightenment. Although the New World took many of its Enlightenment ideas from the Old, it developed a different moral viewpoint concerning education which produced important practical consequences. "While the Old World made science and scholarship the primary instruments of the Enlightenment, in the New it was rather popular education that was thought to be fundamental."[16] The idea that all free men have a right to be educated in order to participate meaningfully in the process of self-government—either directly or indirectly, by knowledgeable choice of their representatives—was essential to the whole idea of natural or equal rights as conceived by Jefferson. In practical application it implied that no artificial aristocracy or class system of education should be permitted to take government away from the people.

One very important but troublesome issue of Enlightenment Ethics involved the matter of slavery. Obviously the institution of human slavery is inconsistent with belief in the natural rights of man. If men are by nature free and equal, the whole institution of buying, selling, and using human beings as slaves is the most outrageous violation of man's inalienable rights. Nevertheless slavery not only flourished during Jefferson's time and in his own state of Virginia, but remained until well after his lifetime. It is also troublesome that Jefferson himself was a slaveowner and in the year 1794 owned about 150 slaves.[17] How is this glaring inconsistency to be explained? How can any sense be made from the fact that the author of the Declaration of Independence and the great defender of the natural rights of man was himself an owner of slaves?

First it must be admitted that the greatest shortcoming of the American Enlightenment was its failure to abolish the institution of slavery. This failure must be shared by all those who played some role in the formation of American democracy. Of all the Founding Fathers, however, none accomplished as much in the cause of abolition as did Jefferson. Jefferson not only believed slavery to be morally wrong and in violation of man's natural rights, but he actually advocated its abolition and introduced legislation to this effect on several occasions. His original draft of the Declaration of Independence contained a strong attack on the King of England for importing slaves to the New World. Referring to George III, Jefferson declared, "He has waged cruel war against human nature itself, violating its most sacred rights of life and liberty in the persons of a distant people who never offended him, captivating and carrying them into slavery in another hemisphere."[18] This passage was omitted by the Continental Congress. In the Virginia Assembly, Jefferson introduced a bill for ending the importation of slaves which was enacted. In addition, he proposed the prohibition of slavery in the Northwest Territory, but this failed in Congress by one vote. Finally "it was President Jefferson who urged, and signed, the bill which, at the earliest moment permitted under the Constitution, permanently outlawed the importation of slaves to the United States."[19]

Despite these efforts Jefferson lamented the lack of interest and action in doing something significant about the problem of slavery. In 1814 he wrote, "The love of justice and the love of country plead equally the cause of these people, and it is a moral reproach to us that they should have pleaded it so long in vain, and should have produced not a single effort, nay I fear not much serious willingness to relieve them & ourselves from our present condition of moral &

political reprobation."[20] Thus although Jefferson was more active than many in the cause of abolition, the fact that he was a slaveowner and his attitude toward the Negro raises a number of troublesome points about his views. In his *Autobiography* he asserted,

> Nothing is more certainly written in the book of fate, than that these people are to be free; nor is it less certain that the two races, equally free, cannot live in the same government. Nature, habit, opinion have drawn indelible lines of distinction between them. It is still in our power to direct the process of emancipation and deportation, peaceably, and in such slow degree, as that the evil will wear off insensibly, and their place be, *pari passu*, filled up by free white laborers. If, on the contrary, it is left to force itself on, human nature must shudder at the prospect held up.[21]

His statement that the two races, equally free, cannot live in the same government was at odds with his Enlightenment views of human nature, as was his claim that the solution to the problem is by emancipation and deportation. Some would indeed interpret Jefferson's views as racist. Whether this is or is not the case, his views were still inconsistent. So also the fact that he owned and used slaves, even though he was by all reports a benevolent master, was inconsistent with his whole philosophy of natural rights. To explain this by reference to the peculiar features of his time and place and by the fact that others such as Washington shared in this inconsistency is also insufficient. The failure to come to grips with the problem of slavery must remain as the greatest serious defect of the American Enlightenment and of Jefferson's ethics as well.

Assessment

That the period of the American Enlightenment was responsible for more important achievements than any other comparable period in American history can hardly be denied. A list and description of these achievements would fill several volumes. Concerning ethics, the most important legacy of the Enlightenment lies in the fact that many of the most enduring and salient features of the American mind and character were formed and given their classic expression during this period. Although the American Enlightenment did not invent the idea of natural rights, its articulation and significant implementation of these rights must count as its greatest contribution to American Ethics. The Enlightenment philosophy of natural rights has very definitely endured as a dominant influence in American life. In 1948 the General Assembly of the United Nations adopted a Universal Declaration of Human Rights as a common standard of achievement for all peoples and nations. This Declaration is similar in many respects to the one conceived by the Founding Fathers. Several prominent American moral philosophers of this century, including John Dewey and Sidney Hook, also acknowledged the contributions of Jefferson's Enlightenment Ethics, and their work shows the continued influence of Jefferson's thought.

We have already seen that the greatest practical shortcoming of Enlightenment Ethics concerned its failure to come to grips with the problem of slavery. On the theoretical side, the greatest shortcoming was the lack of clarity and precision involved in the whole notion of natural rights. Jefferson and other Enlightenment leaders were primarily active men of affairs and did not have the time or take the trouble to refine and explicate their ethical notions. Also Jefferson and others believed that the basic notions of ethics were either self-evident or very simple. This belief that certain basic ethical ideas are self-evident or simply a matter of common sense was perhaps the greatest error of Enlightenment Ethics. It should be pointed out, in fact, that this view was quite inconsistent with the Enlightenment view of human progress through the use of reason and experiment. If certain ethical truths are self-evident, how can men disagree or engage in lengthy disputes about them? Further, how can the basic ideas or principles of ethics be simple or self-evident when the fundamental ideas of the physical sciences, for example, are anything but simple or self-evident? Some ethical ideas may indeed be simpler than others, but since human affairs are much more complex than mere physical or inanimate phenomena, we cannot really expect any ethical ideas to be simple or self-evident.

The notion of natural rights is open to a number of troublesome objections for which we cannot find suitable replies in Jefferson or other Enlightenment thinkers. First, there is an awkwardness in the term "natural" itself. Presumably "natural" refers to something factual or empirically observable, whereas the term "right" refers to something claimed as a value, something normative which is not simply observable but requires thought or some idea to understand. It may be said, for example, that man has certain natural powers or abilities, just as animals have certain powers or abilities by nature. All of these powers and abilities can be empirically observed. But how would one find or observe a natural right in man or animal? And why, we may ask, are natural rights human rights? How is it to be determined that animals have no right to life, liberty, and their own pursuit of happiness? To suggest that animals have no natural rights because they do not need, deserve, or verbally claim them may simply be a prejudice on our part. Legal rights can be verified in the sense that we can determine whether a law has been made to establish a certain legal right. But how are natural rights to be verified if they antedate and do not depend on the existence of any man-made law? The English philosopher Jeremy Bentham (1748-1832), for one, opposed the whole concept of natural rights. He asserted that "there are no such things as natural rights—no such things as rights anterior to the establishment of government—no such things as natural rights opposed to, in contradistinction to, legal."[22] Consequently the view that man has certain natural rights because certain laws of nature exist which guarantee them involves a mistaken view of nature as a legislator. The fact that nature operates according to physical laws certainly does not mean or imply that it likewise makes laws in the sense of norms for man to follow. In many ways and on many occasions man chooses to change, modify, or nullify the operations of nature. If the big fish eats the little fish by nature, one might argue that the bigger or stronger man has a right by nature to subdue or exploit the weaker man. Examples of those who would use exactly such a notion of natural rights to maintain a racist ethics or the natural superiority of certain peoples are plentiful. But this only points up the fallacy hidden in the assumption that nature contains any distinct, self-evident standard of value for man. A moral value or right suggests something right or good that should be chosen or respected. But whether something actually *is* such a moral right or good must be demonstrated or proven.

All advocates of natural rights during the Enlightenment believed that adherence to, or respect for, the natural rights of man would generally and in the long run lead to happiness and well-being. But this is certainly not self-evident. Considerable dispute has, in fact, existed about whether certain things claimed as natural rights really do contribute to happiness or whether we should try to justify them in terms other than happiness. But equally bothersome is the question of deciding which are, and which are not, natural rights. No formula has yet, in fact, been found that satisfactorily determines for everyone what man's natural rights are. Some would claim property as a natural right as in The Declaration of Rights published by the French National Assembly in 1791, for example: "The end in view of every political association is the preservation of the natural and imprescriptible rights of man. These rights are liberty, property, security, and resistance to oppression."[23] But Jefferson, for one, did not include property. Some would claim abortion, suicide, or euthanasia as natural rights, others would not. From this it is hard to see how the notion of natural rights is capable of solving some of man's most pressing moral problems.

Finally we can confidently state that Enlightenment Ethics contributed a number of important moral ideas and innumerable practical goods for man. It did this, however, on very thin theoretical foundations. Its accomplishments in the area of political ethics are considerable. But its accomplishments in the realm of ideas remain confused and quite imperfect.

Chapter 3

Transcendentalist Ethics

American Transcendentalism

American Transcendentalism coincided with the flowering of romanticism and intense literary activity in New England between 1830 and the Civil War. Unlike Puritanism, which counted on the institution of the church or organized religion to expound and express its ideals, and unlike the Founding Fathers of the Enlightenment who utilized the institutions of government and laws to express their beliefs, the Transcendentalists withdrew from institutions and external forms of authority in order to stress man's self-reliance and spontaneous, original relationship to the world. Influenced by numerous European writers including Samuel Taylor Coleridge and William Wordsworth, the New England Transcendentalists sought to create and foster a fresh, creative, native American poetry and prose. Equally important to this development was a strong if unorthodox religious impulse to free man from outworn, arbitrary religious ideas and practices. True, the earlier Enlightenment had achieved a good measure of religious freedom and tolerance, but its espousal of deism or religion based on reason proved uninspiring and impersonal. Unitarian Christianity, which preached a liberal doctrine of man's goodness and moral affinity to the divine being, likewise appeared inadequate to Emerson, Thoreau, and other Transcendentalists. What was sought or needed was not a mere reform or reworking of older ideas, beliefs, and institutions, but a new angle of vision, a new, spontaneous source of inspiration that would enable man to find his own allegiances in ethics, religion, or nature totally from within. Thus the keynote of Transcendentalist Ethics is self-knowledge, inspiration, or intuition; man's excellence or virtue is his own wholeness or integrity rather than outward conformity to some external code or institution.

The term "Transcendentalism" was borrowed from the German philosopher Immanuel Kant whose *Critique of Pure Reason* was published in 1781. Kant had asserted in his Introduction, "I apply the term *transcendental* to all knowledge which is not so much occupied with objects as with the mode of our cognition of these objects, so far as this mode of cognition is possible *a priori*."[1] The key ideas for American Transcendentalism in this passage involve the identification of what is trancendental with the mode of our cognition of objects insofar as this is *a priori*. In other words, Transcendentalism came to mean a new angle of vision or way of looking at things, based not on the senses, but *a priori* on the mind or consciousness itself. Pure, spontaneous consciousness which each man possesses within himself was now to be the center of attention, the source of truth, and the ground of virtue. As Emerson asserted, Kant had succeeded in

> showing that there was a very important class of ideas or imperative forms, which did not come by experience, but through which experience was acquired; that these were intuitions of the mind itself; and he denominated them *Transcendental* forms. The extraordinary profoundness and precision of that man's thinking have given vogue to his nomenclature, in Europe and America, to that extent that whatever belongs to the class of intuitive thought is popularly called at the present day *Transcendental*.[2]

Taking their inspiration and name from Kantian and post-Kantian philosophy, the New England Transcendentalists breathed an essentially new and romantic meaning into this philosophic term. Certainly they were not followers or disciples of Kant or any other philosopher, but used the ideas of previous thinkers insofar as they found them inspiring. They did not actually subject these previous thinkers to probing analysis and investigation. They were interested neither in refuting nor in proving philosophical ideas, but were concerned instead with appreciation and self-knowledge. They studied Plato, Goethe, Shakespeare, and other great authors in order to sharpen and deepen their own creative talents. Plato, for example, was regarded by Emerson as the proper teacher for mankind because he taught that, while all real knowledge was innate within the mind, it had to be drawn out by disciplined questioning. Plato also believed in absolute forms of justice, beauty, and truth which eternally transcend the changing particulars of our experience.

But most of all, the Transcendentalists took their inspiration and moral clues from nature itself. For them the term "nature" signified that which is divine, original, and superbly beautiful. In his *Journal* (1853), Thoreau could boldly assert, "The fact is I am a mystic, a transcendentalist and a natural philosopher to boot."[3] Though they certainly did not always agree on what they understood nature to be or on the best method of approaching it, they were unanimous in their reverent, aesthetic praise of it. The whole natural world calls for spontaneous, free appreciation, at the same time it teaches man the higher moral or spiritual law. The beauties of nature and the great outdoors are inexhaustible and fully in harmony with human nature itself. In fact, man's highest estate is to achieve a sympathetic union or oneness with nature, whether in contemplating trees, landscape, or starry heavens. Emerson believed that everything is moral, everything is divine, when viewed in the right transcendental perspective. This pantheism or deification of nature was clearly intended to pass beyond what was perceived as the inadequate limits of Calvinism and even deism. Every idea or belief that a man has is autobiographical, revealing the nature and character of the man himself. But man, for the Transcendentalists, cannot be hedged in; man and nature have no limits. There are simply lower and higher viewpoints. The higher his viewpoint, the more imaginative and inclusive man becomes. The lower his viewpoint, the more passive and narrow he makes himself. For this reason, the Transcendentalists declared an independence from both empiricism and materialism in their moral outlook. Since all things are moral, the belief in, or study of, ethics itself is not a separate, specialized branch of learning or truth. Materialism as an outlook on life and the world regards the mind and everything else as dependent on matter. When it finds a place for ethics it usually limits this to the question of managing man's sensations or feelings of pleasure and pain. The Transcendentalist does not deny the existence of matter, sensation, pleasure, and pain, but includes them in his larger framework. Matter is indeed something we can perceive and use; experience, including sensation, pleasure, and pain, are accepted as elements or phases of our consciousness. But our consciousness is much broader and deeper than our senses. The senses, including what we perceive, depend on our perspective or angle of vision, and the mind or soul behind every perception is itself not visible, audible, or a product of sensation. The senses reveal particular appearances which are passive, whereas the mind can think or spontaneously comprehend universal laws or principles which are higher than appearances. The purer the thought or mind, the more self-reliant it is; the more self-reliant the mind or soul, the more virtue it contains.

Consequently the ground or standard of moral virtue is neither to be found in utility, as for Jefferson and the Enlightenment, nor in the will or love of a transcendent God, as for Edwards and the Puritans. Man does not need a separate natural or supernatural moral sense in order to apprehend and appreciate what is morally sound. Emerson's famous statement that "nothing is at last sacred but the integrity of your own mind"[4] meant that no external cause or test of virtue can exist. No man *can* consult an authority higher than his own ideals. But man's ideals are metaphysical, not physical; they cannot be weighed and measured, bought or sold. Nor can public opinion or majority rule validly determine what is really just, right, or wrong. Thoreau observed that:

> A government in which the majority rule in all cases cannot be based on justice, even as far as men understand it. Can there not be a government in which majorities do not virtually decide right or wrong, but conscience?—in which majorities decide only those questions to which the rule of expediency is applicable? . . . It is not desirable to cultivate a respect for the law, so much as for the right. The only obligation which I have a right to assume is to do at any time what I think right.[5]

Although the American Transcendentalists did not agree on every issue and held or formulated no systematic ethical philosophy, they did subscribe to a belief in self-reliance as well as a higher moral law. As strong individualists, they did not always agree on the remedies for specific issues of the day—on the issues of anti-slavery and the Mexican War, Thoreau went much further than Emerson. As is well known, Thoreau was jailed for refusing to pay taxes in protest of the Mexican War and slavery. Theodore Parker, by far the most liberal Unitarian minister of his time, believed like Thoreau in the necessity of civil disobedience, the deliberate breaking of immoral laws for a higher moral purpose. Emerson, to be sure, was opposed to slavery in any form and strongly opposed the Fugitive Slave Law of 1850, but Parker went much further. According to Edward Madden's *Civil Disobedience and Moral Law in Nineteenth-Century American Philosophy,* Parker "helped William and Ellen Craft escape from slave hunters and by threats drove the latter out of Boston. Then he went home and wrote President Fillmore what he had done, challenging him to enforce the Fugitive Slave Law."[6] Another member of the Transcendentalist group, Margaret Fuller, became identified as a pioneer of "votes for women" and served as editor of *The Dial* (1840), the first literary journal specifically devoted to expressing Transcendentalist viewpoints. In her 1845 essay *Woman in the Nineteenth Century,* she asserted, "I think women need, especially at this juncture, a much greater range of occupation than they have, to rouse their latent powers . . . . I have urged on Woman independence of Man, not that I do not think the sexes mutually needed by one another, but because in Woman this fact has led to an excessive devotion, which has cooled love, degraded marriage, and prevented either sex from being what it should be to itself or the other."[7]

Another notable aspect of Transcendental enthusiasm was the effort by George Ripley and others to launch a utopian society of communal living at Brook Farm and at Fruitlands. These experiments at idyllic living, though short-lived and ultimately failures, were nevertheless part of the Transcendentalist ethic—escape from the falseness and artificiality of ordinary society and creation of something new and more natural. Emerson could not join these efforts, could not become politically involved or lose himself in any particular act of social reform without, as he believed, scattering his force. One dominant value that Emerson shared with Thoreau was the excellence of solitude. To gather the real fruits of one's own angle of vision, one had to be alone. To achieve a sense of serenity and oneness with nature, one required the leisure and solitude to be free of the business of the world and the noise of the crowd. Solitude and freedom to be about one's own true vocation required, for Emerson and Thoreau, a break with what has been termed the "Protestant ethic." Thoreau was no doubt more extreme and vociferous in his condemnation of the materialism and bustle of the work ethic. Nevertheless both observed that man moves away from the center of his true self by placing too much emphasis on his acquired habits of making money and building reputation. The central features of Transcendentalist Ethics were, after all, the simplicity, naturalness, and unpretentiousness by which one was to live the good life. The real goal of this ethic as Emerson and Thoreau saw it—and there is no doubt that they saw it best—was to transcend or pass beyond all superficial and artificial relations and affiliations, to achieve a richer, more truly human experience and encounter, both with nature and oneself. Such achievement demanded time to tune in, not only to one's own thoughts but also to what were regarded as all the nuances and miracles of nature. For Emerson and Thoreau, all of nature is continually marvelous and miraculous if the viewer will but open up his soul. Every man is a genius, but only the eye of a poet can realize it.

The views that everything is moral and divine and that the "simplest person who in his integrity worships God, becomes God"[8] deliberately transcend the ordinary, accepted ways of viewing things. But this is the very thrust of Transcendentalist Ethics—to find the extraordinary in the ordinary, the supernatural in the natural.

Strictly speaking, no Transcendentalist doctrines exist to which we can point as unifying and defining its theory and practice. At most we can note a number of central tendencies which appear in its best work. The individuals who identified themselves with this romantic outlook prized their own individuality and creativeness. Without doubt, the two individuals who stand out as this group's most talented and famous authors are Emerson and Thoreau. No picture of Transcendentalism would be adequate which ignored either of these quite different thinkers. Each in his own characteristic manner pointed up the central insights and inevitable dilemmas that this movement produced. Emerson was essentially the elder statesman and moral theorist of this enterprise. He believed in preaching and spreading his own understanding about the moral law latent in every man. Thoreau was essentially the younger rebel who frowned on preaching and moralizing, and instead advocated the experience of living and following one's convictions wherever they might lead. Emerson was more detached and cautious in his approach than Thoreau, who threw caution to the winds when presented with issues which really mattered to him.

Ralph Waldo Emerson
and
Henry David Thoreau:
Principal Figures of Transcendentalist Ethics

Not only are Emerson and Thoreau considered the two most celebrated American Transcendentalists, but they were, in their characteristically different ways, the best exponents and spokesmen for the Transcendental moral viewpoint. According to historian Ralph Henry Gabriel, "For both men the central problem was one of ethics, and the task of the moment was to make moral energy effective upon the earth."[9] While this statement is basically true, one must nevertheless realize that Emerson and Thoreau did not share the same view of ethics and its fundamental position in life. Emerson, in a very definite sense, gave a much higher station to ethics and ethical principles in the scheme of things. Thoreau, on the other hand, cherished a more restricted, concentrated view of existence itself and thus found a characteristically narrower place for ethics in the make-up of things. Emerson gave more attention to ethics because he believed in the importance of preaching and moralizing. Everything in life, for Emerson, was an occasion for finding the moral law or lesson. "All things are moral. That soul which within us is a sentiment, outside of us is a law."[10] Thoreau expresses a similar outlook in *Walden* when he declares, "Our whole life is startlingly moral. There is never an instant's truce between virtue and vice. Goodness is the only investment that never fails."[11] Yet in his *Journal* (1842) he had remarked, "What offends me most in my compositions is the moral element in them. The repentant say never a brave word. Their resolves should be mumbled in silence. Strictly speaking, morality is not healthy."[12] Thoreau further indicates his negative feelings about morality: "The best thought is not only without sombreness, but even without morality . . . . Occasionally we rise above the necessity of virtue into an unchangeable morning light, in which we have not to choose in a dilemma between right and wrong, but simply to live right on and breathe the circumambient air."[13] Again, in his record of *A Week on the Concord and Merrimack Rivers,* Thoreau stated, "The conscience really does not, and ought not to monopolize the whole of our lives."[14]

How is this restriction or de-emphasis of moral concerns to be explained? On the surface, at least, there is an inconsistency. *Prima facie* Thoreau is not merely at odds with the main thrust of Emerson's view and the main tendency of Transcendentalism itself, but is apparently contradicting things which he himself maintained at various times. In the same work, Thoreau can maintain that "conscience really does not and ought not to monopolize the whole of our lives,"[15] then later say that the "whole body of what is now called moral or ethical truth existed in the golden age as abstract science. Or if we prefer, we may say that the laws of Nature are the purest morality."[16] To understand this inconsistency, we must realize that Thoreau (and all the Transcendalists, for that matter) did not attempt to formulate or argue a strict, rigid doctrine of moral philosophy. Transcendentalist Ethics, as previously stated, does not constitute a system. Instead, it expresses insights or various tendencies of thought. It was characteristic of Thoreau to leave his reader the task of drawing out the implication and import of his statements. Thoreau had an aversion to preaching or moralizing, hence no desire to be long-winded or to detail all the essential implications of his thought. Thus he could maintain an agreement with Emerson that the laws of nature are the purest morality and that morality is all around us—yet hold that morality in the form of conscience ought not to monopolize our life, since conscience is not the whole of morality but merely the subjective, censoring side of ethics and life. Thoreau believed in the necessity of resignation, obligation, and duty; but he did not believe that these constituted all, or the real essence, of man's existence. Life is not all duty, conscience, or performance of moral responsibilities. For Thoreau, a positive, joyous, even sensuous aspect of life exists that needs to be satisfied. Thoreau had claimed that he was not only a Transcendentalist, but a mystic and natural philosopher to boot. That these vocations are not easy to combine is clear enough. The naturalist or natural philosopher will want to observe, record, and appreciate the details of nature. The mystic will concentrate on the soul or mind in order to achieve a spiritual or higher consciousness.

Emerson had praise for mysticism and naturalism in his philosophy of life as well. He celebrated the great mystics of the world and never tired of talking about the wonders of nature. Compared to Thoreau, however, Emerson's approach to these subjects was detached and intellectual. Emerson's whole approach was cautious and reflective rather than passionate and sensuous; his thoughts and ideas were more radical than he was. Compared to Thoreau, Emerson lived more peacefully. His most radical moves were made early in his life, and even these were accomplished with relative ease and calmness. In 1832, at the age of twenty-nine, Emerson resigned his position as minister of the Second Unitarian Church in Boston because of his growing awareness that his religious convictions were unorthodox and that he could not sustain his faith within the strictures of a single creed. Although this was a radical ethical decision for Emerson, he left the pulpit on the best of terms with his congregation. In 1838 he delivered his famous Harvard *Divinity School Address* in which he declared that "historical Christianity has fallen into the error that corrupts all attempts to communicate religion. As it appears to us, and as it has appeared for ages, it is not the doctrine of the soul, but an exaggeration of the personal, the positive, the ritual. It has dwelt, it dwells, with noxious exaggeration about the *person* of Jesus."[17] These views were extremely offensive to more orthodox members of the clergy, and because of his radical views, Emerson was not invited to speak again at Harvard for almost thirty years. During this period, however, Emerson lived a happy and productive life, wrote most of his famous essays, lectured, and traveled throughout America and abroad, teaching his philosophy of self-reliance and Transcendentalism.

Emerson developed the essential insights of his moral viewpoint on self-reliance and the divinity of nature early in his life, and he continued to embellish these views, finding more and more applications for them. If faith in man and optimism regarding his ability to reform himself and overcome all limitations and adversities is central to Transcendentalist Ethics, Emerson is without doubt its greatest exponent and seer. Consequently Emerson's idealism, his view that all existence is essentially mental or spiritual, is actually predicated on his faith or optimism rather than derived from argumentation or indirect evidence. In his first major work, *Nature* (1836), he endorsed idealism as a metaphysics because it is most congenial to mankind's faith and hope. Idealism is the right view because it supports our best, i.e., loftiest values. It alone allows the valuer to take full credit for his ideals and virtues and encourages him to expand his talents without limit. Every man is potentially great—and the greater each individual becomes, the greater must be the whole of mankind. Emerson never talked down to his listeners; his whole effort was to raise them intellectually up. He taught his listeners a message that he sincerely believed they wanted to hear—that they were wiser than they knew. True, he came down hard on some popular values, but never to ridicule the common man who may have subscribed to them. If, for example, he ridiculed the love of travel or even philanthropy, his purpose was to encourage men to find and help themselves. Travel is only a "fool's paradise" if it takes man away from himself in order to fill him with trivia and pure externals. Philanthropy is only morally inferior to the extent that it fails to give men what they really need—the encouragement to help themselves and go independently about their own best work. Emerson held that what a man *is* is more important that what he has. Possessions are only externals or, at best, outward symbols of inner worth. Likewise Emerson held that the cheater cheats himself, that the thief in effects robs himself of his own integrity and better self. For Emerson, each individual soul is part of a vast universal reality termed the "oversoul." Men are distinct individuals, not carbon copies of one another; yet all men are equal in their inherent, infinite worth. Men are not to compare themselves with one another, for that would be the want of self-reliance. Men must compare themselves with what they can become, with the oversoul that allows each to develop his infinite worth, always from within.

Emerson's ethics presented a simple intuitive solution to the question of virtue and the problem of evil. His ethics, while not denying the existence of evil, taught that it can always be overcome. Evil is limitation, the recognition of the finite. No stronger evidence of Emerson's optimism exists than his faith that things cannot remain wrong or bad for very long. "Things refuse to be mismanaged for long."[18] "You cannot do wrong without suffering wrong."[19] All evils have their compensations in the course of time. Basically Emerson held that man's soul is of such positive strength that it "will not know either deformity or pain. . . . All loss, all pain is particular; the universe remains to the heart unhurt. Neither vexations nor calamities abate our trust. No man ever stated his griefs as lightly as he might. Allow for exaggeration in the most patient and sorely ridden hack that ever was driven. For it is only the finite that has wrought and suffered; the infinite lies stretched in smiling repose."[20]

Emerson's moral message was essentially optimistic and consoling. It is the mind or higher consciousness that Emerson prized, not the passions and senses. Man's greatest power lies in his intuitive consciousness, his angle of vision. What a man *is* is therefore not so much revealed in action and the world (since these are external and particular), but in what he intuitively thinks. All men are builders of ideals, and ideals themselves bring the greatest joys because they are eternal and universal. For this reason Emerson preached and endorsed the worship of great men. The study of Shakespeare, Plato, or Napoleon may reveal a glimpse of their ideals and thus stimulate one's own. If every man is a genius, the payment of respect to the greatness of a Shakespeare is, in effect, the payment of respect to the greatness within oneself. Every man is known by the ideals he keeps, and the wider or more inclusive one's ideals, the richer and more virtuous one's life.

It is well-known that Thoreau was greatly influenced by Emerson's views. Emerson's teachings on the central importance of self-reliance and nature were reflected in all of Thoreau's works. In 1841 Thoreau took up residence in Emerson's home, and in 1845 he began his famous sojourn at Walden Pond which was, in fact, located on Emerson's land. But although Thoreau received his stimulus and start from Emerson, he never became what may be called a follower or disciple. In fact Thoreau carried Emerson's ideas of self-reliance and love of nature to such an extreme that they clearly involved a new departure and break from Emerson's views. Thoreau asserted, "To be a philosopher is not merely to have subtle thoughts, nor even to found a school, but so to love wisdom as to live according to its dictates, a life of simplicity, independence, magnanimity and trust."[21] For Thoreau, neither self-reliance nor nature can be approached without literally living through them. One cannot merely think about them *a priori* or idealize them without living with them. Nature for Thoreau is not like a tame, domesticated animal that can be appreciated through storybooks or zoos. Nature is intrinsically wild and original and must be concretely encountered. In *Walden* he tells us,

> I went to the woods because I wished to live deliberately, to front only the essential facts of life, and see if I could not learn what it had to teach, and not, when I came to die, discover that I had not lived . . . I wanted to live deep and suck out all the marrow of life, to live so sturdily and Spartan-like as to put to rout all that was not life, to cut a·broad swath and shave close, to drive life into a corner, and reduce it to its lowest terms.[22]

In other words, Thoreau was essentially a radical empiricist who wanted to taste and experience the facts of existence for himself. Far from sharing Emerson's view that experience, concrete particulars, and the senses are secondary to the innate intuitions of the conscious mind, Thoreau sought to encounter the pure sensuous richness and fullness of things directly. In this respect, he reversed several of Emerson's basic notions. If Emerson considered the universal and eternal aspect of life primary, Thoreau emphasized the particular and immediate present. "Live in each season as it passes; breathe the air, drink the drink, taste the fruit, and resign yourself to the influences of each."[23] And, as he further declares, "Let me not be in haste to detect the *universal law*; let me see more clearly a particular instance of it."[24] Thoreau expressed his penchant for the present moment as follows: "Nothing must be postponed. Take time by the forelock. Now or never! You must live in the present, launch yourself on every wave, find your eternity in each moment. Fools stand on their island opportunities and look toward another land. There is no other land; there is no other life but this, or the like of this."[25] Emerson had preached a doctrine of intellectual independence, but Thoreau carried this doctrine to the point of attempting an actual experiment in solitary living in the wildness at Walden Pond. Thoreau would build his own shelter with the labor of his own hands, gather and grow his own food, and—above all else—do without the society of men. For Thoreau, putting self-reliance to the test meant confronting life physically and alone, not merely intellectually or in one's thoughts. He asserted, "I find it wholesome to be alone the greater part of the time. To be in company, even with the best, is soon wearisome and dissipating. I love to be alone."[26]

Thoreau's version of Transcendentalist Ethics was by far the most radical and solitary. It involved the severest renunciation of comforts and conveniences in order to better appreciate life in its purity and wildness. He agreed with Emerson that reliance on property and the dependence on governments to protect it involves a lack of self-reliance. He also agreed with Emerson that the less government we have, the better. But in his social ethics Thoreau was much more radical than Emerson, not only in the anarchy of his beliefs but in his own actions. It is well-known that Thoreau believed in, and practiced, civil disobedience. He not only asserted that "this people must cease to hold slaves, and to make war on Mexico, though it cost them their existence as a people,"[27] but he also aided Henry Williams,[28] a runaway slave, and went to jail for refusing to pay taxes in protest of government policy. Thoreau was outraged at the institution of human slavery and especially with the Fugitive Slave Law of 1850. He declared, "I cannot for an instant recognize that political organization as *my* government which is the *slave's* government also."[29] While he claimed that conscience is not the whole of life, he also believed that when conscience calls, talk or verbal commitment is not enough. If one is committed to freedom, one must prove and assert one's freedom in the first person singular. "Even if we grant that the American has freed himself from a political tyrant, he is still the slave of an economical and moral tyrant."[30] And on the question of slavery, Thoreau asserted, "Only *his* vote can hasten the abolition of slavery who asserts his own freedom by his vote."[31] Thoreau strongly attacked that philosophy which would define and justify man's obligations in terms of social expediency. He could not accept the view that one should act in accordance with the interests of the whole society. Morality, when it applies, cannot be a doctrine of calculating the social utility of one's actions. In his opposition to any ethics of mere utility or expediency, Thoreau was in accord with Emerson and Transcendentalism as a whole. But his interpretation of what this demands of the individual was intensely more radical and anarchical than all the others of this group.

Self-Reliance, Civil Disobedience, and the Aesthetic Quality of Life

If Puritanism was primarily a religious movement and the Enlightenment was basically political and social in its impact, it is true to say that Transcendentalism was decidedly individualistic and moral in its focus of attention. As an ethic, Puritanism was preoccupied with what it believed were man's duties to God. Enlightenment Ethics, on the other hand, concerned man's duties to his fellow man and, even more importantly, the freedoms or natural rights that all men were believed to possess. In relation to these earlier developments, Transcendentalism must be viewed as an attempt to transcend all manner of dependencies or intermediaries that would divert man from truly knowing and being himself. Admittedly Transcendentalism was idealistic, but it was a romantic type of idealism that found its clearest expression in literature rather than in theology or politics.

To achieve his proper perspective or angle of vision, the Transcendentalist had to retire, in a sense, from the world. To achieve a finer sensitivity or better perception of the world, the Transcendentalist required the leisure and opportunity to cultivate his moral and aesthetic insights. The integration of these insights was a distinct contribution of the Transcendentalists. By emphasizing the importance of both aesthetic appreciation and creation, they combined their interest in nature and self-reliance, the two major themes found throughout their writings. Thoreau celebrated the aesthetic, and especially the sensuous, qualities of nature in its intrinsic wildness, but at the same time enjoyed the creative powers that these experiences awakened in him. Emerson also celebrated the beauties of nature and drew creative inspiration from its constant freshness and variety.

The aesthetic sensibilities of the Transcendentalists were greatly offended, however, by the low level of politics and commercial materialism of the time. As social critics, they used their moral and aesthetic ideals to lure men away from the vulgarization and trivialization of their lives. When they dealt with matters of politics and religion, they appealed to what they believed were the inherent moral and poetic sensitivities, however hidden, within every person. They sought, in this appeal to the individual's conscience and sense of beauty, to make these unawakened, unused sources of energy effective in the lives of people. Their concern was with the quality of man's life which, by Transcendental standards, was judged too low, crass, and monotonous.

Emerson observed that "our culture is very cheap and intelligible. Unroof any house, and you shall find it. The well-being consists in having a sufficiency of coffee and toast, with a daily newspaper; a well glazed parlor, with marbles, mirrors and centre-table and the excitement of a few parties and a few rides in a year. Such is one house, such are all."[32] America's goals and basic interests are aimed too much toward purely economic, materialistic ends. "We are shopkeepers, and have acquired the vices and virtues that belong to trade. We peddle, we truck, we sail, we row, we ride in cars, we creep in teams, we go in canals—to market, and for the sale of goods. The national aim and employment streams into our ways of thinking, our laws, our habits and our manners. The customer is the immediate jewel of our souls."[33] In Thoreau we find the same complaint, that our life is actually lived with no proper moral or aesthetic principle, consumed instead by an economic or business one. "This world is a place of business. What an infinite bustle! I am awaked almost every night by the panting of the locomotive. It interrupts my dreams. There is no sabbath. It would be glorious to see mankind at leisure for once. It is nothing but work, work, work. I cannot easily buy a blank-book to write thoughts in; they are commonly ruled for dollars and cents."[34] This business ethic of Americans with its concomitant materialism tends to measure values and even the worth of man in terms of quantity and consumption. It leaves no time for the aesthetic appreciation of nature and implies the moral corruption of the individual which includes the awful institution of slavery and the use of war for undeserved gain. The Transcendentalists did not identify their concept of self-reliance with the business ethic of free enterprise, though others interpreted self-reliance in this way. Emerson saw self-reliance as involving or releasing creative energy in a purely moral, aesthetic sense. The quality that makes truly individual, self-reliant action significant must be understood in aesthetic terms. Although beauty is not the only measure of value for the Transcendentalist, it is the highest; as Emerson declared, "We call the Beautiful the highest, because it appears to us the golden mean, escaping the dowdiness of the good and the heartlessness of the true."[35] Beauty is the standard of moral value because it alone is self-justifying and needs no further reason or excuse for being. Unlike material or economic values, beauty and the aesthetic aspect of things cannot be quantified or exhausted by being consumed. For this reason it is regarded as a truly spiritual value. It stands as a finely tuned harmony between the spirit of man and the spirit of the natural world itself. Beauty of all values is the most inexhaustible, directly available, truly sharable, and supremely fresh. When Thoreau declared that "there is an incessant influx of novelty into the world and yet we tolerate incredible dullness,"[36] he pointed up the primary contrast between the aesthetic and unaesthetic manner of perceiving things. For him, the salient feature of the aesthetic manner is its rich particularity and constant variety. For Emerson, the most important feature of the aesthetic is its supreme universal or spiritual dimension which makes all other values pale by comparison.

The most conspicuous clash between Transcendentalist Ethics and American society of the time occurred over the issue of slavery. Though the Transcendentalists were not organized abolitionists, they spoke out in strong, emphatic terms on this violation of man's true freedom. As early as 1844, Emerson delivered an address celebrating the fact of emancipation in the British West Indies.[37] In 1854 he delivered a New York City address that strongly condemned the Fugitive Slave Law.[38] Also, in 1859, he presented an address in Boston pointing up the significance of *John Brown*.[39] And finally, in 1862, he spoke in Boston to celebrate the significance of *The Emancipation Proclamation,* the document signed by Lincoln in September of that year. Emerson's point in all these messages was to illustrate the way in which men rob themselves of their own true virtue by the enslavement of others. The moral lesson to be learned is that man releases himself from moral bondage by his removal of any enslaved person from bondage and by his refusal to sanction an immoral law. But, as Emerson observed, "Liberty is a slow fruit. It comes, like religion, for short periods, and in rare conditions, as if awaiting a culture of the race which shall make it organic and permanent."[40] He pointed out that emancipation, though important and morally necessary, is insufficient and that we should not overly congratulate ourselves on redressing this grievance since emancipation alone does not promise redemption of the black race. He suggested that a more firmly moral age and heightened moral sensitivity will not only defend the independence of these people but will actually give them rank and stature among men.[41]

Thoreau responded to this whole issue with a similar but characteristically different angle of vision. He spoke out against the lack of individual action: "There are thousands who are in *opinion* opposed to slavery and to the war, who yet in effect do nothing to put an end to them."[42] Clearly Thoreau saw less value and had less confidence than Emerson in the collective actions of men. "There is but little virtue in the action of masses of men. When the majority shall at length vote for the abolition of slavery, it will be because they are indifferent to slavery, or because there is but little slavery left to be abolished by their vote. *They* will then be the only slaves. Only *his* vote can hasten the abolition of slavery who asserts his own freedom by his vote."[43] Thoreau complains that, when unjust laws exist, men prefer to wait until the majority can be counted on to act for them. Men tend to hide behind what is perceived as the more secure shield of heavy numbers. They tend to follow and argue from expediency. They hold that one's individual action against an unjust law may do more harm than good. But Thoreau argued that "it is the fault of the government itself that the remedy is worse than the evil. *It* makes it worse. Why is it not more apt to anticipate and provide for reform? Why does it not cherish its wise minority? Why does it cry and resist before it is hurt? Why does it not encourage its citizens to be on the alert to point out its faults and *do* better than it would have them?"[44] What Thoreau meant by action from principle is not abstract and aloof from life and thus unchanging, but "action from principle, the perception and the performance of right, changes things and relations; it is essentially revolutionary, and does not consist wholly with anything which was."[45] A case in point is open civil disobedience, breaking the law by helping a runaway slave or going to jail for refusing to pay taxes which support an immoral or corrupt government.

Nevertheless Thoreau contended that our moral duties primarily extend to the point where they touch the individual. It is not a man's duty to right every wrong, but only those which in some real way touch him.

It is not a man's duty, as a matter of course, to devote himself to the eradication of any, even the most enormous wrong; he may still properly have other concerns to engage him; but it is his duty, at least, to wash his hands of it, and, if he gives it no thought longer, not to give it practically his support. If I devote myself to other pursuits and contemplations, I must first see, at least, that I do not pursue them sitting upon another man's shoulders. I must get off him first, that he may pursue his contemplations too.[46]

With a characteristically different emphasis, Emerson asserts,

> I do not wish to push my criticism on the state of things around me to that extravagant mark that shall compel me to suicide, or to an absolute isolation from the advantages of civil society. If we suddenly plant our foot and say, I will neither eat nor drink nor wear nor touch any food or fabric which I do not know to be innocent, or deal with any person whose whole manner of life is not clear and rational, we shall stand still.[47]

Emerson sees the true and effective method of reform as steady and mounting, but slow. "He who would help himself and others should not be a subject of irregular and interrupted impulses of virtue, but a continent, persisting, immovable person. . . . It is better that joy should be spread over all the day in the form of strength, than that it should be concentrated into ecstasies, full of danger and followed by reactions."[48]

Thoreau's angle of vision was much more impatient with immediate wrongs and with society's slowness to respond in time. "As for adopting the ways which the state has provided for remedying the evil, I know not of such ways. They take too much time, and a man's life will be gone."[49] For Emerson, in contrast, "There is a sublime prudence which is the very highest that we know of man, which, believing in a vast future,—sure of more to come than is yet seen,—postpones always the present hour to the whole life; postpones talent to genius, and special results to character."[50] Thoreau declared, "It is not my business to be petitioning the Governor or the Legislature any more than it is theirs to petition me; and if they should not hear my petition, what should I do then?"[51] On the other hand, Emerson, who never directly participated in acts of civil disobedience, was not averse to petition. As early as 1838, in fact, he sent a letter to President Van Buren protesting removal of the Cherokee Indians from the state of Georgia.[52]

On the question of reform, Emerson's larger, more serene vision made him sensitive to abuses that did not directly touch his person. When the abuses came nearer home, however, it was Thoreau who believed in taking direct, even illegal action, in which Emerson never participated. This contrast points up the fallacies of regarding the Transcendentalists as a united front or as idle dreamers with no influence on the major events of their time. True, they held no high office and engaged in no concerted political action;

but, principally through their writings and by their example, they exercised an influence much greater than their actual numbers. Their moral influence on the countless individuals who heard or read their thoughts must be counted considerable and as lasting well beyond their own time. Though they did not solve all the moral problems of their day, they set a higher tone and standard of conscience than previously existed. In calling for self-reliance, moral reform, and a high aesthetic quality of life, they added a precious ingredient to what was otherwise, at best, a mediocre style of American culture and life.

Assessment

No understanding of Transcendentalism would be adequate or complete without realizing the inspiration it received from William Ellery Channing (1790–1842), the extremely liberal Unitarian minister whose *Unitarian Christianity* was published in 1819 and *The Moral Argument Against Calvinism* in 1820. When Emerson was studying at Harvard, he heard Channing's sermons and came under his liberating influence. Emerson admired Channing's refusal to downgrade human nature or regard it as depraved. In fact, Channing had argued that "a trust in our ability to distinguish between truth and falsehood is implied in every act of belief, for to question this ability would of necessity unsettle all belief. . . . Nothing is gained to piety by degrading human nature."[53] Channing's espousal of man's own potential goodness has to be counted as an important stepping-stone to the Transcendentalist belief in self-reliance.

Equally important for an understanding of the Transcendentalists is the fact that they were not official members of American academic communities of their time. Although they lectured widely, they were neither professors nor administrators of any American college. They were independent of the more conservative, orthodox moral philosophy taught in American colleges during the nineteenth century. In the period following the Revolution, one of the most widely used books on moral philosophy was William Paley's *Moral and Political Philosophy*, published in 1785. This work combined an exposition of Christian morals with a utilitarian defense of what man may gain in the world to come by obeying the will of God. It appears quite obvious why this moral outlook was not congenial to the American Transcendentalists. By defining moral virtue as doing good to mankind in obedience to the will of God and by providing the sanction of moral obligation in terms of self-interest or utility, it clearly placed the essence of morals in external, authoritarian terms. In similar fashion the textbooks in ethics written by many American college presidents and used as sources for senior courses in ethics by such men as Francis Wayland of Brown, Mark Hopkins of Williams, Francis Bowen of Harvard, and Archibald Alexander of Princeton were not congenial to the Transcendental angle of vision. These textbooks, widely used in their day, are now forgotten. "The moral philosophy textbooks were dry and dull. Their moral platitudes about good intentions were more than sufficiently bland, and their authors were, for the most part, temperamentally conservative."[54] In contrast to Transcendentalism, this approach to ethics attempted to indoctrinate true virtue by rational argumentation.

By contrasting Transcendentalist Ethics with the textbook approach to morals, which was the academic vogue at the time, we can clearly observe some of the genuine merits of the Transcendentalist's position. Not the least of such merits is the fact that its leading lights were fine writers whose work deservedly has outlived its time. The writings of Thoreau and Emerson have become American classics, a permanent part of our literary tradition. Emerson's essays on *Self-Reliance* and *Nature*, along with many others, are perhaps more widely read than any other American works of their time. Thoreau's *Walden* and *Civil Disobedience* are also classics of the American literary tradition. The appeal of these works stems in large measure from the fact that they are imaginative and inspiring. Their moral message is presented in such a way that the reader never feels an external moral code of conduct being imposed on him from without; rather, the reader is encouraged to develop his own moral outlook in the highest possible sense.

One of the chief merits of Transcendentalist Ethics is that it did not attempt to present a final doctrine or code of conduct for men to follow. One finds no casebook of ethical answers or decisions which one is expected to follow in the works of Emerson and Thoreau. The whole idea of conforming to some established code of conduct is, in fact, the very antithesis of the Transcendentalist's insistence on self-reliance and creativity. Transcendentalism, by contrast, is thus superior to the aforementioned textbooks whose wooden, artificial moral exercises had little application to real life. The Transcendentalists presented their ethical insights and reflections in order to stimulate others to do the same. And in this they were admirably successful. Emerson touched on an exceedingly wide spectrum of subjects—from farming to religion, from wealth to culture. He was exceedingly open to all sources of ethical insight, including Oriental mysticism, Hellenic philosophy, and the great poets of the world. Thoreau also respected great books because they encouraged the reader to be discriminating in his judgments of all things. Thoreau said that the highest compliment paid to him was when someone asked him what he thought. In this sense, when he spoke out on moral topics, he was clearly trying to stimulate a thoughtful reaction in his readers rather than gain their acceptance or agreement. The Transcendentalist could never do a man's ethical thinking for him, for that in effect would rob the man of his own ethical power and responsibility.

One important contribution of the American Transcendentalists was the opening-up of a more imaginative interpretation of nature, man, freedom, and democracy within the American tradition. Prior to such efforts, the American tradition had not only relied almost exclusively upon past European thinkers; it had ignored any real poetic or aesthetic basis for its interpretation of any of these matters. The authority of Scripture and evidences of the ordinary senses, as well as the use of reason or rational argument, by the Puritan and Enlightenment interpretations had virtually ignored the possibility of grasping the concepts of man, nature, freedom, and democracy in the way the artist sees them—i.e., with poetic or aesthetic feeling and imagination. The Transcendentalists emphasized poetic or aesthetic intuition. What this signified was a warmer if even a sentimental approach to the world that was immediate and carried its own authority with it. The Transcendentalists objected to any cold, impersonal angle of vision that would separate man from his world or the perceiver from what he perceived. Man is involved in, and part of, whatever he sees or cares for.

It is somewhat ironic that the Transcendentalists, in borrowing their terminology from the German philosopher Kant, should have transposed Kant's ideas so radically as to misunderstand and controvert his central teaching. Emerson was the principal source of this misunderstanding. When Emerson alleged that "whatever belongs to the class of intuitive thought is popularly called at the present day Transcendental,"[55] he was following the lead of Coleridge, Schelling, and European romanticism—not that of Kantian philosophy. Kant had denied that intuition or direct awareness is by itself the source of any knowledge or insight. One of the most important ideas in the whole Kantian philosophy is the notion that concepts without percepts (intuitions) are empty and that percepts (intuitions) without concepts are blind. In other words, knowledge or genuine insight and understanding, for Kant, required the union of abstract ideas (concepts) and concrete or immediate presentations (intuitions). Intuitions that are not brought under concepts or general rules of the understanding are chaotic; and general concepts themselves, unless applied to sensory content, have no empirical or testable meaning.

There is a more serious flaw in Transcendentalism than simply mistaken terminology. It is one thing to borrow a term (Transcendental) and give it a new or different meaning. It is quite another matter to claim that any kind of intuition is a source of genuine truth or values without the proper evidence. Transcendentalism, in breaking away from external authority as the source of value and truth, also mistakenly abandoned the necessity of employing objective, independently obtained evidence for supporting any claim to knowledge or moral values. Transcendentalism is consequently tinged with subjectivism in its notion that we all see the world from our private vantage points with no objective evidence indication that any one of these different views is true or valid. In its insistence on individual inspiration and personal conscience, Transcendentalism failed to provide anything like an adequate analysis or elucidation of our basic moral concepts. Not all inwardly sincere ideas of right, wrong, good, or bad are equally cogent. Without the proper qualifications, the idea of self-reliance or relying exclusively upon one's own ideas can end in sheer confusion or absurdity. That no one is completely self-reliant goes without saying. But whether increasing one's self-reliance also increases one's virtue is problematic to say the least. The fanatic or moral zealot may be exceedingly self-reliant or unheeding of any advice or external evidence, but this does not mean that moral fanaticism or zealousness is morally sound or valid.

The principal failing of the Transcendentalist approach to ethics was its oversimplification of the whole idea of the moral life. The Transcendentalists erroneously believed that the voice of individual conscience or intuition was all that was needed to gain moral insight or understanding. They failed to provide any real analysis of moral concepts; in fact they even disparaged careful, analytical thinking as too indirect or remote from what they cherished as the center of man's moral life. Even Thoreau, who was more subtly analytical than Emerson, did not trust the continuous consultation of experience along with rational argument as relevant to the prime matters of ethics. When Thoreau wrote in his *Journal* (1842) "Who is old enough to have learned from experience?,"[56] he displayed an impatience with empirical investigation that made this seem unnecessary and paltry compared to the lively freshness of imagination or new intuition. Emerson, in exalting man's higher consciousness, was likewise impatient with experience and empirical evidence as showing us only the surface of things.

The Transcendentalists, with their doctrine of ethical intuition or conscience, were consequently unable to handle the whole problem of ethical or moral disagreement. If ethics rests on intuition or unaided, uncriticizable insight, how can we decide when intuitions disagree? And even when and if our intuitions happen to agree, how do we know when they are sound or right? In a similar way the Transcendentalists essentially ignored the existence of moral perplexity. Because they erroneously assumed that moral issues were simple and straightforward, they could not countenance the view that man does not actually know what is right. And for one to be told simply to consult one's conscience or self-reliance when a moral perplexity arises is rather unhelpful, to say the least.

In a similar fashion Emerson's solution to the problem of evil and the Transcendentalist's glorification of nature raise serious questions. To assert as did Emerson that "all loss, all pain, is particular; the universe remains to the heart unhurt . . . . No man ever stated his griefs as lightly as he might . . . . For it is only the finite that has wrought and suffered; the infinite lies stretched in smiling repose"[57] is no real consolation or solution to this problem. The mere classification of loss, pain, or suffering as particular and finite does not make them any less real. To suggest that these are merely parts of the whole, swallowed up by that which is universal or infinite, is no better than saying that good things are also fragments contained within a larger, infinite, or universal evil. Extreme pessimism is just as tenable by this form of reasoning as uncritical, extreme optimism. Emerson did not really seek to explain or critically evaluate the odious facts of pain, loss, or suffering. He simply classified them as imperfect, meaning that they are imperfectly, only apparently real. This is clearly a metaphysical solution to the problem of evil, in the sense of metaphysical which denies or bypasses the actual facts.

Regarding the Transcendentalist's exaltation of nature, it is one thing to find more in nature than common sense or unimaginative perceptions allow, but quite another to be carried away by the imagination and overestimate what nature really is or contains. Somehow one must distinguish between nature and the beauty or value it may afford. To identify nature with whatever beauty or value it may contain only creates confusion. To deify nature consistently would imply acceptance or worship of its discords, catastrophes, ugliness, death, and decay. Even Thoreau was troubled by the naturalness of disease and decay. That disease and death are just as natural as health and life certainly gives no warrant for overestimating or glorifying the original wildness of the natural world. Wildness may have its rightful place and value but not at the expense of man's attempts to tame and control certain of these wild forces. Only civilized man can afford the leisure and gain the perspective to appreciate nature as something wild at all. It must be remembered that, when Thoreau tried to live as simply and purely in nature as he could, he brought much civilization and cultivation with him. His two years at Walden Pond did not start from "scratch" but from all the education, society, and civilization that he had assimilated up to that point.

Finally we should observe that while the Transcendentalists were indeed perceptive social critics, were even heroic in some of the positions they took or examples they set, their social ethics is fraught with a number of difficulties. We may applaud their tendency to warn man against a false or vain identification of himself with narrow causes or reforms. In this sense the Transcendentalists were clearly humanitarians, not simply enthusiastic patriots or overzealous reformers. But their views of society and government tended to be based on oversimplification and false comparison. Their argument that the less government we have, the better—or the fewer laws, the better—is not necessarily true. This position suggests that the quality of government or of laws is a simple function of size or number. Government and laws of some kind are necessary for any civilization. Imperfections in any government and its laws cannot automatically be cured by reducing the number of laws or even the size or influence of government. Emerson suggested that "to educate the wise man the State exists, and with the appearance of the wise man the State expires. The appearance of character makes the State unnecessary."[58] But this position imposes a hiatus between morality and politics. To suggest that character specifically, and moral qualities generally, pertain only to the individual and not to collective bodies or institutions is inconsistent. A state or an institution can be better or worse than many of its actual members. Good men can in fact make bad laws, and bad men obviously violate or fail to live up to good laws. The appearance of character does not make the state unnecessary—far from it; rather, the appearance of character or individuals of good will requires all the resources of good government and laws to protect and serve the interests of themselves and others. Character or moral qualities cannot function in a vacuum. To make moral qualities purely internal or spiritual and politics and society purely external or even superfluous is mistaken. In order to evaluate or criticize society and government, one must suppose that responsibility can be shared, that responsibility does not apply exclusively to individuals acting alone. But the whole idea of sharing guilt or credit is foreign to the Transcendentalist belief in self-reliance. In a sense it can be said that the Transcendentalists actually had no social ethics. No wonder, then, that as time passed their belief in self-reliance was both misunderstood and considered irrelevant to America's increasing social complexity and industrialization. Transcendentalist Ethics was not really in tune with the advancements in science, technology, and society occurring in the last half of the nineteenth century.

Chapter 4

Pragmatist Ethics

American Pragmatism

Pragmatism represents the first major indigenous or original philosophy to appear in the United States. Prior to the development of pragmatism, American philosophies including Transcendentalism, the Enlightenment, and Puritanism were largely borrowed from European sources. In particular, moral philosophy in America prior to the inception of pragmatism was not based on the origination of any new methods of inquiry, but derived from various attempts to reformulate and defend much older, previously held moral beliefs. What characterized early American ethics was the attempt to locate, live by and defend what its partisans believed were absolute, fixed moral truths and certainties. Whether one appeals to a supernatural sense (Edwards), to a natural moral sense (Jefferson), or even to the higher intuitions of one's own self-reliance (Emerson), the result is very much the same. Each of these positions maintained that a fixed, universal moral order exists which man can apprehend and live by if he will only use the proper method.

Pragmatism represents a radical departure from this viewpoint of fixed assurance. Less concerned with what man should certainly and steadfastly believe, pragmatism inquired into the practical consequences of any supposed belief—what is the difference in terms of one's future experience whether he believes this or that idea? Instead of beginning with the assumption that some important truth or certainty exists for us to believe in, the approach of pragmatism was to ask what a belief actually means or signifies in terms of practical, testable outcomes. Pragmatism from its very inception signified a method of approaching issues rather than a doctrine or set of beliefs. Such an inquiry cannot be genuinely launched with the initial assumption that any self-evident, certain, or infallible answers can actually be attained. The idea that we can know or apprehend anything with certainty would, in fact, halt or block further inquiry; what is more, it would assume that the truth is fixed rather than changing and evolving.

The development of pragmatism in the United States must be understood in terms of the rise of natural science during the latter half of the nineteenth and early part of the twentieth centuries. Specifically, it must be viewed in the context of the leading scientific idea of the last century—evolution. Although this idea was neither absolutely new nor the exclusive origination of any single thinker, it was quite properly identified with Charles Darwin, whose *Origin of Species* was first published in 1859; *The Descent of Man* appeared in 1871. Darwin's factual detail brought together a number of tendencies in natural science that would challenge anew man's conception of himself and the world. Just as Copernicus and Galileo in an earlier age had challenged traditional medieval concepts by daring to suggest that the earth is neither at rest nor the center of the universe, so Darwin challenged some old, well-established moral and religious beliefs. This challenge appeared in terms of a naturalistic rather than a supernaturalistic conception of life, its various forms, and the means by which they emerged. "Struggle for existence," "natural selection," "accidental variation," and "survival of the fittest" were the dramatic new phrases used to usher in the theory of evolution. The main implication of this theory was that the natural world could no longer be viewed as comprising fixed natural kinds or species. All species including man have evolved over long periods of time by a process of natural selection. In the struggle for existence encompassing all living things, there occurs a slow, natural weeding-out process by which organisms adaptive to their environments manage to survive. In even broader terms, the idea of evolution suggests that the whole physical universe, rather than completed and operating according to fixed, eternal natural laws, is in the very process of creation or development into something new.

This idea of evolution gave added importance and prestige to the development of natural science and a naturalistic outlook on all things. It also gave greater attention to the importance of change as opposed to permanence, to the importance of contingency or even accidental variation as opposed to necessity and certainty. The originators of pragmatism—Charles Sanders Peirce (1839-1914) and William James (1842-1910)—were greatly influenced by the idea of evolution and sought to develop an appropriate philosophic interpretation of, and response to, this idea. In the early 1870's, Peirce, James, Chauncey Wright, John Fiske, and several others met in a group known as "The Metaphysical Club"[1] to discuss current philosophic topics including the idea of evolution. John Fiske became famous during the latter part of the nineteenth century as an expositor and defender of Herbert Spencer's evolutionary philosophy, which enjoyed a great vogue in America at the time. In 1874 Fiske published his *Outlines of Cosmic Philosophy* in which he sought to explain the concept of evolution and also to reconcile it with religion and ethics. Chauncey Wright, whose untimely death in 1875 cut short a brilliant career, actually published very little. Nevertheless his keen analytical mind and scientific interests had great influence on Peirce and James. Wright objected to vague metaphysical speculation, especially concerning the topic of evolution, as premature and unwarranted by the actual facts. He criticized the attempt of English philosopher Herbert Spencer to apply a general law of evolution to man, society, and the whole physical universe. He asserted,

Mr. Spencer's law is founded on examples, of which only one class, the facts of embryology, are properly scientific. The others are still debated as to their real characters. Theories of society and of the character and origin of social progress, theories on the origins and the changes of organic forms, and theories on the origins and causes of cosmical bodies and their arrangements, are all liable to the taint of teleological and cosmological conceptions—to spring from the order which the mind imposes upon what it imperfectly observes rather than from that which the objects, were they better known, would supply to the mind.[2]

But Peirce believed that metaphysical speculation could be united with scientific methods and logic. He thought that, with the proper methods of inquiry, the concept of evolution could be used metaphysically to explain the most general features of reality. Although Peirce published very little during his lifetime, his writings were quite extensive. Some years after his death those writings appeared under the title *Collected Papers of Charles Sanders Peirce* in eight volumes. When he died in 1914 he was generally recognized neither as the founder of pragmatism nor as an acute philosopher of the first rank. He made extensive studies in logic and the philosophy of science and actually attempted to construct an entire system of philosophy. By 1878 Peirce had published two important essays: "The Fixation of Belief" and "How to Make Our Ideas Clear." Although not really recognized at the time, they contained germinal ideas of what was later to be known as "pragmatism." In discussing the difference between belief and doubt, Peirce had said, "There is a practical difference. Our beliefs guide our desires and shape our actions."[3] Pragmatically considered, in other words, a belief is an idea we are prepared to act upon, or simply a rule or habit of action. Looked at functionally or pragmatically, a belief is what it accomplishes. Also, Peirce had observed that our conceptions of objects are, when we clarify them, conceptions of their effects.[4] Thus to the question "how are we to clarify our ideas?," the proper answer would trace out the practical consequences or effects that our ideas can have. When we understand the practical consequences or effects of our ideas, we *ipso facto* understand what our ideas mean. In his famous *Pragmatism* (1907), William James gave full credit to Peirce for originating the idea of pragmatism. He stated:

> The term is derived from the same Greek word πράγμα, meaning action, from which our words "practice" and "practical" come. It was first introduced into philosophy by Mr. Charles Peirce in 1878. In an article entitled "How to Make Our Ideas Clear," in the "Popular Science Monthly" for January of that year Mr. Peirce, after pointing out that our beliefs are really rules for action, said that, to develop a thought's meaning, we need only determine what conduct it is fitted to produce: that conduct is for us its sole significance.[5]

James added, however, that this idea "lay entirely unnoticed by anyone for twenty years, until I, in an address before Professor Howison's philosophical union at the University of California, brought it forward again and made a special application of it to religion. By that date (1898) the times seemed ripe for its reception."[6]

Peirce illustrated his pragmatic method by explaining "what we mean by calling a thing *hard*. Evidently that it will not be scratched by many other substances. The whole conception of this quality, as of every other, lies in its conceived effects. There is absolutely no difference between a hard thing and a soft thing so long as they are not brought to the test."[7] What Peirce sought thereby to introduce into philosophy was essentially an experimental or operational test of the meaning of our general concepts or ideas. Philosophy and also science depend upon the use of general ideas or concepts. But every general idea tends to be vague and may also be ambiguous. What is needed, then, is a method for pinning ideas down, a method that will locate insofar as possible exactly what each idea says or implies. Before we can test or determine the truth or validity of any idea, we must know in some clear sense what that idea means. Disputes in philosophy, for example, could never be settled without a clear understanding of what the ideas in the dispute may be asserting. Consequently Peirce regarded his own brand of pragmatism as an exercise in logic—or, more particularly, in what he termed "abductive logic." An experimental approach to meaning, according to Peirce, does not treat meanings as definitions found in dictionaries or as subjective impressions in people's heads. To approach the question of meaning, one must treat ideas as hypotheses or sets of inferences. This becomes clear with the realization that, in order to state the pragmatic meaning of an idea, one must translate the idea into a set of conditional propositions: if A signifies some experimental operation performed, B is an observed result or practical consequence of that operation. To explain what the idea of acid means, for example, one might venture the experimental hypothesis that (A) if we placed blue litmus paper in acid, (B) we expect or predict that the blue paper will turn red. If this experiment can be successfully repeated, we have gone far toward identifying this substance and determining exactly what we mean by calling it an acid. But it should also be noticed that no experimental test is definitive or infallible. Consequently, for Peirce, the logic of the pragmatic method can only give a probable conclusion. Peirce united his notion of pragmatism with what he called "fallibilism," the view that error is always possible in any genuine experimental inquiry. Fallibilism does not assert that any experimental hypothesis is actually false and therefore to be discarded; rather it says that any experimental hypothesis is tentative rather than final and that testing and search for further results should be continued. Consequently the pragmatic method for testing meaning will never give us the absolute or final meaning of any concept, but it will give us the most reliable meaning possible, subject to further testing and refinement.

Peirce was primarily interested in what he termed the "logic of pragmatism" and in using this idea toward construction of a scientific philosophy. His major concerns included logic, the philosophy of science, and the development of a scientific metaphysics. Peirce understood metaphysics as a speculative study of the most basic features of reality. Although he made room for ethics as a branch of what he termed "normative science," he gave no extensive attention to ethical questions and never developed what might be termed a Pragmatist Ethics. Peirce's importance for Pragmatist Ethics lies in the fact that he originated a general method which William James and others applied to the topics of morality.

William James was greatly influenced by Peirce and by Peirce's statement of the pragmatic method. Most important, however, is the fact that James radically transformed Peirce's pragmatism and turned it into a form of humanistic philosophy. In so doing, James not only originated pragmatism as a moral and humanistic outlook, but he succeeded in making pragmatism world-famous. What we must understand, therefore, are the new elements or ideas which James introduced into Peirce's original conception, and the elements or ideas he discarded. In this way we will better comprehend why James is credited for originating what is known as the pragmatic movement in twentieth-century thought—and why this movement has a decided moral emphasis.

Although they shared numerous points in common, including adoption of a pragmatic or experimental method for determining the meaning of ideas or concepts, Peirce and James had basically different conceptions of philosophy. Peirce thought of philosophy primarily in theoretical, logical, and systematic terms; whereas James' orientation was more practical, psychological or humanistic, and antisystem-building. In a sense Peirce had a narrower conception of the pragmatic method than had James. Peirce did not consider that the pragmatic method intended to clarify the meaning of all ideas, but restricted it to intellectual concepts.

> I understand pragmatism to be a method of ascertaining the meanings, not of all ideas, but only of what I call "intellectual concepts," that is to say, of those upon the structure of which, arguments concerning objective fact may hinge . . .

the qualities of hard and soft strikingly contrast with those of red and blue; because while red and blue name mere subjective feelings only, hard and soft express the factual behavior of the thing under the pressure of a knife-edge. (I use the word "hard" in its strict mineralogical sense, "would resist a knife-edge.") My pragmatism, having nothing to do with qualities of feeling . . .[8]

Peirce further held that his pragmatism concerned only the rational purport of concepts. It is therefore important to notice that what Peirce meant by practical consequences are not consequences of importance in any personal, moral, or humanistic sense. Instead they are consequences that have scientific significance in furthering inquiry or leading to the discovery of new facts or an actual scientific law. He emphasized the point that all of his pragmatic or practical consequences are essentially general, not subjective or particular. He thought that his pragmatism entailed the truth of realism and the denial of nominalism. Peirce's realism held that real, objective general laws or facts exist which cannot be exhausted by, or reduced to, particular instances. Nominalism asserts that general terms such as "hard," "soft," "man," or "force" are mere names representing collections of particulars. The nominalist holds that all existences are particular; there are no general facts, but merely groups or collections of particulars.

James was a nominalist and a pluralist. He began in philosophy as an empiricist and was greatly influenced by the nominalism of Chauncey Wright and the whole tradition of British empiricism. An empiricist regards ideas as deriving from, and pertaining to, experience. But a basic fact about experience is that it is always particular. All of our ideas are themselves particular, and all of their contents point or refer to particular existences. General ideas are only symbols of convenience—shorthand approximations for bundles of particular facts. The general idea of "man," for example, does not refer to some general essence or nature (human nature), but refers to all particular men. Only particular men exist; there is no way we can find in experience anything like "man" in general or an abstract person. The nominalist as an empiricist refuses to reify abstractions and therefore holds that universals or general concepts have no literal existence, but are merely symbols of particular things which do in fact exist. As a pluralist, James held that our experiences and the world which we experience are much richer and fuller than any of our mere general ideas or intellectual conceptions. Experience contains variety and detail which our general concepts leave behind or cannot contain. Further, our concepts tend to become fixed or changeless, whereas experience and reality are always changing and moving. James held, therefore, that, for our concepts to have any real meaning, we must continually apply them to experience. He termed his view "radical empiricism" to call attention to his belief that traditional empiricism was too limited, static, and compartmentalized.

Radical empiricism emphasizes the essential point of pragmatism, that the meaning of our ideas is not given in terms of past experience but must be found in terms of future consequences. The meaning of an idea, for James, must be located by tracing its practical consequences, but the only consequences which are practical are those still to come. Practical consequences imply those over which we can have some actual control, while past experience is gone and beyond our control. Radical empiricism means that "the only things that shall be debatable among philosophers shall be things definable in terms drawn from experience"[9]; but, he adds, "the relations between things, conjunctive as well as disjunctive, are just as much matters of direct particular experience, neither more so nor less so, than the things themselves."[10] The older forms of empiricism were based too much on the idea of past experience and not geared to the future. These older forms also failed to note that the relations between things are not alien to experience or imposed on it by the mind but are found directly within it. Thus James can say "that therefore the parts of experience hold together from next to next by relations that are themselves parts of experience. The directly apprehended universe needs, in short, no extraneous transempirical connective support, but possesses in its own right a concatenated or continuous structure."[11]

James interpreted Peirce's pragmatic rule in a radically empirical and pluralistic way. As interpreted by him, the pragmatic question became: What particular difference does any idea make for you or me in our actual life experiences? To have pragmatic meaning for James, an idea must make a difference in terms of someone's actual and future experiences. Peirce construed the practical value of ideas in terms of the theoretic interest of furthering inquiry and finding more objective reasonableness and increasingly better general laws. James broadened the practical usefulness of ideas to include not only their theoretical usefulness but their humanistic value in enhancing man's life morally, religiously, and aesthetically. The theoretic interest in ideas is only one among many others. We use ideas as instruments not only to lead us to new facts or to enhance our understanding of things, but also as instruments which have a definite usefulness in helping us make better life adjustments. Pragmatism, for James, was more than a method for clarifying the meaning of our ideas because it provided a way of finding truth and value as well.

In this way James broadened Peirce's original conception of pragmatism and turned it into a humanistically centered life philosophy. Although James still considered pragmatism as essentially a method and not a final or finished doctrine, this method was important for its moral usefulness. Far from remaining neutral or disinterestedly objective in the pursuit of facts, James saw the pragmatic method as a way of dealing with, and deciding, man's choices of values and commitments to them. He also held that, in dealing with these problems, the pragmatic method could not claim absolutely certainty or finality; but it could claim to lead toward progress. Pragmatism, as James saw it, can help us to decide whether we are fated or free, whether we have a right to believe in religion, or whether we can justify any optimistic attitude toward existence at all. As it applies to the personal problems of everyday living, pragmatism can offer us a justified moral outlook. But it must be realized, according to James, that insofar as these problems have a personal meaning, they cannot be answered or handled in purely intellectual terms. Pragmatism cannot offer us a rational proof of free will or of any moral belief, for that matter. James held that the important value questions concerning what goals man ought to pursue or how he should live his life are not intellectual puzzles that can be solved merely by recourse to logic or fact. For James, the most important thing about a human being is his outlook on life, his personal philosophy. No actual, living philosophy is purely based on reason or is a sole product of one's intellect. Philosophy is fundamentally an expression of one's temperament, feelings, and whole personality. Every philosophy has its psychological roots in the makeup, needs, and concerns of the individual person. How we view the world depends upon our selection of facts and our arrangement of them into some kind of coherent picture. Every philosophy is humanistic in the sense that some "human" interest has selected the facts and arranged them into a picture of the world. Even all scientific efforts are humanistic in this sense. It is in fact impossible, according to James, for man to adopt a purely objective point of view that has no connection with human interests. The abstract and physical sciences quite properly attempt to remove subjective bias in order to discover the truth, but the pursuit of truth itself must be understood as a fundamental human concern. Truth, no matter how abstract or remote, is not some colorless, neutral, and static term. Truth, in its fundamental makeup, is a species of value, a very important kind of good.

William James was responsible for originating what is known as the "pragmatic theory of truth." After publication of his *Pragmatism* in 1907, he followed in 1909 with *The Meaning of Truth, A Sequel to Pragmatism.* Clearly this theory was a sharp departure from Peirce. Peirce thought of truth in terms of impersonal, scientific methods of investigation. For Peirce, truth was to be defined in terms of the entire scientific community of investigators. Truth for him signified that end upon which all serious investigators would converge if they carried their inquiries to the ideal limit. James developed a quite different concept; instead of thinking of truth as an impersonal ideal confined to the scientific community, he regarded it as having personal and moral significance. "The truth of an idea is not a stagnant property inherent in it. Truth *happens* to an idea. It *becomes* true, is *made* true by events. Its verity *is* in fact an event, a process, the process namely of its verifying itself, its *verification.*"[12] In other words, truth is to be defined in terms of an idea's functional value, its capacity for leading us to the facts. True ideas are those which work toward leading us to their facts; whereas false ideas or lies do not work in this fashion. Because he defined true ideas as those which work, James' theory occasioned considerable controversy and criticism. It was alleged that this kind of pragmatism glorified action and expediency at the expense of honesty and other moral values. Some critics even claimed that this way of looking at truth was simply an expression of the American business mentality with its vulgar interest in gaining profit and advantage. If ideas are true because they work or are efficient, it would seem to follow that lies, which often work to deceive people, would be pragmatically true. But James' point was that, in order to be true, ideas must work specifically in leading us to their facts.

Admittedly a lie may work to deceive people or even to gain a profit, but this does not mean that lies are pragmatically true; for they do not lead us to their facts. James tried to dispel misunderstandings of his theory of truth and devoted an entire chapter of *The Meaning of Truth* to this very problem.

By the time he published his pragmatic theory of truth, it had already gained support—in America, principally in the work of John Dewey's philosophy— and, in England, from F. S. C. Schiller. Pragmatism was now launched as an important philosophical movement that gained worldwide attention. Dewey preferred to call his version of pragmatism "instrumentalism." He asserted, in fact, that James "regarded conceptions and theories purely as instruments which can serve to constitute future facts in a specific manner. But James devoted himself primarily to the moral aspects of this theory . . ."[13] Dewey was primarily responsible for continuing the humanistic tendency of pragmatism after James' death. His version of pragmatism, in contrast to that of James, contained a decided social emphasis with specific relevance to the development of what has become known as "progressive education."

One of James' most important contributions to Pragmatist Ethics was his concept of the will to believe. In his essay *The Development of American Pragmatism,* Dewey made special mention of this fact: "William James accomplished a new advance in Pragmatism by his theory of the will to believe, or as he himself later called it, the right to believe. The discovery of the fundamental consequences of one or another belief has without fail a certain influence on that belief itself."[14] James argued that our efforts of will or our beliefs in certain ideas can themselves be effective in helping those beliefs come true. In fact James held that certain truths may not be realizable at all without our definite belief or faith in them. This is particularly true with respect to moral and religious matters. From the standpoint of his pragmatism, James claimed that our desires, choices, and acts of faith must be viewed functionally in terms of their ability to help produce certain results. By believing that one can accomplish a certain action or result, a person may help bring that action or result into existence. This is not certain or guaranteed, of course. James did not claim that we can perform courageous or heroic deeds simply by wanting or trying to do so. But he did claim that without faith or belief there could be no real moral life at all. Faith and willpower, he claimed, can be effective and help bring desired results. He contended that viewing faith and will as merely subjective or static phenomena enclosed within someone's mind or private experience is not sufficient. The will to believe in certain moral values must be viewed in terms of the practical consequences that follow from our acts of desire or choice. In this manner James hoped to show how an ethics of pragmatism is indeed possible and even desirable for man. Pragmatism in ethics calls for a healthy respect for the facts; it must be empirical. At the same time pragmatism must apply to things that are practical and of real importance; and, it must thus address itself to values and morals since it must be humanistic.

This is exactly what James sought to develop in his moral philosophy—a harmonizing of man's interest in, or need for, both values and facts. James gave the name "meliorism" to the tendency of his pragmatism to balance tough-minded concern with brute facts and tender-minded concern with moral values and ideals. Facts without values would be humanistically worthless; at the same time, values ungrounded in facts would be vain and irresponsible. James accepted the challenge to try reconciling the tough-minded scientific craving for facts and evidence with the tender-minded or idealistic concern for values or meaningful goals. Indeed, the success of his Pragmatist Ethics must stand or fall on this very attempt.

William James: Principal Figure of Pragmatist Ethics

William James was one of the foremost pioneers in the development of modern psychology. After receiving his M.D. degree at Harvard in 1869, he began teaching anatomy and physiology there in 1873. In 1875 he began teaching psychology and by 1879 his interests had turned to philosophy. At this time he started work on his famous *The Principals of Psychology,* which was finally published in 1890. This work, a pioneering effort in the field, established James as a major figure in philosophical psychology. He sought to apply empirical and naturalistic methods of inquiry to an understanding of man's whole mental life including consciousness, the emotions, volition, and human conduct. This involved the application of the concept of evolution to man's whole mental life. Man's "mental life is primarily teleological; that is to say, that our various ways of feeling and thinking have grown to be what they are because of their utility in shaping our *reactions* on the outer world."[15] Consequently mental phenomena and activities cannot be understood *a priori* or intuitively, but must be studied empirically in terms of their practical consequences. Not only does psychology offer many practical applications that can help enhance man's life, but the whole study of psychology must be viewed pragmatically in terms of tracing the effects that man's mental life produces. To understand what consciousness is, we must understand what it does in helping the organism adapt or function in its different life situations. Consciousnessness—and all mental activities, for that matter—will remain an unfathomable mystery as long as we tend to regard them as entirely self-enclosed or cut off from the natural world. Consciousness has appeared mysterious because man has tried to find its rational essence—what it is in terms of itself alone. But such a purely transcendental or introspective method is unscientific and doomed to failure. "Mental facts cannot be properly studied apart from the physical environment of which they take cognizance. The great fault of the older rational psychology was to set up the soul as an absolute spiritual being with certain faculties of its own by which the several activities of remembering, imagining, reasoning, willing, etc., were explained, almost without reference to the pecularities of the world with which these activities deal."[16] James further added, "But the richer insight of modern days perceives that our inner faculties are *adapted* in advance to the features of the world in which we dwell, adapted, I mean, so as to secure our safety and prosperity in its midst."[17]

Consequently the proper study of man's mental as well as his moral life must be pragmatic; i.e., both functional and relational. Consciousness is obviously essential to morality, since if no one had any moral interests or concerns—if no one felt any difference between that which is good or bad, right or wrong—morality would be an entirely meaningless term. Morality is, then, functionally related to consciousness. Any morality worthy of the name must consider the feelings, sensitivities, needs, and demands that appear in individual consciousness. This means, of course, that no absolute, fixed, objective moral order exists independent of man's preferences and conscious concerns. Morality comes into existence to the extent that it is sought or desired. There can be no purely rational or intellectual refutation of a thoroughgoing moral skepticism. In mathematics, for example, we can answer the skeptic who asks for rational proof. Whether $2 + 5 = 7$ or whether the area of a circle is πr^2 does not depend on anyone's desires or feelings, but on discovery of abstract, objective sets of relations. In ethics, however, if the skeptic asks for a rational proof that courage is morally good or that justice is morally right, no purely rational or *a priori* demonstration can be effective.

For James, "The first thing to grasp in moral philosophy is the volitional rather than the purely intellectual character of the whole enterprise."[18] In his essay *The Moral Philosopher and the Moral Life* (1891), he tried to answer three fundamentally different but related questions in ethics which he termed the psychological, metaphysical, and casuistic: "The psychological question asks after the historical *origin* of our moral ideas and judgments; the metaphysical question asks what the very *meaning* of the words 'good,' 'ill,' and 'obligation' are; the casuistic question asks what is the *measure* of the various goods and ills which men recognize, so that the philosopher may settle the true order of human obligations."[19] James refused to allow that the origin of all our moral ideas can be explained simply on the basis of past experience. Our moral ideas have many sources, but they cannot all be defined in terms of past utility or "as signifying corporeal pleasures to be gained, and pains to be escaped."[20] Our higher moral values and concerns "present themselves far less in the guise of effects of past experience than in that of probable causes of future experience, factors to which the environment and the lessons it has so far taught us must learn to bend."[21] Moral ideas form a complex plurality which refuses to be pinned down to any simple form of hedonism. James argued that many of our best moral ideas are new, even revolutionary. They are anticipations of our possible moral future rather than records of our moral past.

To the metaphysical question, James offered a simple but radical, even paradoxical, answer:

> The only possible reason there can be why any phenomenon ought to exist is that such a phenomenon actually is desired. Any desire is imperative to the extent of its amount; it *makes* itself valid by the fact that it exists at all. Some

desires, truly enough, are small desires; they are put forward by insignificant persons, and we customarily make light of the obligations which they bring. But the fact that such personal demands as these impose small obligations does not keep the largest obligations from being personal demands.[22]

James refused to separate the validity and the bare existence of any moral obligation or claim. No moral values can exist unless they are demanded or required by some concrete, conscious agent. But no abstract, impersonal standard of validity can possibly sit in judgment on any moral desire or demand. No moral desire's validity can be decided *a priori* or by any standard which is external or extraneous to that desire itself. Here James' pluralism asserted itself in the strongest possible terms. But the problem this view must face is the contention that it leads to moral bankruptcy by way of moral anarchy or chaos.

James noted that many answers have traditionally been given to the casuistic question. "Various essences of good have thus been found and proposed as bases of the ethical system. Thus, to be a mean between two extremes; to be recognized by a special intuitive faculty; to make the agent happy for the moment; to make others as well as him happy in the long run; to add to his perfection or dignity; to harm no one; to follow from reason or flow from universal law; to be in accordance with the will of God; to promote the survival of the human species on this planet. . . ."[23] But none of these are completely satisfactory answers because no moral philosophy or principle can actually be formulated in advance. The only principle that will work in every case, according to James, is "that *the essence of good is simply to satisfy demand.*"[24] This principle at least leaves the ultimate decisions of ethics open to revision. But it nevertheless insists that there can be no ethical goods at all unless they are demanded or unless someone cares about having them. James accepted the implications of this principle that the real casuistic question is tragically practical. Legitimate conflicting demands in man's moral life do, in fact, exist; and these cannot be resolved by the pretension that they do not exist or that one principle or demand takes precedence over all the others. The "ethical philosopher's demand for the right scale of subordination in ideals is the fruit of an altogether practical need. Some part of the ideal must be butchered, and he needs to know which part."[25] Every ethical choice or decision is taken at a risk with no guarantee of success. Not only may an ethical decision fail to achieve the particular good it aims for, but it may fail to achieve a greater good as a whole. The only ethical ideal that we should all aim for, according to James, is inclusiveness "so as to vote and to act as to bring about the very largest total universe of good which we can see."[26] According to James, the only actual moral order is one that is in the process of being made, hence is still quite imperfect. Man can actively participate in seeking to perfect the tragically practical ethical universe in which we actually live. It is just because this universe is riddled with competition and conflict that the pragmatic method is best suited to deal with it. The pragmatic approach to the moral life calls for testing our ethical concerns by the practical results to which they will lead in the future. It calls for a strenuous ethic because it encourages as great a plurality of concrete ethical interests as men are capable of promoting. It places a high moral premium on effort since, without the effort or will to have certain values, man's goals cannot be achieved at all. James admitted that

> Of course we measure ourselves by many standards. Our strength and our intelligence, our wealth and even our good luck, are things which warm our heart and make us feel ourselves a match for life. But deeper than all such things, and able to suffice unto itself without them, is the sense of the amount of effort which we can put forth. Those are, after all, but effects, products, and reflections of the outer world within. But the effort seems to belong to an altogether different realm, as if it were the substantive thing which we *are*, and those were but externals which we *carry*.[27]

The most distinctive note in James' ethics is the central role he gave to the moral effort or energies of men. "Thus not only our morality but our religion, so far as the latter is deliberate, depend on the effort which we can make."[28] He wanted to show not only that moral effort can be effective in shaping our future; but that only moral effort or the will to believe in a better future makes our future worth having in moral terms. In order to come to terms with the claims of moral effort, however, one must face the free-will controversy head on. In *The Dilemma of Determinism*, he tried to show how this problem could be solved. In *The Principles of Psychology*, he admitted "that the question of free-will is insoluble on strictly psychologic grounds. After a certain amount of effort of attention has been given to an idea, it is manifestly impossible to tell whether either more or less of it *might* have been given or not."[29] Determinism claims that choices already made and actions already completed could not have been otherwise. Indeterminism claims just the opposite—that other choices and actions were indeed possible and could have been undertaken instead. The whole issue here, according to James, depends on the notion of possibilities—what could or could not have been done. James contended that science deals in facts or actualities and cannot rule on such matters as "could," "might," or "possibility." Once a choice has been made, science may try to find what led to it or caused its occurrence. But science can never prove that, once a choice has been made, no other choice *could* have occurred. It is the same with respect to actions: Once an action has been performed, science can try to find the antecedent causes which probably led to that action. But science is powerless to prove that no other choice or action could have been undertaken. Such a claim would have to be decided *a priori* or postulated without real empirical proof. But science is just as incapable of proving the indeterminist's thesis—that other choices and actions could have been undertaken instead. Consequently the dispute between determinists and indeterminists is metaphysical; it goes beyond any purely factual accumulation of evidence; it pertains to one's entire outlook on life and the world. It is just this kind of dispute that the pragmatic method is suited to resolve. The method of pragmatism is designed to cut through verbal entanglements and resolve such fundamental disputes that might otherwise be unending. Thus if no purely intellectual or theoretical solution to this problem exists, perhaps there is a practical solution. What practical difference will it make in anyone's actual future experience if he believes in determinism or indeterminism? For pragmatism, it should be remembered, a belief is an idea upon which one is prepared to act. A belief provides us with a rule for expectations of future facts. "Hard determinism"[30] as opposed to "soft determinism" adopts a thoroughly tough-minded attitude toward future facts; it holds that they are rigidly governed by universal law or simply fated to happen. Nothing is allowed to chance, and "possibilities that fail to get realized are, for determinism, pure illusions: they never were possibilities at all."[31] Indeterminism, on the other hand, pictures an open future with things not already fixed in their course. It involves a real belief in chance happening and adopts a tender-minded hope that man's goals and values can count for something. In a practical sense indeterminism leaves room for faith, hope, and even regret; whereas determinism can find no practical or theoretical value for such ethical concerns. Thus an important moral difference exists between determinism and indeterminism. Determinism essentially turns our moral judgments into illusions. "Calling a thing bad means, if it means anything at all, that the thing ought not to be, that something else ought to be in its stead. Determinism, in denying that anything else can be in its stead, virtually defines the universe as a place in which what ought to be is impossible—in other words, as an organism whose constitution is afflicted with an incurable taint, an irremediable flaw."[32]

The practical outcome of determinism is that it leads to pessimism as far as the moral life is concerned. It cancels any hope that man's moral efforts may make any difference in what is yet to come. But such pessimism is incapable of being proven; it is not grounded in the facts. Total moral pessimism is based on emotion, a feeling of despair in the face of what is viewed as a pointless universe.

The practical outcome of indeterminism, according to James, is at least a piecemeal type of moral optimism. It does not pretend to know that the future will be better, nor does it claim that every human effort will arrive at its chosen goal. But it does claim sense for the belief that the future can be *made better*. Indeterminism gives man a right to believe in his own efforts and most cherished interests. James, however, wanted to avoid the idea that indeterminism leads to sentimentality or subjectivism. The practical outcomes of what James called "nerveless sentimentality" or "sensualism without bounds" are both morally bankrupt. Morality is not simply a matter of feeling; it requires an objective factor regarding conduct. The feeling of courage or honor cannot in reality be separated from the performance of courageous or honorable actions. Moral values, in short, cannot be isolated from the tragically practical world where hard decisions must be made, where disappointments must be met, and where real loss is essential to any feeling of regret.

Consequently James could not accept any simple solution to the problem of evil and suffering in the world. He could not accept Emerson's romantic outlook which managed to evaporate the evils and sufferings of life in the wake of some absolute or infinite good; nor could he allow that evil and suffering are justified as a punishment for original sin. Pragmatically there is no *absolute* justification for the evils, sufferings, and disappointments of life. The pragmatic approach to these things is to see them always as specific defects, losses, or challenges in the moral life. Pragmatist Ethics knows no moral good or bad apart from specific, concrete situations that may and do arise. The practical character of this ethics is that it involves specific issues and concerns that cannot be conveniently pigeon-holed under any available universal rules. This does not mean that general ideas are useless in ethics; but it does mean that general formulas are only as good as the particular instances they coincide with or enlighten.

A sound Pragmatist Ethics must inevitably place a high value on moral tolerance. While it must take sides and have its opinions about the interests of others, it cannot pretend to make judgments for them or compel them to submit or subscribe to what it finds to be good. Tolerance in ethics goes hand in hand with moral plural-ism. Tolerance would be unnecessary in morals if all men had the same sensibilities, interests, or wants. But tolerance would not require any great moral effort or energy if men did not have a certain blindness to the feelings and situations of others. That man does have such a blindness is a stubborn fact that must be faced in the moral life. But equally, the fact exists that man has great resources of moral energy that can and should be called upon to enhance the total good.

Moral Individualism, Science, Evolution, Religion and The Gospel of Success

As Ralph Barton Perry has observed, "The most perfect philosophical expression of American individualism is to be found in the thought and personal characteristics of William James."[33] James succeeded in creating and popularizing a pragmatic approach to both philosophy and psychology that placed the highest premium on individual initiative. James had a knack of writing in a vivid, dramatic style that always maintained the reader's interest. Whether he dealt with abstruse philosophical topics or technical psychological ones, he always remained the perfect individualist and pragmatist in his search for concrete applications of ideas with meaning for the individual. As a champion of moral individualism, James did not identify his own position with any extreme formulation. He did, of course, defend the rights of others to their views. But his own brand of moral individualism tried to uphold a delicate balance between the opposite extremes of what he called "tough-mindedness" and "tender-mindedness." The tough-minded side of James' individualism called for verification or grounding of our ideas in the facts. The tender-minded side required a searching for, and definite allegiance to, human values. Moral individualism claims that the concrete individual is always the basic, irreducible unit of moral discourse and meaning. The individual may indeed be explained by certain laws and generalizations, but he cannot be explained away or simply reduced to his environment or some abstract principle. Morality for James was nothing if not personal and depended on individual choice, commitment, and conduct. In terms of moral priorities, the individual comes first; the society or group is only secondary. In his famous analysis of the stream of human consciousness, James found clear support for this view: "The first and foremost concrete fact which every one will affirm to belong to his inner experience is the fact that *consciousness of some sort goes on* . . . . Consciousness, then, does not appear to itself chopped up in bits. Such words as 'chain' or 'train' do not describe it fitly as it presents itself in the first instance. It is nothing jointed; it flows. A 'river' or a 'stream' are the metaphors by which it is most naturally described."[34] How does consciousness function? James answers: "(1) Every 'state' tends to be part of a personal consciousness. (2) Within each personal consciousness states are always changing. (3) Each personal consciousness is sensibly continuous. (4) It is interested in some parts of its object to the exclusion of others."[35] That human consciousness is intensely personal and selective does not, of course, exclude the existence of mental habits and common experiences shared by individuals. Without habits and common experiences, practical life could not continue; communication between people would be impossible. Consciousness has a subjective as well as an objective existence. In pragmatic terms, consciousness is subjective to the extent that it functions as a subject, perceiver, or selector within experience. A private dimension to experience exists which can never be made public or purely objective. Qualities of feeling are perfect illustrations of subjective experience. But consciousness also has an objective function and dimension; it cannot be consciousness without contents of some sort. "As 'subjective' we say that the experience represents; as 'objective' it is represented. What represents and what is represented is here numerically the same; but we must remember that no dualism of being represented and representing resides in the experience *per se*. In its pure state, or when isolated, there is no self-splitting of it into consciousness and what the consciousness is 'of.' Its subjectivity and objectivity are functional attributes solely."[36] By regarding consciousness as pragmatically functional, we can study it in terms of the way it works. Instead of regarding it as a static substance, James preferred to regard consciousness as a dynamic set of relations within experience.

The difference, then, between what we call the mental and the physical is solely a matter of their having different functions within experience. James was neither a materialist nor an idealist, since he refused to reduce the mental to the physical, as materialism does; and he refused to reduce the physical to the mental, as in idealism. Matter and mind are only known to us in terms of experience. Consequently pure experience itself is the only raw material or data on which we can fall back in our philosophy. Our world is one of pure experience which we divide or interpret in many different ways. The diversity of concrete detail and incessant changes that occurs in experience is its most prominent feature, which rules out any single, fixed principle that can cover all of its facts. Consequently monism and absolutism are completely incongruous with a pragmatic philosophy faithful to experience. As James asserted, "The pragmatism or pluralism which I defend has to fall back on a certain ultimate hardihood, a certain willingness to live without assurances or guarantees."[37] But piecemeal, practical guidelines can be devised. One such precept which James offered concerns the control of emotions:

> In rage, it is notorious how we "work ourselves up" to a climax by repeated outbreaks of expression. Refuse to express a passion, and it dies . . . There is no more valuable precept in moral education than this, as all who have experience know: if we wish to conquer undesirable emotional tendencies in ourselves, we must assiduously, and in the first instance coldbloodedly, go through the *outward movements* of those contrary dispositions which we prefer to cultivate.[38]

It will do no good to think or brood about an undesirable emotion; that will only make it worse. To control our emotions, we must control our behavior, and of the two our behavior is more readily controllable. We cannot turn our emotions on and off at will, but we can more easily change our postures, movements, perceptions, and expressions. According to James, our emotions are not self-contained but are rather the feelings of complex bodily states. If emotions are caused by the arousal of bodily stimuli, we can change our emotions by changing those stimuli. Common sense assumes that we cry because we are sorry or that we strike or insult someone because we are angry. But James' theory of emotion reverses this commonsense position. "The hypothesis here to be defended says that this order of sequence is incorrect . . . the more rational statement is that we feel sorry because we cry, angry because we strike, afraid because we tremble."[39] In other words, our emotions result from certain responses of our body to external cues or stimuli. We do not freely choose to experience the emotions we do, but we can voluntarily control the conduct or behavior which will automatically make us experience certain emotions. The moral point here is that we cannot overcome undesirable emotions such as envy, hatred, or despair by making mental resolutions not to feel these emotions. Instead of intellectualizing or theorizing how useless or morally bad these emotions are, a more effective method is to directly engage in a different behavior that will, in turn, make us feel contrary or different emotions. If we want to get rid of despair, according to James, we must engage ourselves in constructive activities—stop crying and start smiling, stop tearing ourselves down and start building ourselves up. James admitted that this type of moral therapy is not easy, of course, and in fact requires us to be quite hard on ourselves. If we fail to check a bad impulse in time or yield to an undesirable emotion, that emotion becomes much more difficult to modify in the future.

Moral individualism implies a strenuous ethic, because the individual must bear the weight of moral responsibility. While moral individualism implies a belief in free will, free will only has pragmatic meaning to the extent that the individual acts in accordance with a definite faith in his own freedom. The first act of individualism or free will is the "existential leap" that affirms one's individuality or freedom. But the first act is never the last and must in fact be reaffirmed in every moral situation. One feature that distinguishes a moral situation or question is its characteristic inability to wait for proof. *"Moral questions* immediately present themselves as questions whose solution cannot wait for sensible proof."[40] By suspending judgment or putting off a moral question, we have in fact already responded to it. Moral questions are practical, not theoretical, issues. By the time we study them or locate sufficient evidence for their solutions, they may no longer exist or may have changed. This is why moral decisions were tragically practical for James; viewed in terms of the ideal good, some part of that ideal must be lost or butchered. The concrete individual is the only source of moral interests or demands. But it is a notorious fact that not all individual demands can be satisfied.

One of the most serious moral issues concerns the persistence of war in human history. There is no need to catalog the brutality, suffering, and waste that war has produced. But also according to James, there is no need to accept war as inevitable. In a 1910 essay called *The Moral Equivalent of War*, James explored the possibility of finding a moral substitute for the horrors of war. He admitted that "militarism is the great preserver of our ideals of hardihood, and human life with no use for hardihood would be contemptible."[41] He stated that "so far, war has been the only force that can discipline a whole community."[42] If we grant that the military virtues of courage, honor, loyalty, and service are worthwhile, the problem is whether we must also have the evils of war in order to have these virtues. To supply these virtues, is it necessary that thousands or millions of human beings must combat, maim, and destroy one another? James did not think so; he championed another alternative. Why can not man employ his energies and military virtues to subdue and harness nature, James asked, rather than to fight wars?

> If now—and this is my idea—there were, instead of military conscription, a conscription of the whole youthful population to form for a certain number of years a part of the army enlisted against *Nature*, the injustice would tend to be evened out, and numerous other goods to the commonwealth would follow . . . To coal and iron mines, to freight trains, to fishing fleets in December, to dishwashing, clotheswashing, and window-washing, to road-building and tunnel-making, to foundries and stoke-holes, and to the frames of skyscrapers, would our gilded youths be drafted off, according to their choice, to get the childishness knocked out of them, and to come back into society with healthier sympathies and soberer ideas.[43]

One of the more important issues of James' day concerned the possible conflict between science and evolution on the one hand and between religion and morals on the other. The dispute actually centered on the alleged conflict between various philosophical interpretations of science and evolution and their relation to certain humanistic values and ideas taught by religion and morals. James addressed himself directly to a number of these problems, especially in *The Will to Believe* (1896) and *Great Men and Their Environment* (1880).

During the last half of the nineteenth century, the British philosopher Herbert Spencer enjoyed a great vogue in the United States. "Spencer's philosophy was admirably suited to the American scene. It was scientific in derivation and comprehensive in scope. It had a reassuring theory of progress based upon biology and physics . . . It offered a comprehensive world view, uniting under one generalization everything in nature from protozoa to politics."[44] Spencer's approach was, in many ways, opposite that of William James. Spencer's view of philosophy was deductive and deterministic, attempting to infer particular changes in nature and human society as absolutely necessary or inevitable. He believed that a general law of evolution, everywhere at work in the universe, guarantees inevitable progress. There is inevitable movement everywhere from the homogeneous to the hetereogeneous, from the simple to the complex. It was Spencer who coined the phrase "survival of the fittest," which was used to champion a ruthless evolutionary ethic in which all weak, unfit, or poor members of society were judged as naturally inferior, hence dispensable in the drive for progress. Spencer also attacked the "great man theory of history."

> The genesis of societies by the action of great men may be comfortably believed so long as, resting in general notions, you do not ask for particulars. But now, if dissatisfied with vagueness, we demand that our ideas shall be brought into focus and exactly defined, we discover the hypothesis to be utterly incoherent. If, not stopping at the explanation of social progress as due to the great man, we go back a step, and ask, Whence comes the great man? we find that the theory breaks down completely.[45]

Spencer argued that "the genesis of the great man depends on the long series of complex influences which has produced the race in which he appears . . . Before he can remake his society, his society must make him."[46] James took strong exception to this theory and declared,

The causes of production of great men lie in a sphere wholly inaccessible to the social philosopher. He must simply accept geniuses as data, just as Darwin accepts his spontaneous variations . . . The mutations of societies, then, from generation to generation, are in the main due directly or indirectly to the acts or the example of individuals whose genius was so adapted to the receptivities of the moment, or whose accidental position of authority was so critical that they became ferments, initiators of movement, setters of precedent or fashion, centres of corruption, or destroyers of other persons, whose gifts, had they had free play, would have led society in another direction.[47]

Social changes, according to James, are not inevitable or simply determined in a mechanical way by antecedent conditions. The more carefully we look, the more we discover accidental variations and individual initiative which play vital roles in social evolution. Social change is due to the interplay between individuals and their environments, but this interplay is plastic, complex, and changing. It cannot therefore be completely plotted in advance nor explained as simply the result of vague general laws of history. "The evolutionary view of history, when it denies the vital importance of individual initiative, is, then, an utterly vague and unscientific conception, a lapse from modern scientific determinism into the most ancient oriental fatalism."[48]

James was strongly critical of the evolutionary ethics popular during his day. "The philosophy of evolution offers us today a new criterion to serve as an ethical test between right and wrong. Previous criteria, it says, being subjective. . . . Here is a criterion which is objective and fixed: *that is to be called good which is destined to prevail or survive.* But we immediately see that this standard can only remain objective by leaving myself and my conduct out."[49] The survival of the fittest, that which is destined to prevail, is an empty, useless ethical criterion since it leaves out individual initiative in the true sense. The efficacy of individual initiative is just the sort of thing that cannot be calculated or established in advance. If individual effort, interest, and conduct are simply subsumed by the inevitable forces of fate or progress, they can have no real, i.e., individual, effect. Any such ethical rule "would lead to its practical refutation by bringing about a general deadlock. Each good man hanging back and waiting for orders from the rest, absolute stagnation would ensue."[50] No laws of history plot out the inevitable road to progress or collapse. All genuinely scientific laws, James pointed out, are conditional. They do not state that such and such will inevitably occur; rather they assert that certain things will happen *if* certain other things are true. Science, in other words, affirms the contingency of cause and effect, not any kind of fatalism. James distinguished sharply between any fatalistic philosophy of evolution and our special knowledge of particular causes of change. The former, he alleged, is a metaphysical creed, an emotional attitude, while the latter is true science. Science is painstaking in its search for particular, definite causes and evidence. It rightly seeks to be patient and dispassionate in its search for truth.

There is a fundamental difference between the interests of science and those of morality and religion. *"We must know the truth; and we must avoid error,—*these are our first and great commandments as would-be knowers; but they are not two ways of stating an identical commandment, they are two separable laws."[51] In morality and religion, unlike science, we cannot suspend our judgment until we have sufficient evidence. Scientific questions are not personal and valuational; they are factual. Morals and religion present forced and momentous options to us. We have a personal stake in what we believe—our personal well-being or salvation is necessarily involved. Strictly speaking, there should be no conflict between the scientific attitude and morals and religion. To believe in a scientific truth on the basis of insufficient evidence would indeed be improper. Avoidance of error and inaccuracy are so important in science that the scientific attitude must avoid jumping to conclusions in order to make its best advance. But in morals and religion, where human life or well-being is at stake, suspension of judgment for lack of sufficient evidence would be ridiculous. We never have sufficient scientific evidence for our beliefs. In these areas it is quite rightly imperative that we cultivate and act on personal faith. For James, this did not mean that morals and religion are inherently occult or superstitious. Rather it signified that they deal with values, sentiments, and vital interests. "Morality says some things are better than other things; and religion says essentially two things. First, she says that the best things are the more eternal things. . . . The second affirmation of religion is that we are better off even now if we believe her first affirmation to be true."[52]

Pragmatism asserts that we have a genuine right to believe in our moral and religious values despite insufficient evidence. For pragmatism contends that our active beliefs in values can help bring about those very goods. To believe in justice, courage, or saintliness, for example, is essential to realization of the goods that these virtues can bestow. Science or intellectual analysis can never tell us how to measure or estimate the relative worth of justice as compared to mercy. Individual choice or initiative is required here. The value of individual initiative lies not in any law or preordained pattern, but in the fact that it can be creative—it can, by experience, be shown to help bring about various goods which otherwise would not exist at all.

A notorious fact about pragmatism is that it became easily identified with American commercialism and worldly success. Its rapid rise to fame and popularity in the twentieth century stems in large measure from this identification. James had indeed declared, "On pragmatic principles we can not reject any hypothesis if consequences useful to life flow from it."[53] It is understandable how this and similar formulations were taken by the popular mind to signify a philosophy best suited for businessmen, lawyers, doctors, and men of action. When James declared that "any idea upon which we can ride, so to speak; any idea that will carry us prosperously from any one part of our experience to any other part, linking things satisfactorily, working securely, simplifying, saving labor; is true for iust so much, true in so far forth, true *instrumentally*,"[54] he seemed to encourage the identification of pragmatism with worldly success. Thus it is not surprising that the earliest critics of pragmatism seized on this identification. The well-known British philosopher Bertrand Russell made this criticism when he declared, "I find love of truth in America obscured by commercialism of which pragmatism is the philosophical expression."[55] William James was well aware of this interpretation and considered it an unfortunate mistake. "The name 'pragmatism' with its suggestions of action, has been an unfortunate choice, I have to admit, and has played into the hands of this mistake."[56] But James further added that no word could protect the philosophy of pragmatism from being narrowly interpreted to apply primarily or exclusively to money-making or gaining of some similar advantage. James admitted that pragmatism certainly does apply to the business world and to practical affairs; ideas do indeed work commercially, legally, medically, and so on. But, he added to think that pragmatism as a philosophy is primarily concerned with the commercial working of ideas or with providing a rationale or justification for a gospel of worldly success is a serious mistake. Ideas work theoretically and morally as well, and it is these workings on which pragmatism mainly focuses. As a philosophy or philosophical method, pragmatism is not concerned with buttressing or defending already firm beliefs or commitments. Rather it is a method of inquiry to help find what is cognitively true and morally good for us to believe. For James, pragmatism had a cognitive and moral purpose rather than a crassly commercial, material aim. Ideas are important in a pragmatic sense because they are cognitively and morally useful; cognitively useful insofar as they serve as intellectual instruments that lead us to the facts; morally useful insofar as they function to raise the quality of our lives. Pragmatism does not signify a penchant for success at any cost or a drive to "get ahead" with no thought of where we are going. In one of his strongest utterances, James condemned "the exclusive worship of the bitch-goddess Success. That—with the squalid cash interpretation put on the word success—is our national disease."[57] In his moral outlook James was, in fact, a champion of the underdog and against every aspect of bigness:

> I am against bigness and greatness in all their forms. . . . The bigger the unit you deal with, the hollower, the more brutal, the more mendacious is the life displayed. So I am against all big organizations as such, national ones first and foremost; against all big successes and big results; and in favor of the external forces of truth which always work in the individual and immediately unsuccessful way, under-dogs always, till history comes, after they are long dead, and puts them on the top.[58]

Assessment

Well before he published his famous *Pragmatism* in 1907 and well before the term "pragmatism" became identified with a major American philosophical movement, James had already formulated many of the key ideas that comprised his Pragmatist Ethics. As early as 1879 in the essay entitled *The Sentiment of Rationality*, James had declared that

> every way of classifying a thing is but a way of handling it for some particular purpose. Conceptions, "kinds," are teleological instruments. . . . It is far too little recognized how entirely the intellect is built up of practical interests. . . . Faith is synonomous with working hypothesis. . . . the highest good can be achieved only by our getting our proper life; and that can come about only by help of a moral energy born of the faith that in some way or other we shall succeed in getting it if we try pertinaciously enough.[59]

It is a serious mistake, however, to interpret James' ethics as simply another form of utilitarianism. Utility is *a* test for moral actions, but it is not *the* test, as its proponents suppose. James admitted that it is reasonable to try satisfying as many demands as one can. Inclusiveness, if that means striving to achieve the greatest amount of satisfaction or happiness of the greatest number of individuals, is certainly *a* worthy ethical goal, however imprecise or vague it may be. But it is certainly not the only moral goal and is definitely not the highest. As John Wilde has correctly noted, "The ethics of inclusiveness often attributed to James levels down all desires and claims to the same qualitative level, so that only quantitative considerations remain."[60] For James, "The deepest difference, practically, in the moral life of man is the difference between the easy-going and the strenuous mood. When in the easy-going mood the shrinking from present ill is our ruling consideration. The strenuous mood, on the contrary, makes us quite indifferent to present ill, if only the greater ideal be attained."[61] Hedonism and utility are standards that govern or apply to the easy-going, conventional moral life. But moral heroism, the ethics of the strenuous moral life, clearly goes beyond the calculations of pleasure or utility and all so-called conventions of ordinary morality.

The strenuous moral life calls for innovations rather than conventions, creation of new ideals rather than calculation of how to achieve old ones. But this strenuous type of life is still pragmatic in the Jamesian sense since individual risk taking always entails a hope of success along with the possibility of disappointment and failure. Personal risk taking in the attempt to realize any truly heroic moral ideals cannot be explained in purely utilitarian terms. Such actions are not even practical, if by practical one means efficient or safe. These heroic efforts are indeed pragmatic insofar as they involve a higher than ordinary exercise of moral energy with the consequent chance of a finer moral success. The very idea of aiming high in one's moral life, although containing no guarantee of success, gives the whole idea of success and the struggle to reach it a greater personal meaning and significance.

It is interesting to observe that James' distinction between the easy-going and strenuous moral life has greater affinities with Nietzsche and existentialism than perhaps any other tradition. As the contemporary psychologist Rollo May has pointed out,

The existential approach, for example, is very close to the thought of William James. Take, for example, his emphases on the *immediacy of experience* and *the union of thought and action.* . . . . Another aspect in William James that expresses the same approach to reality as existential psychology is the importance of *decision* and *commitment*—his argument that you cannot know truth by sitting in a detached armchair, but that *willing* and *decision* are themselves prerequisites to the discovery of truth.[62]

Existentialism, in common with William James, emphasizes the primary importance of man's individual existence, the immediate way in which each person encounters his world. Of all the American pragmatists, including Charles Peirce, George Herbert Mead, and John Dewey, James uniquely emphasized the importance of man's private and personal individuality. As James asserted "As soon as we deal with private and personal phenomena as such, we deal with realities in the completest sense of the term."[63] In this sense, James was a true nominalist and held that, when we consider universal or general features of things, we deal only with the symbols of reality. This view stands in sharp contrast to that of Peirce, who not only held that "a thing in the general is as real as in the concrete,"[64] but also that "the absolute individual cannot only not be realized in sense or thought, but cannot exist, properly speaking."[65] Also, in contrast to James, the pragmatism of Mead and Dewey contained a decidedly social emphasis—the view that human individuality not only cannot develop without social influences but that man as we understand him cannot be separated from his social interactions or transactions. Dewey not only claimed that societies are "definite aspects of the natural world, but all existence is *associated* in character, and existents are never found in total isolation from one another."[66] He used "the social as a ranking philosophic category on the ground that it is indicative of the widest and richest range of association empirically accessible. . . . I do not say that the social as we know it is the whole, but I do emphatically suggest that it is the widest and richest manifestation of the whole accessible to our observation."[67] In contrast to this social emphasis, James was always a champion of the individual, considering associations and societies secondary or as primarily dependent upon the individuals who comprise them. For James, "A concrete bit of personal experience may be a small bit, but it is a solid bit as long as it lasts; not hollow, not a mere abstract element of experience. . . . It is a *full* fact, even though it be an insignificant fact; it is of the *kind* to which all realities whatsoever must belong."[68]

This explains why James was opposed to viewing morality and religion in institutional and rational terms. Morality and religion for James were intimately connected in many ways. They both depend on faith rather than intellectual evidence, and they both emphasize the importance of personal meaning. James did not deny that morality and religion have been institutionalized. Clearly they have been supported by, and identified with, churches, laws, and governments. He claimed, however, that any institutional support of morality and religion lives at second-hand on the individuals who comprise these groups.

James claimed that specific religious experiences have the most powerful energizing effect on the moral life of individuals. Religious experiences are pragmatically real because they are not mere contemplations of ideals; they produce effects in this world. Religious experiences confirm the reality of the unseen or spiritual because they produce real effects, as in saintliness and conversion. James was willing to say that "God is real since he produces real effects."[69] In pragmatic terms, God is real, not merely ideal, since this reality "exerts an influence, raises our centre of personal energy, and produces regenerative effects unattainable in other ways."[70] Pragmatically it must always remain an option for one to deny any supernatural reality and its influence. For James, this option had to remain a matter of personal decision.

James' greatest contribution to ethics is not to be found in his having devised any kind of system—or even in having devised a so-called "pragmatic movement" followed by Dewey and others in the twentieth century. His importance lies in the fact that he opened up fresh approaches to ethics by using his own brand of pragmatic and psychological insights. He broadened the base and application of Peirce's original pragmatism, but in so doing destroyed the scientific character of Peirce's idea. In no sense of the term can we say that James' Pragmatic Ethics is scientific. But the whole effort of what has been identified as Dewey's pragmatism was to reinstate scientific methods, not only in ethics but in all areas of philosophy and important human concerns. Of all the American pragmatists, James was the least scientific in the principal thrust of his philosophy. This is all the more remarkable when we consider that James was not only a pioneer of modern psychology but was the only pragmatist who actually produced a classic work in the field of science, *The Principles of Psychology*. It is consequently understandable that Dewey, with his overriding interest in scientific method, should have been most impressed with, and influenced by, James' studies in psychology. Dewey did not subscribe to the individualism and unscientific, existentialist tendencies in James' brand of pragmatism. Similarly understandable is Peirce's actual coinage of the term "pragmaticism" to distinguish his type of pragmatism from that of James. Peirce's pragmaticism, Dewey's instrumentalism, and James' humanistic or individualistic pragmatism actually represent three distinct tendencies of thought. It is true that all three philosophers shared the view that the meaning of ideas is to be found in their practical consequences and that this meaning is contingent or fallible rather than *a priori* necessary. But the differences between these varieties of pragmatism are of great significance since they point to the originality and distinctness of thinking in these three most famous pragmatists. Dewey's philosophy has a greater affinity to James' than that of Peirce since moral concerns are central to the philosophic endeavors of Dewey and James. James achieved a real advance in pragmatism by bringing moral problems to the fore. And although Dewey gave a different analysis to the problems of ethics, it is indeed a tribute to James that he influenced Dewey and encouraged his work.

James was remarkable for the contacts he maintained and the influence he exerted on other philosophers. He had an eye for recognizing talent and a sympathetic interest in helping and promoting the work of other thinkers, even when those thinkers markedly disagreed with his own ideas. He befriended Peirce and tried to obtain for him a position in the academic world. James was mainly responsible for bringing Josiah Royce to Harvard, and he clearly influenced the development of Royce's moral philosophy. Although Royce was a rationalist and idealist in philosophy, he admired the humanistic pragmatism of James. Royce even went so far as to call himself an "absolute pragmatist." It was primarily through James' influence that Royce sought to construct a system of idealism that was as pragmatic and voluntaristic as possible. Because James called other people's attention to Peirce and because he widened the base of pragmatism, he was actually the key figure in bringing American philosophers to an appreciation of one another's work, away from sole reliance on European and other sources. James was the first American moral philosopher of marked influence on the philosophic thinking of other American philosophers. He was also the first American philosopher to have a real impact on European philosophy.

Although he liked to describe himself as a "piecemeal supernaturalist," James had a pronounced influence on the development of naturalism as a philosophy in the twentieth century. Both Santayana and Dewey, the two leading American naturalists of this century, were influenced by William James. Santayana accepted James' contention that any value ultimately depends on interest or desire rather than on reason or thought. Santayana, in his own fashion, also agreed with James that goods or values are ultimately relative and pluralistic. Santayana, however, saw James' naturalism as inconsistent and incomplete. For Santayana, naturalism could not really contain any "piecemeal supernaturalism" without contradicting itself. Santayana found pragmatism generally, and James specifically, lacking a true appreciation for the importance of a life of detachment and aesthetic values. In Santayana's view, pragmatism, with its emphasis on future, practical consequences, lacked a sense of the timeless quality of beauty and every true enjoyment.

By influencing the philosophic thought of Royce, Santayana, and Dewey, James became the central source of American philosophy arriving at its own maturity. James was the first American philosopher to achieve the status of both philosopher's philosopher and people's philosopher. Any fair estimate of his work must recognize both the popularity of his writings and their definite impact on other major thinkers.

One of the most troublesome notions in James' ethics was his view that the essence of good is simply to satisfy demand, and that demand and obligation are coextensive terms. Granted that a preference, interest, or demand is a necessary condition of any value or good, why should the presence of interest or demand be sufficient? Is there not some distinction between the existence of a demand and its validity? Are we really obligated in any sense to attempt the satisfaction of every or any demand? James' refusal to distinguish between the existence of a demand and that demand's validity stems from his antirationalism, his refusal to allow reason or critical thought to play a vital role in making and sustaining any value judgment. The point is, however, that we do use our rational powers for these purposes, and one cannot easily see how we could proceed very far in any moral life without them. Clearly, to hold that the essence of good is simply to satisfy demand is an extreme, even self-refuting, position. This kind of pluralism has no real answer to the counterdemand—that the essence of good is not satisfaction of every or any demand, but only of the right or proper ones. Any moral philosophy that makes demand or interest basic and uncriticizable must necessarily lead to a stalemate or dead end. Unless all demand and interest are subject to thoughtful criticism, we simply have irresolvable conflicts and chaos in any moral life. It is one thing to admit that conflicts exist, but quite another to allege that they can never be resolved by any rational means. It is one thing to assert that some good things must be sacrificed; quite another to say, as James did, that some part of the ideal must be butchered.

In his moral philosophy James clearly identified moral concerns with feelings and volitions, not with thought or reason. But reflective thought and reason are also needed for identification of our moral concerns and for consideration of their goals and implications. James clearly did not advocate a thoughtless moral life; but unfortunately his premises did not enable him to advocate or build a thoughtful one. The most serious defect in his ethics is that he saw only contrast or conflict between thought and volition, rather than the possibility of coordination between them. His mistake was to come down hard on the intellect in morals; and thereby he threw away the possibility of making thought or intellect pragmatically useful in the moral life. His fear, of course, was that if reason is given a hold it will simply dominate the passions and will, or at least conceive them as subservient to its interests. Rationalism, as James saw it, must necessarily move in the direction of monism, of claiming one single, absolute, universal principle to govern all the rest. Ethical monism for James was unacceptable because it is intolerant and not faithful to experience. But the claim that thought or reason is relevant to the moral life is not necessarily a claim that nothing else is relevant. Reason in ethics does not have to lead to monism, nor must it be unfaithful to the facts.

James' views that moral questions present themselves as questions whose solutions cannot wait for sensible proof—and that skepticism in morals is actually an active ally of immorality—are further indications of his basic impatience with the use of reason or critical thinking in ethics. Certainly, not all moral questions must be answered immediately; in any case, how would we know that sensible proofs cannot be found without attempting, at least, to find them? Some moral dilemmas may indeed be irrational in the sense that the situations in which they arise may actually afford us no time to think. But the fact remains that many of the greatest moral questions have existed for a very long time, suggesting that what is really needed to answer these questions is not simply stronger commitment to one's goals or even more thought about them; but better, more relevant ideas. One of the most serious problems in man's moral life is to know what is relevant to the answer of any moral question. Quite often we are inundated with opinions and feelings, but seldom are we presented with a clear view of what is relevant to meet any challenge.

James found no real place for skepticism or detachment in the moral life, since he saw them as threats to the will to believe. We must believe, hence we cannot really adopt a neutral stance. As he said, referring to moral matters, "Who is not for is against. The universe will have no neutrals in these questions."[71] Granted that one cannot remain detached and neutral on every moral question, that does not mean that detachment and doubt have no essential moral function. Clearly, doubt and the suspension of judgment are just as useful in ethics as in science or anyplace in life. To counteract believing too quickly or with prejudice, skepticism has an equally important role to play in ethics as in any other area of life. To overcome one's illusions, one *must* practice a certain amount of detachment and doubt. Disillusionment may not be the only value in a moral life, but its value must count for something and cannot seriously be denied.

We can accept James' notion that one has a right to believe in moral values on the basis of insufficient evidence, but this is not the same as saying that one has a right to believe in the face of overwhelming evidence to the contrary. James was wrong in suggesting that integrity of belief has its place in science but not in morals. In morals, it is important for us to identify what is meant by a responsible belief. While James quite rightly held that a moral belief is one that we are willing to take personal responsibility for, this is not enough. A responsible belief is also one for which we are willing to consider the evidence for and against. To be responsible, a moral belief must have more than an existential leap of personal faith, since such a leap of faith can easily be fanatical or absurd. A responsible belief can be based on personal faith and, at the same time, be open to intelligent criticism. Personal faith can, in fact, be increased or enhanced by intelligent criticism. If criticism is allowed to include creative thought and imagination, there is no sound reason to suppose, as James did, that it must be opposed to action based on faith.

Criticism is basically essential to any advancement or refinement in the moral life. While criticism, analysis, and careful thought are not the sole ingredients of any moral life, any moral life without them is bound to be subhuman and irrational. When James announced that there can be no final truth in ethics until the last man has had his experience and his say, he left the doors open for advancement and refinement in man's moral life. Clearly, James was correct in holding that ethics is not a closed book wherein all the important issues have already been decided. But when he came to the important question of exactly how these issues can be decided, James saw only a single avenue of help. He saw that moral questions do pertain to man's personal and passional interests. He also saw that man's passional commitments can be effective in helping him achieve moral results. To all of this passion, commitment, and moral energy, however, James was reluctant to add any rational factors. As a consequence, his Pragmatist Ethics is deficient in its lack of a rational side. Since he held that "claim" and "obligation" are coextensive terms, he offered no real analysis of moral obligation. For James, a moral obligation was simply a moral claim or demand. He went so far as to assert that "any desire is imperative to the extent of its amount; it makes itself valid by the fact that it exists at all."[72] But such an indiscriminating proposal is clearly useless as far as man's moral life is concerned and only shows the need for careful analysis. The existence, intensity, or persistence of desire does not confer any validity on that desire except in a purely verbal, rhetorical sense. What a desire is, is one thing; whether it has any real value is quite another, and a much harder question. Determining the value or estimating the worth of desires is not equivalent to notice of their presence or assent to them. If it were true that what we *do* in fact desire were always what we *should* desire—or if each actual desire were *ipso facto* morally valid—there would, of course, be no need for moral reflection or philosophy at all. The fact is, however, that the need for moral reflection and philosophy exists specifically because our actual desires are not automatically valid or simply what they ought to be.

Chapter 5

Idealist Ethics

American Idealism

Idealism in America is at least as old as Jonathan Edwards' Puritanism, and it continued as a prominent feature of Emerson's Transcendentalism. Not until the latter part of the nineteenth century, however, did American idealism develop any full-fledged philosophical systems of thought. It is important to note here that only in the work of Josiah Royce (1855-1916) do we find any complete, systematic treatment of ethics. Edwards and Emerson both held that reality is basically spiritual in character and that moral virtue involves the love of an ideal or spiritual kind of beauty. Similarly, both Edwards and Emerson held that the visible natural world is merely an appearance or outward display of a higher spiritual reality. They differed, of course, in their interpretations of the character of this spiritual reality and its relation to man. Emerson upheld a pantheistic form of idealism in which man and nature directly participated in the higher divine or spiritual reality. Edwards, on the other hand, maintained a theistic form of idealism wherein man and nature are clearly separated from, and subordinate to, that which is divine. Another important difference between these two earlier varieties of idealism is found in the fact that Edwards based his idealism on empirical foundations, particularly an analysis of the English philosopher John Locke—whereas

Emerson could not accept the notion that the mind is a blank tablet on which experience writes. For Emerson, the mind was intuitive, spontaneous, and the source of its own ideas. Although both men believed that mind or spirit is the only ultimate reality, Edwards did not believe that the human mind contains any innate ideas. Emerson, on the contrary, held that, since man is inherently divine, all of his ideas are innate or possess a spark of originality.

But neither of these two early forms of idealism exercised pronounced influence on later American idealists. American idealism as it developed in the latter half of the nineteenth century came under the influence of German philosophers, primarily Kant and Hegel. In 1866 a group of German intellectuals formed the St. Louis Philosophical Society under the leadership of W. T. Harris to promote the translation and study of the works of Kant and Hegel. The purpose of this enterprise was to encourage the study and development of speculative philosophy in the United States. Harris, who later served as United States Commissioner of Education, had a major influence in advancing the study of German idealism throughout America. In 1867 he established *The Journal of Speculative Philosophy*, which

> . . . was the first American journal specifically devoted to original thinking on distinctively philosophical topics. It provided a forum for the discussion of metaphysical and epistemological questions, such as had never been available in America. Although the journal was organized by men sympathetic with German idealism (Kant and Hegel in particular), spokesmen for many diverse and original philosophic viewpoints were given the opportunity to present their positions in the journal's pages. The greatest American pragmatists—Charles Peirce, William James, and John Dewey—all contributed to the journal, as did America's greatest idealist Josiah Royce.[1]

George H. Howison (1834-1916), an early member of the St. Louis Philosophical Society, eventually moved to the University of California where he began, in 1884, a long and distinguished teaching career in philosophy. But "his chief influence, for all the value of his publications, was upon those whom he taught in person. . . ."[2] He developed a philosophy which he termed "personal idealism." "The aim of Personal Idealism . . . is to present, and, in one way or another enforce, an idealistic system that shall be thoroughly personal. . . . Instead of any monism, it puts forward a Pluralism, an eternal or metaphysical world of *many* minds, all alike possessing personal initiative, real self-direction, instead of an all-predestinating single Mind that alone has real free-agency."[3] Although Howison admired the pluralism of William James and James's emphasis on personal initiative, he could not accept James's view that no mind is public or universal. For Howison, mind was essentially objective and social, for without these characteristics any "moral ideal would be nothing but an empty egoism, incapable of transcending solipsism, and leading only to a self-centered culture. Justice and benevolence would have no place in such a life, but only aesthetic self-refinement and self-poise. . . ."[4] Howison claimed that his objective view of personal idealism "puts altruism into the very being of each spontaneous self, and lodges his necessary recognition of others in the very primal intelligent act whereby he defines himself and gives intelligible meaning to his saying *I*."[5] This view of man's mind as primarily social, in its interest in the well-being of other persons, involves an acceptance as well as a reformulation of the German philosopher Immanuel Kant's famous categorical imperative. As reformulated by Howison, it asserted, *"So act as to regard humanity, whether thine own or that of another, as an End withal, and never merely as a means."*[6] For Howison, this imperative became the foundation for all knowledge as well as morality, since it regards each distinct person as capable of discerning what is true and what has absolute value.

Borden Parker Bowne (1847-1910), who taught philosophy at Boston University for more than thirty years, also developed a form of personalistic idealism which he called "personalism." "It is a personal and social world in which we live, and with which all speculation must begin."[7] For Bowne, a law of reason existed which is valid for all, and a world of common experience existed within which our personal lives take place. Everything real must either be a self or an idea belonging to a self. He held that impersonal ideas are pure fictions. "All actual ideas are owned, or belong to some one, and mean nothing as floating free."[8] In his principal work *Personalism*, published in 1908, he argued that two main sources of the "fallacy of impersonalism," as he called it, remove the personal quality of all our experiences. One source is naturalism, which regards our senses as presenting objects in the external world, objects which are mere material bodies moving in an impersonal space. The other source is idealism itself, when it commits the fallacy of abstraction and improperly tries to explain things, including man's mind and personal self, in terms of purely abstract categories of thought. Bowne distinguished between naturalism as applying to the natural sciences or scientific method; and naturalism as a philosophic doctrine. It is the latter that he severely criticized. He raised the question,

> Can life and mind and morals and society be explained on a naturalistic basis? . . . The space and time world of phenomena explains nothing; it is rather the problem itself. The real account of anything must be sought in the world of power; and this world eludes us altogether, unless we raise power to include intelligence and purpose. The unpicturable notions of the understanding, as substance, cause, unity, identity, etc., elude all spatial intuition, and vanish even from thought when impersonally taken.[9]

Bowne argued that it is illogical to attempt to derive the personal from the impersonal; rather, man's personal existence needs to be explained or grounded in the notion of a Supreme Person who produces and maintains man's personal, finite spirit.

> The objections to affirming a Supreme Person are largely verbal. Many of them are directed against a literal anthropomorphism. This, of course, is a man of straw. Man himself in his essential personality is as unpicturable and formless as God. Personality and corporeality are incommensurable ideas. The essential meaning of personality is selfhood, self-consciousness, self-control, and the power to know. These elements have no corporeal significance or limitations. Any being, finite or infinite, which has knowledge and self-consciousness and self-control, is personal; for the term has no other meaning.[10]

James E. Creighton (1861-1924), professor of philosophy at Cornell University and editor of such scholarly journals as the *Philosophical Review* and *Kant Studien*, was a founder of the American Philosophical Association and served as its first president (1902-1903). Although best known as a teacher and editor, he developed a form of what he termed "speculative idealism," which he distinguished from mentalistic or subjective idealism. He attacked what he saw as the main thrust of mentalistic idealism: reduction of the objective order of the external world to states of consciousness. He argued that "it is obviously impossible to reduce material things to states of consciousness in an individual mind."[11] It is also impossible, he argued, to reduce material things to any states of consciousnessness of an absolute mind. "To assert that things exist as elements in an Absolute experience is then in itself only an appeal to a mechanical device which explains nothing, and is in addition unmeaning and arbitrary."[12] What Creighton termed "speculative idealism" does not separate the mind from the external world. "It knows no egocentric predicament, because it recognizes no ego 'alone with its states,' standing apart from the order of nature and from a society of other minds. It thus dismisses as unmeaning those problems which are sometimes called 'epistemological,' as to how the mind as such can know reality as such."[13] For Creighton, philosophy was to be understood as an absolutely free form of inquiry. It is

. . . without presuppositions in the sense that it is able to criticize and transcend any category that falls short of the complete range and scope of the whole mind and the whole of reality. . . . Philosophy is accordingly just intelligence coming to full consciousness of itself, turning back upon itself and becoming critically aware of its working principles; looking forward and taking a more comprehensive view of its own purposes, trying all things, proving all things, and holding fast to that which critical experience reveals in regard to the nature of the world and of intelligence.[14]

Certainly American idealism as it developed in the late nineteenth and early twentieth centuries did not present a united platform of beliefs. We can, however, find several tendencies of thought which characterize its major thrust and which also distinguish this philosophy from naturalism, realism, and pragmatism. The best work of the American idealists can be characterized as a form of humanistic rationalism; idealist philosophers tended to view man principally as a social, rational being. Man is that being who lives and grows by virtue of the ideas he forms and by the interpersonal contacts and communication he achieves with his fellow man. Thus the idealist tends to place great emphasis on the historical nature of man and on the study of historical traditions of thought—principally philosophy. The idealists were, in fact, the first in America to cultivate a serious study of the history of philosophy and philosophical systems. Mostly scholars and teachers, they were responsible for establishing philosophy as a distinct subject or department in American colleges. They were, of course, sympathetic to religion but tended to view it as a rational phenomenon in need of philosophical elucidation and scrutiny. Since they placed great emphasis on the importance of the human self and its power of self-consciousness, they tended to view the concept of divinity as both a

real and an ideal form of self-consciousness. They opposed, however, any mechanical or abstract notion of a divine being as
inconsistent with the ideas of selfhood and intelligence. The divine
being was not conceived as simply a causal power nor a merely
abstract ideal, but as a perfectly actualized self-consciousness.

Idealism was definitely opposed to commonsense realism,
which it regarded as naive. The external world is indeed objective,
but is nevertheless intimately related to mind or consciousness.
Mind has the power to objectify itself in the sense of being able to
conceive and fashion forms of order in a publicly verifiable sense.
Governments, societies, churches, and works of art are all examples
of objectified mind, mind working to create forms of definite order
and meaning in the external world. Everything that exists displays
some level of mind activity seeking to achieve order. To say that any
existing thing has meaning or significance implies that it has a
reason for being or has some degree of objective mind. Objective
idealism is therefore not content to say that all existence is mental,
since this could be taken simply to mean that a thing is whatever we
think or feel it is. Objective idealism holds that there are degrees of
truth and error. The more rationally complete our ideas, the more
objectively true they are. Our commonsense ideas of the world have
some degree of truth, but they are also vague and imprecise. In a
similar fashion our commonsense morality has some hold on moral
truth, but not a firm, really adequate grasp. Commonsense morality
believes that justice, honesty, or loyalty are good, but when asked to
explain precisely how or why, it is unable to give coherent answers.
Common sense may tend to accept pragmatic, realistic, or even
naturalistic proofs or justifications for its moral beliefs. But when
questioned for a coherent explanation, it will inevitably become
caught up in contradictory ideas. It may believe that justice is
absolutely good, yet should be tempered with mercy; it may believe
that truthfulness is good for all, yet that sometimes it is expedient to
tell a lie; or it may believe that loyalty to one's country is morally
good even when loyalty may work against the legitimate loyalties of
other nations. These and other possible examples emphasize the
point that morality cannot be made to rest simply on conscience or
common sense. Morality or moral values are just the sort of things
that are really important and cannot be left to chance or unreflective
thought. The only morality worth having is one that is achieved by
careful, coherent thought. Here the idealists parted company with

all forms of irrational or nonrational moral outlooks. Any morality that is simply satisfied to accept an external authority on faith (Edwards), to accept the voice of one's moral sense or conscience (Jefferson), to accept the voice of intuition (Emerson) or, to accept even the pragmatic faith of one's will to believe (James) is essentially morally backward or undeveloped. Morality is an intellectual achievement requiring hard work and thought; it is not the sort of thing that can merely follow the heart rather than the head. This does not mean that man should discard his feelings or sentiments— but it does mean that he cannot accept them at face value as a guide to his moral life. The moral life is easy neither in practice nor theory. The value of moral ideals is, in fact, demonstrated by the great efforts required for one to realize and understand them. Morality is clearly a pursuit of ideals, not an acceptance of easy formulas or the *status quo*. As an intellectual achievement, morality must be able to ex- plain and overcome conflicts and problems that emerge in man's moral life. But clear, logical thought and speculative reason must focus on these problems in order to accomplish this.

William James, it will be remembered, held that moral ques- tions cannot wait for sensible proof and that moral issues are basically volitional rather than intellectual concerns. Since James held that truth itself is that which works or satisfies our need to know, there could be no fixed, universal, or absolute moral truth or answers. James could not give the entire notion of a final absolute, inflexible truth any practical or pragmatic meaning. Thus he believed that man can find no real moral law or permanent moral order. If everything undergoes incessant change, any moral idea or order will at best be tentative and only relative. In strong contrast to these views, idealism attempted to bring absolute and relative, eternal and temporal, universal and particular, as well as intellectual and volitional concerns into proper relation with one another. To accomplish these reconciliations between pairs of conflicting opposites, the idealist used what is termed "dialectical reason." He attempted to locate a third idea which would transcend the two conflicting ideas and which would provide a synthesis of whatever truth they contain. Dialectical reason is essentially a triadic process of thinking that enables our understanding to advance toward grasping a higher truth which includes smaller, lower truths.

This method, made famous by the German philosopher Hegel, was especially practiced and cultivated by Josiah Royce. Royce sought to improve on Hegel's method by construing all thoughts or ideas as signs that require an infinite series of interpretations for making their meanings complete and coherent. Moral ideas, for example, are not self-contained; as signs, they require an intelligent interpreter seeking to give them a meaning that both he and others can understand. Interpretation is essentially a triadic process, since it requires first a sign or idea to be interpreted; second, an interpreter of the sign; and third, someone to understand the interpretation. The idea of loyalty is a case in point. To understand the moral significance of this idea, it is not sufficient for one merely to perceive or conceive what loyalty is. At best we can perceive certain acts or examples of loyalty, but that gives no complete understanding of the idea's moral meaning. We can also abstractly conceive loyalty in general terms, but this gives us no concrete understanding of where and how this idea applies in any actual moral life. A third process is needed that involves an interpretation of the full moral meaning and significance of this idea. Interpretation, as Royce conceived it, is philosophically a higher, richer way of approaching ideas than either perception or conception. Interpretation is a triadic process that is ongoing or continuous; it ideally tries to unite in one coherent insight all of the concrete and particular, as well as abstract and universal, meanings of our ideas. This means that our moral ideas are neither simple, self-evident, nor capable of easy definition. They must be unravelled by a rational process of interpretation.

Royce, of all the American idealists, was the philosopher who gave by far the most careful, complete consideration to the meaning of man's moral life. He was most strongly influenced in his thinking by the pragmatism of James and Peirce. Although he studied in Germany and came under the influence of Kant, Hegel, and German idealism, the stimulation and challenge of American pragmatism was what caused him to rethink and reformulate his basic commitment to idealism. He agreed with Peirce that philosophy must remain objective and committed to the demands of hard thinking and logical precision. Along with Peirce, he believed that philosophy must not only engage in metaphysical speculation but that the goal of such thinking is the articulation of a fullfledged philosophical system, which is needed for an understanding of how all parts fit into the larger whole. But a genuine system must result from hard inquiry; it cannot arbitrarily or surreptitiously be imposed on the facts. Royce was really the first major American thinker to develop a philosophic system and defend it at length in a series of published works.

He also agreed with James that philosophy must have practical application to the concrete and moral concerns of everyday life. Philosophy cannot remain merely an academic, theoretical discipline detached from the vital problems of society, religion, or morality. Philosophy must be able to furnish us with a way of life or plan of living, must definitely concern itself with the concrete human person. For Royce, ideas were volitional, as well as intellectual, processes. They express the purposes we try to achieve as well as our cognitive grasp or understanding of things. If ideas are expressions of purpose as well as cognitive instruments, certainly they must be studied in terms of their future consequences. This sense of pragmatism is clearly acceptable to Royce. In order to be true or valuable or to possess any meaning at all, ideas must succeed in leading us to their facts. Meaningful, true, or valuable ideas cannot merely happen to work; we must have a way of testing them to see that they absolutely do, or will always continue to, work. What Royce found lacking in pragmatism was its refusal to permit any conception of the absolute. Pragmatism is committed to the parts, but not to the whole. Because pragmatism is overcommitted to empirical results and fallibilism, it can find no real place for the *a priori* and what is infallible. Royce considered this mistaken, a definite limitation of this philosophy. It is particularly disastrous in ethics, he thought, since this area needs something more than tentative, partial truths and values. Man cannot be content to live a moral life that is only partially right and good. In ethics especially, Royce demanded from philosophy an attempt, at least, to furnish us with real wisdom, something solid, lasting, and fulfilling. Royce contended that man can indeed find absolute, solid truths. We recognize, for example, that a deed once done can never be undone. This is an absolute, infallible truth about past deeds that is verified both by our reason and experience. Other absolute truths also exist, and philosophy's task is to find and justify them. Some of our ideas are indeed fallible, but not all; some of our ideas are only partial or relative, but not all. Royce was fond of asking whether fallibilism is itself fallible, whether the belief in relative truth is itself only relatively true, or whether the denial of any absolute is itself an absolute denial. These questions pointed up the important task of testing the consistency and coherence of all our ideas to make sure we do not contradict ourselves.

It is important in ethics to make certain that our beliefs have an inherent integrity. It would be ludicrous and self-defeating to profess one thing and do something else. In ethics, we must above all else be rational and coherent lest we make a mockery and shambles of any attempt to live a moral life. If we assume, to begin with, that no absolute, final truth in ethics can be found, we in fact adopt an absolute belief in skepticism which is contradictory. If we try to rule reason out of ethics, we must do so with the use of reason. If we try to have an ethics without idealism, we must still live by *this* ideal. The question for ethics is not whether to be idealistic or not, or whether to have ideals at all—but which ones to have, and how. We need to find the right and best ideals, which are those that are most relevant, complete and consistent. The moral life, like logic and science, can only proceed by use of precise tests and standards.

For Royce, we can make no real headway in ethics if we rely entirely on the empirical dimensions of ideas and deny the *a priori*. Pragmatists and others have denied the *a priori* in ethics and relied entirely on purely empirical considerations. The assumption behind this effort is an ethics based entirely on experience. But this is clearly shortsighted, according to Royce and the idealists. A moment's reflection will teach us that even the concept of experience itself is not an empirical concept.[15] Only thought is wide and deep enough to give us an understanding of what experience really is. Clearly we must transcend experience and go beyond it in order to see its boundaries and nature. No particular experience will cover all experiences, and no finite sequence of experiences will give us an adequate conception of what experience *en toto* really is. If we rule out any *a priori* dimensions of experience, we must do so on *a priori* grounds.[16] If we rule out *a priori* reasoning in ethics, we have no means of testing our beliefs for their consistency and completeness. True morality, as the German philosopher Kant maintained, must pertain to experience but cannot be grounded in experience. Morality concerns what ought to be, and cannot be founded simply on what is or happens to be. Empirical attempts to build an ethics must inevitably fail, as they have no valid way of establishing the whole idea of "ought," responsibility, or moral obligation. The fact that we do demand or desire certain ends certainly does not prove that we should or that those ends are really good. To determine what we should or ought to desire—to determine what is really good—there is no substitute for hard, reflective thought. This becomes, then, the central mission of an Idealist Ethics such as we find in Josiah Royce: to elucidate and justify a rational ethics, grounded in reflective thought, that is still relevant to the concrete details of our lives.

Josiah Royce:
Principal Figure of Idealist Ethics

Josiah Royce was the first American philosopher to develop a complete system of thought that included a systematic treatment of ethics. After several years of study at the University of California and in Germany, Royce entered Johns Hopkins University, where he received his doctorate in philosophy in 1878. In 1882, mainly due to the influence of William James, he was appointed Instructor in Philosophy at Harvard. Royce remained at Harvard for a long, distinguished career in teaching and writing philosophy. In 1885 he published the first major statement of his position in *The Religious Aspect of Philosophy*.

In this work he formulated a number of characteristic arguments for his absolute or objective idealism and was to use them again and again in his later writings. Although his position would undergo development and modification on certain points, he never wavered from his initial absolute idealism. He argued that any attempt to deny the whole, absolute truth ends up as contradictory—as, in fact, affirming the very thing it tries to deny. "'No absolute truth exists,'—can you say this if you want to? At least you must add, 'No absolute truth exists *save this truth itself, that no absolute truth exists.*' Otherwise your statement has no sense. But if you admit this truth, then there is in fact an absolute distinction between truth and error."[17] But outside of thought or mind, there is no truth or error. It is equally contradictory to say that we know there is some unknowable truth or some truth that is not related to a knower. The mind or knower does not create the truth by his thoughts or ideas—truth must be discovered. But truth could never be discovered without a mind or consciousness with the power or purpose of grasping it. Royce further argued that no finite mind actually apprehends the whole or absolute truth. The whole truth is something ideal in relation to any finite mind, but this ideal is something actual to the all-encompassing, infinite mind. The whole or absolute truth cannot be grounded in the thoughts or ideas of finite minds, but must be grounded in nothing short of an all-inclusive infinite mind. "*'All reality must be present to the Unity of the Infinite Thought.'* There is no chance of escape. For all reality is reality because true judgments can be made about it.... You and I and all of us, all good, all evil, all truth, all falsehood, all things actual and possible, exist as they exist, and are known for what they are, in and to the absolute thought."[18] Royce insisted, of course, that proof of this principle cannot be given by empirical evidence, by appeal to the senses. The proof or justification for such an all-encompassing principle must be given *a priori* if at all. Absolute idealism cannot be justified empirically because empirical evidence is always partial or piecemeal. There is actually very little that we can prove at all if we rely exclusively on empirical evidence. Consider past or future events, for example. How can we justify our belief in the reality of the past? Not by observation or experience, since the past is now gone. Or how do we justify our belief in the reality of future events? We cannot now observe or experience them since they have not happened yet. Basically our belief in the past or future can only be justified by *a priori* thought or reason. We postulate the reality of both past and future because it is consistent or coherent to do so. Thought or reason, therefore, is more powerful or more extensive than experience. We actually need thought or reason to link our various experiences together, to give them any true meaning or coherence. Our experiences of things are intermittent and full of gaps. We never see all sides of any object at one time, nor can we experience any object for very long. Our senses and experiences by themselves give us only superficial, scattered reports. Consequently we must rely on our concepts and thoughts to see things as orderly and coherent. Royce's point was that more of our ideas and knowledge of things is *a priori* than we ordinarily realize. Only when we become truly reflective and philosophical can we realize how much of our awareness of things is *a priori* or independent of actual experience. Consider the reality of the human self. We take for granted that each person is a distinct self or unified mind. We assume that we can communicate with and know other people as distinct minds or selves. But how are these beliefs to be verified? We cannot actually observe any self, including our own, with our senses. To ask the color, shape, or sound of a human self or mind doesn't make sense. Nor is any self given to us intuitively as a datum of any immediate experience. Why do we attribute the character of a self to our own experiences and to other people as well? The only reasonable answer, according to Royce, is that it is consistent or coherent to do so. By postulating a human self that unites our own and other people's experiences, we come to see ourselves and others in a more orderly, coherent fashion. This way of viewing things makes our practical, social transactions with people intelligible. By reflecting on what we mean by self, we see that it is not given to us ready-made but is something that must develop—and that it does not and could not develop without the powers of memory, thought, and volition. A self without a history is a contradiction in terms. But so is a self without any social awareness—an isolated self with no relation to other selves is just as contradictory. "We are all aware, if we have ever tried it, how empty and ghostly is a life lived for a long while in absolute solitude. Free me from my fellows.... I am no longer friend, brother, companion, co-worker, servant, citizen, father, son; I exist for nobody; and erelong, perhaps to my surprise, generally to my horror, I discover that I *am* nobody.... In the dungeon of my isolated self-consciousness I rot away unheeded and terror-stricken."[19] Thus Royce went on to argue, "Within myself the rule holds that I live consciously only in so far as I am known and reflected upon by my subsequent life. Beyond what is called my private self, however, a similar rule holds. I exist in a vital and humane sense only in relation to my friends, my social business, my family, my fellow-workers, my world of other selves. This is the rule of mental life."[20] The self is just that sort of thing that cannot exist or be known in isolation and without reflective thought. "Each one of us is what some other moment of his life reflectively finds him to be.... No one of us knows what he now is; he can only know what he *was*. Each one of us, however, is *now* only what hereafter he *shall* find himself to be. This is the deepest paradox of the inner life."[21] Our whole mental life flourishes or exists insofar as it is "reflected upon, viewed from without, seen at a distance, acknowledged by another than itself, reworded in term of fresh experience."[22]

Royce's view that the human self only exists through reflective thought or consciousness and in relation to other selves has important implications for ethics. First, it implies that any moral values or truths that we can find must be based on reason and cannot be derived from the senses or anything else. The only ethical principles that can apply to an essentially reflective self or person must themselves be based on reflective thought. This means that empirical ethics is impossible. We can never find any valid moral law or principle applicable to a human self except by *a priori* reasoning. What a human self or person should choose to do in a moral sense, what goals or ends he should seek, cannot be discovered by simply consulting this or that experience or his senses.

Secondly, the view that the human self only exists insofar as it is related to other selves implies that morality must be essentially social in character. A moral agent, if such exists, can only exist by having duties, obligations, and moral relations with other selves or persons. This immediately implies a denial of what is sometimes called "moral individualism." If moral individualism means that each person is a self-contained island who makes choices and decisions only for himself and his own good, this view is clearly unreasonable. "Individualism, viewed as the tendency to hold that the ideal of life is the separate happy man, is itself very naturally the normal tendency of unreflecting strong natures."[23] But this is just the point: Individualism only seems satisfactory as long as it remains unanalyzed. Royce argued that the postulate of the absolute worth of individual satisfaction leads to its own practical refutation. "Everybody has tried to realize the ideal of individualism, this ideal of a happy or satisfied self, either for himself or for some loved one; and everybody finds, if he tries the thing long enough, what a hollow and worthless business it all is."[24] Self-satisfaction or even the utilitarian goal of individual happiness for everyone cannot be the valid goal of morality—since this goal cannot be achieved. It is unreasonable to uphold an impossible goal. Obviously not every self or desire can be satisfied, since some desires can only be satisfied at the expense of others. Even William James, who held that the essence of good is to satisfy demand, admitted this point. But the real objection to this view is not simply that it cannot in fact be attained—but that it *should* not be pursued, since a superior goal exists that *can* be attained. The only reasonable moral goal in life, according to Royce, must be one that both can and ought to be realized. A rational moral ideal must be possible for us to attain, since it is contradictory to assert that one ought to pursue an unattainable goal. But a rational moral ideal must also be characteristically worthy of attainment because of its superior value. It is not enough that someone or even everyone may want or desire this goal; it is also necessary that they be obligated or duty-bound to attain it. It is for this very reason that hedonism must always fail as a moral incentive. To say that people ought to seek pleasure or that they have an obligation to enjoy themselves makes no sense. Hedonism can never supply a correct sense of moral obligation. That we forego our pleasures or willingly suffer pain in order to fulfill our higher moral obligations, in fact, is often a reasonable demand. To be honest or just is our moral duty, not because it invariably brings us pleasure but because it is an expression of good will. Where morality is concerned, according to Royce, "Only the good intention is truly moral."[25]

The question remains whether a suitable moral goal or principle can be found, a principle that all persons ought to pursue, one that will actually unify or harmonize all of man's legitimate moral concerns. In 1908 Royce published *The Philosophy of Loyalty* in which he claimed, *"In loyalty, when loyalty is properly defined, is the fulfillment of the whole moral law."*[26] Royce sought to show that all of the traditional moral virtues including justice, charity, courage, and integrity are in fact definable in terms of loyalty. Without loyalty there can be no moral value at all. Loyalty is, in other words, necessary for moral goodness. But loyalty is also, when properly conceived, a sufficient principle to cover all of moral goodness or rightness from the standpoint of reason. First, it will be noticed that loyalty can apply only to a self or person that is essentially related to other selves or persons. Loyalty is a state of the person or self that binds that person or self to others in a common cause. Innumerable examples include loyalty to one's family, friends, country, or religion. Second, it will be noticed that loyalty is essentially practical in the sense that it inspires or requires action or the performance of loyal deeds. In other words, loyalty requires the individual to put his devotion to his cause into motion, not only by joining that cause but by actually working for it and even making personal sacrifices when necessary. Third, loyalty is not only inherently social and practical;

it is also ideal or spiritual. When an individual practices loyalty, he affiliates himself with something much larger and greater than himself. It is not one's personal or selfish interest that one serves with loyalty; one must have a cause distinct from oneself that other persons can serve as well. No arbitrary limit can be imposed on the number of individuals who can serve a cause. The more genuine and ideal the cause, in fact, the more numbers of individuals who can actually be devoted to it.

A further ingredient of loyalty is that it involves freedom of choice or autonomy of the will. One cannot actually be compelled to be loyal to a cause. External compulsion or force can indeed control people's behavior or make them conform to certain commands. But mere obedience to authority or mechanical behavior is not loyalty. Loyalty is a quality of devotion that only applies to a self that determines its own goals; it does not apply to a machine or to blind acceptance of orders. According to Royce, loyalty must be self-imposed. The individual must take the responsibility for devoting himself to whatever cause he is loyal. For this reason loyalty can never be something wholly impersonal. One cannot be loyal to a mere abstract principle or pure power that has no personal meaning. No matter how universal or infinite one's chosen cause may be, it must have the character of a larger self or community of selves that can conceivably understand, need, and appreciate any loyalty. It would be illogical to devote oneself to a cause that could not notice or appreciate one's devotion to that cause. This does not mean that one's loyalty is always in fact recognized or appreciated by those included in its scope. One's loyalty to friends or country may in fact go unappreciated or unrewarded—but this does not mean that one's loyalty *cannot* be appreciated. Whether one's loyalty is in fact known or appreciated, nevertheless it ought to be.

Royce defined loyalty as "*the willing and practical and thoroughgoing devotion of a person to a cause.*"[27] What Royce meant by "thoroughgoing" was a decisive commitment that the individual makes which removes any vacillation or wavering. When one is really loyal to a cause, one is wholly devoted to it in terms of one's whole personality or self. This does not mean that one cannot change or abandon one's loyalties, but it does mean that, while the individual is loyal, he is thoroughly committed to his cause. But obviously "nobody can be equally and directly loyal to all of the countless social causes that exist."[28] Some loyalties do conflict with one another. Some loyalties are, in fact, bad in the sense that they involve the destruction of other people's loyalties. Loyalty to a band of thieves may be useful to the thieves, but it is not good for the victims. Even patriotism, loyalty to one's country, is not absolutely good when it involves the willful destruction of other people's lives and loyalties. Thus a higher principle is needed that can harmonize loyalties with one another. This Royce found in the principle he termed "loyalty to loyalty." "And so, a cause is good, not only for me, but for mankind, in so far as it is essentially a *loyalty to loyalty*, that is, is an aid and a furtherance of loyalty in my fellows."[29] Loyalty to a cause is good because it it an expression of free choice that raises a person above mere self-interest and binds him to the service to others. But loyalty is not completely or absolutely good unless it involves a devotion to all legitimate loyalties that can be made consistent with one another. Loyalty to loyalty involves a devotion to furtherance of the principle of loyalty itself. The more that one is loyal to the idea of loyalty itself, the more one helps everyone to cultivate and increase his loyalty.

But loyalty to loyalty is not merely an abstract principle, for it involves an actual community of selves or persons united in a common cause. Universal loyalty is not simply an ideal for mankind to aim toward, but is a practical principle that can and ought to be enacted. A person who is honest out of principle, for example, is giving expression to loyalty to loyalty—as is a person who gives kindness or help to others when that kindness or help is based on a genuine interest in others' welfare. Royce claimed that innumerable examples of loyalty to loyalty exist and that every truly moral action falls under this principle. The concept of loyalty to loyalty is sufficiently broad to encompass all moral actions because it actually involves what Royce called an "infinite community." "Whoever is concretely loyal, that is, whoever wholly gives himself to some cause that binds many human souls in one superhuman unity, is just in so far serving the cause not only of all mankind, but of all the rational spiritual world."[30] This universal loyalty, Royce held, is not only the source of genuine morality, but is the essence of true religion as well.[31] The cause of universal loyalty binds individuals together in what Royce regarded as an eternal, infinite community of rational endeavor. The cause of true morality or religion cannot be limited in terms of duration or numbers of actual members. A genuine community, Royce held, is not merely a collection of people. "It is essentially a historical phenomenon, having both a past and a future which are connected with one another through the lives of its individual members who remember a common past and aspire to a common purpose or future goal. A community requires a time process in order to come into being, but only an eternity of time will suffice to enable any truly religious or moral community to realize itself fully or reach its goal."[32] Royce sharply contrasted what he meant by a genuine community with a mere mob or crowd. A mob or crowd "means merely a company of people who, by reason of their sympathies, have for the time being resigned their individual judgment."[33] In a mob or crowd "The good sense of individuals is lost in a blur of emotion, and in a helpless suggestibility."[34] In a community the minds or selves of its individual members are not lost or submerged, but are united to the mind or spirit of the whole community. A community not only functions as a unit, but functions as a mind or self—it produces customs, language, values, morality, and religion. A community is a larger, objective mind or self wherein its individual members identify and unify their own personal lives and values. "The individual member may love his community as if it were a person, may be devoted to it as if it were his friend or father, may serve it, may live and die for it."[35] According to Royce, the individual may come to regard his community "as if it were a sort of super-personal being, and as if it could, in its turn, possess the value of a person or some higher level. One who thus loves a community, regards its type of life, its form of being, as essentially more worthy than his own."[36]

In his idea of loyalty to a universal or infinite community of interpretation, Royce believed he had found not only the key to man's moral life but also a way of reconciling science and religion. Man cannot be moral or religious alone or in isolation. Only in a larger community can the human self find the opportunities for moral virtue, service, religious concern, or salvation. But a community only exists by interpretation. No moral, religious, or scientific community can exist without the minds of its individual members who must continually translate that community's meaning into significant, understandable terms. No community can exist without the use of signs or symbols which its individual members use to interpret and communicate the essential meaning of that community. Science originates and progresses by the loyal efforts of individual scientists who interpret one another's work and pool their studies. Science is impossible without the formation of a community of investigators united in the common cause of discovering truth. No human individual can do all the work of science alone. The individual efforts of any single human scientist are meaningless and worthless apart from the efforts of other investigators who test, criticize, and expand his work. As Royce remarked, "Practically I cannot be saved alone; theoretically speaking, I cannot find or even define the truth in terms of my individual experience, without taking account of my relation to the community of those who know. This community, then, is real whatever is real. And in that community my life is interpreted. . . . My life means nothing, either theoretically or practically, unless I am a member of a community."[37]

In his later works, Royce sought to develop the insight that everything real is part of an infinite community of interpretation. Royce's theory of interpretation as a higher mental process than either perception or conception was markedly influenced by the work of Peirce. In fact Royce placed particular stress on the importance of Peirce's influence when he states, "I now owe much more to our great and unduly neglected American logician, Mr. Charles Peirce, than I do to the common tradition of recent idealism."[38] Perception ends in an object perceived, and conception ends in a definition or universal type—but interpretation is not self-limiting. "By itself, the process of interpretation calls, in ideal, for an infinite sequence of interpretations. For every interpretation, being addressed to somebody, demands interpretation from the one to whom it is addressed."[39] Royce carried Peirce's idea well beyond Peirce's original meaning, however. Royce was particularly interested in the moral, social, and religious significance of this idea. Where human values are concerned, Royce believed that a rational method is needed for comparing and resolving conflicts between ideas. Problems of racial prejudice, war, and evils of all kinds require a triadic method of interpretation to show how all evils can be overcome. In his later philosophy especially, Royce tried to give more concrete meaning to his absolute idealism by showing how, if viewed in terms of an ongoing community of interpretation, it could help resolve the practical, moral, and social problems of man.

The Moral Role of Reason
and the Problem of Evil

In agreement with William James, Josiah Royce viewed the moral life of man in terms of struggle, conflict, and even tragedy. When James asserted that some part of the ideal must be butchered, he clearly meant to offer only a piecemeal form of optimism in the face of possible pessimism and despair. But Royce clearly could not be satisfied with the mere hope of some partial or small moral success. Royce indeed was a complete rationalist in ethics—and, oddly enough, for the very same reason that James was not. James thought a sufficient refutation of any rational type of idealism in ethics is that evil simply exists, that some part of the ideal good must be lost or given up. James considered that, once we admit the positive presence of evil and tragedy in the world, the idea that the world constitutes a complete, perfect moral order must be abandoned. But for Royce, the real existence of suffering, evil, or tragedy was necessary to the existence of a truly complete and perfect moral order. Suffering, evil, and tragedy in man's life confront him with a challenge to overcome these very things and to create a stronger, more perfect order. For Royce, a world without conflict, suffering, and evil would not be a moral universe at all. In the absence of anything positively bad, the notion of anything positively good would lose all meaning. Just as error is a necessary contrast for the definition and meaning of the very idea of truth, so evil is dialectically necessary for the recognition of any genuine goodness or moral order. Royce wanted to show that opposition, conflict, and all the evil, irrational factors of life are actually needed for the development of a more perfect, rational order or whole. "The dialectical method, as we remember, has especially insisted upon the fact that the practical life of the spirit depends upon developing and overcoming opposition."[40] If no oppositions and conflicts existed for man's reason and moral efforts to overcome, reason and morality would have no essential functions in life. The function of reason in life is to arrange our ideas and judgments so as to achieve a more intelligible and complete order than is ever immediately given. If things immediately or automatically arranged themselves for the best without any real effort on our part, reason would have no practical or moral task to perform. But for Royce, there was obviously much work for reason to do. Our ideas and lives are not automatically harmonious and sound. He affirmed that empiricism, pragmatism, and idealism all agree on this point. But he further claimed that only idealism offers a completely rational solution to this problem. The other philosophies merely acknowledge the existence of disorder and the irrational features of life. But dialectical idealism, as he saw it, demands or actually exploits the existence of these various features. "We must maintain with Hegel that extremely lofty rational interest both of the will and of the whole spiritual nature are such as to demand the presence of conflicting motives and even of essentially tragic contests in all the higher spiritual life."[41]

A common criticism of idealism is the allegation that it offers only a barren intellectualism or a totally abstract account of life that leaves out all the concrete detail. Royce admitted that this criticism may indeed apply to some older forms of idealism, but he denied that it applies to all of the modern forms, especially his own. "The truth, whatever it is, is certainly not expressible in merely abstract, or in merely harmonious terms. If it is the truth of life, i.e., if the truth is a living and not a merely bloodless realm of abstract categories, then the truth must involve issues, struggles, conquests, and conquests over aspects of life that, when viewed in their abstraction, are distinctly evil and irrational."[42] Idealism cannot succeed as a philosophy by denying the reality of irrational, less than ideal things or by leaving them functionless and unexplained. To demand a reason for anything's existence is clearly the point of both reason itself and any rational philosophy. To suggest that things do not need or have a reason for existence is philosophically unacceptable, since we can always ask how this is known or why it is true. How do we know that some things happen merely by chance or accident? How can we prove that so-called purposeless or irrational events have no rational explanation? Merely by raising these questions, according to Royce, we see that acceptance of anything irrational as final or ultimate is contradictory. Things may not, often do not, fulfill the purposes that we have in mind for them. Often, in fact, our human understanding is confounded and unable to find sound reason for a thing's existence. Perplexity and lack of complete knowledge are very real conditions of the human scene. But, according to Royce, we would not really be perplexed if we did not assume that a more complete, rational account ought to be found. The facts of human error and lack of knowledge only make sense against the background of a more complete picture still to come.

Perhaps the strongest role of rationalism in Royce's ethics is contained in his view that values take logical precedence over facts, that the notion of *ought* is logically prior to, or more fundamental than, the notion of what *is*, or is real. "'How ought I to conceive the real?' is logically prior to the question, 'What is the real itself?' . . . the *ought* is prior in nature to the real, or the proposition: 'I ought to think thus,' is prior to the proposition: 'This is so.' This whole view of the problem of reality is one which is characteristic of idealism."[43] The notion of *ought* is indispensable to ethics. Without the contrast between what ought to be and what is, or between what we ought to do and what in fact we do, morality and moral injunctions would have no point. But is is characteristic of man's thinking about morality that he tries to derive values from facts. Moral obligation and virtue, it is believed, can have no better, more solid foundation than some suitable facts. This mistake is a very old one and has many varieties. Hedonism, for example, is a very old moral outlook based on the mistake of trying to ground the validity of moral values and obligations on those facts that provide some kind of satisfaction or pleasure. William James was also guilty of this fallacy insofar as he held that the essence or foundation of good is simply to satisfy demand. Royce did not claim that this view is completely mistaken; in fact it has, in common with every erroneous judgment, some degree of truth. To discover its degree of truth and error, we must examine what Royce termed its "internal and external meaning." All ideas or judgments have an internal and external meaning. Internal meaning refers to the idea's purpose or aim. In order to function at all, an idea must aim toward some objective. This holds for true ideas as well as for false ones. I can certainly think that 2 + 3 = 7—but as soon as I consider the external meaning of this idea, I realize that my purpose or aim cannot be fulfilled. External meaning refers to what would actually fulfill that idea's aim or purpose. Now if we consider James's idea that the essence of good is simply to satisfy demand, we observe that the internal meaning of this idea actually has a very narrow aim. Its aim or purpose is to make all good things or experiences consist only in the fact that they satisfy someone's demand or interest at some time. But when we examine the external meaning of James's idea, we realize that this aim cannot be completely carried out. James's idea is true, of course, insofar as *good* pertains to demand or interest. James rightly insists that the essence of good is vitally related to the satisfaction of people's demands. But this is far from proving that the relation is one of identity or that satisfaction of demand coincides with what is meant by saying that anything is good. Satisfaction of a demand is often not good; we often regret, upon later reflection, that a demand was indeed satisfied. Now if no demands or interests were ever satisfied, nothing would ever be good. This much of James's view is valid; it simply means that appreciation is necessary to any value. But for Royce, appreciation was not sufficient for value because not all values or goods are on the same level, and also because no limited appreciation or finite number of appreciations can add up to everything that is valuable or should be experienced. What ought to be demanded or appreciated is always higher than what is in fact demanded or appreciated. Our present demands and interests are always finite, hence imperfect. Our finite demands and interests actually presuppose a higher set of values that ought to exist and which we ought to strive for. "The consciousness of the more rational purpose beyond my present impulses . . . is what we mean in Ethics by the Ought. . . . The practical Ought of Ethics is thus the fuller determination of my own will, viewed at once as mine and yet as superior to my present capricious and imperfect expression of my purpose."[44]

Royce admitted that a paradox is involved in his view that man's moral life must be viewed as something not temporal but nevertheless occurring in time, as not finite and individual but nevertheless pertaining to finite persons. Royce asserted: "For the Ethical Self, as we have already seen, has its meaning defined in terms of an activity to which no temporal limits can be set without a confession of failure."[45] This means that an ethical self or moral agent must be regarded as rational, as having purposes and duties that are universal and not limited to any particular time or place. An ethical self is capable of acting on principle, e.g., the principle of loyalty to loyalty, which transcends any present interests and defines an ideal interest that ought to be pursued at all times. But although the ideal purpose or rational meaning of any truly moral action is independent of any particular time, such purpose or meaning must apply to actions which do occur in time. "Moral acts, as I have pointed out, occur in time."[46] There is no contradiction in maintaining that, while the ideal principles of moral action are themselves eternal, the applications of these principles must be temporal. This is analogous, according to Royce, with the principles or eternal truths of mathematics. $A=\pi r^2$ is an eternal truth or principle defining the area of a circle. But this eternal principle also works or is valid for determining the area of any empirical circle that one may draw at some time or other.

The same logic applies to the relation between the finite and the infinite in ethics. Any genuine moral obligation or virtue must pertain to both the infinite community of moral agents and the finite lives of individuals as well. The duty to be loyal to the furtherance of universal loyalty defines the goal of all moral actions, yet this standard can and must be met in specific examples of moral action. An act of kindness, done not for the sake of reward but simply from a genuine thought to help another human being, is a concrete instance of an absolute moral good. The act in terms of its particular circumstances is finite, but it is such an action that has infinite worth. In a material sense, the moral benefit of benevolent actions may be very small; but in an ideal or spiritual sense of value, such actions help all humanity. Thus the moral benefit of an action cannot really be measured in material or empirical terms. But this does not mean that the moral benefit cannot be measured or determined at all or that it must be considered a mystery. The fact that a moral action benefits the infinite community of loyal selves implies that this benefit is indeed supernatural, according to Royce. But Royce refused to identify the supernatural with the miraculous or the mystical: "Man needs no miracles to show him the supernatural and the superhuman. You need no signs and wonders, and no psychical research, to prove that the unity of the spirit is a fact in the world."[47] While the infinite community of loyal selves may be invisible, this certainly does not mean that such a community is unverifiable and irrational. The infinite community of loyal selves involves a community of rational interpretation that is clearly open to rational inspection and testing in terms of our *a priori* reasoning. Man's uniqueness as a moral agent is clearly linked with his ability to think and form ideas that clearly outrun the senses. Man's ethical strength and stature, according to Royce, comes exactly from his power to think and act rationally, i.e., his ability to take an infinitely long run of moral consequences into consideration. Man can know the difference between an action which benefits only himself or some special group and one that benefits all rational beings. In fact Royce claimed that "reasonable" and "unreasonable" are essentially moral terms. Not merely neutral terms of description or abstract analysis, they pertain to standards of value that ought to be realized because it is universally or impartially good to realize them. *Reasonable* means unbiased or unprejudiced, and unreasonable means just the opposite.

> When we speak of an ill-tempered or of a prejudiced man as "unreasonable" we do not merely mean that he is unable to form or to define abstract ideas, or that he cannot analyse the meaning of his own statements. For sometimes such a man is contentiously thoughtful, and fond of using too many one-sided abstractions, and eager to argue altogether too vehemently. No, when we call him unreasonable, we mean that he takes a narrow view of his life, or of his duties, or of the interests of his fellow-men. We mean, in brief, that he lacks vision for the true relations and for the total value of things.[48]

It is instructive to note that Royce's emphatically rationalistic form of idealism contrasts sharply with the Calvinistic idealism of Edwards and the Transcendental idealism of Emerson. The basis of moral virtue for Edwards was supernatural, but this did not mean that it was based on *a priori* reason. For Edwards, reason was insufficient as a substitute for divine intervention and revelation. In contrast to Royce, Edwards held that man's power of reason was unequal to the task of furnishing a true basis for morality or moral insight. Also, Emerson believed that moral virtue transcended anything that could be furnished by the senses or mere experience. And although he held that the moral law can be known by man, such knowledge came by intuition rather than by reflective thought. In contrast to Royce, Emerson upheld the value of mystical insight or union wherein he believed each man was in direct contact with the divine.

The problem of evil posed a serious moral problem for Royce's idealism. He could not accept James's piecemeal optimism or meliorism as a solution to this problem. Neither James, Emerson, nor Edwards before him had adequately explained why evil exists in the world or what meaning it has for man's moral life. These philosophers had left the problem essentially where they found it. Perhaps worst of all, in Royce's view, was Emerson's evasion of the problem by making evil only a false appearance which disappears when we achieve the right transcendental angle of vision. Emerson had, in effect, denied the reality or existence of evil when he declared, "The soul will not know either deformity or pain.... All loss, all pain, is particular; the universe remains to the heart unhurt."[49] One might suppose that Emerson's view is the most consistent with idealism. If idealism holds that all existence is mental and that all realities depend on the mind, the conclusion should follow that the reality of evil depends on the mind. If evil is something odious, something that mind is opposed to or shrinks from, what better way to solve the problem than by having mind simply deny its existence? If evil cannot exist without mind and if mind cannot appreciate or justify its existence, the only sensible course for any mind is to banish evil from consciousness. Transcendental Meditation is the name often identified with the quest to discipline our states of consciousness so as to banish all struggle, worry, pain, and evil in order to achieve a higher state of consciousness that is entirely peaceful and serene. Royce admitted some degree of truth in this transcendental approach to the problem of evil. This form of "romantic idealism," as Royce termed it,[50] is on the right track in its optimistic belief in the ultimate triumph of universal good will—but it is wrong in what it ignores. For this viewpoint is not truly universal, since it "refuses to grapple by the throat the real ills of life."[51] Romantic or mystical idealism is unable to solve the universal problem of evil because its viewpoint is too tender and narrow. Evil, tragedy, and sorrow play no significant role in achieving the ideal good; so, in a practical sense, this ideal good is only ideal, not concrete and real.

According to Royce, any real solution to the problem of evil must take the insights of pessimism into consideration. Pessimism is a natural, meaningful alternative to idealism in ethics; and the more profound the pessimism, the truer is its insight into the real sorrow, tragedy, and evil of life. Pessimism is intimately connected with ethical skepticism. Skepticism in ethics signifies the failure of finding any meaningful way to harmonize all of man's desires and goals. Skepticism sees each apparent good as only an appearance and doubts that any real, substantial good exists behind what appears. Many so-called good things are only transient or fleeting—what if *all* good is of this character and only an illusion? If extreme ethical optimism turns evil into an illusion, it is to be expected that extreme ethical skepticism that ends in pessimism should turn good into an illusion and make evil the essential reality of the world. Ethical pessimism in the full sense is based on the insight, according to Royce, that every finite creature not only inevitably suffers but ultimately loses both life and any chance of perfecting itself as finite. This is a real fact about the world that cannot be denied or ignored. Hence evil and suffering are not mere episodes or chance occurrences; they are universal conditions of existence. It is the very inevitability and universality of suffering and evil that pessimism emphasizes. Happiness and goodness are only illusions, myths that men use or fabricate, to hide the real suffering and badness of life. For pessimism, man's fate is to be born, to struggle, suffer, and die; and no moral justification can be found in this gloomy picture. Royce admitted a degree of truth in the doctrine of pessimism. When clearly viewed, pessimism in fact helps us see the errors involved in trying to base moral values on the desire for pleasure or happiness. The goals of individual and collective happiness are illusory and cannot be realized. But pessimism only partly sees what is wrong with hedonism in ethics. It only finds fault with the pursuit of happiness because it cannot be attained and gives no thought to the more fundamental question of whether it *ought* to be sought or is *worthy* of being pursued. Pessimism, in other words, would have us give up the pursuit of happiness as our primary goal in life in order to minimize our disappointment with life. But if life itself is as inevitably disappointing and pointless as pessimism holds, any maxim to reduce pain and sorrow is itself bound to be self-defeating and full of disappointment. Pessimism fails to see that real moral and spiritual values are inevitably bound up with struggle, discord, and suffering. Royce quoted the German philosopher Hegel as demonstrating this necessary point for the realization of a higher ethical insight: "Virtue is not without strife, but is rather the highest, the fulfilled strife."[52] Moral value is not to be found in flight from strife and suffering but rather in surmounting them. Suffering and evil are only pointless if no self acknowledges them and works to overcome their influence. Ample evidence shows that these very undesirable things play an important role in strengthening man's moral fiber and insight, indicating that the correct solution to the problem of evil is not the fatalistic or pessimistic one of mere resignation. The higher moral insight, according to Royce, is to realize that, although evil is certainly not good in itself, it is morally good that evil should exist in order to be overcome. What Royce called "the moral insight" "involves from its very nature, for those who have it, the will to harmonize, so far as may be possible, the conflicting wills that there are in the world"[53] Royce even asserted that "it becomes our duty to labor to increase pain, whenever pain is the *best* means of fostering the moral insight.... it is right that we ridicule all pretentious mediocrity that is unconscious of its stupidities.... it is right that we should criticize unsparingly all pretenders, however much they may be pained by our criticism."[54]

Royce's absolute moral truth or insight did not simply consist of one abstract principle or aim. Truth in morals must include the existence of many aims, since it must contain the proper resolution of conflicting purposes or points of view. Dialectically, the conflicting views are not simply dropped or forgotten when they are resolved through a higher synthesis. As partial truths, they are retained, though transformed, in the synthesis. In this sense, errors, misconceptions, and even sins perform a worthwhile function insofar as one uses them to move to a higher moral understanding and order. Thus if man did not sin or go astray in his moral life, he could not be redeemed. The moral values of forgiveness and atonement are rightly given a high place in the moral life, according to Royce, because they are so difficult to attain. "To sin is *consciously to choose to forget*, through a narrowing of the field of attention, an Ought that one already recognizes.... all sin is a free choosing of the *sort* of narrowness which ... we found to be, in one aspect, the natural fate of the human being."[55] For Royce, men have a natural inclination to sin insofar as it is easier for them to act from selfish interest than to take the interests of others into consideration. Men "have in this world no rights as individuals."[56] Moral rights and values pertain to men only insofar as they assume the duties of loyalty to others, including the infinite community of rational selves. "We must live united with each other and the world. Therefore must we do our part to find work vast enough to bring us all in so far as may be into unity, without cramping the talent of any of us. Each then is to do his work, but so as to unite with the work of others."[57] The moral goal of cooperative action and universal harmony is not defeated or refuted by the fact that men fail to cooperate or live united. Moral failures and impediments are incentives for greater efforts, incentives needed for enabling man to realize the values of correcting his errors and atoning for his sins.

Assessment

A prominent feature of what we have identified as Idealist Ethics consists of the intimate connection between morality and religion. Clearly, whether we go back to the early idealism of Jonathan Edwards, examine the Transcendentalism of Emerson, or consider the moral philosophy of Josiah Royce, all of these viewpoints agree in seeing the real meaning and value of moral life in principally religious or spiritual terms. The main moral problem as it appeared to Royce, in fact, was that of finding an adequate reconciliation between man's moral responsibilities and his religious aspirations. For Royce, "Morality gives us counsel as to our duty., Religion, pointing out to us the natural poverty and failure which beset our ordinary existence, undertakes to show us some way of salvation. Ethical teachings direct us to a better mode of living. Religion undertakes to lead us to a home-land where we may witness, and, if we are successful, may share some supreme fulfillment of the purpose for which we live."[58] In his first major work, *The Religious Aspect of Philosophy* (1885), Royce was concerned with examining and resolving the principal problems and conflicts that appear in man's moral and religious consciousness. Royce discovered the key to these problems in the idea of loyalty. In *The Philosophy of Loyalty* (1908), he attempted to define and defend the principle of "loyalty to loyalty" as the universal core of any truly rational religion and moral life. He was never satisfied, however, that he had succeeded in interpreting the idea of loyalty so as to encompass all the concrete facts and situations of life. Consequently he continued to rework and reformulate his whole philosophic position during his later years. In *The Sources of Religious Insight* (1912) and especially in *The Problem of Christianity* (1913), he sought to give fresh meaning and application to the idea of loyalty as not merely man's devotion to a cause but as man's devotion to that divine community of selves which is the only worthy, lasting cause.

Perhaps Royce's greatest achievement as a moral philosopher was his devotion and skill in exposing one dialectical problem after another that beset man's moral life. Every moral problem, he believed, had its answer; answers, however, were not resting places, but sources of new dialectical challenges and insights. Like William James, he was dissatisfied with any mere abstract, static view of man's moral life. But, unlike James, he could not adopt an ethical pluralism of individual moral volitions or faiths. For Royce, the individual only develops through social influences, to the extent that the strongest kinds of individuality only occur as direct results of contrasts and conflicts within their social environments. The morally independent individual therefore constituted a problem, rather than a solution or goal, in Royce's outlook.

> High social cultivation breeds spiritual enmities. For it trains what we in our day call individualism, and, upon precisely its most cultivated levels, glories in creating highly conscious individuals. But these individuals are brought to consciousness by their social contrasts and conflicts. Their very consciences are tainted by the original sin of social contentiousness. The higher the cultivation, the vaster and deeper are precisely the more spiritual and the more significant of these inward and outward conflicts. Cultivation breeds civilized conduct; it also breeds conscious independence of spirit and deep inner opposition to all mere external authority.[59]

Royce struggled throughout his philosophical writings with the problem of exactly how the individual person is related to the universe as a whole. To his credit, he could never accept any single formula as an expression of this relation. If individuality is something which must be developed in relation to, and even in conflict with, its social context and is not something preestablished or ultimate, its positive value as well as its defects or negative aspects are important for us to understand. A world without distinct individuals is no world at all. Any type of meaningful order, harmony, or unity logically requires that individuals exist to constitute such order, harmony, or unity. Any living community, for example, has an undeniable individuality. An actual community of persons cannot be a mere unity. As much as Royce tended to emphasize loyalty and community, it is mistaken to consider that he emphasized these values at the expense of individuality and autonomy. In 1902 Royce delivered an address at Iowa State University on provincialism, in which he defended the need for what he termed a "wholesome provincialism" or a healthy pride in local independence to combat the undesirable aspects of leveling tendencies which he saw as too prevalent in America. "The time has come to emphasize, with a new meaning and intensity, the positive value, the absolute necessity for our welfare, of a wholesome provincialism, as a saving power to which the world in the near future will need more and more to appeal."[60] He claimed that tendencies toward national unity and local independence cannot prosper without one another. "We tend all over the nation, and, in some degree, even throughout the civilized world, to read the same daily news, to share the same general ideas, to submit to the same overmastering social forces, to live in the same external fashions, to discourage individuality, and to approach a dead level of harassed mediocrity."[61] A narrow provincialism that insulates and isolates communities from one another and even fosters intolerance and prejudice is indeed morally unhealthy, even disastrous for mankind. But a vigorous pride in one's local community, Royce claimed, is clearly compatible with a healthy respect for, and cooperation with, other communities and mankind at large. Morally speaking, man has not only a duty to develop and improve his loyalty toward communities to which he belongs, but has an equal moral responsibility to respect the loyalties of others as far as possible. A basic principle of Royce's ethics was that no group or community has a right to establish and maintain any type of allegiance or loyalty that would weaken or destroy other people's legitimate claims to loyalty. To his credit, Royce spoke out in clear, emphatic terms against the actions of Germany at the outset of World War I. Germany's unjust invasion of Belgium and sinking of the *Lusitania* were clear instances to Royce of violations of the very principles of "loyalty to loyalty" and international morality. Germany's actions, according to Royce, showed us "one great classic example of the rejection, by a great and highly intelligent nation, of the first principles of international morality—the rejection of international duty, the assertion that for its own subjects, the State is the supreme moral authority, and that there is no moral authority on earth which ranks superior to the will of the State."[62] Loyalty to any political state cannot be made absolute without denying loyalty to the infinite community. To turn loyalty toward any state or community into an absolute is not only a metaphysical error but a crime against humanity as well. Royce claimed that man has but one inalienable right: a right to the opportunity to do his duty. "I fully agree with those who believe that men can reasonably define their rights only in terms of their duties. I have moral rights only in so far as I have duties. I have a right to my life because it gives me my sole opportunity to do my duty. I have a right to happiness solely because a certain measure of happiness is needed to adapt me to do the work of a man."[63] This is indeed a stern moral outlook that places duty ahead of happiness and service to a higher cause ahead of one's personal life. But it is clearly not fatalistic or pessimistic about man's moral abilities. Unlike Calvinism, it attributes freedom and the power of self-determination to man's conscious choices. Man's choices are not simply mechanically determined by his strongest motives or desires, but are consciously carved out by man himself; they are creations of man's freedom. Royce, to his credit, emphasized that moral choice implies the conscious effort of mental attention in the pursuit of ideals or ideal purposes. Freedom is therefore not negated or refuted by causation. Causation is a matter of impartial description, but freedom operates on an entirely different level: the level of appreciation, aspiration, and prescription. To deny man freedom of the will is thus tantamount to denying him possibility of action according to his love of ideals or principles that ought to regulate his life. Man indeed is subject to causes, and he operates in terms of natural laws. But he also appreciates and pursues ideals. A distinct, positive contribution of Royce's ethics was its insistence that values cannot be reduced to purely descriptive causes or facts. This further implies that freedom is not something to be merely assumed or taken as an article of blind faith but that man's freedom is something rational. It can only exist and flourish in terms of intelligence and self-controlled thought.

Royce did not begin a new philosophical movement like Peirce and James; his achievement in moral philosophy lies rather in his solid, rich interpretation of older philosophical traditions. Nor, as a rationalist and idealist, did Royce found a new type of moral philosophy. It is in fact unfortunate that his reputation has suffered because of his identification with older, even outmoded philosophical traditions. Although he exercised an influence on twentieth-century philosophers including W.E. Hocking, J. Lowenberg, and C.I. Lewis, his impact on James, Santayana, and Dewey—and on pragmatism and naturalism in American philosophy—has been almost entirely negative. Realism, pragmatism, and naturalism in America had, by the early part of this century, clearly gained an ascendency over idealism. It was in fact the absolute idealism of Josiah Royce that defined a common philosophical enemy for these more empirically oriented philosophical views in the United States. James argued strongly against Royce that an absolute mind or self can really have no history: "*As such*, the absolute neither acts nor suffers, nor loves nor hates; it has no needs, desires, or aspirations, no failures or successes, friends or enemies, victories or defeats. All such things pertain to the world quâ relative, in which our finite experiences lie, and whose vicissitudes alone have power to arouse our interest."[64]

Dewey complained that Royce's type of philosophy was inherently irrelevant and false to the world of actual experience: "The claim to formulate *a priori* the legislative constitution of the universe is by its nature a claim that may lead to elaborate dialectic developments. But it is also one that removes these very conclusions from subjection to experimental test, for, by definition, these results make no differences in the detailed course of events."[65]

Santayana, a colleague of Royce at Harvard, criticized Royce for inventing rather than finding genuine problems—especially the problem of evil:

> There is certainly a truth about evil, and in this case not an unknown truth; yet it is no solution to the "problem" which laid the indomitable Royce on the rack. If a younger son asks why he was not born before his elder brother, that question may represent an intelligible state of his feelings; but there is no answer to it, because it is a childish question. So the question why it is right that there should be any evil is itself perverse and raised by false presumptions. To an unsophisticated mortal the existence of evil presents a task, never a problem. Evil, like error, is an incident of animal life, inevitable in a crowded and unsettled world, where one spontaneous movement is likely to thwart another, and all to run up against material impossibilities.[66]

Peirce, in a review of Royce's book *The World and the Individual*, alleged that Royce's greatest fault as a philosophical thinker involved the error common to metaphysical thinkers who

. . . have always taken mathematics as their exemplar in reasoning, without remarking the essential difference between that science and their own. Mathematical reasoning has for its object to ascertain what would be true in a hypothetical world which the mathematician has created for himself—not altogether arbitrarily, it is true, but nevertheless, so that it can contain no element which he has not himself deliberately introduced into it. All that his sort of reasoning, therefore, has to do is to develop a preconceived idea; and it never reaches any conclusion at all as to what is or is not true of the world of existences. The metaphysician, on the other hand, is engaged in the investigation of matters of fact, and the only way to matters of fact is the way of experience.[67]

Clearly Royce's moral philosophy rests on his metaphysics, and his metaphysics in turn rests upon his claim that *a priori* or dialectical reason can establish and justify absolute truths that apply universally and eternally to our world of experience. Royce did not merely claim that *a priori* thinking can present us with possible hypotheses or ways of arranging any facts—he went much further to claim that *a priori* reasoning can determine, settle, or establish all of the most important kinds of truth. Royce, like Kant before him, was impressed by the successful use that mathematics makes of *a priori* or deductive reasoning. Two plus two is not *probably* equal to four, or *sometimes* equal to four; it is *necessarily* equal to four. As Peirce correctly pointed out, however, mathematical statements *per se* contain no factual information; they are purely hypothetical. If someone has four dollars in the bank, that is a matter of fact to be determined by empirical evidence. But to tell someone that, if he adds two dollars to two dollars, he will have four dollars does not inform him about an actual amount of money; it simply makes a hypothetical inference. Deductive or *a priori* reasoning by itself can never establish any factual truths. Only from factual premises can we deduce factual conclusions; it is the factual premises, not *a priori* reasoning, which determine what those factual conclusions shall be. We can start with factually false premises and by *a priori* reasoning arrive at consistent, logical conclusions which will, of course, be factually false. This clearly shows that deductive or *a priori* validity with respect to ideas is factually empty. *A priori* reasoning is valid not because its conclusions are factually true but because they are formally consistent. Thus it is illicit to use *a priori* or mathematical models of reasoning to establish, as Royce attempted, ultimate truths about God, the world, and man. Royce's favorite method of argumentation was the *reductio ad absurdum*. For Royce, the best and simplest way to prove that an absolute truth or moral order exists was by means of denying these very notions and finding that this denial inevitably results in the necessity to reinstate what was just denied. Certainly the *reductio ad absurdum* method of argument is legitimate when properly used—which means that one must realize its limitations. As a formal deductive technique, its use is purely hypothetical; i.e., it cannot be used independently of factual information to prove factual or existential conclusions. We cannot use this method to prove that an absolute moral order must exist. It is not self-evidently clear as to exactly what an absolute or perfect moral order is. There is considerable disagreement, in fact, as to just what should be included in any moral order. Should a perfect moral order contain sin or evil within it or not? Royce held that a perfect moral order must contain these things. But they are obviously blemishes, signs of imperfection, the very features which indicate that the moral world we actually live in and experience is not absolute or perfect. How, therefore, does it follow that the imperfect moral order of experience is contained in, or part of, a perfect, unblemished moral order? The only answer Royce could give was to assert that a perfect moral order must be blemished or imperfect in order to overcome these very evils. But this does not prove that such an all-inclusive moral order exists, nor that it has any so-called absolute value. The fact that the overcoming of evil may be good does not prove that any evil should have existed to be overcome. If no sicknesses or diseases existed, for example, we could not develop cures for them. But it does not follow from this that we should try to increase disease in order to have more diseases to cure. To alleviate suffering is morally good, but it is certainly not morally good to torture people so that we can then alleviate their suffering. Royce was clearly wrong to maintain that it is morally good for suffering and evil to exist so that we can work to overcome them. What is faulty in this thinking is to confuse the admitted good of alleviating suffering with the causes that are responsible for its existence. Man has learned how to eliminate certain diseases. But in Royce's logic, this means that man has cut off his possibility of profiting from any more suffering from those ills. Numerous instances of human progress imply that certain evils, errors, and hardships have effectively been eliminated. But elimination of an evil, for Royce, must imply the loss of any further benefit from the effort to conquer and control that very evil. Overcoming an evil is thus only good in a relative sense; quite obviously the time and effort expended in

overcoming this evil could be better spent in some other constructive or worthwhile activity. War is a notorious case in point. Some
good lessons and results are gained from the horrors of war. War
teaches us keen appreciation of peaceful existence. But how does it
follow that the evils of war will necessarily be overcome, or even
that the good lessons learned from war could not have been learned
in some other way? Any benefits derived from actual wars are
contingent, not necessary, since the only logically necessary things
are purely hypothetical.

Royce's main moral principle, which he termed "loyalty to
loyalty" or loyalty to an infinite community of selves, cannot
specifically inform us about exactly what ought to be done on
particular occasions. This principle is quite clearly abstract and
general. Whenever we act, we must engage in specific actions in
specific circumstances, which in turn will have particular effects on
particular persons and their circumstances. A general, abstract
moral principle is at best only hypothetically good to act upon, since
it may produce worthwhile results in certain circumstances but not
in others. But the question itself of whether any specific results are
themselves morally worthwhile calls for a value judgment or moral
appraisal and cannot simply be decided by a general principle.
Telling the truth, for example, may be generally good and
desirable—but not if we know beforehand that those to whom we
tell the truth will make immoral, even disastrous use of the truths we
furnish. Similarly, loyalty may, in many cases, be morally good or
desirable; but disloyalty to bad or improper causes may also be
good and desirable. To be told that we should be loyal to all good
causes and disloyal to all bad ones is rather empty advice. What we
want to know are the specific causes which are worthy of being
served and what specific causes we should shun. But no abstract or
general principle will furnish us with that information.

Royce's claim that all the specific moral virtures (e.g, justice,
mercy, benevolence, autonomy, courage) are all specific forms of
loyalty is not necessarily true. Some virtues by their very nature are
exceptions to rules or only have value in exceptional circumstances
and cannot be erected into universal principles that always apply.
Sometimes mercy may be good; at other times it may be irrelevant
or actually bad. If mercy were erected into a universal principle,
justice itself would be eliminated. Some virtues are needed to

counterbalance or augment others. But to know, in specific cases, how, where, and when to apply them is not the sort of thing that can be decided *a priori*. The whole center of any moral judgment or decision is, in fact, the knowledge in specific situations of how to make use of any general principles—and this cannot be decided completely *a priori* without trivializing the whole decision making process.

Royce's greatest mistake, which is characteristic of philosophical or dialectical idealism, is to have overestimated the use of logic or reason in man's moral life. He is to be credited for showing, contrary to the skeptics and empiricists, that reason does have its moral uses. Royce claimed it as an absolute truth, for example, that once a deed is done it cannot be undone. But the only thing absolute about an accomplished deed is that it is accomplished. To suggest that once done a deed cannot be undone is a play on words if it means that we cannot correct our mistakes. A deed done is done— that is an absolute certainty—but it is also a perfectly trivial statement, since it says nothing about any important consequences of the deed. Deeds that are done are important because they continue to have consequences, and these consequences can be changed and undone. If a man has stolen some money, he may be able to replace it. If a person has broken a chair or even a confidence, he may be able to restore them. In a factual sense, it is possible for one to undo a deed or a harm that has been done. Only the act of abstracting a deed away from its empirical consequences makes the undoing of that deed impossible.

In his penchant for an ethics of duty and loyalty, Royce underestimated the possible values of happiness and moral independence. He claimed that we have a right to be happy only insofar as this enables us to do our moral duty. But there is no sound reason why happiness must be subordinated to duty, no more than duty must be subordinated to happiness. Both are values; while they are often hard for us to coordinate, there is no reason why they cannot be given equal status. Happiness divorced from responsibility or duty may be morally undesirable, but responsibility without happiness of some kind seems pointless and unnecessarily barren. Similarly, while the welfare of others or the larger community of people must be included in our moral decisions, each person's independence from others is also a source of moral value. While service to others may be good, it is also true that, by cultivating enlightened self-interest, one may need less of those services that others may provide. The conscious desire always to be searching for something to do for others may, in fact, make a man quite useless to both others and himself. In any case, what must be faced and decided are particular facts and situations—and no abstract rule of loyalty will furnish us with ready-made answers to our moral problems.

Chapter 6

Naturalistic Ethics

American Naturalism

In the first half of the twentieth century, naturalism established itself as the most prominent form of philosophy in America. Its ascendency was primarily due to the impact of modern science plus influence of the comprehensive philosophies of John Dewey and George Santayana. As one contemporary philosophical naturalist has observed, "'Naturalism' came into vogue as the name for a recognized philosophic position during the great scientific movement of the nineteenth century, which put man and his experience squarely into the Nature over against which he had hitherto been set."[1] In its most definite meaning, naturalism stands opposed to any form of supernaturalism or idealism that would interpret the natural world as a mere appearance or fragment of some higher, invisible spiritual reality. For naturalism, the world of the senses—the world studied by all the natural sciences—is not only fully real and tangible, but is in fact the source of man's total interests and activities including his problems and ideals. According to Dewey, human "experience is *of* as well as *in* nature. It is not experience which is experienced, but nature, stones, plants, animals, diseases, health, temperature, electricity, and so on. Things interacting in certain ways *are* experience; they are what is experienced. Linked in certain other ways with another natural object—the human organism—they are *how* things are experienced as well."[2] Naturalism as a broad philosophic label is consequently in clear harmony with empiricism and realism. Since naturalism accepts the methods of natural science as the most reliable ways of gaining knowledge, it views all human knowledge as based on experience and the discovery of real, independently existing facts or events in the external world. Naturalism, broadly considered, is also in harmony with many features of pragmatism. The pragmatism of Peirce and James had insisted that all of our factual knowledge is fallible, to be construed in a functional or experimental manner. Naturalism accepts this view of the fallibility of our knowledge as well as the corollary for ethics: that our moral ideas are not absolute but are subject to correction and criticism.

In 1905, Santayana published *The Life of Reason*, which contained a classic formulation of the naturalistic position and which exercised considerable influence on later American naturalists. Santayana asserted that "everything ideal has a natural basis and everything natural an ideal development."[3] Clearly Santayana's assertion of naturalism was materialistic in the sense that he held matter as the ground of all existence and as the sole source of power or causation. Love and beauty are perfect illustrations of Santayana's principle. Love cannot exist as a disembodied force or form, but is generated by biological or animal impulses. No matter how idealistic or spiritual love may be in its quality or objects of affection, it nevertheless has a natural, material basis or ground. But even though love is an expression of animal interests, it can at the same time be greatly idealized. Animal impulses can be transformed by the imagination and reason in such a way as to include or apply to universal, even timeless considerations. Love of truth and love of mankind both have their basis in animal interest or impulse; but for both, the impulses or interests have been made coherent and enlightened. Although man is inevitably situated in the natural world, he is mentally able to detach himself from its influence. Man can conceive, portray, or imagine other worlds and things than the particulars of his own situation. For Santayana, it was perfectly natural that man strive to modify his natural environment in ways that suit his interests and aspirations. Nature is certainly not immediately or invariably congenial to man's interests or survival. As a consequence, man modifies or transforms the natural world in order to achieve a happier or better relation with it. Art is the name Santayana gave to the human activity of transforming material things and conditions into more useful, beautiful forms. Architecture, as a case in point, has a natural basis; it is based on man's animal need to protect or shelter himself from the vicissitudes of nature. But shelter building also has an ideal fulfillment—since man, not satisfied merely to live or survive, strives to live well and to surround himself with forms of beauty. Beauty itself, not only a chief source of value in human life, is a perfect illustration of the natural or material ground of all value. In *The Sense of Beauty* (1896), Santayana defined beauty as "value positive, intrinsic, and objectified. Or, in less technical language, Beauty is pleasure regarded as the quality of a thing."[4] We say, for example, that beauty is in the music we hear or the landscape we see. But beauty is not literally in the music as physical sound waves or in the landscape in any material sense. The beauty actually lies in our own experience of the sound waves or in our own experience or view of the landscape. Existentially, in terms of its occurrence, beauty is subjective, clearly dependent on the eye or ear of the beholder. Beauty is not actually an objective, primary quality of a tree (like its height) or a river (like its depth). Although beauty is subjective in terms of the feeling of its pleasure, it becomes objectified, according to Santayana, in the sense that we idealize it and regard it as a quality of the music or landscape. Beauty is thus distinct from ordinary or merely sensual pleasures since these are not commonly objectified or regarded as the quality of a thing. The taste of an apple may bring pleasure, but we do not normally regard this pleasure as a quality of the apple; it is simply a quality of our taste or experience. Any aesthetic quality or feeling of beauty requires detachment from the object viewed. Beauty is not itself a material thing of tangible existence, but simply a form—what Santayana termed an "essence"—that material things may evoke in us. "The most material thing, in so far as it is felt to be beautiful, is instantly immaterialized, raised above external personal relations, concentrated and deepened in its proper being, in a word, sublimated into an essence."[5]

For Santayana, essences "or pure enjoyable qualities are not out of place in a naturalistic philosophy. It would be out of place, however, to confuse mere essences or symbols with existing powers or substances. Naturalism would be incomplete as a philosophy if it restricted itself to what merely happens to exist. It would thereby lose all those possible themes which only the imagination and intellect may see."[6] For Santayana, "Existence would not be worth preserving if it had to be spent exclusively in anxiety about existence."[7] The beginning of wisdom, therefore, is the ability to distinguish the detachable essences or forms of things from their natural, material ground or existence. The important thing about existences is that they display or involve detachable qualities or forms which man can appreciate or enjoy. These qualities themselves, as in any quality of beauty, are not substances or forces with any material location or function. They do, however, have moral or aesthetic meaning. Man can appreciate and enjoy only the forms or qualities of things. "Man has a definite tendency to be carried away by the symbols he uses, the ideas he thinks, and the beauty he experiences. He confuses the way things appear with the way they really are. To mark off this important difference Santayana insists upon what he calls the distinction between *essence* and *existence*."[8] Naturalism will break down or be turned into mere mythology if we confuse the words we use or the symbols and ideas we think with actual forces and substances that comprise the world. The natural world is not compacted by the ideas and thoughts we may form of its shape or structure. Our ideas are not literal copies or transcripts of the natural world; at best they can only be relevant to, or indicative of, this world. Idealism has this very fault of confusing essence with existence—of confusing the forms with which we think about the world with the natural world itself. Even our best scientific ideas, according to Santayana, are not literal transcriptions of the world, but are at best verifiable interpretations that make sense in terms of our natural powers of understanding. Santayana observed that "men became superstitious not because they had too much imagination, but because they were not aware that they had any."[9] Human reason is the conscious effort to discern order in the midst of change and confusion. But the power of human reason is limited and impossible without imagination. Reason, when guided by observation and fidelity to facts, is indeed a source of knowledge and understanding. But reason guided by imagination, while it may contain great poetic beauty, is not a reliable source of truth. For this reason, naturalism cannot accept the tenets of any form of supernatural religion as valid or factually correct. Religion may indeed be morally inspiring and aesthetically beautiful, but that is not the same as being factually true. "Poetry is called religion when it intervenes in life, and religion, when it merely supervenes upon life, is seen to be nothing but poetry."[10] Poetry and religion involve imaginative, symbolic interpretations of existence. Consequently neither offers a literally true picture of things, but both offer a view that has aesthetic and moral value. Naturalism neither denies the reality of religion nor cancels its humanistic value. Religion is natural and congenial to man because it defines values and ideals for him to cherish and pursue. But to take religion for an imaginative or supernatural substitute for science is mistaken, since the true place and value of religion is to offer man aesthetic and moral inspiration.

Religious philosophies such as we find in the idealisms of Royce, Emerson, and Edwards involve an illicit use of mere symbols or ideals to determine matters of fact or existence. Even the piecemeal supernaturalism of William James involved an improper use of beliefs about the function of values to determine or regulate matters of fact. Man's values, including his moral beliefs, have their basis in natural fact; but that is not the same as saying that they themselves depict or describe any facts about the world. Man's illusions and errors certainly have natural causes or origins; but that does not mean that such errors or illusions are true in any factual sense. Moral values such as loyalty, justice, and benevolence also have natural causes and conditions. Unless men actually cared about pursuing moral ideals, these ideals would have no meaning or function. The whole point of any moral ideal for Santayana, however, was not to describe some truth or fact, but to express a preference or prescribe a mode of living. Hence, while moral values can be enlightened, coherent, and sincere, they cannot actually be literally true or false. "The worst mistake in ethics, according to Santayana, is to fail to see that values are relative to natural, animal interests. This error not only leads to fruitless controversy, but actually encourages the worst forms of intolerance and fanaticism."[11] Santayana insisted that naturalism in ethics implies not only the relativity of all beliefs about values—that no values are absolute or unconditioned—but also implies the skeptical conclusion that values cannot be proved or established as valid by the use of either reason or empirical fact. "The ultimate intuitions on which ethics rests are not debatable, for they are not opinions we hazard but preferences we feel; and it can be neither correct nor incorrect to feel them."[12]

Other naturalists agreed with Santayana that moral values or values of any kind are not absolute or unconditioned. All naturalists generally agree that moral values have a natural basis. Values involve preferences that are intimately related to biological conditions or facts. Not all naturalists, however, share Santayana's skeptical position that value judgments are incapable of empirical proof or justification. Dewey, for one, considered it one of the major tasks of his whole philosophy to show how values or valuations can be brought within the purview of scientific method, hence be empirically tested and verified. So-called facts and values have been falsely separated or isolated from one another; the real problem for philosophy, according to Dewey, is to show how facts and values can be connected or coordinated. "The problem of restoring integration and cooperation between man's beliefs about the world in which he lives and his beliefs about the values and purposes that should direct his conduct is the deepest problem of modern life. It is the problem of any philosophy that is not isolated from that life."[13] Dewey termed his own philosophy a form of "empirical naturalism,"[14] as well as "instrumentalism."[15] In contrast to Santayana—whose naturalism was in many ways opposed to, and critical of, pragmatism—Dewey's naturalism was strongly pragmatic in character. Santayana rejected James's pragmatic theory of truth including his conception of pragmatism as a philosophy of involvement in human affairs. Dewey, on the other hand, while also critical of certain ideas in James's pragmatism, accepted the premise that philosophy should properly be involved in human affairs, not detached or removed from man's basic concerns. Far from rejecting either the pragmatism of Peirce or James, Dewey sought to improve upon their ideas and formulate a more comprehensive, adequate type of pragmatism. Neither Peirce nor James formulated a complete, explicit form of naturalism, although elements of naturalism existed within their views. James's philosophy, according to Dewey, lacked any proper social emphasis or consideration of the social factors in existence. Both James and Peirce regarded the scientific method in much too narrow terms and did not see this method as relevant to the solution of all of man's problems. Dewey accepted that all ideas are to be viewed in terms of their future, practical consequences. The only way to find or test the meaning, truth, or value of any idea is to treat that idea as an experimental hypothesis. In this sense, Dewey was a pragmatist. He insisted that "it lies in the nature of pragmatism that it should be applied as widely as possible; and to things as diverse as controversies, beliefs, truths, ideas, and objects."[16] This means that no essential difference exists between the pragmatic method and the method of intelligence in science. Neither pragmatic nor scientific methods can be limited or defined in terms of some special subject matter. What is essential to these methods is intelligent experimentation rather that any fixed, special object of investigation. The virtue of the scientific method is its self-correctiveness. In seeking to resolve questions and find answers, it asserts that inquiry must be continuous so that no results are accepted as final or uncriticizable. For Dewey, the success of the experimental method in natural science must be carried over to philosophy and the humanities. Instrumentalism must be combined with naturalism so that ideas are studied operationally in terms of continuous inquiry—and so that no false dualisms are erected between theory and practice, experience and nature, values and facts, or the humanities and natural sciences.

One major emphasis in Dewey's naturalism was his repeated opposition to what he termed "false dualisms" that distort our understanding of how things are actually related to one another.

> It is his view that many traditional philosophic problems that have caused endless controversy are predicated on the basis of false dualisms. The quest for certainty and the search for an absolute in philosophy are both based upon falsely disparaging ordinary experience.... Dewey argues that nothing positive is gained by disparaging sense experience. What is really needed is a method of integrating the senses with intelligent thinking so that our experiences can become more continuous and relevant to one another. Experience does not exclude thought and no thoughts can be so pure that they outrun experience.[17]

The rationalists in philosophy allege that experience is inferior to thought or reason, and the empiricists insist on just the opposite. What is true, of course, is that some experiences are better than others and that some thoughts are less adequate than other thoughts. But if thought or reason is capable of being experienced and if experience itself can be controlled by intelligent thinking, then to separate and oppose these very things is false and pointless.

One very important false dualism is that which concerns the study of values, including moral philosophy. This dualism involves the separation of facts from values and means from ends. It is commonly asserted that judgments of value cannot be based on, or derived from, judgments of fact, since judgments of fact are merely descriptive and neutral whereas judgments of value are prescriptive and involve taking sides. Judgments of value are said to be concerned with what ought to be, while judgments of fact only concern what is. To say that "water contains hydrogen and oxygen" is a factual or descriptive judgment; but to say that "water is good to drink" is a value judgment. Dewey admitted that plain judgments of fact are not value judgments even when they concern desires and preferences or likes and dislikes. Mere preference for one thing rather than another or the mere desire for some object certainly does not establish the value or goodness of that object. A person who likes or enjoys a thing does not establish the value or goodness of the thing by his mere liking or enjoyment of it. On the other hand, nothing could be of value if no person could find satisfaction or interest in something. Desire, interest, and preference do not establish values, according to Dewey, but they are necessary to the meaning and existence of any values. Without the existence of preference, interest, or enjoyment, there could clearly be no values. Values, therefore, are not opposed to so-called facts, but only come into existence because of certain facts.

> Valuations exist in fact and are capable of empirical observation so that propositions about them are empirically verifiable.... The notion that valuations do not exist in empirical fact and that therefore value-conceptions have to be imported from a source outside experience is one of the most curious beliefs the mind of man has ever entertained. Human beings are continuously engaged in valuations. The latter supply the primary material for operations of further valuations and for the general theory of valuation.[18]

Dewey used the term value "to designate whatever is taken to have rightful authority in the direction of conduct."[19] A genuine value does not merely indicate something desired or enjoyed, but something desirable and enjoyable. In other words, value judgments concerning the goodness or rightness of anything involve predictions about what will prove, upon careful examination, to be sound guides to conduct. This means that values are testable insofar as they involve assertions about observable means of achieving certain ends. To judge that a certain building material is good for constructing a certain bridge is to predict that this material will serve to support traffic on that bridge under specifiable conditions; that this material is available, economical, and so on. To say that justice or democracy are morally good is likewise to predict that, under specifiable and testable conditions, they will foster or promote harmony and healthful growth among human beings. But as empirical judgments about the relations of means to ends, value judgments depend upon seeing that means and ends are continuous with one another. Nothing is good merely as an end, irrespective of the means available for bringing that end into existence. For Dewey, there can be no genuine final ends in ethics or in life that are unconnected with further ends. In order that value judgments may be verifiable or testable, all ends and means toward those ends must be open to criticism. To assume that certain ends or values are ultimate and not subject to further criticism and proof is to block further progress or inquiry. The scientific method can only work in ethics or the determination of values if all supposed value beliefs are open to investigation and continued testing. For this reason, Dewey held that "not only is science itself *a* value (since it is the expression and the fulfillment of a special human desire and interest) but it is the supreme means of the valid determination of all valuations in all aspects of human and social life."[20]

The naturalistic philosophies of Dewey and Santayana in the first half of the twentieth century exercised marked influence on other American philosophers and naturalists. Ralph Barton Perry, who was greatly influenced by William James, developed an extensive theory of value in such works as *General Theory of Value* (1926) and *Realms of Value* (1954). Perry sought to defend a naturalistic conception of value as based on interest: "A thing—any thing—has value, or is valuable, in the original and generic sense when it is the object of interest—any interest."[21] Perry's conception of value as any object of any interest, although naturalistic, clearly conflicted with Dewey's conception: that a value is not simply any interest or preference, but only an interest or preference that has rightful authority in the direction of conduct. Morris Cohen, whose *Reason and Nature* (1931) and other works in logic, philosophy of science, and legal philosophy was also a leader of American naturalism in this century. Although Cohen never wrote a treatise on ethics or theory of value, he was concerned with the problem of how a science or organized knowledge of ethics and values is possible. Cohen's position on ethics resembled Dewey's insofar as he regarded preferences as necessary but not sufficient for ethics or the establishment of genuine values. He asserted, "Now the fact that some things are liked and others are disliked is necessary but not sufficient for ethics—for, like any other science, ethics must be rational, that is, able to give reasons for such differences of attitude. When grounds of preference are made explicit, we call such formulations 'norms' and the systematization and clarification of such norms is the basic subject matter of ethics."[22]

Two leading contemporary American naturalists who show the influence of Dewey and Santayana are Sidney Hook and Ernest Nagel. Sidney Hook, whose views most closely agree with Dewey's, has made extensive contributions in defending a pragmatic, naturalistic interpretation of issues in social and political philosophy in such works as *Political Power and Personal Freedom* (1959), *The Paradoxes of Freedom* (1962), and *The Quest for Being* (1963). In ethics, Hook has sought to defend the position that "a moral ideal is a prescription to act in a certain situation or class of situations in determinate ways that will organize the human needs and wants involved so as to fulfill a set of other values which are postulated as binding in relation to the problem in hand."[23] Ernest Nagel, defending a naturalistic conception of philosophy in recent times, has become a leading figure in dealing with problems in the philosophy of science. His major works include *Sovereign Reason* (1954), *Logic Without Metaphysics* (1956), and *The Structure of Science* (1961). Nagel asserted that

> . . .to a naturalistic philosophy, man occupies no central position in the flux of events. He is part of the flux; and in that trivial sense, nature would not be what in fact she is if man were not what he happens to be. The order of the flux must clearly be favorable to man's existence if he is to exist. But this tautology cannot validly be interpreted to mean that the order of nature is in any way concerned with man's continued existence. There is no cosmic plan which aims at man's survival or at achieving his ideals, for to his lot the universe is morally indifferent. All philosophies which conceive nature as concerned with human values or as developing toward some end in view, seem to me unregenerately romantic and immature.... Desires, needs, or their objects are not primarily moral or immoral. Moral considerations arise only when, as a consequence of the structure of the human body and society, an organization of various interests is attempted. The discovery of what is good is thus as arduous a task as is the discovery of a scientific law.[24]

American naturalism in this century has made sizable contributions to moral philosophy, but this movement is not without serious disagreements and problems. Although naturalists agree that any ethics or values must have a basis in natural, biological facts, considerable disagreement exists as to how and even whether our moral judgments can be confirmed or validated. Naturalists have, in recent years, given serious attention to the problems of determining how value judgments, including moral judgments, can be cognitive—how they can be justified without either a fallacy in logical reasoning or the prior assumption of what one is in fact trying to prove.

George Santayana and John Dewey: Principal Figures of Naturalistic Ethics

One feature common to the Naturalistic Ethics of both Santayana and Dewey was their deployment of the term "moral" in the broadest human sense. Moral concerns, the whole subject matter of moral philosophy, do not comprise a narrow class of special problems or issues; the range of moral philosophy includes the entire scope of human interests and actions. Dewey expressed this point clearly in his *Human Nature and Conduct* (1922): "In the eighteenth century, the word Morals was used in English literature with a meaning of broad sweep. It included all the subjects of distinctively humane import, all of the social disciplines as far as they are intimately connected with the life of man and as they bear upon the interests of humanity. The pages that follow are intended as a contribution, from one point of view, to Morals thus conceived."[25] Santayana, in *The Realm of Truth* (1938), declared that "moral judgments of some sort are inevitable in man. He cannot help having some radical preference.... Reflected in the living soul, all the rays of nature instantly acquire a moral colour. Nothing can happen that will not be good or bad in a thousand directions.... The root of morality is animal bias: and to renounce that bias would be to renounce life."[26] Since the sphere of morality contains the whole range of human interests and actions for both Dewey and Santayana, their ideas on ethics are expectably located throughout their written works, not only in those writings explicitly addressed to moral topics. It is also important to notice that both Santayana and Dewey believed that the real task of philosophy fundamentally involves the careful criticism of ideas and human culture. Thus it is fair to characterize both their positions as forms of critical naturalism, since neither held that any naturalistic belief or philosophical conclusion is inherently immune from criticism. Nevertheless Santayana and Dewey did not develop identical forms of naturalism; they clearly disagreed on a number of major points, including their treatment of ethics. These disagreements are significant insofar as they reveal the breadth and richness possible in a naturalistic philosophy and expose several difficult problems to which this type of thinking is prone. The philosophical writings of these men are remarkable for their sheer quantity and quality, which clearly outdistance the efforts of earlier American philosophers. For well over half a century, both Dewey and Santayana published noteworthy works. Dewey published his *Outlines of a Critical Theory of Ethics* as early as 1891; as late as 1939, he published his *Theory of Valuation*. Santayana published his first book in philosophy, *The Sense of Beauty*, in 1896; as late as 1950, he published his *Dominations and Powers, Reflections on Liberty, Society and Government.*

While both men were educated in the United States and spent many years teaching and lecturing in American universities, Santayana was born in Spain and lived in Europe for approximately the last forty years of his long life. He came to the United States at the age of nine and received his education at the Boston Latin School and Harvard University. "He pursued his graduate studies in philosophy at Harvard under the guidance of both James and Royce and joined them in 1889 to form what was for about twenty years Harvard's, and perhaps America's, most renowned department of philosophy."[27] In 1905 he published the first major statement of his philosophical position in *The Life of Reason*, a philosophic classic of American naturalism. The five-volume work discussed what Santayana termed the "phases of human progress," or the principal ways in which man has used his power of reason to achieve order, harmony, and well-being in his life. The phases of human progress wherein reason can be discerned include common sense, society, religion, art, and science. "Reason is understood throughout this work to be simultaneously an intelligent observer and an imaginative interpreter capable of enlightening and guiding the human animal in the process of living. Reason signifies animal sagacity raised to the power of discerning general patterns and symbolic forms on the one hand, and imagining ideal harmonies on the other."[28] While reason is inherently realistic and practical as based on common sense and respect for the world of external fact, it is also distinctly imaginative. The way in which reason interprets the facts of experience is often highly poetic and never completely loses a metaphorical, emotionally colored manner of conceiving things.

For Santayana, ideas had an aesthetic as well as a factual or cognitive aspect, suggesting that poetry, art, religion, and all of man's values or ideals are perfectly natural in representing extensions or idealizations latent within human nature. Following Aristotle, Santayana assumed that a life of reason is natural to man since it represents a union or harmony of the rational and animal sides of human nature. To forget or neglect either the rational or the animal in human nature is to bypass or override the facts and cut off the very idea of progress in human life. Human life has both a material and an ideal or spiritual dimension, each of which is necessary and complementary to the other. Often, however, these dimensions are misunderstood or even mismanaged in relation to one another. The more crass forms of materialism in philosophy and everyday living virtually reduce man to his physical body and sensuous needs. Likewise the more absolute, romantic forms of idealism virtually ignore or deny that man has a body or material needs. How, then, could Santayana assert that "the most brutal form of naturalism is materialism, and I have repeatedly confessed that I am a materialist"?[19] Romantic or poetic naturalism as found in Emerson, for example, may involve or express a sincere love of nature and its beauty, but it is nevertheless shortsighted and confused. Sights and beauties of the natural world may inspire the poet and dreamer, but inspiration and poetry are not identical with knowledge and philosophy. Santayana was even willing to admit that to be inspired or to feel beauty intuitively may be better than knowledge but, in fact, is no substitute for it. The philosopher cannot wish to be deceived or carried away by his enthusiasms. While philosophy can never hope to know all the facts, it must try to find the most important, central facts and not confuse these with fancy. Skepticism is a healthy intellectual exercise in philosophy— whereas, in the poet or mystic, it may indeed be irrelevant. If the philosopher does not push skepticism to its ultimate limits, he cannot really engage in critical thought or analysis. If commom sense tells us that not all of our ideas are true or that sometimes we are deceived, any philosophy worthy of the name must try to determine the difference between knowledge and error, truth and illusion. The idealists and pragmatists, especially Royce and James, offered conflicting theories of truth that are both inadequate, according to Santayana. For both, truth was a function of ideas or opinions; but for pragmatism, truth is never eternal or absolute; for idealism, real truth is always absolute or that which omniscience comprehends. According to Santayana truth cannot be an idea or opinion, since ideas and opinions are mental events; if they are to discern or report any truth at all, they must be logically distinct from that which they represent or report. Every idea or opinion, as a mental event that occurs at a definite time, logically implies by its simple occurrence a truth about itself which is distinct from that occurrence. If I have, for example, the idea or opinion that the earth is round rather than flat, the truth of this opinion does not at all depend on my idea or even on my idea's success. Truth simply depends upon the existence of factual relations or characteristics which are quite independent of anyone's ideas or opinions about these relations. My opinion or idea that the world is round is true, just in case the world is round. My idea is not true because it works or leads me to a successful prediction of future experience, as James would assert. Nor is my idea true because it agrees with, or is part of, what the divine or omniscient mind would assert. Truth is entirely contingent, wholly dependent upon existence or fact. Santayana held that existence cannot occur without manifesting some form or character. We say the earth is round rather than flat, but roundness or flatness are simply "forms" or "essences," in Santayana's terminology. Numbers are also forms or essences. But there is a difference between a pure number and a numbered thing—between the quantity *four* and four trees. Numbers are ideals or universals that do not exist in time and space, but they may characterize things such as men, rocks, or trees that do exist in time and space. By themselves, essences or universals do not exist—they are detached from existence. Actually countless numbers of essences are purely fanciful in the sense that they never characterize any facts or existences. The square root of minus one is a perfectly good essence, but it does not refer to the existent length, height, or width of anything. Even the essence "round," which does characterize the shape of the earth, does not characterize the shape of everything, and no guarantee exists that even the earth will always have that shape. Santayana insisted that we can always doubt whether any form or essence applies to any actual, existent thing or event. We do not know for certain that the earth is round, though we have good evidence that it is. Knowledge is therefore not equivalent to truth but is a presumption or belief that some form or essence actually applies to some existence. Truth, as a relation between essence and existence, is quite impersonal. Many truths are beyond our powers to know, and many others are perfectly trivial or unimportant to know.Man can doubt or question any truth, but that skepticism has no effect on the truth itself. Skepticism or doubt is a purely human phenomenon that may help to clear man's mind of error and illusion. Skepticism based on doubt or disbelief, however, can only be partial, since Santayana held that doubt itself is a form of belief. To doubt anything seriously involves a belief in one's own doubt, at least; to doubt or disbelieve any fact involves the real act and existence of doubt or disbelief itself. Consequently Santayana concluded that one cannot logically doubt all existences. We cannot remove or get rid of facts or existences by doubting them all—since, as long as we believe in our own act of doubting, we are believing in a fact or existence.

But another form of skepticism can be more complete than the one based on doubt. This form of skepticism is based on suspension of judgment. We can mentally detach ourselves from belief in any facts. Instead of doubting or denying their existence, we can simply refrain from belief or disbelief. Santayana called this "detached suspension of judgment"—the intuition of or direct acquaintance with some essence. We can simply appreciate or observe some quality or form without presuming to judge whether or not it is true to any facts. Intuition is pure awareness or consciousness of some quality or essence; but since it involves no truth or falsity, it provides no knowledge or error. Merely to listen attentively to a sound or to observe some colors without presuming to judge how they originated or what they factually mean is to have an aesthetic experience. Ultimate skepticism, therefore, is reached by detachment of one's mind from belief in any existence and by simple contemplation of some essence. Santayana held that, since essences are not material or mental things that exist in time, they are basically timeless, eternal qualities that man may appreciate and enjoy. Real enjoyment must, in fact, involve the contemplation of timeless essences since, as long as man is aware of time's passage, he is in some sense distracted. One cannot really experience true happiness or enjoyment if one is distracted by the clock or anxious about the facts of existence. To really enjoy oneself, one must lose oneself in the timeless quality of some form of beauty or essence. Of course man cannot spend all his time in such aesthetic experiences. He cannot simply absorb himself in the contemplation and enjoyment of timeless essences and forget or denounce his animal needs and nature. Man has instincts, drives, and impulses that cannot consciously or for long be neglected. Man must, in other words, pay attention to nature and existences simply because they automatically assert themselves and provide the ground or basis for his mind and enjoyments. Intuition or aesthetic appreciation is not self-sustaining. It clearly depends upon animal organs and a physical world. "Existence would not be worth preserving if it had to be spent exclusively in anxiety about existence."[30] For Santayana, the point was that "unless man can detach himself from existence and become absorbed in the enjoyment of timeless essences or forms, his life would not be worth having."[31] But Santayana denied that values, enjoyments, and anything good are objective and universal. "My critics suppose, apparently, that I mean by the good some particular way of life or some type of character which is alone virtuous, and which ought to be propagated. . . . I have no wish to propagate any particular character, least of all my own. . . . The good, as I conceive it, is happiness, happiness for each man after his own heart, and for each hour according to its inspiration. I should dread to transplant my happiness into other people; it might die in that soil."[32]

The worst mistake in ethics, according to Santayana, is failure to see that all goods or values are relative to particular animal or vital interests. Without prerational or original preferences, nothing would possess value. Values are not discovered by reason or science—they must be felt or preferred. Reason and science may attempt to show us the causal antecedents and eventual consequences of our values or preferences; but if we are indifferent to these conditions or outcomes, we will be indifferent to the counsels of any reason or science. Reason may even attempt to discover how our preferences or interests may be harmonized, but unless we take an interest in harmony itself, it can have no value. For Santayana, to suggest that anything which one finds good or valuable ought to be admitted as universally good by everyone else was unmeaning. The utilitarian theory of ethics, for example, asserts that those actions are right or morally good which tend to produce the greatest happiness of the greatest number of people. Santayana admitted that this may be a sincere and somewhat enlightened belief on the part of the utilitarian. At the same time, however, no utilitarian can impose this belief on others or demand their agreement with its statement of moral value. Such a principle is only imperative for those who actually desire or seek it. John Stuart Mill, who defended this principle of ethics, admitted that the only possible reason why anything is desirable is that people actually desire it. In agreement with the relativity of values, William James also asserted that the essence of good is simply to satisfy demand.

Consequently Santayana asserted, "As for my own judgment, since the first principle of my ethics is relativity, I cannot admit that . . . elementary differences might be reconciled morally, from the point of view of either party."[33] Santayana could not agree with Royce that moral disagreements can be resolved by appeal to any principle of reason. The initial desire to settle any disagreement is not based on reason; also, the constitutional unanimity of human beings can only be stretched so far. Even if men were unanimous in supporting some principle of value, this would not "tend to show that the good they agreed to recognize was independent of their constitution."[34] For Santayana, as for Spinoza before him, things are not desired or valued because they are good—things are good or valued because they are desired.

In adopting a naturalistic and relativistic conception of good or value, Santayana also adopted what may be termed a noncognitive interpretation of ethical judgments; i.e., moral judgments about what is right or good cannot be described as either valid or invalid, true or false. Santayana admitted that moral judgments are usually "hybrid." Thus they may contain descriptive or factual material along with prescriptive or evaluative elements. The simple judgment that someone is an honest person may be partially descriptive insofar as it implies that the person judged does not steal or can be trusted. As a moral or value judgment, however, the belief that someone is honest is not simply descriptive; it is also normative and implies that it is good to be honest or that the person is good because he is honest. This part of the judgment is what makes it a moral judgment. It expresses a preference or endorses some definite value. "The nerve of moral judgment is preference: and preference is a feeling or an impulse to action which cannot be either false or true."[35] In a moral sense, there is no way to prove that the judgment "honesty is good" is true. We cannot adduce in its favor that most people think or claim that honesty is good because it is socially useful. These may be facts, but as facts they are only descriptive and, as such, have no prescriptive force. Unless we feel that honesty is good or unless we prefer it, no external fact about honesty will prove that we ought to prefer it or ought to consider it a moral value.

To say that moral judgments cannot be true or false, Santayana admitted, goes against common sense and sounds strange. But this is only true because common sense does not bother to distinguish carefully the descriptive and prescriptive elements in moral judgments. In ordinary life there is no real need to be exact about such things. But in philosophy the case is different. Just as the science of astronomy may have to revise man's common sense opinions about the heavens, so philosophy, which is primarily concerned with man and his ideas and values, may have to refine and revise our unsophisticated, common sense moral beliefs. In an indirect or secondary sense, Santayana admitted that "an ethical proposition may be correct or incorrect, in a sense justifying argument, when it touches what is good as a means, that is, when it is not intrinsically ethical, but deals with causes and effects, or with matters of fact or necessity."[36] One may, for example, show the correctness of the beliefs that milk is nourishing for children and that, by feeding those who are starving, we can prevent them from dying. But this involves no moral judgment until we assert such things as "it is good to nourish children" and "it is good to feed those who are starving." Ethical judgments are not intrinsically assertions of means toward ends, but are convictions or preferences for certain ultimate ends themselves. Ethics is concerned with what is good or what should ultimately be chosen. "But to speak of the truth of an ultimate good would be a false collocation of terms; an ultimate good is chosen, found, or aimed at; it is not opined. The ultimate intuitions on which ethics rests are not debatable, for they are not opinions we hazard but preferences we feel; and it can be neither correct nor incorrect to feel them."[37]

While truth in terms of agreement with outside facts was not the basis of morality or moral value for Santayana, another sense of truth comes closer to this whole matter. We often speak about a person being "true to himself" or "sincere." Sincerity is certainly a moral quality, one not based on external fact. Sincerity is something inward, based on a person's self-knowledge or conception of his own motives and interests. Santayana admitted that, in this sense, "truth and error may be possible in morals, in so far as they are truths or errors in self-knowledge."[38] Moral beliefs may be judged in terms of their sincerity or integrity; à man may judge whether he is true to himself or not. But this only serves to reinforce the whole relativity of moral values. Ethics "cannot pronounce it sinful in a serpent to be a serpent; it cannot even accuse a barbarian of loving a wrong life, except in so far as the barbarian is supposed capable of accusing himself of barbarism. If he is a perfect barbarian he will be inwardly, and therefore morally, justified."[39] If we admit the importance in ethics of sincerity or integrity, we must also admit that individuals can be true or faithful to different values and ideals.

Santayana claimed that a genuine appreciation of the relativity of values, far from inducing moral chaos, would "tend to render people more truly social than would a belief that things have intrinsic and unchangeable values."[40] Moral tolerance, a respect for other people's values, is perfectly consistent with the belief that values are relative to individual interest. Moral dogmatism, the belief that only certain things are right or good in themselves, is the very thing, in fact, that produces intolerance and moral fanaticism. To attempt to impose one's values on someone else is the height of moral egotism and folly. This does not mean, of course, that reasonable persuasion in ethics has no place. Reason and persuasion are quite consistent with the idea that values are relative. The fact that values are relative does not imply that people often cannot or do not agree on what they find good. Nor does the discovery that values are relative imply that reason and enlightenment are not useful in any moral life. Reason and enlightenment are extremely useful, according to Santayana. They are, in fact, necessary to any development of a human sense of values, since only through enlightenment and reason can man really achieve the goals of sincerity and harmony in his life.

If the main idea in Santayana's naturalism is the distinction he drew between essence and existence, the main idea in Dewey's naturalism concerns the notion of continuous interaction between all things in nature, including all human affairs. Santayana's naturalism was ontological and materialistic; Dewey's naturalism, by contrast, was instrumental or pragmatic, not materialistic. Santayana composed an elaborate ontological framework consisting of four distinct realms of being. He alleged that "the simple dissolution of superstition yields three of my realms of being: matter, as the region and method of power; essence, as the proper nature of appearances and relations; and spirit, as the witness or moral sensibility that is subject to the double assault of material events and of dramatic illusions. There remains the realm of truth, which is the total history and destiny of matter and spirit, or the enormously complex essence which they exemplify by existing."[41] Dewey never constructed an ontological system. His whole philosophical approach was in fact opposed to making speculations about, or distinctions between, different orders of being. While Santayana insisted on drawing ontological distinctions between form (or "essence," as he called it) and matter, and between consciousness (or "spirit") and matter, Dewey considered this whole procedure false to experience, only successful in separating and opposing aspects of nature that are never actually found isolated from one another. For Santayana, the forms of matter were detachable, nonexistent, and timeless essences or universals. But for Dewey, only a false abstraction would lead us to regard the forms of actual material things as nonexistent, timeless, and as having a different kind of being or ontological status than the things of which they are the form. For Dewey, a basic fact about the natural world was that all existences are found to be interacting and associated with one another. Existing things are never found in total isolation.

Associated existences or groupings of things are found throughout all nature and not merely in human societies. Electrons and animals, insects and plant life do not exist in isolation from one another. The tendency of philosophers to look for ultimate data is not only false to the way things exist, but it also leads to unverifiable controversies and thwarts the integration of our knowledge in theory as well as practical application.[42]

Santayana, in contrast, considered matter and mind ontologically distinct. For Santayana, mind or consciousness had no spatial location or causal power; spatial location and causal efficacy are two of the most important features of matter. For Santayana, mind is only epiphenomenal, i.e., its existence is entirely dependent on matter, since mind by itself has no power to produce either itself or any physical effects. Consciousness or human experience represents particular or subjective perspectives that arise or can be seen from a particular individual's point of view. In nature or the material world, there are no human or personal perspectives. While human ideas or experiences arise from nature, Santayana wanted to insist that nature itself is not a set of human experiences or ideas. Human ideas may be clear or confused, true or false—and certainly, as

Santayana insisted, nature is not compacted or constructed according to any of our *false* ideas of it. Even our true ideas are ontologically distinct from nature, since ideas are not literal copies of external things but are only more or less relevant to them. Human experience and ideas are emotional, personal, selective, and shifting; and to suppose that nature itself is all of these would be a dramatic illusion or sheer superstition.

In 1925, Santayana published his estimate of Dewey's naturalism, titled *Dewey's Naturalistic Metaphysics*, in *The Journal of Philosophy*. Santayana claimed that the crux of Dewey's naturalism involved what Santayana termed "the dominance of the foreground."

> In nature there is no foreground or background, no here, no now, no moral cathedra, no centre so really central as to reduce all other things to mere margins and mere perspectives. A foreground is by definition relative to some chosen point of view, to the station assumed in the midst of nature by some creature tethered by fortune to a particular time and place. If such a foreground becomes dominant in a philosophy naturalism is abandoned. Some local perspective or some casual interest is set up in the place of universal nature or behind it, or before it, so that all the rest of nature is reputed to be intrinsically remote or dubious or merely ideal.[43]

Santayana, in short, claimed that, since Dewey combined his naturalism with a pragmatic interest in the social and moral usefulness of ideas, his naturalism is dominated by this merely practical foreground. The pragmatist interprets and reduces nature to man's transactions and manipulations of it. For the pragmatist, nature has no meaning apart from the ways in which it can be confronted and used by human beings. "The pragmatist becomes, or seems to become, a naturalist only by accident, when as in the present age and in America the dominant foreground is monopolized by material activity."[44]

In his reply to Santayana's criticism, Dewey contended:

> To me human affairs, associative and personal, are projections, continuations, complications, of the nature which exists in the physical and pre-human world. There is no gulf, no two spheres or existence, no "bifurcation." For this reason, there are in nature both foregrounds and backgrounds, heres and theres, centers and perspectives, foci and margins. If there were not, the story and scene of man would involve a complete break with nature, the insertion of unaccountable and unnatural conditions and factors.[45]

Dewey claimed that man and human experience are as much parts of nature as trees and stones. Human ideas, interests, and perspectives, as well as entire societies or cultures are not outside of, or exceptions to, nature—but are, through and through, part and parcel of nature. Dewey did not suggest that human experience comprises all of nature or that human and social experience are more real than physical or inanimate nature. He insisted on the presence of real continuity in nature, so that man and nature or mind and matter are not to be regarded as opposed to one another but as interacting and empirically involved with one another. As Dewey asserted, "I have tried to bring together on a naturalistic basis the mind and matter that Santayana keeps worlds apart."[46] Human societies and man's moral interests, for example, are not mere conventions or arbitrary perspectives with no basis in fact. On the contrary, man's values and social life are the richest, most complex forms of nature that are empirically discoverable. The important thing about man's ideas, values, and social life is that they can be made intelligent and responsibly controlled. It was Dewey's thesis, however, that as long as man's mind, ideas, and values are falsely regarded as subjective and isolated from the rest of nature, no real understanding and progress can occur in man's life. To separate man and his ideas from the rest of nature is to close any true avenues to the experimental or scientific method. For Dewey, the experimental method is the only truly reliable, progressive method with which to study all aspects of man and nature. It is not sufficient to allow that experimental methods are proper in physical science but do not apply to the study of man. To suggest that man's ideas, values, and whole social life are best known by intuition, introspection, or the mere dialectical manipulation of concepts not only cuts man off from the rest of nature, but makes the whole panorama of human affairs unverifiable and a sheer mystery. What may even be worse, for Dewey, is to adopt a form of skepticism such as Santayana's, wherein nothing can be truly known or verified. Dewey admitted that the experimental method is not infallible, but he also maintained that it is not arbitrary or illusory. Experimentation is inherently practical and natural in the sense that it requires actions and the testing of outcomes located objectively in the natural world. No experimental idea is to be accepted merely because the experimentor would like it to be true. Experimental ideas become acceptable only to the extent that careful, intelligent testing discloses empirical evidence in support of them.

Any acceptable form of naturalism, according to Dewey, must be consistent with the development of natural science and the use of scientific methods, which are the only reliable instruments of progress in science and human life. Naturalism, as an intelligent philosophic outlook, cannot be based on pure speculation or mere faith. For this reason, unlike Santayana, Dewey did not characterize his own form of naturalism as materialistic. Dewey preferred not to use the term "materialism," since he considered it associated with certain speculative or metaphysical beliefs about matter and substance that are unsupported by empirical evidence. He was willing to admit that "all the subject-matter of experience is dependent upon physical conditions."[47] But this implies no single, all-inclusive material substance in any metaphysical or ultimate sense. The idea of matter as used in physical science has verifiable meaning, but no one would suggest that physics, chemistry, or biology are forms of materialism or imply the truth of materialism. Materialism, for Dewey, was a philosophical position which states that a single material substance constitutes ultimate reality. This view, he found, not only asserts more than naturalism but is untestable and inconsistent with experimental methods of inquiry.

The main thrust of Dewey's experimental naturalism or instrumentalism was to show how man and nature, as well as facts and values, can be intelligently integrated through the use of scientific methods of investigation. The main traditions in Western philosophy and American thought have too frequently denied that scientific methods of inquiry have real application to the problems of human experience and ethics. Dewey found this situation mainly due to the influence of religion and the reliance on outmoded traditions and customary ways of viewing things. Dewey lamented the fact that, while science has made great progress in the realms of physical nature and technology, its use in relation to understanding and controlling human nature, society, and moral values has lagged sadly behind. Man still lives in fear of change, in bondage to his emotions, when confronted by questions of establishing values and making decisions concerning the course of human affairs. Human affairs are often said to be too complex, variable, and even subjective to allow analysis by scientific methods of study. True, a scientific approach to human affairs will necessarily seem inadequate if we expect it to furnish us with certainties or definitive answers. But this is only to misjudge the value of experimental inquiry by holding up false standards for it to meet. Royce and all of the idealists made this mistake when they suggested that we must pass beyond mere empirical methods to *a priori* ones in order to arrive at any absolute or complete understanding in ethics. Royce was right, according to Dewey, to emphasize the social character of any truly human, moral life. Royce also rightly emphasized the need for logical, intelligent techniques for solving man's problems. But Royce's views on society and logic were distorted by his penchant to analyze and synthesize these concepts in terms of the *a priori* and the infinite at the expense of the empirical and the finite. In pretending to give us absolute and final answers, a rationalistic approach to ethics makes these very answers untestable and unworkable. The rationalist in ethics overestimates the function of general rules or principles in relation to human conduct. Every ethical situation is specific, and therefore no ethical rule can be absolute or can absolutely determine a course of action under particular and even changeable circumstances. Ethical rules are useful; they can simplify a situation and furnish us with possible ways of responding to it. But any rule or principle taken as absolute needs no further qualification or investigation in order for us to be able to use it. No intelligent rule can be absolute in this sense, since such inflexibility only inspires blind obedience rather than any thoughtful moral concern. In his first book on ethics, *Outlines of a Critical Theory of Ethics* (1891), Dewey discussed the nature of moral commands and rules. Here he pointed out that even the seemingly clear and simple command "Thou shalt do no murder" is not really a definite command, since "it allows questioning as to what is murder. Is killing in war murder? Is the hanging of criminals murder? Is taking life in self-defense murder?"[48] Dewey argued further that even the Golden Rule does not tell a person how to act in a specific situation. His point was that commands, rules, or principles in ethics are not final truths or absolute forms of advice, but are rather instruments of analysis. They can be useful only if they are properly qualified and subjected to further analysis and questioning. Dewey claimed that "it is of the very nature of moral conduct to be progressive. Permanence of *specific* ideals means moral death. We say that truth-telling, charity, loyalty, temperance, have always been moral ends and while this is true, the statement as ordinarily made is apt to hide from us the fact that the content of the various ideals (what is *meant* by temperance, etc.) has been constantly changing, and this of necessity."[49]

In science, what Dewey called the "changed attitude toward change" meant that changes are no longer feared or passively accepted but are studied and even deliberately introduced in order to allow experimentation. Once a thoroughgoing experimental approach to all ideas and experiences is adopted, ideas and experiences can be studied in the widest sense to discern their bearing on one another. An experimental or instrumental approach finds no barrier between the theoretical and the practical, between man and nature, or between facts and values. All intelligent thinking, according to Dewey, is problem-solving. Thought only arises because something is presently unsatisfactory and problematic. Thus Dewey insisted on contrasting thought with impulsive behavior, which is an immediate, undirected type of response. Thinking is always a form of doing something and has practical consequences. As a form of behavior, thinking is essentially an indirect or delayed response, since time is needed for one to think and investigate the problem at hand. William James, it will be remembered, had declared that moral problems cannot wait for proof, that they present themselves with an urgency that demands an immediate response. Dewey could not allow that this view represents a true picture of moral situations. A moral situation is practical in the sense that it is specific and refers to the field of action. But one is certainly wrong to consider that moral action does not (1) involve an intellectual component, and (2) require mental effort in order to achieve the best practical success. There is nothing particularly moral or practical in mere reaction to a situation or in jumping to conclusions. The so-called will to believe or faith in one's convictions will only be practical and moral to the degree that it is intelligently controlled and anticipates future consequences. We never infallibly or completely know, of course, what the future consequences of our decisions and actions will be. Knowledge grows by degrees, since it depends on warranted judgment—judgment backed up by some degree of evidence. Knowledge is not properly described, as Santayana would have it, as a kind of animal faith. Human knowledge is just the opposite of blind faith or the impulse to believe anything that presents itself. Knowledge always involves, to some degree, a thoughtful, intelligent appraisal and anticipation of consequences. The mark of intelligent judgment is that it welcomes correction and criticism.

Real knowledge assumes that the only path to real progress or practical success is by continuous inquiry.

The frequent fault of empirical theories of value and ethics, according to Dewey, is that of identifying value with mere interest or desire. These theories hold down "value to objects *antecedently* enjoyed, apart from reference to the method by which they come into existence; it takes enjoyments which are casual because unregulated by intelligent operations to be values in and of themselves. Operational thinking needs to be applied to the judgment of values just as it has now finally been applied in conceptions of physical objects. Experimental empiricism in the field of ideas of good and bad is demanded to meet the conditions of the present situation."[50] Empirical theories correctly connect values with preference, desire, or interest; but they are wrong in excluding any intellectual factors in the discernment or judgment of what constitutes real value. Both views—Santayana's that things are good because they are desired, and James's that the essence of good is to satisfy demand—are wrong because they mistake a mere indeterminate starting point for values with the determination of full-blown values themselves. "The view which connects valuation (and 'values') with desires and interest is but a starting-point. It is indeterminate in its bearing upon the theory of valuation until the nature of interest and desire has been analyzed, and until a method has been established for determining the constituents of desires and interests in their concrete particular occurrence."[51] To assert that one desires or has an interest in a certain thing does not establish that the thing has any positive value. It may have such value, but this can only be disclosed by examining the bearing of any desire or interest on the facts of future experience. To assert, however, that a certain thing is desirable or interesting is to make a positive value judgment which future experience and examination may confirm. Thus value judgments, including moral judgments, are not mere statements of present interest or subjective preference; rather they are predictions of what will either be confirmed or disconfirmed as enjoyments or satisfactions in the future. This signifies that moral values involve judgments about how certain means are instrumental in leading to definite or chosen ends. To claim that justice is morally good signifies that, under specifiable conditions, it can reliably produce worthwhile human results. To say that injustice is a disvalue or not morally good is to imply the very opposite. When construed in terms of means in relation to chosen ends, values obviously can be tested or confirmed to see whether they imply or instrumentally lead to those ends.

Santayana, for one, admitted that "an ethical proposition may be correct or incorrect, in a sense justifying argument, when it touches what is good as a means."[52] We can verify that honesty is morally good if by "good" we only mean that honesty is a useful means of achieving harmony and peaceful relations among human beings. But this does not prove that peace or harmony themselves are good or that honesty is intrinsically good. In other words, good (in the sense of that which is a means to an end) is not intrinsically ethical, according to Santayana, since ethics is concerned with the value or desirability of ultimate ends. A hammer is good for driving nails, and dynamite is good for creating an explosion. Many things that are good in a purely instrumental sense are not good at all in any specifically moral sense. Moral values concern what we should, or ought to, choose as our ultimate ends in life. Judgments of expediency or means to ends are only moral if we claim that expediency is intrinsically good and we make it our final aim. But, according to Santayana, there is no way to prove or verify that expediency, altruism, benevolence, or any other ethical aim is intrinsically good.

Dewey acknowledged that the standing objection to his view of the instrumental nature of all values "is that it applies only to things *as means*, while propositions that are genuine valuations apply to things as *ends*."[53] A further objection to any completely instrumental conception of values is that it involves an infinite regress. "If, so it is said, there is no end which is not in turn a means, foresight has no place at which it can stop, and no end-in-view can be formed except by the most arbitrary of acts—an act so arbitrary that it mocks the claim of being a genuine valuation-proposition."[54] Dewey frankly admitted that no final ends or values in the sense of isolated, detached, and uncriticizable goods can exist. To hold, however, that any meaningful human ends or values are intimately related to the means by which those ends can be realized is not to say that no ends, in fact, exist. On the contrary, ends divorced from means or the facts of human life are, in the true sense, purely arbitrary or no ends at all. The value of any end is appraised in terms of the available or possible means that can be used to reach that end. Thus no end can have intrinsic or ultimate value in itself, if this means independence from its impact on human experience and the conditions needed to realize that end. Means are properly evaluated in terms of their use in achieving their ends. How do we know that a particular end is good or worthwhile to pursue? The only intelligent answer is that such an end, instead of being a finality, is itself instrumental or useful as a means of producing satisfactory results. Ends must be evaluated as means to satisfaction if they are to bring any value at all.

Nevertheless the conditions of existence are changeable, and satisfaction of any kind is variable, found only in connection or interaction with other things in the environment. Neither means nor ends can be appraised once and for all. They must be judged continuously in relation to one another and to the ongoing, changing conditions of existence. Certain forms of punishment, for example, may be socially useful at certain times in retarding crime and keeping order. In one sense, then, those forms of punishment have an instrumental value in relation to certain ends and existent conditions. But this does not mean that those same forms of punishment are always good without qualification—nor, certainly, that any specific form of punishment is intrinsically or absolutely good. Obviously it would be better to prevent crime and not need any form of punishment at all. To suggest that punishment or anything else in human life does not require evaluation and judgment, both as a means to other ends and as an end to be chosen or pursued, is perfectly ridiculous.

Moral ends and values, according to Dewey, are just those concerns in life that are the most far-reaching and important. The less deeply any interest or concern affects human beings, the less that interest or concern is likely to have any moral significance. For this reason, Dewey declared that "growth itself is the only moral end."[55] Happiness, pleasure, loyalty, or any form of virtue only assume real moral significance insofar as they are able to grow or enrich the lives of men. What is sought is not a final happiness or pleasure, but an enriching, expanding series of ongoing satisfactions. For this reason, moral values cannot be divorced or separated from aesthetic, political, economic, and other values. An aesthetic value is one that is found in enjoyable experiences that are continuous and harmonious, thus running their course to fulfillment. This means that experiences of beauty or aesthetic value, instead of being rarefied or detached, are extremely useful and fruitful in human life. The more that work takes on aesthetic value, the more worthwhile, enriching, and productive it tends to be. To work merely for money or for completion of the job with no experience of satisfaction in doing the work itself is morally tedious and stultifying. For this very reason, pleasure is neither to be denied nor pursued as the only end that is good. Pleasures are to be judged instrumentally in terms of how they serve or fail to serve the enrichment of human experience. No pleasure can be judged in isolation from the cost or means of obtaining that pleasure. Pleasure or any supposed good must be appraised in terms of its potential to enrich human life and to maintain further growth in the widest possible sense.

It is a biological fact that man can live only by continuing to grow. To stop growth is tantamount to stopping life. This is no less true in a moral, cultural, and intellectual sense than in a biological sense. Man's moral life can only flourish by increasing knowledge, by increasing the intelligent control of his personal and social life, and by increasing the quality of the satisfactions he finds in experience. To stand still, in a moral sense, is simply to lose ground. Yet not every change is good or for the better. Mere change or growth lacking in intelligent direction is not desired or needed. One can indeed change for the worse, or a whole society can grow in size and complexity but still be oppressive, unsatisfactory, and demeaning. This fact indicates the vast difference between intelligent or experimentally controlled growth and sheer change or increase in dimensions. The most difficult and important problems of moral life concern the assessment of the quality or qualities capable of enriching and improving that life. These qualities cannot be known *a priori*, nor can they be discovered by mere passive intuition. It was Dewey's claim that these qualities can only be discerned by the cultivation of intelligent, scientific methods of investigation.

The Naturalistic Fallacy and
the Good Life for Man

The deepest problem for any naturalistic ethics is to explain or coherently account for the exact relation between nature and value—between the facts of the natural world and claims about what is morally good or right. Obviously naturalism cannot simply argue that anything is morally good because it is natural or morally bad because it is unnatural. For naturalism, everything that exists is in some sense an aspect of, or dependent upon, the natural world. Everything that exists, whether good or bad, right or wrong, is natural in the sense of being some part of nature. There is thus no sufficient basis for calling anything right or wrong, good or bad, merely because it is some part of nature. If nature comprises the whole of existence, to say that man ought to live in accordance with nature or its laws can make no sense, since whatever way man lives will be in accordance with nature. Thus the most frequent criticism of any naturalistic ethics is that it has no way of grounding or explaining moral values or imperatives. Naturalism seems caught in the dilemma that either everything is a value (since everything is equally natural) or nothing is a value (since nothing is more distinctly natural than anything else). This means that nature is value-neutral; that nature simply is or exists; and that any attempt to ground or derive some value, ideal, or statement from nature itself of what "ought to be" is bound to fail or involve fallacy.

Hedonism, utilitarianism, and evolutionism as forms of ethical naturalism would seem, therefore, clearly fallacious. Each goes astray in basically the same fashion; each attempts to derive values from neutral facts. If the hedonist argues that pleasure is the goal or standard of morality because all men pursue it, he illicitly infers a value from mere facts. If the utilitarian argues that the greatest happiness of everyone is morally desirable since each person desires his own individual happiness, he (also illicitly) infers a normative conclusion from a purely factual or descriptive premise. Finally the evolutionist who argues that, since all life is a struggle for existence, the morally superior forms of life are those that represent survival of the fittest or the more highly evolved organisms also commits the same fallacy. The pragmatic ethics of William James apparently commits the same fallacy, insofar as James argued that a thing is good because it satisfies demand. Perhaps the clearest instance of this fallacy is found in the naturalism of Ralph Barton Perry, who defined a value as any object of any interest.

Although neither Santayana nor Dewey actually asserted that a thing is good or has value because it is natural, certain of their formulations of the relation between natural facts and values indicate that they too were prone to this same fallacy. Santayana held that things are good because they are desired, rather than desired because they are good. Dewey, on the other hand, held that, while values cannot be reduced to past facts or experiences, they can nevertheless be understood in terms of predictions about future experiences or about things to be brought into existence. It is appropriate, therefore, to examine what has become known as the "naturalistic fallacy," to see exactly what this alleged fallacy is and to what extent it may apply to the views of Santayana and Dewey; and to see whether it is a serious threat to the very idea of a naturalistic ethics.

In 1903, the English philosopher G. E. Moore published *Principia Ethica*, which subsequently became an extremely influential work in moral philosophy. Moore argued that the question of what "good" means is the most fundamental question in ethics. He further argued that good is basically a simple, unanalyzable, and nonnatural quality. "My point is that 'good' is a simple notion, just as 'yellow' is a simple notion; that, just as you cannot, by any manner of means, explain to anyone who does not already know it, what yellow is, so you cannot explain what good is."[56] Moore admitted that good is a property of certain natural objects, but he denied that good itself is a natural property. His test of whether anything is a natural property concerns its existence in time. "Can we imagine 'good' as existing *by itself* in time, and not merely as a property of some natural object? For myself, I cannot so imagine it."[57] He argued that even if "good were a feeling, as some would have us believe, then it would exist in time. But that is why to call it so is to commit the naturalistic fallacy. It will always remain pertinent to ask, whether the feeling itself is good; and if so, then good cannot itself be identical with any feeling."[58] This amounts to saying that the "naturalistic fallacy," as Moore termed it, is a mistake of identifying the property "good" with some natural property or phenomenon with which it is not in fact identical. To say, for example, that "good means pleasure" is to commit the naturalistic fallacy by confusing good with the natural phenomenon of pleasure. If one merely asserted that "pleasure is good," no identification of good and pleasure would be implied; hence such an assertion would not exemplify this fallacy. If, however, one identifies good with pleasure, desire, or any natural phenomenon, one commits the naturalistic fallacy by confusing two different properties and considering them identical. Moore claimed that good is good and not any other thing, not pleasure, happiness, survival of the fittest, nor any natural property of any kind.

One important consequence of Moore's view is that good is an objective property in the sense that it cannot be defined in terms of one's interest or preference but must be independent of natural or psychological needs, feelings, or preferences. Thus any subjectivistic or relativistic interpretation of good must also be a consequence of committing what Moore called the "naturalistic fallacy." Good in the intrinsic sense is not only indefinable, but is objective, independent of anyone's opinion. To say, therefore, that something is intrinsically or ethically good is to assert an intuitive judgment— i.e., a judgment, incapable of proof, that must stand by itself. It is impossible, according to Moore, for one to show evidence why something is good in itself or has intrinsic value. If something is intrinsically good, any extrinsic evidence in terms of natural facts would be irrelevant to its being good-in-itself.

In 1911 Santayana published his *Hypostatic Ethics*, which analyzed the ethical views of G. E. Moore and Bertrand Russell. Santayana admitted that the abstract quality "good" is indefinable; but this does not imply that "good" is unconditioned or exists independently of our opinions and interests.

> Pleasure, and its rivals, are not synonyms for the abstract quality "good," but names for classes of concrete facts that are supposed to possess that quality. From this correct, if somewhat trifling, observation, however, Mr. Russell, like Mr. Moore before him, evokes a portentous dogma. Not being able to define good, he hypostasises it. "Good and bad" he says, "are qualities which belong to objects independently of our opinions, just as much as round and square do; and when two people differ as to whether a thing is good, only one of them can be right."[59]

Santayana argued that right and left are indefinable, but nevertheless relative. So good and bad, while indefinable, are nevertheless relative to some point of view or preference. Santayana further argued that Moore's view, rather than the naturalistic one, "renders reasoning and self-criticism impossible in morals; for wrong desires, and false opinions as to value, are conceivable only because a point of reference or criterion is available to prove them such."[60] As value terms, "good" and "bad" have meaning only to the extent that some individual takes interest in, or shows a preference for, one thing rather than another. As terms of evaluation, "good" and "bad" are as extensive and variable as the actual and possible preferences of people. Consequently hedonism, for example, goes astray—not because it commits the naturalistic fallacy, but because it narrows its interest to pleasure alone and thus misses all other interests that may be taken. "The impossibility which people labour under of being satisfied with pure pleasure as a goal is due to their want of imagination."[61] When Santayana affirmed that things are good because they are desired rather than being desired because they are good, he wanted to claim that values are caused or created by the various acts of interest taken in particular objects. To believe that things can be desired because they are good would involve a false hypostasis of good, implying that things are good before anyone values them or whether anyone values them or not. To say that things are good because they are desired is not a moral or normative judgment, since it does not pretend to tell us what things are good. Santayana claimed that good is indefinable and that good qualities are all different in kind. He did not reduce good to some merely natural fact or identify it with some other, different property. Yet he did insist on *relating* it to natural feelings, desires, or interests. Good, he insisted, "is not an intrinsic or primary quality, but relative and adventitious."[62] As a mere form or timeless essence, good is a static, changeless universal. But all pure universals are changeless and timeless since they do not exist in time. To hypostasise these universals and treat them as absolute or independent existences is mistaken. Good is good in the same sense that round is round or square is square—in the perfectly tautological and trivial sense of logical identity, which asserts no existence of anything at all. But moral or ethical assertions about what is good are not tautologies. In an ethical sense, to assert that charity is good or not good is not to assert a mere identity or stipulation of abstract terms, but to make a claim about natural facts or existences. Thus if one person believes that charity is good and another person denies this, the conclusion does not at all follow that one is wrong and the other right. Goodness is not a primary or intrinsic quality that inheres in some things rather than others—no more than is beauty. If one person finds an object beautiful and another person does not, this does not mean that one must be wrong. A person who fails to find goodness or beauty in a certain thing may indeed be missing what someone else has found, but to conclude that the one view is right and the other wrong is a false hypostasis of value.

For this very reason, according to Santayana, it is fallacious to think that we can legislate values. Values are only found where a suitable interest or sensitivity obtains. We can no more require or demand that other people accept our moral values than we can require others to like the same food or have the same tastes we do. People do not always disagree, of course, and constitutional uniformities and similar preferences exist. But people's agreement that something is good does not mean that their view or perception of value is correct; it only means that their perspectives are the same.

In *Principia Ethica*, G. E. Moore accused John Stuart Mill's utilitarianism of committing the naturalistic fallacy by confusing what is desirable with what is desired.[63] If we argue that happiness is good or desirable because people actually desire it, then, according to Moore, we have illicitly identified the moral, nonnatural sense of good with the natural, nonmoral fact that someone has a desire. The fact that someone has a desire does not imply that this desire is good in any moral sense. Dewey, in *The Quest for Certainty* (1929), asserted: "There is no value except where there is satisfaction, but there have to be certain conditions fulfilled to transform a satisfaction into a value."[64] In other words, Dewey admitted that desire and satisfaction are not identical with good or value—but not because desire and satisfaction are natural phenomena and good and value are not. Dewey insisted that values are just as much natural phenomena or parts of the natural world as are desires, preferences, or any given interest. There is nothing nonnatural or absolute about the meanings of the terms "good" or "value." For Dewey, the assertion that anything is good or has value, if it is to have any verifiable meaning, must refer to certain facts about the world. Dewey agreed with Moore that what is desirable cannot simply be reduced to whatever happens to be desired. "The fact that something is desired only raises the *question* of its desirability; it does not settle it."[65] On the other hand, the statement that something is good or desirable cannot be divorced from natural, observable facts without making value judgments unverifiable or purely arbitrary. As a nonnaturalist in ethics, Moore wanted to claim that judgments about what is good in itself, judgments about intrinsic value, are intuitive, incapable of being proved. This is exactly what Dewey's form of naturalism excepted. A judgment about what is good or has value that cannot be supported by evidence was, for Dewey, no moral or value judgment at all. To believe, for example, that honesty is intrinsically good and that no factual evidence is relevant in support of this belief is completely fallacious. One cannot, of course, prove that honesty is good simply on the basis that people tend to prefer or desire it. But there is vast difference, according to Dewey, between mere thoughtless, uncriticized desires and desires that are thoughtful and regulated by inquiry. Desires are not all of equal footing. One can never discover the difference between good and bad desires by moving away from the natural world to some absolute or intrinsic nonnatural object. The only way one may discover any meaningful difference between good and bad desires is to engage in experimental testing of these desires and their consequences. If so-called good desires invariably lead to the same consequences as bad ones, no factual or real difference would exist between them. If honesty leads to the same consequences as dishonesty, one would have no basis for calling honesty morally good and desirable and dishonesty bad and undesirable.

Dewey claimed that older empirical and naturalistic conceptions of value failed to take into consideration the notion of future and experimentally testable consequences. These older theories falsely identified what is good or valuable with "objects *antecedently* enjoyed, apart from reference to the method by which they come into existence."[66] What is good cannot be decided on the basis of past experience or in terms of preconceptions of what must be good. It is a notorious fact that man's value judgments are infected and influenced by prejudice. Men hold that certain things are good, not because they have conducted an inquiry to discover what is in fact good, but because they cherish certain preconceptions or dogmas about values independently of any test or inquiry. Dewey alleged that the belief in so-called intrinsic values—things good in themselves—as final ends without relation to the means by which they can be realized is completely fallacious and unscientific. Nothing is good in itself apart from its relation to experience and other things. Nothing is good as an absolute end in itself apart from intelligent and testable means by which that end may be realized. It is a mistake, for example, to believe that pure enjoyment or pleasure is good in itself or is, as hedonism claims, the ultimate goal of living. Pleasure does not exist by itself alone, and any meaningful appreciation of pleasure is not a bare enjoyment; but is rather, according to Dewey, a consummation of previous processes and responses. A meaningful enjoyment or pleasure is not an end in itself or something isolated from other experiences, but is a cultivated appreciation that intelligently joins many elements into a harmonious, integrated whole. We cannot enjoy the beauty of a melody, if we forget or lose consciousness of the preceding notes.

It is interesting to note that Santayana and Dewey, while agreeing that the concept of good or value only has meaning in a naturalistic sense, disagreed concerning the cognitive status of value and moral judgments. Santayana agreed with Moore that judgments about what is intrinsically or ethically good cannot be established by empirical evidence or proven at all. But Moore held that such judgments can be intuitively true, whereas Santayana held that such judgments can only be enlightened or sincere, not correct or incorrect. Dewey, in disagreement with both Moore and Santayana, held that any naturalistic theory of value or ethics must be consistent with the natural sciences and experimental proof. Consequently he claimed that value judgments must be capable of proof and that such proof must be entirely empirical. This suggests serious internal disagreements among naturalists themselves. A further problem that emerges for any Naturalistic Ethics concerns how value judgments can be both cognitive and normative within the strictures of scientific methods. Normally we think of biologists, chemists, or physicists as making no moral or value judgments in performance of their scientific work. Explanation of how to produce an atomic explosion is one thing but explanation of how and where such power should be used is quite another. Certainly science implies or raises moral issues, but the claim that the same methods used to explain chemicals and animal organisms can also be used for moral regulation of their use in human life is, to say the least, rather strong. If the success of science in achieving objective, testable results depends on its adherence to impartial and impersonal methods of inquiry—on its success in refraining from making moral or value judgments about its objects of study—one cannot easily see how moral judgments can be assimilated into experimental science and proof. Dewey wanted to avoid any false divisions between science and values, between theory and practice. He wanted to claim that science must use and test value judgments in order to carry on its work. According to Dewey, questions of value (e.g., What constitutes a good experiment in a particular context? What constitutes a good measurement of a certain phenomenon?) all lead to instrumental, operationally testable judgments. A good measurement is one that will provide reliable, accurate results. A good experiment is one that will advance further inquiry and throw light on more and more facts. In other words, Dewey's interpretation of naturalism was clearly pragmatic, he conceived all genuine inquiry to be a form of practice or action with testable, observable results. According to his conception, it is always wrong to import judgments of value independently of inquiry. No value judgment is immune from testing and criticism, and all values must be basically tested by the same experimental method. Dewey declared that, so far as social or political values are concerned,

> . . . the evils in current social judgments of ends and policies arise . . . from importations of judgments of value from outside of inquiry. The evils spring from the fact that the values employed are not determined in and by the process of inquiry: for it is assumed that certain ends have an inherent value so unquestionable that they regulate and validate the means employed, instead of ends being determined on the basis of existing conditions as obstacles-resources. Social inquiry, in order to satisfy the conditions of scientific method, must judge certain objective consequences to be the end which is *worth* attaining under the given conditions.[67]

While determination of ends or goals on the basis of existing conditions may be instructive, we should note that those ends are not necessarily suitable or sufficiently determined by existing conditions. Existing conditions may well be more important in science than they need be in morals. In any case, a serious problem is indicated here for a scientific ethics. Dewey's theory must place a heavy premium on existing conditions in any moral situation. However, careful appraisals of moral situations require consideration of vast periods of time and place, even of all times and places. Whether a scientific or experimentalist conception of ethics can give such consideration or sufficient attention to any *universal* conditions of man is a serious problem for Dewey's ethics. The tendency to bring science and morals closer together, along with the tendency to view both as essentially practical affairs, may result in a blurring of important distinctions. Dewey insisted that "the conduct of scientific inquiry, whether physical or mathematical, is a mode of *practice*; the working scientist is a practitioner above all else, and is constantly engaged in making practical judgments: decisions as to what to do and what means to employ in doing it."[68] We make a moral distinction between experimenting on animals and experimenting on humans but one cannot see how this distinction could arise if based exclusively on experimental methods of inquiry. The purpose of inquiry is to find out as much as possible. Blocking or halting inquiry before certain facts are gained is bad for the purposes of inquiry. But obviously other purposes exist besides those of knowledge and inquiry. How, then, does one decide between them? To allow any scientific method of inquiry to decide how far its own purpose (in relation to other purposes) will be pursued would only seem to prejudge the whole issue. On the other hand, to suggest that no real difference of kind but only a difference of degree exists between various purposes that can be pursued seems plainly false. To construe science as practical and the scientist as mainly a practitioner only seems to blur the distinction between the theoretical, speculative side of science and the practical, technological aspect of scientific research. While the aims of theory do not necessarily oppose the aims of applied science or technology, they can and sometimes do conflict with one another. The freedom of inquiry necessary for the imaginative efforts involved in advancing scientific theory may, in fact, require a complete disregard for existing conditions that would be disastrous in experimental or technological work.

Equally important to the forms of critical naturalism developed over many years by both Santayana and Dewey are the epistemological and normative questions of ethics. The epistemological questions of ethics refer to such matters as the cognitive status of moral judgments; how these judgments can be proven or justified. The normative questions of ethics are concerned with what can possibly constitute the good life for man and what kinds of goals or values make sense for him to pursue. Although Santayana and Dewey agreed on the need to ground moral values in terms of the natural world—and further agreed on the need to examine and criticize proposed values and forms of life—they did not agree on either the cognitive status of moral judgments or on conceptions of the good life for man. As already seen, Santayana did not believe that moral beliefs can be made scientific; whereas Dewey not only believed that they can, but, if they are to play a constructive role in building any good life for man, that they *must*. For Santayana, moral beliefs could be more or less enlightened, coherent, and sincere, but he found no meaning in calling them true or false in any scientific, verifiable sense. He pointed out that moral judgments and beliefs are usually hybrid, that although the nerve or center of any moral judgment is animal preference, such a judgment may contain beliefs about external facts as well as important items concerning self-knowledge. For Santayana, in fact, the only sources of moral enlightenment stemmed from man's attempt to learn and clarify what his interests or preferences really are and how they are related to the natural world. Clarification, coherence, and harmony are thus the ideals or goals of any rational approach to ethics. But any basic interest in the use of reason in any moral life cannot itself be grounded in reason. No interest is inherently reasonable—even the interest in being reasonable itself—since all interests are relative to the biological equipment and sensitivity of any organism. No logical or rational argument can show man that he must or ought to be reasonable unless he first assumes an interest in the use of reason. Consequently Santayana drew a distinction between what he called "rational ethics" and "rational morality." The former is only a sketch or blueprint of the latter, since a completely rational morality or life lived wholly in terms of reason is unattainable by man. A perfectly rational morality would depend on perfect self-knowledge and a harmony of interests so that no potential good would be missed and no actual good would be misplaced or confused. This is not to be hoped for. Instead, what makes sense for man to pursue is a rational ethics. "An ethics in the manner of Socrates, Plato, or Aristotle is only a sketch of a rational morality. Hence, a rational ethics is neither dogmatic nor final, but makes use of critical or dialectical thinking to discover not what is good once and for all but to discover the consequences of whatever estimations of value a man may make."[69] As Santayana asserted "This method, the Socratic method, consists in accepting any estimation which any man may sincerely make, and in applying dialectic to it, so as to let the man see what he really esteems."[70] In this way the function of reason in ethics is only relative and structural; it does not itself create or enforce any values, but simply discovers possible harmonies among them. Such a rational approach to ethics requires leisure and detachment, of course, from the distractions and troubles of the world. For Santayana, it would be folly to suppose that all men at all times and places can or ought to attempt cultivation of such a rational ethic in their lives. One of the most serious impediments to any life based on reason is the tendency of man to be swayed by his emotions, to become a victim of his own illusions and self-deceptions. Man naturally becomes involved with a multiplicity of changing existences and fashions that he neither completely controls nor understands. The hardest lesson for every man to learn is to comprehend and live within his own potentialities and limitations. Men have a proclivity to exceed their own grasp, to imitate the lives and goals of others. Consequently two of the most important items for any life of reason to cultivate are disillusionment and freedom from distraction. If a man seeks a life of reason and harmony, he must learn to respect the sources on which his values and life really depend. Santayana was willing to call this respect or reverence for the sources of one's very being by the old-fashioned name of "piety." But he insisted on giving piety a naturalistic, rather than a supernaturalistic, interpretation. Piety is a "man's reverent attachment to the sources of his being and the steadying of his life by that attachment."[71] The proper objects of piety in a naturalistic sense are "parents first, then family, ancestors, and country; finally, humanity at large and the whole natural cosmos."[72] Man's natural environment must be conserved and respected, not exploited or defiled, if man hopes to live any life of reason. The whole modern interest in progress, industry, and technology is in many ways destructive of, and incompatible with, any leisurely, rational attempt to live the good life. What made this point even clearer, for Santayana, are the dehumanizing, unspiritual dimensions of modern industrialized existence. Just as Santayana gave the name "piety" to man's respect for the natural grounds of his own existence, so he gave the name "spirituality" to the higher side of man's life, to those ideal goods which would fulfill man's existence and make it worth having. "Spirituality is nobler than piety, because what would fulfil our being and make it worth having is what alone lends value to that being's source."[73] Any disillusioned spirituality or rational spiritual life must be based on the understanding that spirit or consciousness is neither a supernatural nor material power or substance. "Spirit is invisible, intangible, unapproachable from the outside. . . . What I call spirit is only that inner light of actuality or attention which floods all life as men actually live it on earth. It is roughly the same thing as feeling or thought; it might be called consciousness."[74] Spirit is an epiphenomenon of matter and depends on the body for its very existence. But even though vitally dependent on its natural body, it presents a new, extremely important quality of existence. The nature of mind or spirit is to form ideas or perspectives; to see, feel, think, or imagine in some selective manner. Memory, for example, is a purely spiritual phenomenon in terms of its own quality of existence, though it depends on the brain and other material things for its source. The past is gone and cannot literally be recovered; but in memory, the past comes alive by virtue of the forms or essences that mind or spirit is able to retain. Spirit has a natural affinity for ideas or essences which are timeless, eternal qualities. Only some detached essence is before our mind whenever we think or experience anything. Our mind cannot in any physical sense literally possess the things we claim to know or the things that consciously interest us. All of our enjoyments, insofar as they are conscious, are spiritual in the sense that only the essence or quality of material things can enter our awareness. Thus it is true that material things are only valuable for the spiritual uses to which they can be put. Material things in themselves have no values, no better or worse, beauty or ugliness. Only when they appear to some conscious observer can any classification or category of values arise. Matter by itself has no appreciation, one way or another, of any aspect of its existence. But it is the very nature of spirit to feel that some things are good and some things are bad in relation to itself. But to suppose that what is good or bad for spirit is intrinsically and universally good or bad is only an illusion. In its enthusiasm for what it loves or in its antipathy to what it deplores, spirit is prone to assume that its ideals are everyone's and that its relative enjoyments are absolute.

What is most congenial to spirit is simply to live in the presence of things eternal. When spirit or mind enjoys itself, it loses any real sense of time insofar as it is concentrated or absorbed in some object of beauty or satisfying experience. "If it be frivolous to live in the present, is it not vain to live for the future? And how many are concentrated and contemplative enough to live in the eternal?"[75] Santayana did not of course believe that any detached, disillusioned preference for a spiritual life can simply be imposed on mankind. He did not suggest that man is under any moral obligation to detach himself from the distractions of existence in order to become as much absorbed as possible in the enjoyment or contemplation of essences. He pointed out, however, that we do in fact find satisfaction at various intervals in our lives by simply absorbing ourselves in the beautiful or timeless qualities that find their way into our experiences. "It is by reaching, at moments, this absorption of life in eternal themes that spirit is liberated from the hindrances that envelop it at its birth and distract it in its career."[76] In this sense Santayana thus remained a staunch critic of the pragmatism of William James and John Dewey. Their conceptions of the good life found no genuine place for the inward cultivation of man's mind or for the enjoyment and contemplation of anything eternal. As philosophies of action and progress, they were geared always to a receding future and an ever-changing world. The philosophies of James and Dewey, in short, made no place for spirit and essence. Santayana observed that "an unfortunate peculiarity of naturalistic philosophers is that usually they have but cursory and wretched notions of the inner life of the mind."[77] Man's spirit or inner life is too frequently judged as useless or as fantasy because his thoughts and ideals tend to be pragmatically judged in terms of their relevance or use for things outside the mind. But Santayana alleged that "the use of experience, to my mind, cannot be to prepare us for further experience; somewhere this experience must be self-rewarding, else all would be a democracy of unhappy tyrants making slaves of one another. There is a concomitant fruit to be gathered during this journey, experience at another level, the level of reflection, of spiritual self-possession, of poetry, of prayer. This is not a parasitic growth or expensive luxury."[78] Santayana agreed with the pragmatists in their pluralism, that no single good exists that all men should pursue. "In truth good qualities are all different in kind, and free lives are different in spirit. Comparison is the expedient of those who cannot reach the heart of the things compared; and no philosophy is more external and egotistical than that which places the essence of a thing in its relation to something else."[79] Santayana definitely agreed with Emerson in his preference for beauty, individuality, and the inner quality of the mind or spirit. But, unlike Emerson, Santayana was not a romantic idealist. Santayana could agree with Emerson that democracy is only a relative good—that as a form of social order or government, it is far from perfect or universally good. Santayana observed that the

> . . . ideal of a perfect ultimate democracy rests on two assumptions: that human nature in all men is essentially similar, and that consequently mankind could not fully develop its vital liberty without coming to a unanimous vision of the world and a cooperative exercise of the same virtues. I think this is a biological error, and that what is identical in all life is only its germ, from which all plants and animals have developed centrifugally, as circumstances have allowed them to develop.[80]

For Santayana, dissatisfaction with any government was inevitable "because any real government that does not let things merely drift must impose sacrifices, some severe and some universal."[81] To be real, a government must act. Every government is monarchical in its actions, since the expectation that everyone will agree with what it does or that everyone can be equally consulted is unrealistic. In sharp opposition to the whole American tradition, Santayana held "that monarchy, if good, is the ideal of good government follows from the nature of government, which must be an exercise of intellectual and moral synthesis in a living mind; this can exist only in one person; and it follows also from the possibility of instinctive representation of many children's interests in one disinterested paternal mind, and its impossibility in a collection of many children's minds, each bent on its special interests."[82] When a monarchy is good (since obviously it can be bad), what makes it good is simply the excellence of the monarch in imposing necessary sacrifices impartially and distributing "them in the way that would make them most tolerable all around."[83] A benevolent, enlightened monarch who understood the relative, naturalistic character of all goods or values could be expected to enforce a set of conditions that would let each man find his own true good, although he could not automatically enforce or create a good life for his subjects.

The most distinctive quality of human life lies in its capacities of imagination. Though man's imagination and all of his mental life are rooted in nature or material causes, it is only through a rational exercise of his imaginative powers that man can transcend the accidents of time and change and live in the presence of the ideal. What Santayana called the "inward landscape of imagination" constitutes man's proper happiness. "By their mind, its scope, quality, and temper, we estimate men, for by the mind only do we exist as men, and are more than so many storage-batteries for material energy."[84]

Dewey agreed with Santayana on the importance of imagination in any appreciation of the good life for man. For Dewey, "Imagination is the chief instrument of the good."[85] But imagination is not to be interpreted as something purely personal or subjective. A most important feature of imaginative experiences is that they can be shared. Imagination is not only a source of personal enjoyment but is a most useful means of bringing people closer together. Only through the use of imagination, since we have no direct acquaintance with other people's experiences, can we put ourselves in another person's place. Since every ideal is an imaginative construction and not a literal representation of any situation, "the ideal factors in every moral outlook and human loyalty are imaginative."[86] But for Dewey, moral ideals could not simply be imaginative; they must also be instrumental in giving what he termed "deep and enduring support" to the processes of living. In this way moral ideals are also religious in quality and involve no supernatural revelation or special worship of fixed objects. "Any activity pursued in behalf of an ideal end against obstacles and in spite of threats of personal loss because of conviction of its general and enduring value is religious in quality."[87] Dewey distinguished between the noun "religion" and the adjective "religious." He claimed that, while the general noun "religion" is associated with all the various and sundry denominations, cults, and sects throughout the world which have little if any common meaning, the adjective "religious" can be given an important moral, operational meaning independent of any sect or denomination. Dewey preferred to interpret the term "religious" as applied to any human life or experience as meaning simply a richly sharable, enduring value. To Dewey, "religious" signified just the opposite of whatever is exclusive, self-centered, and transient. Religious values and experiences are those which people can share widely and deeply. This is why Dewey held that "faith in the continued disclosing of truth through directed cooperative human endeavor is more religious in quality than is any faith in a completed revelation."[88] Here Dewey agreed with Royce and those idealists who viewed religious experience in terms of its social import or tendency to foster a sense of community and cooperation. But he sharply disagreed with Royce and those idealists who interpreted this sense of community as something final, transcendent, and absolute. Dewey's overriding value in his whole philosophy was continued growth, not some final end or changeless goal. Naturalistically conceived, life means growth, and Dewey saw no empirical way of establishing any limits or ultimate boundaries for human potential and growth. Countless empirical obstacles and limitations to the development of human life, of course, exist. Practical limitations and problems accompany the whole development of man's moral life. But practical difficulties are never final; in principle, they are always capable of solution through the exercise of improved intelligence and planning. A cardinal point of Dewey's instrumentalism insisted that the experimental approach to problem solving implies that new problems are created by the very effort of solving old ones. The experimental, scientific approach to the solution of man's problems must initiate changes in any given situation so that new problems originate as an inevitable result of any given problem's solution. This is true in a theoretical as well as in a practical sense. Any advance in knowledge creates new problems, opens up new, previously unknown, or neglected areas of inquiry. The history of mathematics is replete with examples of new problems and whole branches of study gained as a result of solving previous problems. This, of course, only serves to indicate the continuity of intelligent research or inquiry itself; every stage of knowledge is only a stepping-stone to the next, with no final resting place. The solution of practical problems also involves the creation of new problems and challenges. Development of new technologies, for example, makes man's life easier and his labor more efficient, but it also creates new problems by outdating and eliminating previous forms of labor and tools. Every new practical innovation or result alters man's material and social environment in some way; thus man must learn to adapt to these new, rapidly changing circumstances.

An indispensable dimension of any truly good life for man is, of course, its aesthetic quality. Dewey mentioned that "the Greek identification of good conduct with conduct having proportion, grace, and harmony, the *kalon-agathon,* is a more obvious example of distinctive aesthetic quality in moral action."[89] But Dewey refused to view aesthetic quality as a special type of experience set apart from practical, everyday occurrences. An aesthetic experience is not a passive enjoyment or contemplation of beauty detached from practical, social, and intellectual concerns. Any experience with unity of form that is enjoyed as it runs its course to fulfillment has aesthetic quality. "The esthetic is no intruder in experience from without, whether by way of idle luxury or transcendent ideality, but . . . is the clarified and intensified development of traits that belong to every normally complete experience."[90] Certain experiences in life are unaesthetic because they are incoherent, tedious, rigidly coerced, or aimless. Thus an aesthetic experience is never a mere indulgence or mindless pleasure. While any aesthetic experience, of course, involves pleasure or enjoyment, such experiences must have a coherent form in order to be genuine. They cannot be mere mechanical repetitions, isolated emotions, or sensuous feelings. Dewey lamented the fact that, with the advent of the machine age, the aesthetic quality of experience is conspicuously lacking. "The mechanical stands at the pole opposite to that of the esthetic, and production of goods is now mechanical. The liberty of choice allowed to the craftsman who worked by hand has almost vanished with the general use of the machine."[91] Consequently he argued that "the labor and employment problem of which we are so acutely aware cannot be solved by mere changes in wage, hours of work and sanitary conditions. No permanent solution is possible save in a radical social alteration, which affects the degree and kind of participation the worker has in the production and social disposi-tion of the wares he produces."[92] Here Dewey's concern with the problem of the good life appeared not as a problem of how the individual can detach himself from the undesirable features of existence—but how man and society can devise intelligent ways of interacting or participating in the challenges of actual life.

Of primary importance in improving man's life in all its aspects, Dewey insisted, is the necessity of improvements in communication and education. No philosopher since Plato paid more attention to the problems of education and exercised a larger worldwide influ-ence in this regard than Dewey. From the socially involved, widely instrumental character of his naturalism, Dewey became the acknowledged leader of what is known as "progressive education."

> Plato hit upon the idea of an educational program as necessary to the pursuit of knowledge and the good society as well. However, Plato's idea of education involving the establishment of an intellectual elite or leadership class, as well as including a separation between the practical and the theoretical, was based on mislocating the true social value of education as guided by scientific methods. Plato disparaged sense experience, physical doing or making, as well as democracy. In their place he upheld purified rational thought, perfect immaterial forms, and an intellectual aristocracy. For Dewey, Platonic educa-tion and philosophy was based on a whole series of untenable dualisms.[93]

Similarly Dewey noted that education in the twentieth century is defective because it too is based on a number of untenable dualisms. Education is falsely identified with certain traditional subject matters and formal studies in schools isolated from the practical, concrete situations in society where this learning is supposed to be applied. The whole point of Dewey's progressive approach to education insisted that real education involves an intelligent, experimental interaction with all the important phases of personal and social life. The student only learns by doing; therefore not only must theory not be separated from practice, but the greatest care must be exercised in controlling and planning what the student actually does and learns. Learning, in one sense of the term, is always occurring; but miseducation or the learning of bad habits and ideas involves the very isolation or separation of items in experience that need integration with one another. The hardest yet most important lesson in education is the cultivation of a sense of critical judgment so that experiences can be decisively used in relation to one another. "The business of the educator—whether parent or teacher—is to see to it that the greatest possible number of ideas acquired by children and youth are acquired in such a vital way that they become *moving* ideas, motive-forces in the guidance of conduct. This demand and this opportunity make the moral purpose universal and dominant in all instruction—whatsoever the topic."[94] Dewey admitted that it is, of course, impossible to keep direct moral considerations always uppermost in education. If moral ideas are treated as positive and constructive rather than as merely negative and restrictive, however, they gain a better chance toward integration with other ideas and the rest of life. Too often "stress is laid upon correcting wrong-doing instead of upon forming habits of positive service. Too often the teacher's concern with the moral life of pupils takes the form of alertness for failures to conform to school rules and routine. These regulations, judged from the standpoint of the development of the child at the time, are more or less conventional and arbitrary."[95] Dewey lamented that "the idea and the practice of morality are saturated with conceptions that stem from praise and blame, reward and punishment. Mankind is divided into sheep and goats, the vicious and virtuous, the law-abiding and criminal, the good and bad."[96] To identify morality with rule-following—and thus to suppose that morally good action means conduct that is praised and rewarded, while morally bad behavior means conduct which is blamed and punished—is a mistake not only in the school but in the rest of life as well. Rule-following, praise, and blame are restrictive finalities. Instead of indicating that any truly moral life depends on judgment, initiative, and constructive action, they imply that moral life is inhibiting, "cut and dried." Dewey saw Puritan Ethics and its survival in America as representing a false, morbidly obsessive conception of moral values that prevents intelligent understanding and handling of moral issues, which are viewed as final, absolute categories that carry only emotional weight. Dewey, in fact, criticized any view of morality that would reduce it to emotional meaning or rely on simple feelings as the basis or cause of our moral choices. Jonathan Edwards falsely analyzed man's moral life and judgment insofar as he placed heart above head, sentiments ahead of reason and experience. More recently, Dewey strongly criticized those theorists, including Santayana and C. L. Stevenson,[97] who claimed that the emotional meaning of ethical terms is in some sense primary. Stevenson argued that "when a person *morally approves* of something he experiences a rich feeling of security when it prospers and is indignant or 'shocked' when it does not. . . . In the moral usage, as well as in the nonmoral, 'good' has an emotive meaning which adapts it to suggestion."[98] Stevenson distinguished two kinds of disagreement— disagreement in belief and disagreement in interest—and claimed that the latter kind occurs in ethics. Ethical disagreements on such issues as whether suicide or abortion are morally wrong involve no mere disagreement in belief or about facts of the case, but involve the holding of contrary interests about the matter. Disagreements in belief can be resolved by more careful study of, and appeal to, the facts. But when an ethical disagreement is based on no disagreement in belief about facts, does any method exist by which it can be resolved? Stevenson answered by saying, "If one means by 'method' a *rational* method, then there is no method."[99] In the absence of any empirical or rational way of settling an ethical dispute, Stevenson urged that a persuasive way may be by the use of emotions. One party in the dispute "may pour out his enthusiasms in such a moving way—present the sufferings of the poor with such appeal—that he will lead his opponent to see life through different eyes."[100] One disputant may, in fact, change or influence the other disputant by the use of emotive language. Stevenson alleged that "this is often the only way to obtain ethical agreement, if there is any way at all."[101] Stevenson's position was in substantial agreement with Santayana's view that basic ethical differences express basic differences of feeling, which can be countered by other feelings but cannot be resolved by empirical facts or reason.

Dewey took issue with this emotive view on two principal points: one theoretical or analytical, the other practical and moral. Dewey alleged that "to take the cases in which 'emotional' factors *accompany* the giving of reasons as if this accompaniment factor were an inherent part of the judgment is, I submit, both a theoretical error and is, when widely adopted in practice, a source of moral weakness."[102] Dewey argued that isolation of emotive meaning from descriptive meaning is impossible. If we speak about expressing or venting an emotion, we must be able to identify what we are talking about—and this is only possible if we locate the facts or empirical situations in which these emotions actually occur. We cannot actually locate bare emotions or pure expressions of emotion; all we can empirically locate are emotional situations. To suggest, therefore, that emotional meaning or expression can be analyzed apart from empirically describable facts is psychologically and empirically false. When this false separation of emotive meaning from empirically describable facts is applied to the analysis of ethics or ethical language, it necessarily leads to a fallacious result: that ethical beliefs as emotive expressions are noncognitive or cannot be validly supported by empirical evidence. Purely emotive expressions are untestable in any ethical sense because they are unconnected with all the surrounding facts that comprise any ethical situation. Dewey denied Stevenson's view that "ethical terms cannot be taken as fully comparable to scientific ones. They have a quasi-imperative function."[103] According to Dewey, it is fallacious to oppose or contrast scientific terms and imperatives. Science cannot exclude experimental imperatives, for otherwise it could not establish and perform its own testing situations. Some philosophers, including Kant and Royce, have supposed that what distinguishes ethical imperatives from mere hypothetical imperatives is the categorical or purely *a priori* status of the former. But Dewey denied that moral imperatives are absolute or independent of empirical considerations. If moral imperatives are construed as absolutes, they will, of course, be opposed and not comparable to scientific imperatives. Only by making ethics fully empirical can it be brought into proper relationship with scientific methods.

The practical consequence of viewing ethical terms and judgments as principally emotive is a kind of moral laxness or weakness, according to Dewey. If widely adopted, this view would discourage the effort to locate sound empirical evidence for moral decisions. Further, it would actually tend to discourage the search for intelligent, rational solutions to moral disagreements. If one adopts the view that moral problems and disagreements cannot be resolved by rational or empirical means, one opens the doors to less responsible ways of settling the issues. For Dewey, a basic principle of sound philosophy was not to close any avenues to further inquiry. Finding solutions to moral problems is admittedly no easy matter. But if it is decided *ab initio* that ethical disputes cannot be settled rationally, the relevant or needed evidence will not, of course, be sought.

Like Thomas Jefferson before him, Dewey tied his own moral views to the concept of democracy. Dewey credited Jefferson for stating the principles of democracy in clearly experimental and moral terms. Dewey declared: "As believers in democracy we have not only the right but the duty to question existing mechanisms of, say, suffrage and to inquire whether some functional organization would not serve to formulate and manifest public opinion better than the existing methods. It is not irrelevant to the point that a score of passages could be cited in which Jefferson refers to the American Government as an *experiment*."[104] Dewey affirmed that "the source of the American democratic tradition is moral—not technical, abstract, narrowly political nor materially utilitarian. It is moral because based on faith in the ability of human nature to achieve freedom for individuals accompanied with respect and regard for other persons and with social stability built on cohesion instead of coercion."[105] Dewey could not agree with Santayana that democracy, as a working social experiment and moral ideal, is inherently defective because moral unanimity is impossible or even undesirable. Democracy does not imply that everyone will or must have identical interests. But it does imply that genuine interests can be shared and that differences of opinion can be respected. Santayana's preference for monarchy represented at best a preference for an aesthetic ideal at the expense of the moral. Dewey asserted that "a democracy is more than a form of government; it is primarily a mode of associated living, of conjoint communicated experience. . . . A society which makes provision for participation in its good of all its members on equal terms and which secures flexible readjustment of its institutions through interaction of the different forms of associated life is insofar democratic."[106] Worthwhile, sharable human goals cannot be achieved by undemocratic means. Dewey pointed out that recent history, including the devastating results of two world wars, patently shows that ideal human ends cannot be served or achieved by totalitarian means. No social ideal or form of government can be judged simply in terms of the ideal ends it *promises* to achieve. Social ideals and governments must also be judged in terms of the characteristic means to be utilized in arriving at its ideal ends. The value of democratic ends is thus directly related to the democratic means used to achieve those ends. Freedom, growth, respect for individual persons, and increased prosperity cannot be worthwhile democratic ends without the use of intelligently democratic means toward their achievement. Democracy cannot assume that any particular form of freedom is absolute and independent of other forms; nor can individual freedom be assumed as innate and unchangeable, but must be seen as something to be developed. Concerning economic freedom, Dewey lamented that democracy has been falsely identified with *laissez-faire* individualism. The belief that freedom simply means a lack of restraint—or that social prosperity and progress are the inevitable results of politically unrestrained or unregulated economic forces—fails to take into account the specifically human or moral aspect of society. Lack of restraint or freedom to act only assumes moral significance when critical, intelligent judgments are made concerning how such freedom or lack of restraint is to be used. If unrestrained freedom implies a growing prosperity for the few or for some persons at the expense of others, it cannot be considered democratic or good in any moral sense. The democratic ideal implies much more than freedom; it implies the intelligent, controlled formation and exercise of freedom so that this freedom may progressively be shared and enabled to grow.

Assessment

Any careful consideration of ethical naturalism must recognize the great variety of different, even divergent theories classified under this label. In the American tradition itself, thinkers as different as Jefferson, Emerson, Thoreau, James, Santayana, and Dewey have, in one way or another, been identified in this category. Utilitarian and nonutilitarian, pragmatist and nonpragmatist, hedonist and nonhedonist, evolutionary and nonevolutionary, as well as cognitive and noncognitive theories have all, in different ways, been identified as forms of naturalistic theories of ethics. As a consequence, it has been suggested that naturalism is too elusive or unwieldy a category for identifying any ethical theory and that use of the term should therefore be dropped. Elusiveness, however, is not peculiar to

naturalism as a philosophical term. Pragmatism, empiricism, idealism, and most other widely used philosophical labels involve a
similar lack of clear-cut precision. Any general label must be used
with caution and, wherever possible, with proper qualification.
Labels do wear out—or rather they become replaced with newer
ones. Yet some form of identification will always be needed for
discussion or reference to theories which, however complex and
even divergent, may nevertheless possess certain important features
in common. As long as naturalism or any other philosophical
category is seriously employed for purposes of discussion and
argument of important issues, we can say that it has a definite philosophical use. That naturalism as a philosophical category has been
so used in this century is without doubt. There can be little doubt
too that ethical naturalism in the twentieth century, especially in the
work of Santayana and Dewey, represents a richer, far more
sophisticated accomplishment than earlier varieties. Earlier criticisms of naturalism—that it reduces everything to matter and
motion, that it disregards the higher, more significant aspects of
human life and experience—are certainly not true of the philosophical efforts of Santayana and Dewey. One of the most notable
accomplishments of their comprehensive forms of naturalism was
the extensive, insightful attention they gave to art, religion, science,
society, and virtually every significant aspect of human life and
experience. It is indeed unusual that Santayana as an avowed
materialist gave so much philosophical attention and importance to
immaterial things. Three of his four realms of being—essence, truth,
and spirit—are all immaterial in the quality of their being, though
any instantiation or human use of these immaterial things depends
on matter or must be grounded in the natural world. It is equally
unusual that Dewey as an avowed empiricist gave so much philosophical attention and importance to rational, intellectually determined means and ends in every aspect of life. No philosopher in
modern times was so thoroughly critical of irrationalism in all its
forms as Dewey, but Dewey always insisted that reason and thought
must always be grounded in experience and the facts of the natural
world. He has even been criticized for overintellectualizing experience; in ethics he has been criticized for overintellectualizing the
emotional urgency of moral terms.[107] Santayana, on the other hand,
has been charged with overemphasizing the purely spiritual, aesthetic dimensions of man's life and with failing to integrate these

detached ideals with the more concrete, realistic facts of the natural world.[108] Santayana complained that Dewey's naturalism was not sufficiently detached or disinterested, that it represented a false dominance of a pragmatic foreground in nature—whereas nature, in Santayana's view, has no foreground or moral center at all. Dewey, in turn, complained that Santayana's naturalism is ruined by its aesthetic detachment which falsely prefers to contemplate nature merely in terms of eternal essences rather than confront it intelligently with experimental methods of study. From such disagreements, one cannot easily see how these two divergent approaches to naturalism can be reconciled. If they cannot be reconciled—if each can be a genuine, possible form that naturalism may take—if the internal divisions within naturalism are as great as those between Santayana and Dewey—a serious question concerning the meaning and validity of any naturalistic approach to ethics is raised. If naturalists divide on a question as important as the cognitive versus noncognitive status of moral judgments or beliefs, perhaps it is only trivial or inconsequential that they agree on the grounding of moral ideas in terms of the natural world. Of course no ethical naturalist can consider the grounding of all moral ideas on facts of the natural world trivial or unimportant. But *how* they are so grounded and whether moral ideas are cognitively significant are even more important questions. The disagreement among naturalists on these questions makes the cogency of any Naturalistic Ethics as a whole— or even the merits of criticisms already made against this kind of ethical theory—difficult to assess. For example, the contemporary English philosopher, R. M. Hare in his book, *The Language of Morals*, has charged that "what is wrong with naturalist theories is that they leave out the prescriptive or commendatory element in value-judgments, by seeking to make them derivable from statements of fact."[109] This criticism is similar to G. E. Moore's in its attack on so-called naturalistic theories in terms of the alleged form of their reasoning, claiming that derivation of normative or ethical terms and conclusions from purely descriptive, nonnormative terms or premises is invalid. The trouble with this criticism is that, while it may apply to some forms of naturalistic argumentation, it does not apply to *all*. In fact it applies to neither Santayana nor Dewey—but for different reasons. Santayana did not leave out the prescriptive or commendatory element from value judgments by attempting to derive them from factual statements. According to Santayana, we do not infer that anything is good; we feel it or prefer it. If Santayana had inferred that something is morally good because it has certain factual characteristics, he would not be a non-cognitivist. But Santayana's point in moral theory is that our value judgments are neither factually true nor false—which, if derived from factual premises, they would be. When we make a genuine moral judgment that honesty is good, for example, Santayana insisted that no external facts can be found to validate this judgment. Such a judgment certainly has prescriptive or commendatory force, but it has no descriptive force in terms of any public or external facts.

It can also be claimed that Dewey did not leave out the prescriptive or commendatory element from value judgments by attempting to derive them from factual statements. Here the case is different, however, since Dewey did attempt to infer or derive value judgments from factual evidence—not simply from any factual evidence, but only from the facts he considered relevant. Dewey denied that we can derive the conclusion that something is desirable or morally good simply from the facts that people desire or prefer it. Desires and preferences *per se* are not prescriptive, although they can be transformed on the basis of analysis and inquiry into meaningful prescriptions or valuations. Dewey's point was that beliefs about what is desirable or morally good cannot be left "up in the air" but must be based on factual evidence. Since he also held that only warranted or relevant facts can provide the basis for any moral conclusion or value judgment, he insisted that facts relevant to the drawing of any normative conclusion will carry *legitimate* and *practical* prescriptive and commendatory force. For Dewey, it was not enough for value judgments to be prescriptive or commenda-tory, since not all prescriptions or commendations are equally useful or sensible. Since Dewey assumed that every value judgment is practical in the sense of prescribing some way of guiding conduct or action, all value judgments must necessarily be judged in terms of how well they perform this task. To suggest that any value judgment need not meet this test or to assume that no factual ways exist of determining their applicability would, according to Dewey, be perfectly ridiculous.

The contemporary American naturalist Sidney Hook defended Dewey's claim that relevant factual propositions have a normative status in relation to moral and other choice situations. Hook declared that "Dewey's contention is that every true proposition *in use* in a concrete situation provoking choice does have a normative status, because wherever relevant it determines in some degree what we should choose. But the great body of scientific propositions at any time are not in use."[110] In other words, there is no opposition or inconsistency in holding that factual or descriptive statements may have a normative or prescriptive use. In the light of Dewey's instrumentalism, in fact, all statements are to be viewed in terms of how they are or can be used to solve problems. No statement is inherently or intrinsically descriptive or prescriptive; rather, statements *become* descriptive or prescriptive in terms of their usage, and nothing prevents a statement from being used in both ways. Dewey denied the existence of two separate, uncombinable classes of statements that he referred to as the "so-called descriptive" and "so-called prescriptive." It is instructive to note that the contemporary English philosopher G. J. Warnock made this same point in his analysis of certain criticisms against ethical naturalism. Warnock argued that the trouble with the allegation that evaluative expressions are not definable in terms of descriptive expressions

. . . is that there do not exist the two distinct classes of expressions ostensibly referred to. It is possible, no doubt, to distinguish evaluating from describing. . . . But it is not, in general, possible to make this distinction merely on the basis of the expressions used; for it is probably true to say that any expression which occurs in the context of the evaluation of something could also occur in the context of the description of something, and vice versa—this distinction is simply not a distinction of *vocabulary*.[111]

A somewhat different criticism of Dewey's ethical naturalism was made by C. L. Stevenson, who alleged that Dewey neglected the emotive meaning of ethical terms[112] and thereby underplayed what Stevenson called "disagreement in attitude" by absorbing all such disagreement into disagreement in belief.[113] This fault, according to Stevenson, resulted from Dewey's dwelling on the descriptive aspects of language. It is not true, however, that Dewey neglected the emotive meaning of ethical terms and judgments. What is true is that Dewey offered a different analysis of the role that emotions or feelings play in relation to any evaluation or value judgment. Dewey admitted that "a moral judgment, however intellectual it may be, must at least be colored with feeling if it is to influence behavior."[114] Thus there was no question for Dewey that moral judgments do have emotive meaning and force. But emotive meaning or force, though often persuasive and influential, is obviously not cognitively significant in the sense of being valid or invalid, true or false. A *bona fide* moral judgment cannot be construed as simply expressing a feeling or as merely containing emotively prescriptive force. For Dewey, the force of emotion by itself is not indicative of anything specifically moral, any more than the force of wind or electricity. Only by connection with empirically disclosable facts of some thoughtful human concern can any emotion have moral meaning or significance. In addition, however, it must be noted that, even in a factually determined moral situation or context, the force of emotion is no substitute for cognitive interests and the serious analysis of facts; it may rather become a source of prejudice and confusion if left unanalyzed or uncriticized. Emotions are noncognitive or extracognitive factors, and if they "enter into the subject-matter or content of sentences purporting to be legitimately ethical, those sentences are by just that much deprived of the properties sentences should have in order to be genuinely *ethical*."[115] Here we should note a fundamental disagreement between Dewey and some of his critics on the very question as to what constitutes a *bona fide* moral or value judgment. Stevenson wanted to allow for cases where moral judgments, as value judgments, conflict with other moral judgments; where no factual judgments or beliefs are relevant; or where none can be of effective use in deciding the dispute. Dewey, while admitting that unsettled cases may very well exist, could not admit that such cases are incapable in principle of resolution. This is the same issue that divided Dewey's whole approach to ethics from that of Santayana. When Santayana declared that "since the first principle of my ethics is relativity, I cannot admit that . . . elementary differences might be reconciled morally, from the point of view of either party,"[116] Dewey could only admit that such differences may go undecided or be extremely difficult to resolve. Dewey could not admit that any moral disagreement is, in principle, incapable of cognitive resolution, i.e., by the use of relevant facts. This issue concerning the cognitive status of moral judgments, including the cognitive status of fundamental moral disagreements, has emerged in recent discussion as perhaps the single most important and difficult question in all of moral philosophy. If one asks who is right—Dewey or his critics, cognitivists or noncognitivists—no simple answer can be given. One should observe, however, that both parties to this dispute have in one sense apparently overstated their claims. Neither cognitivists nor noncognitivists have proven or demonstrated their conclusions. Thus it is logically possible, though undemonstrated, that what are termed basic moral differences or disagreements are both capable and incapable of resolution. This is not a contradiction; for what one party termed as basic moral differences were not so termed by the other. Thus both cognitivists and noncognitivists disagree as to what shall constitute a moral disagreement. The present author's view is that this issue cannot be settled by logical analysis alone. For it is not enough to establish the logical possibility that all moral disagreements can or cannot be settled. One must show that all can actually be settled or that all cannot be settled. Dewey, for one, did not show that all moral disputes can *actually* be settled by scientific or cognitive means;[117] at best, he demonstrated that cognitively determined facts are relevant to the *possible* solution of such disputes. On the other hand, Santayana and others have not shown that moral disputes cannot be settled by appeal to the relevant facts; at best, he demonstrated the *logical possibility* that cognitively determined facts are not decisive to the actual solution of moral disputes. Santayana in fact overstated his own noncognitivist position; he is rightly regarded as a dogmatic noncognitivist because of his claim that differences cannot be cognitively reconciled owing to the intrinsic nature of moral or value disagreements. But this is a metaphysical stance, for it is not a matter of evidence or logic that shows moral disagreements as intrinsically incapable of resolution on cognitive grounds. Santayana's position represents a refusal to allow and seek supporting evidence because of his preconception that moral judgments cannot possibly be cognitively supported or proved. Dewey also overstated his own case, perhaps in a more subtle way. He did not say that value or moral judgments, because of their intrinsic nature, can all be proven or that all disputes can be settled. Dewey did not speak of things as having an intrinsic nature at all, since this idea was anathema to his instrumentalism or experimental type of naturalism. Because of his peculiar, unformal view of logic itself, Dewey did not or could not allow that the noncognitivist position is a logically possible one. While it would be wrong or misleading to label Dewey as a dogmatic cognitivist in ethics, he did refuse to take seriously the view that alternative ways exist of regarding logical principles themselves. He refused to allow or seriously consider a purely formal or hypothetical conception of these principles that is radically distinct from, or independent of, any empirical or experimentally determined findings. Thus Dewey would have rejected the idea that it is "logically possible," in one sense of the term, that moral judgments cannot be proved or that not all *bona fide* moral disputes can be resolved. Dewey somehow assumed that admission of the possibility that factually cognitive evidence is not always relevant to the settlement of any ethical dispute implies moral bankruptcy or weakness. But this is surely to overstate the case. From the simple notion of the logical possibility that not all ethical disputes can be settled or meaningfully adjudicated by factual evidence, no logical conclusion follows as to how we should respond to this impasse. Certainly we cannot conclude that we should adopt some irrational method of solution or any kind of moral detachment or withdrawal. I would suggest that, when Dewey accused the noncognitivist position of leading to moral weakness, he was simply responding to its tendency toward dogmatism and overstatement of its case. Santayana, for one, did not maintain that any kind of moral weakness or withdrawal is logically implied by his position. His own preference for detachment and the aesthetic contemplation of essences was nothing that Santayana wished to impose on others. But certainly Santayana, as James before him, wanted to preserve what he saw as the inherent right of every moral agent—to assert his own moral preferences independent of any obligation to bring these in line either with empirical inquiry or another person's views. But this is exactly where Santayana became a moral dogmatist and thus provoked criticism, along with the charge of moral weakness, from Dewey. Santayana flatly refused to allow any kind of empirical evidence or inquiry to adjudicate what he termed "elementary moral differences." But how do we know when moral differences are elementary? And what is meant here by the term "elementary" itself? These questions were only obscurely answered by Santayana.

A further difficulty is involved in Santayana's claim that the first principle of his ethics is relativity. Santayana was much too brief in his elucidation of exactly what this relativity means and involves. He asserted that "maintaining, as I do, that morality is relative, and that the ideal moves like the zenith above the head of the traveller, I respect and require pre-rational preferences, to be the nerve of all contrasts between good and evil, and of all virtue. Yet such preferences are vital not rational, psychic not spiritual; they express particular interests, that are legitimate relatively but are expressed absolutely, as befits a call to arms for the home forces."[118] But he did not explain the grounds on which these prerational preferences are both relative and legitimate. They have not been legitimatized by any kind of empirical test or analysis. Presumably they are legitimate in the sense that they are real or really occur, are not fabricated or make-believe. But why should any preference be legitimate merely because it occurs? There is no need to assert that a preference or anything else, for that matter, is legitimate simply because it exists. Such an assertion in Santayana's eyes may have represented the height of tolerance, but it is also rather empty and virtually meaningless. Absolute tolerance, if this means acceptance of anything that happens to exist, cannot be made coherent, since it must include a tolerance of existing intolerance. In any case, one cannot easily see how absolute tolerance is any different than the refusal to make any judgment at all. Santayana compared the relativity of any moral sense of good to the relativity of concepts like right, left, or green. His point was that nothing is good, green, right, or left in the absence of any conditions; but that things are good, green, right, or left only on condition that they are viewed in a certain way or from a certain perspective. But this only shows that these terms are relational, not subjective or solely dependent on the view that happens to be taken. A biased or irrelevant judgment, for example, is subjective, not objective—in the sense that it depends only on the perspective taken. If, for example, a questioner asks whether a certain hat is green or not and someone replies that he doesn't like or even wear a hat, that judgment is irrelevant to the point at issue. Santayana seemed not only to imply that judgments about moral good are relational, but that they are subjective in the sense that they depend entirely on the viewpoint taken. But he failed to show how such moral judgments are subjective on the basis of being relational. In other words, Santayana does not appear to make any distinction between a thing's relativity (in a purely relational sense) and its subjectivity—or at least he considered that such a distinction has no bearing on the whole question of the status of moral values. But it does, of course. To claim that all moral judgments are subjective makes no more sense than to say that all judgments about motion or relative humidity are subjective. Honesty is morally good may very well be a relational judgment, but it does not follow that it must be subjective or cannot be objective.

"Objective" is not synonymous with "absolute." To claim that anything (including the concept "good") is objective does not imply its independence of all relations; but only that it does not depend solely upon any relation taken at random—that it depends on certain specifiable relations that can be publicly or interpersonally identified.

Concerning this point, it is interesting to note that the famous English philosopher, Bertrand Russell, was presumably led to reject more than he had to reject by Santayana's position. Russell declared, "When I was young, I agreed with G. E. Moore in believing in the objectivity of good and evil. Santayana's criticism, in a book called *Winds of Doctrine*, caused me to abandon this view, though I have never been able to be as bland and comfortable without it as he was."[119] Apparently Russell failed to distinguish between good as absolute and good as relational since Santayana, as indicated, only showed that good is relational or not absolute, not that it is subjective—i.e., not objective.

The claim that morality or moral beliefs and judgments are relative loses much of its sting and perhaps all of its controversiality when the concept of what is relative is pinned down to the concept of what is relational, and when it is realized that relational does not necessarily imply either arbitrariness or subjectivity. Thus to say that "stealing is wrong," for example, is indeed *related* to an interest in owning and keeping property; as so related, however, no inference logically follows that this interest must be arbitrary or subjective. The relational character of moral terms or concepts leaves open the possibility of marshaling evidence or giving reasons for moral judgments or beliefs; it neither precludes such evidence nor decides any moral issue one way or another.

In considering the conceptions of what has been termed "the good life for man" as presented by Santayana and Dewey, one must be impressed by the richness and extensiveness of their views. It can safely be said that these two philosophers developed the richest and best statements of this good life to be found in American naturalism. The acuteness and wisdom of many of their observations have been well recognized and appreciated, and such high regard I believe, continues. Unfortunately the emphasis that both Santayana and Dewey placed on careful, critical thinking about what constitutes the good life for man has been rarely pursued by other, more recent American moral philosophers. Moral philosophy in the larger sense practiced by Santayana and Dewey has markedly gone out of fashion in favor of a narrower, presumably more manageable endeavor to analyze ethical concepts and language. This narrower interest, though regrettable, is nevertheless understandable in view of the great difficulty or unmanageability that some philosophers perceive in the pursuit of moral philosophy in this larger sense. It is also understandable that moral philosophers have narrowed their efforts to the analysis of concepts and language, due to the genuine intricacy and complexity of problems involved, in the attempt to clarify the meanings and implications of moral terms or discourse. Nevertheless it is philosophically as well as culturally regrettable that few recent philosophers have ventured upon the study of ethics in a normative or larger sense. Santayana's early investigation of the life of reason and his later portrayal of the spiritual life place him more in the tradition of Plato, Aristotle, and ancient moral philosophers than in the framework of recent American thinkers. Santayana's detached view of man's possibilities for a spiritual life still within the confines of naturalism is either misunderstood or virtually neglected.[120]

One contemporary American philosopher has seen the importance of developing a naturalistic, even materialistic conception of spirit and its meaning for man's life. James K. Feibleman, a naturalist as well as a system builder in philosophy, like Santayana made an ontological distinction between essence and existence.[121] But Feibleman's ontological system departed from Santayana's approach in many important ways and was actually closer to Peirce's system of categories. Contrary to recent tendencies in ethics, Feibleman did not restrict his efforts to analysis of ethical concepts and language but addressed himself to normative questions and to ethics in the larger sense.[122]

Outstanding for his work in carrying forth many ideas of John Dewey, especially in the areas of social and political philosophy, is the previously mentioned contemporary naturalist Sidney Hook. Hook has not only sought to defend Dewey against many of his critics, but has gone far toward showing how a philosophy of critical naturalism can meet such problems as the threat of communism and nuclear war, desegregation, academic freedom, and many others.[123] In sharp contrast to Santayana, whose penchant for detachment and moral tolerance kept him aloof from taking sides and passing moral judgments on many social issues, Sidney Hook has emphatically spoken out, as did Dewey, on many important issues of the day.

Though Santayana lived in the United States for more than forty years and in Rome during World War II, he asserted:

> I was not bound to any type of society by ideal loyalty nor estranged from any by resentment. In my personal contacts I found them all tolerable when seen from the inside and not judged by some standard unintelligible to those born and bred under that influence. Personally I might have my instinctive preference; but speculatively and romantically I should have been glad to find an even greater diversity; and if one political tendency kindled my wrath, it was precisely the tendency of industrial liberalism to level down all civilizations to a single cheap and dreary pattern.[124]

Dewey, by contrast, was directly and personally involved in many social and political issues of his day. His active work on behalf of progressive education and his defense of liberalism and democratic institutions confirm the following observation made about him: "John Dewey is unquestionably the pre-eminent figure in American philosophy; no one has done more to keep alive the fundamental ideals of liberal civilization; and if there could be such an office as that of national philosopher, no one else could be properly mentioned for it."[125] In contrast to Santayana, Dewey considered the problems of democracy and the industrial age as challenges to build a better liberalism and free life for man. Dewey declared that "ideals, including that of a new and effective individuality, must themselves be framed out of the possibilities of existing conditions, even if these be the conditions that constitute a corporate and industrial age. The ideals take shape and gain a content as they operate in remaking conditions. We may, in order to have continuity of direction, plan a program of action in anticipation of occasions as they emerge."[126] Dewey's ethical naturalism, which placed such heavy emphasis on serious, intelligent attempts to remold the actual conditions of life, was clearly incompatible with Santayana's counteremphasis on the importance of detachment and spiritual or aesthetic contemplation for the good life. But perhaps this very incompatibility suggests that something extremely important and valuable for man may be gained through clear, emphatic statements of what these diverse life-styles are and can mean to us.

Chapter 7

Recent Directions in Ethical Analysis

The Emotive Theory: C. L. Stevenson

The forms of philosophical naturalism of Santayana and Dewey, as previously noted, tended to view the province of morality and moral philosophy rather broadly. All human concerns and problems that pertain to value judgments in relation to the whole of man's life fall within the realm of morality. Hence moral philosophy involves not only an epistemological analysis of moral terms and ideas, but also a normative study and interest in what constitutes the good life for man. Dewey's defense and analysis of democratic and experimentally determined ideals and Santayana's portrayal of a detached, disillusioned spiritual life are clearly forms of ethics in the normative sense. By 1952, the year they both died, moral philosophy in America had already turned to a pronounced if not exclusive interest in epistemological problems. For some years prior to World War II and continuing virtually to the present, the dominant interest among moral philosophers in the United States has been engaged with problems concerning the meaning and cognitive status of moral judgments and discourse. Although normative ethics has not entirely disappeared, it is true that what came to be called "meta-ethics" assumed center stage. Metaethics, as the term is used in recent philosophy, is not concerned with making or proposing moral judgments or standards of value for any good life; rather, it is concerned with clarifying and analyzing the terms, concepts, or ideas used in moral discourse. Hence metaethics is to be contrasted with normative ethics or ethics in the broader sense, which *is* concerned with propounding principles of virtue or guidelines for pursuit of the good life. This does not mean that metaethics is totally unconcerned with normative issues or normative ethics. As one recent influential proponent of metaethics stated, "There is a marked distinction between the conclusions that are drawn *about* normative ethics and those that are drawn *within* it."[1] Metaethics must indeed discuss and analyze moral judgments and norms; but discussion and analysis of moral judgments and principles is not the same as propounding or recommending any particular moral judgment or general standard of value. Metaethics can be viewed as the investigation preliminary to normative ethics or as an inquiry to replace the pursuit of a normative ethics. Considerable disagreement exists on this point. Some philosophers favor a narrow conception of metaethical analysis in which this type of investigation would actually replace normative ethics; while others would view normative ethics as still genuine and possible, but in definite need of preliminary clarification. Controversy and disagreement about the very province or scope of moral philosophy constitutes, in fact, a major problem of recent ethics in the United States.

The dominance of metaethics, the logical analysis of moral discourse, was greatly influenced by developments in British philosophy in this century. We have already noted that G. E. Moore's *Principia Ethica* (1903) exercised pronounced influence on British and American thinkers. Rather than Moore's normative views or conclusions, however, his major influence on other philosophers lies in his *method* of analyzing and isolating simple questions concerning the meanings of terms like "good" and "right"; and concerning how and whether certain ethical assertions can be substantiated or proven.

The work of the logical positivists, particuarly the views of A. J. Ayer, have also exercised a pronounced influence on American philosophy and ethical analysis. In 1936, Ayer published his famous *Language, Truth and Logic*, which defended philosophy as exclusively logical analysis and also presented a brief but emphatically stated emotive view of ethics. Ayer argued that it is not the business of philosophy to compete with science or to override its work by attempting to construct a speculative system or metaphysics. Any attempt to explain the ultimate nature of things by virtue of so-called first or transcendent principles is not so much false as cognitively meaningless. Cognitively significant or meaningful assertions are those that can conceivably be brought to a test or verified. To be cognitively significant or meaningful, a statement does not actually require verification, but it must, at least in principle, be capable of verification. Although Ayer and the logical positivists encountered a number of serious problems in attempting to formulate their principle of verifiability,[2] Ayer continued to adhere to this principle as well as to its implications for ethics. As a criterion of cognitive meaning, this principle essentially asserts that the meaning of a statement is the method of its verification. According to this criterion, ordinary factual statements are meaningful in terms of verification through their sense contents. The statements "people disapprove of murder" or "people approve of honesty" are empirical. Whether people approve or disapprove of these things can be tested by actual research. Statements such as "murder is a form of killing" or "lying is a form of dishonesty" are also cognitively meaningful, though they are not tested by reference to experience or sense contents; such statements are said to be either true by definition or by a logical consequence of definition. Once we discern the ordinary meaning or definition of murder, we can see that it is a tautology to say that "murder is a form of killing." Such a statement is said to be analytically true or true simply by virtue of analysis of what the statement implies, not by reference to any external empirical facts. But if we ask the meaning of the statement "murder is morally wrong"—and how we know whether this statement is true or false—we discover that no factual or logical way exists to determine the answers. By empirical means or observation we can determine that people disapprove of murder, or even that people consider murder to be wrong; but from the fact that people generally believe murder to be wrong, the conclusion does not follow that murder *is* wrong. We can observe all the facts involved with actual murders, as well as people's opinions and reactions, but such observation is not equivalent to any moral judgment stating that murder is wrong. The assertion that "murder is wrong," on the other hand, is not tautological or true simply as a consequence of our definition of murder. Thus the conclusion would apparently follow that moral judgments such as "murder is wrong" are capable neither of logical nor empirical verification and that moral judgments are thus neither true *a priori* nor *a posteriori*. But then they can be neither true nor false, since no other tests of truth and falsity exist except by means of logical analysis or empirical observation. One might think that they can be tested by empirical means, but that they are too complicated to be brought under any simple test or observation. But according to Ayer, in no way can such moral judgments be rendered even probably or possibly true in terms of future evidence. Further, more refined empirical testing can only reveal more facts. But the assertion of any moral judgment is not a set of facts, complex or simple—but a value. Ayer admitted that value judgments, including moral judgments, are meaningful in some sense; they have a kind of meaning that is not cognitive or descriptive, but is emotive. When someone asserts that "murder is wrong," he is simply expressing his feeling of disapproval for murder and perhaps trying to influence others to feel the same way. Thus moral judgments, although cognitively meaningless or unverifiable, are emotively meaningful and perfectly capable of having influence. It is one thing for a person to assert his feeling that murder is wrong, and quite another for him merely to express or evince this emotion. The statement that "one feels that murder is wrong" is an empirical assertion that can be tested; it is not a moral judgment. The judgments "murder is wrong" or "honesty is good" are value judgments. As such, they merely express approval and disapproval without stating this as an actual fact. This point is important because it implies that moral judgments are not even subjectively true, as some philosophers have claimed. Subjectivism and relativism in ethics, if taken to mean that moral judgments are true or valid for the persons who hold them but not necessarily for anyone else, are completely untenable, according to Ayer. If moral judgments have emotive meaning only and lack any cognitive or descriptive sense, they cannot be true or valid for any person or group.

One important consequence of this pure emotive theory is that ethical disputes cannot be settled by rational or cognitive means. If one person holds that abortion is always wrong and another disputes that sometimes it is morally good and right, this dispute can be settled in no verifiable way. Any appeal to empirical facts or logical argument, while perhaps psychologically persuasive or convincing, is not cognitively relevant to this kind of dispute. There is a difference between establishing a conclusion or agreement by the use of evidence and by simply influencing people or persuading them to believe something. The former is a purely cognitive or rational affair; the latter is either noncognitive or extracognitive (sometimes referred to as "conative"). Ayer held that no cognitive evidence is ever relevant to the rational settlement of any ethical dispute simply because no ethical dispute depends upon rational considerations—considerations for which any verification or evidence can be given. If the parties to any ethical dispute are simply expressing contrary emotions, it is pointless to expect any logically determined evidence to have any bearing on the situation. To feel a certain emotion is neither correct nor incorrect. Why do people believe that they possess evidence for their ethical beliefs? Why do people persist in believing that certain ethical judgments are correct while others are incorrect? These questions, according to Ayer, are not philosophical, but psychological or sociological questions. What causes people to believe what they do is an empirical question with no logical bearing on the validity or truth of what they believe.

Cognitively, from Ayer's analysis, moral judgments are pseudo-judgments—judgments that may appear to be valid or invalid, true or false—but actually they can have none of these characteristics. The conclusion does not at all follow from this analysis that people should stop making moral judgments or that such judgments should be considered unimportant. Ayer's theory recommends neither that one should nor should not make moral judgments, since the whole purpose of his analysis is metaethical, not normative. For Ayer, however, it is not the business of philosophy to make moral judgments or formulate normative principles. Philosophy has no special competence to make moral judgments since its sole purpose is to seek clarification of conceptual issues by logical analysis. Once the 'philosopher has discovered that moral judgments have only emotional meaning and that they cannot be proved or disproved, his work in ethics is, for all practical purposes, finished. The only possible work remaining for the philosopher would be refinement of this theory, answering of possible objections to it, and dispelling of misunderstandings. This is, in fact, what Ayer has done in the forty years that have elapsed since he developed his pure form of emotivism.

Discussion of Ayer's pure form of emotivism has been necessary in order to present a background for understanding recent developments in American ethics, especially C. L. Stevenson's more complex version of the Emotive Theory. In 1937, Stevenson published an important, subsequently famous article in *Mind* entitled "The Emotive Meaning of Ethical Terms." This was followed by other important essays on persuasive definitions and ethical disagreements,[3] as well as Stevenson's influential book *Ethics and Language* (1944), in which he made clear that his approach to ethics is restricted to metaethics. Stevenson asserted that "this book deals not with the whole of ethics, but with a narrowly specialized part of it. Its first object is to clarify the meaning of the ethical terms . . . Its second object is to characterize the general methods by which ethical judgments can be proved or supported."[4] Stevenson granted that the normative questions of ethics are the most important, but he also insisted that any careful metaethical analysis of moral discourse runs the risk of distortion or confusion if mixed with normative concerns. Consequently he chose to keep his own analysis free from proposing or promoting any particular moral code or normative principles, and he concentrated exclusively on metaethical issues.

Stevenson maintained that any adequate analysis of ethical terms must not only be relevant but must be completely relevant to the meaning of those terms. For example, it is not enough that an analysis of ethical terms point out that "good" in a moral sense is related to approval, interest, or desire. The question is whether any of these naturalistic terms are completely relevant to the meaning of "good" in a moral sense. Naturalistic theories or theories which attempt to explain ethical notions in terms of some kind of interest seem only to concern themselves with the descriptive meaning of moral terms while neglecting any dynamic or emotive meaning that those terms have. Moral terms appear to have a kind of imperative ring—to the effect that something termed "good" is not merely asserted as approved or desired by someone or even most people. The implication is also that one *should* approve, desire, or take an interest in what is judged to be good. Consequently Stevenson argued that any adequate analysis of moral terms such as "good" or "just" must satisfy three principal conditions: First, the analysis must make disagreement about whether something is "good" possible for people; second, moral terms must preserve a certain "magnetism," as Stevenson termed it, so that a person who apprehends something as "good" must "ipso facto acquire a stronger tendency to act in its favor than he otherwise would have had";[5] and third, "the 'goodness' of anything must not be verifiable solely by use of the scientific method."[6] What is implied by insistence on these three conditions? And why did Stevenson insist on them? The first condition implies that interest theories which define or analyze "good" in terms of some personal or group desire are to be ruled out, since both personal and group desires imply that significant, intelligent disagreement is impossible. If the declaration of something as "good" simply means that a particular person desires that thing, one person may say that something is good and another person say it is not—but both are only asserting different desires, and not contradicting one another. Also, to define "good" as *desired by my community,* is also excluded, for how could people from different communities disagree?"[7] The second requirement, that ethical terms must carry a certain magnetism, rules out those interest theories which imply that ethical terms are purely descriptive in meaning or have no imperative force in implying a person's tendency to act in favor of what he judges to be good. And the third requirement, that ethical terms cannot be verifiable solely in terms of scientific method, finally rules out all of the traditional interest theories. Stevenson cited G. E. Moore's objection to all interest theories: "No matter what set of scientifically knowable properties a thing may have (says Moore, in effect), you will find, on careful introspection, that it is an open question to ask whether anything having those properties is *good.*"[8] Stevenson claimed that traditional interest theories, including those based on the scientific method, hold that ethical statements are essentially descriptive of people's interests—that they only give us information about such interests. "(More accurately, ethical judgments are said to describe what the state of interests is, was, or will be, or to indicate what the state of interests *would* be under specified circumstances.) It is this emphasis on description, on information, which leads to their incomplete relevance."[9] Stevenson admitted, in contradistinction to Ayer's pure Emotive Theory, that every ethical judgment contains descriptive elements within it. But his main point was that "their major use is not to indicate facts but to *create an influence.* Instead of merely describing people's interests they *change* or *intensify* them. They *recommend* an interest in an object, rather than state that the interest already exists."[10] Stevenson distinguished two different purposes, which he called "descriptive" and "dynamic," in using language. "On the one hand we use words (as in science) to record, clarify, and communicate *beliefs.* On the other hand we use words to give vent to our feelings (interjections), or to create moods (poetry), or to incite people to actions or attitudes (oratory)."[11] An intimate relation exists between the dynamic use of language and emotive meaning. "The emotive meaning of a word is a tendency of a word, arising through the history of its usage, to produce (result from) *affective* responses in people. It is the immediate aura of feeling which hovers about a word."[12] Emotive meaning and the dynamic use of words are not identical, but emotive meaning is said to assist dynamic usage. But how does this concern the meaning of moral terms? Stevenson claimed that the word "good," for example, "has a laudatory emotive meaning that fits it for the dynamic use of suggesting favorable interest. But the sentence 'we like it' has no such emotive meaning."[13] Moral terms have an essential element of emotive meaning which assists or enables them to have a dynamic use. To neglect this emotive component is to distort or miss the distinctive meaning, which amounts to their imperative force, that moral terms actually have. Actually Stevenson apparently held that dynamic usage or imperative force is what really distinguishes moral discourse and that emotive meaning is only secondary in assisting this dynamic function. This raises the question as to whether emotive meaning is essential or always necessary in order to produce a morally imperative force. If we grant that moral terms and discourse not only have a merely descriptive function but also a dynamic, imperative one, it is important for us to know what kind of imperative function this is and whether emotive meaning fits this kind of imperative function. In other words, it is instructive for us to ask the same kind of question about emotive meaning that Stevenson asked about interest theories: i.e., the question of relevance. Is emotive meaning completely relevant to the distinctive dynamic usage or imperative force of moral judgments? There is no doubt that emotive meaning does assist the dynamic function of language; emotive language affects people and can create an influence. But this only means that it is causally relevant or effective in producing or tending to produce certain effects. It does not mean that emotive meaning is *morally* relevant in producing any appropriate *moral* consequence in an appropriate moral manner. Even to raise these questions, of course, entails the act of stepping out of the completely neutral or nonnormative metaethical framework within which Stevenson operated. From the outset, Stevenson assumed that to give a completely neutral or nonnormative analysis of the meaning of ethical terms and discourse is possible and even necessary. But what if this is *not* really possible? What if, in the attempt to render a nonnormative analysis of the admittedly normative content of ethical discourse, we inevitably end by distorting that discourse? Surely ethical discourse is not simply effective or influential, nor is it simply normative or prescriptive. One would like to say that moral discourse is or can be normatively effective. But this is not sufficiently precise, since it neither specifies what an effective *moral* norm is nor what is required for a specifically moral norm to be effective. Emotive meaning, while effective in producing certain results, is clearly not inherently normative; it is, in fact, irrelevant or even disturbing to the achievement of certain goals or aims. Emotive meaning is irrelevant and disturbing to the achievement of cognitive, legal, and scientific aims. In a court of law, certain emotional language is specifically disallowed, not only because it distorts cognition or understanding of the facts, but because it is believed to distort the proper legal evaluation of evidence. This suggests that, just as emotive meaning may be irrelevant and damaging to a proper understanding and evaluation of proper legal issues and discourse, emotive meaning may likewise be irrelevant and damaging to a proper understanding and evaluation of moral issues and discourse.

In order to pursue this question further in relation to Stevenson's theory, we must explore his conception of the nature of ethical disagreement, as well as his views on the concepts of cognition and validity as these relate to ethical discourse. Stevenson claimed that his own version of the emotive theory "finds much more to defend in the analyses of Carnap, Ayer, and the others, than it finds to attack. It seeks only to qualify their views—partly in the light of Dewey's—and to free them from any seeming cynicism. It hopes to make clear that 'emotive' need not itself have a derogatory emotive meaning. And in particular, it emphasizes the complex descriptive meaning that ethical judgments can have, in addition to their emotive meaning."[14] According to Ayer's pure Emotive Theory, as previously mentioned, ethical judgments are neither true nor false, but pseudojudgments; and consequently cannot be supported by factual reasons. Stevenson's more cautious, highly qualified theory is not completely noncogntive. His theory allows that ethical judgments can be regarded as true or false and "recognizes the possibility of giving factual reasons for evaluative conclusions."[15] For Stevenson, ethical judgments have both a descriptive element and an emotive one; to say that ethical judgments can be neither true nor false is consequently erroneous and misleading. "It is more accurate and illuminating to say that an ethical judgment *can* be true or false, but to point out that its descriptive truth may be insufficient to support its emotive repercussions."[16] Stevenson admitted that the emotive meaning of ethical judgments *per se* has no bearing on truth or falsity, with the possible exception that one may use the expression "that's true" to indicate agreement with someone else's attitude or feeling about a certain thing judged to be good.[17] If someone affirms it true that honesty is morally good and worthy of respect, this use of "true" implies no special sense of moral truth in contradistinction to scientific truth but merely indicates agreement in ethical attitudes. Insofar as an ethical judgment has descriptive meaning in reference to beliefs about facts, the notions of truth and validity have clear application. But "for the steps which go beyond these, and use beliefs in their turn to alter *attitudes*, questions about validity, in any helpful sense of the term, are irrelevant."[18]

Moral judgments are complex phenomena insofar as their descriptive meaning affects cognition and belief and their emotive meaning affects feelings and attitudes. For Stevenson, cognitive activities include believing, thinking, supposing, and presuming; whereas the more dynamic, emotional types of human activity involve approval, disapproval, persuasion, and alteration of attitudes. In order to view this difference more clearly, it is instructive for us to see what Stevenson meant by ethical disagreement—how this relates to cognitively describable beliefs on the one hand and emotively influential attitudes on the other. Arguments that arise in ethics usually involve disagreement concerning what the parties believe about the facts; and they also involve disagreement in attitude. These are two different kinds of disagreement. Disagreement in attitude involves an opposition of attitudes, both of which cannot be satisfied; whereas disagreement in belief involves an opposition of beliefs, both of which cannot be true. Disagreement in belief can exist without disagreement in attitude, as when two legislators approve of the same law but disagree about its long-term effects. Similarly, according to Stevenson, disagreement in attitude can exist without disagreement in belief, as when two people disagree on the merits of a certain novel but essentially agree in their beliefs about what it means and concerns. Though Stevenson admitted the difficulty of specifying exactly how attitudes and beliefs differ, some distinction between them can be noted in everyday practical affairs. That they are intimately related is partially indicated by the fact that they are causally efficacious in a reciprocal manner. Beliefs influence or cause us to change our attitudes, and attitudes themselves influence or cause us to change our beliefs. But this does not mean that a certain belief or change of belief will automatically produce a change in attitude or that a certain attitude is logically justified because it is based on a certain belief. If agreement in belief could automatically produce agreement in attitude, ethical disagreements could be settled by the scientific method. That this is not true was one of Stevenson's most important points. Stevenson held that disagreement in attitude is the most important feature of ethical arguments. For it is attitude rather than belief which determines the beliefs that are relevant to the issue and to any hope of settlement. "To be relevant, any belief that is introduced into the argument must be one that is likely to lead one side or the other to have a different attitude, and so reconcile disagreement in attitude."[19] Stevenson further argued that ethical disputes usually end when disagreement in attitude is removed, even though some disagreement in belief may remain. This indicates that attitudes and disagreement in attitude play a fundamental role in ethics and that any theory which ignores attitudes by attending exclusively to beliefs is certain to be inadequate. Stevenson admitted that attitudes are complex phenomena; hence they defy any simple definition or explanation. Attitudes are complex emotional states involving a complicated conjunction of dispositional properties.[20] Most importantly, attitudes involve a definite personal interest in approving or disapproving, favoring or disfavoring, a particular thing. Attitudes in this sense are not neutral, but are either for or against something. Attitudes do not merely express an impartial description of facts, but involve taking a definite interest in something; and they serve as a source of evaluation. To notice and describe a painting in terms of its colors and shapes in the form of a landscape, for example, is not to express an attitude toward that picture but merely to express a factual belief. But to judge a painting as a great work of art, worthy of placement in a museum for all to appreciate, is to make a value judgment that expresses one's attitude about that painting.

One thing to note about attitudes is that they are, in a certain sense, impervious to purely rational or scientific methods of influence. If a prospective juror in a law court, for example, is definitely biased in his attitudes toward certain people, that bias is sufficient to disqualify him as a juror. The court clearly assumes that even the presentation of strong factual evidence may be insufficient to overcome an original biased attitude. Likewise a judge is not permitted to officiate at the trial of one of his relatives; again, the assumption is that the judge's attitudes toward his family may or will prevent his impartial judgment. Stevenson did not deny that beliefs or factual evidence may influence people's attitudes; he even allowed that factual reasons may be given for our evaluative or ethical conclusions. But he did deny that such beliefs or evidence can "be judged by the rules of deductive or inductive logic. That is precluded by the very notion of reasons for approving, which fall outside logic simply because they require inferences (if I may call them that) from belief-expressing sentences to attitude-expressing sentences. The truth of the reasons themselves can be tested by logic, but their bearing on the evaluative conclusion is neither logical nor illogical. It is simply nonlogical."[21] Thus, although we may attempt to justify a moral judgment (i.e., attempt to find factual reasons to support it), such an activity "is itself an evaluative inquiry, and indeed, one that if fully developed would require us to take a stand on each and every evaluative issue that could ever confront us."[22] We cannot prove or justify a moral judgment by the use of reason or logic because a moral judgment requires us to adopt an attitude, take an interest, or express a preference—which are the very things that are nonlogical or nonrational. This is the heart of Stevenson's noncognitivism. His view, however, must not be misunderstood to imply that it is pointless or to no avail to give factual reasons or rational support to moral judgments. There is a point in trying to support evaluations with factual reasons, but this is not to try to *prove* them logically. The point rather is to make them more convincing or acceptable to others as well as to oneself. The purpose of holding values and taking serious interest in them is to make them influential. There would be no point in holding any value or moral judgment if it could never be accepted. Insofar as rational methods of supporting moral judgments can be persuasive, they will have a useful, serious function. Stevenson claimed that "whatever else the emotive conception of ethics may do it does not imply that evaluative decisions must be thoughtless."[23] Ethical judgments can be thoughtful insofar as thoughts or reasons are instrumental in influencing behavior or modifying the actions to be judged. This dynamic or influencing function of ethical judgments enables us to explain, according to Stevenson, why ethical judgments only apply to avoidable matters. Unavoidable matters do not come under the purview of ethical judgment simply because they cannot be changed or influenced. To blame or praise a person for an unavoidable action would be pointless and senseless, for then praise and blame would only be labels. If ethical judgments are regarded as kinds of performances instead of mere descriptions, they can serve such purposes as prevention and reformation. "An adverse ethical judgment is a kind of blame."[24] When we say that "murder is wrong," our purpose is not to describe murder but to strongly oppose it and prevent its occurrence. To achieve this aim, the use of persuasive methods assisted by emotive meaning is then quite appropriate, for such methods can be effective where purely cognitive or rational methods may entirely fail.

Stevenson's theory was, of course, stated in much greater detail than is outlined here. This presentation has tried to state the substance of his views with a fair indication of his many qualifications. His influence on other American and British thinkers has been quite extensive, but too often, unfortunately, he has been indiscriminately grouped with other emotivists whose views he did not share. It is regrettable that Stevenson, in his major work *Ethics and Language*, did not place greater emphasis on distinguishing his own views from those of other emotivists. Oddly, Stevenson asserted that he found much more to defend than to attack in the analyses of Ayer and others. A careful reading of Stevenson seems to indicate just the opposite. Regrettably he did not, in fact, subject Ayer's pure Emotive Theory to thorough and direct criticism; for, although Stevenson's departures from Ayer were subtle, they were nevertheless major. Ayer not only left many essential points of his emotivism unanalyzed—which, in his own theory, Stevenson did not—but Ayer actually exaggerated or overstated the noncognitive status of moral judgments—whereas Stevenson was much more careful.

Any appraisal of Stevenson's work must admit that he helped cause a change, even a revolution, in ethical theory by exhibiting the importance of metaethics or a careful study of the language of morals. This does not mean that Stevenson proved metaethics to be the only kind of authentic moral philosophy or that metaethics is independent of normative ethics. The question of the relation between metaethics and normative ethics is a much disputed issue in recent moral philosophy. One recent author claims that "the thesis that metaethics is not itself ethically partial was naive and hardly alive to the complexity of ethical disputes."[25] In this regard, one cannot easily see how a meaningful ethical or linguistic analysis of moral terms is possible without first deciding how the concepts of what is ethical or moral are to be construed. How can we know that we are actually analyzing *moral* judgments or *ethical* terms, rather than merely investigating *what are called* or commonly believed to be *ethical* terms and *moral* judgments? We cannot define the terms "moral" or "ethical" simply on the basis of usage, since usage is often conflicting. Apparently any ethical analysis must face the seemingly normative question at the outset of its own inquiry: how *should* the terms "moral" and "ethical" be construed? Consequently it is understandable why the problem of what can be identified as a moral matter (i.e., what does "moral" as opposed to "nonmoral" mean?) has loomed as a major issue in recent philosophy.

One problem regarding Stevenson's theory concerns its relation to ethical naturalism. Apparently Stevenson viewed naturalistic theories in rather narrow terms and was thus not alive to the emotive, noncognitive possibilities or varieties within naturalism. He asserted: "Naturalistic theories, for instance, identify an ethical judgment with some sort of scientific statement, and so make normative ethics a branch of science."[26] This remark may be true of Dewey and some varieties of ethical naturalism, but it is not true of Santayana nor of other recent theories including that of Paul Edwards.[27] Santayana's analysis of ethical terms and judgments was not as detailed as Stevenson's, but there can be no doubt that Santayana sought to defend a noncognitive, naturalistic analysis. A number of interesting similarities exist, in fact, between Santayana's analysis (especially as found in his *Hypostatic Ethics* and *Moral Truth*) and Stevenson's, which indicate that Santayana's approach may be much closer to Stevenson's analysis than to Dewey's. Santayana explicitly denied that moral judgments can be identified with scientific or descriptive statements insofar as they are based on preferences we feel rather than on opinions or beliefs capable of logical or empirical proof. Santayana also admitted that moral judgments are usually hybrid in the sense that they do contain descriptive content as well as hortatory or prescriptive elements. Like Stevenson, Santayana emphasized the primacy of the expressive or emotive side of ethical judgments in exerting influence over any cognitive or descriptive components. An important difference between their analyses, however, is that Santayana insisted on ethical relativism, whereas Stevenson apparently repudiated any form of relativism as contained in, or implied by, his Emotive Theory. Because Santayana connected ethical relativism with an attitude of tolerance toward other people's moral views, he was less interested in any persuasive function of moral discourse, which Stevenson deemed important and essential.

This raises an important point about Stevenson's insistence that the major use of ethical language is to create an influence or to change or intensify an interest. In this connection Stevenson apparently failed to distinguish moral discourse adequately from political, legal, or other forms of persuasive argument and rhetoric. Moral judgments can, no doubt, be used to create an influence or to change or intensify someone's attitude. But this does not demonstrate the major use of moral judgments or show that this use is characteristically a moral one. The term "major use" is ambiguous, at least in the sense that it means either (1) most frequent use, or (2) most important or characteristic use. Sense (1) can be empirically determined, in theory at least, by some kind of count, but sense (2) cannot be determined in this way. Even if moral judgments are most often used to create an influence (which I do not think is empirically true), this does not establish that such use is their only, or most important and characteristic, one. Certainly it makes sense to ask how a moral judgment can or should be used simply as a moral judgment or for moral purposes. But this is not a simple question to be answered by a poll. We cannot begin to research how moral judgments can be used to achieve any moral purpose unless we know what a moral purpose is. Moral judgments can be used to create an influence that is either nonmoral or immoral. Clearly we would have to know the distinctions between moral as opposed to nonmoral purpose, as well as between moral as opposed to immoral purpose. Certainly not all influences are morally significant or good. An additional point is that one does not have to make a moral judgment in order to create an influence or to change or intensify people's attitudes. One would like to say that the major use of moral judgments, in the sense of their most important and characteristic function, is the assessment or evaluation of a situation in terms of some moral standard or point of view. After all, a moral judgment is a judgment and therefore involves some mental act of assessment or evaluation. But no mental act of assessment could be identified as a moral judgment without some use of a presumed moral norm or standard. One can, of course, always debate and question any moral standards that are used; but the point that a moral standard of some kind is needed in order for us to make and identify a moral judgment is *not* debatable. Clearly an attitude or interest is not itself a moral norm or standard, although certain attitudes or interests may be intimately connected with a moral point of view. One may claim to have a moral attitude about a certain thing, but not unless that attitude involves some moral norm or standard. But one can also claim to have a neutral or noncommittal attitude toward a certain thing, which means that one's attitudes are not always pro or con expressions of evaluation. Two people can differ in their attitudes toward abortion, for example; where one person is solidly against it and the other person is neutral or noncommittal. Here the disagreement concerns whether abortion can or should be judged on moral grounds at all. This differs from a dispute in which the two parties agree that an action or situation should be judged on moral grounds but disagree on what those grounds are. Thus moral disagreements exist on several different levels, but never is the disagreement simply one of attitude; it always presumes the use of moral norms of some kind.

Stevenson assumed that disagreement in attitude may exist without any disagreement in belief. But this is certainly not obvious. Stevenson admitted that "perhaps every attitude must be accompanied by some belief about its object; but the beliefs which attend opposed attitudes need not be incompatible."[28] Many beliefs exist that can attend opposed attitudes, but one cannot easily see how all of them can be compatible with opposite attitudes. Some beliefs are not particularly relevant to certain attitudes; other beliefs are. A belief may quite possibly influence one's attitude or judgment, even though that belief is logically irrelevant to that attitude or judgment. Stevenson only allows causal relevance between attitudes and beliefs. Speaking of the relation between a man's value judgment and the reasons given in support of that judgment, Stevenson declared, "His reasons do not 'entail' his expression of approval, of course, or make it 'probable.' An expression of attitude cannot stand in these logical relationships to descriptive statements but only in causal relationships."[29] A causal relationship is clearly not normative, but the relation between a moral attitude or judgment and the reasons given for that judgment are normative. If the reasons given for a moral attitude or judgment have merely causal relevance but no logical relevance to that moral judgment, it is hard to see how those reasons could serve as *moral* ones or be *morally* relevant to the judgment made. Logical relevance does not mean conclusive evidence or strict deductive proof. Logical relevance means that a belief or idea is not irrelevant to a supposed conclusion but can furnish *some* evidential support for it. Any particular belief or reason for a moral judgment or attitude can always be specifically questioned as to how well or poorly it furnishes evidential support. But to reject any and all beliefs as candidates for evidential support is purely arbitrary and indiscriminating. No belief or reason can possibly have any logical relevance to the support of a moral judgment apart from the presumption of moral norms. No belief can be relevant in itself, but only in relation to certain established standards. Norms or standards can, of course, be questioned in terms of their relevance or adequacy to serve as moral principles. But a question or dispute about norms is on a different level than a dispute about a particular moral judgment or about the relevance of reasons for a particular moral judgment.

One cannot easily see how attitudes or interests divorced from any possible moral norms could have any moral significance. But attitudes, judgments, and interests that are connected with some moral norm can come into logical relationship with beliefs or reasons that may be used to support those attitudes, judgments, or interests. Stevenson claimed that when an ethical disagreement or argument involves attitudes, "disagreement in attitude determines what beliefs are *relevant* to the argument. . . . To be relevant, any belief that is introduced into the argument must be one that is likely to lead one side or the other to have a different attitude, and so reconcile disagreement in attitude."[30] Here again Stevenson interprets relevance as causal, as that which can have an influence. But this clearly misses the point that moral disagreements are not simply contests or struggles for power and gaining acceptance; they are also concerned with the integrity of whatever is believed or accepted. In certain kinds of dispute, the question as to whether an agreed-upon conclusion violates any principle of integrity or any moral principle may not arise. But a so-called moral dispute that construed the relevance of any introduced belief into the argument only in terms of its likelihood to lead either side toward a different attitude, thus to reconcile disagreement in attitude, would clearly have failed as a moral dispute—since it lacks any concern for the moral integrity or quality of what is believed or accepted. One can agree with Stevenson that no easy, guaranteed method of solving moral disagreements exists; but on the other hand, no agreement or disagreement would be particularly moral in its basic character if it paid no heed to the moral integrity or quality of what is accepted or believed. It is, of course, pertinent to ask: What is the point of caring whether an agreement or reconciliation of attitudes possesses any integrity? Is it not sufficient that an agreement in attitude has been achieved? The only answer is that we can indeed reconcile attitudes without resolving any moral issue at all; but if moral attitudes themselves are the matters of disagreement, then the moral integrity or rightness of any resolution to the disagreement becomes relevant simply because this is what moral attitudes are all about. Here we can further agree with Stevenson that no descriptive facts are sufficient to establish any moral attitude as good or right. Stevenson is clearly correct in holding that moral judgments are not simply descriptive or scientific. But certainly some moral attitudes are dogmatic, and some are better supported by reasons than others. When attitudes remain dogmatic or unsupported by reasons, there is no room for any moral resolution of a dispute. It would seem that the sense in which any attitudes, or feelings of approval and disapproval have any relevance to morals is only insofar as they are subject to responsible or intelligent control. To the extent that any attitude, emotion, or feeling remains impervious to possible criticism and control, it remains nonmoral or amoral. One recent critic of Stevenson's theory makes the following remark in this regard: "The attempt, as, for example, in Stevenson, to combine emotivism and imperativism must fail simply because of the impropriety of directing or commanding anyone to acquire attitudes, emotions, tastes, feelings, and the like, which cannot be deliberately adopted and which, nevertheless, may be appraised."[31] Similarly J. O. Urmson, in his book *The Emotive Theory of Ethics* (1968), criticized Stevenson's whole conception of emotive meaning and attitudes. Urmson asserted,

"When one wishes to change a person's evaluative attitude one does not wish to change only, or most importantly, his emotions, but rather the whole pattern of his thinking and behavior."[32] Urmson also criticized Stevenson's refusal to allow any distinction between logically relevant and irrelevant considerations in relation to moral evaluation, as well as between valid and invalid arguments in any evaluation. Urmson thought Stevenson guilty of "the fundamental error of the definition of evaluative force in purely causal terms."[33] To support his criticism Urmson insisted that it is necessary to regard moral judgments or evaluations in relation to standards or norms; and Urmson believed it important to distinguish between *setting* and *using* standards, a distinction which Stevenson neglected. Urmson claimed that this distinction has important implications concerning the possibility of valid and invalid arguments for moral judgments. He asserted, "Where there are no standards of merit it is no doubt idle to distinguish between valid and invalid grounds for a preference. But when we are using standards, which have been agreed as a result of the success of standard-setting proposals, the case is different."[34] Stevenson's views—that no fact is logically more relevant than any other fact to a disagreement in attitude and that no distinction can exist between valid and invalid arguments in support of evaluations—may, according to Urmson, be true if applied to standard-setting or when no standards are set at all, but they are not necessarily true and may even be clearly false when the use of existing standards is involved.

A recent American philosopher, Paul Edwards, has sought to develop and defend a metaethical analysis that combines naturalism with emotivism. In his book *The Logic of Moral Discourse* (1955), Edwards declared, "My own view, rejecting intuitionism and all forms of subjectivism, combines features of objective naturalism with features of emotive theories."[35] When we judge or claim that a person or action is good, according to Edwards, our approval of certain objective qualities of that person or action is what determines our moral judgment. But "in saying that the person or the action is good one refers to the qualities and not to the approval. This is the most important point of my whole treatise."[36] Edwards's concession to, or agreement with, emotivism is contained in his statement that the referent of a moral judgment is *determined* by the speaker's attitude; but Edwards's concession to, or agreement with, naturalism lies in his claim that the referent of a moral judgment is not the speaker's attitude but the natural facts or qualities of the action or situation that is presented for approval. Edwards departed from Stevenson's Emotive Theory on a number of important points. For one, he argued that it is possible for one to give reasons for moral judgments that go beyond mere causal factors. For another, he argued that moral disputes can be settled in a number of ways, not "simply if both parties *have come to hold the same view*, whether that view has been proven or not."[37] While Edwards wanted to claim that moral judgments do have emotive or expressive meaning, their descriptive or referential meaning is not incidental to the moral character of the judgment. "When I say 'X. Y. is a good person,' for instance, my sentence would count as a moral judgment and the word 'good' in it as an ethical predicate not only because of its expressive, but also because of its referential meaning. The sentence would be considered 'moral' *both* because it expresses my approval and also because I am referring to such qualities as her kindness, gentleness, and lack of envy and not to her figure, income, or excellence in ping-pong."[38]

Problems concerning the objectivity and cognitive status of moral judgments and all normative discourse have loomed large in recent moral philosophy in the United States. Perhaps the foremost American exponent of the objectivity of moral judgments and the full cognitive status of value judgments since World War II has been Clarence Irving Lewis. In sharp opposition to the Emotive Theory and noncognitive approaches to ethics, Lewis insisted that "no manner of behavior wholly untouched by thinking could be right or wrong; and it is only such thinking as is bent upon the determination of fact and has the intent of some objective reference which is subject to normative assessment."[39] We will examine Lewis's contributions to these problems in the next section.

Rational Imperatives in Ethics: C. I. Lewis

Having studied under James, Royce, and Santayana, Clarence Irving Lewis (1883-1964) received his doctorate in philosophy at Harvard in 1910. Lewis developed an early interest in logic under the influence of Royce, and his first major publication was *A Survey of Symbolic Logic* (1918). He continued his logical studies, developing his own concept of strict implication. In 1929 he published his first major work in epistemology, *Mind and the World-Order: Outline of a Theory of Knowledge*. But not until 1946 did he publish the major formulation of his theory of value based on his epistemological studies, *An Analysis of Knowledge and Valuation*. This was followed by his venture into the fundamental questions of ethics, *The Ground and Nature of the Right* (1955), and *Our Social Inheritance* (1957). Five years after Lewis's death, a collection of his papers bearing on his further studies in ethics was published under the title *Values and Imperatives: Studies in Ethics* (1969). Lewis, in his basic philosophic framework, sought to combine the best elements of logical empiricism with those of pragmatism and naturalism. While he sharply distinguished the analytic truths of logic from the synthetic truths of experience, he insisted that these two fundamentally different kinds of verifiable knowledge are both related to action and ultimately depend upon a pragmatic justification. For Lewis, knowledge, action, and evaluation were intimately related. With the pragmatists, he insisted "The primary and pervasive significance of knowledge lies in its guidance of action: knowing is for the sake of doing."[40] But he further insisted that action itself is grounded in evaluation. "For a being which did not assign comparative values, deliberate action would be pointless; and for one which did not know, it would be impossible. Conversely, only an active being could have knowledge, and only such a being could assign values to anything beyond his own feelings.'[41] Philosophy, in Lewis's view, was fundamentally criticism or critique. It is not so much concerned with the psychological description of the mental states of knowing, deciding, and evaluation as with an analysis or critique of their cognitive claims, the assessment of their validity, and the finding of criteria by which any knowledge or value claims can be justified. In his last reply to his critics, Lewis asserted, "The best brief characterization of my ethical position . . . is that I am a naturalist with respect to the good but a rationalist with respect to the right."[42] Lewis insisted that questions of evaluation, of what is good, must be distinguished from questions of ethics, of what is right. "Determination of values is essential for, and must be antecedent to, any concrete application of the principles of ethics; but value determinations are not sufficient by themselves for any solution of ethical problems, in general or in particular. . . . Valuation is always a matter of empirical knowledge. But what is right and what is just can never be determined by empirical facts alone."[43]

Important to note in this regard is that Stevenson's Emotive Theory of ethics made no fundamental distinction between the terms "good" and "right." Stevenson declared, "Certain theorists are accustomed to make a sharp distinction between 'good' and 'right,' as though the terms involved quite disparate problems of analysis. The present writer can find little ground for such a distinction, either in common usage or elsewhere. There are slight emotive differences, and different ranges of ambiguity for the more specific senses; but that is true of any pair of ethical terms."[44] Lewis's whole theory of ethics turned upon his careful distinction, as well as the relationship he drew, between the notions of right and good. First, Lewis insisted on distinguishing the terms "right" and "good" in the sense that "the achievement of the good is desirable but conformity to the right is imperative. And second, nothing is strictly right or wrong except some possible activity or the manner of it, whereas in an equally strict sense anything under the sun may be good or bad."[45] The terms "good" and "right," of course, apply to things beyond the province of ethics or moral concerns. But despite this broad application of both terms, "good" has a wider sense than "right" since the latter term applies only to things subject to deliberation or things which lie within our responsible control. Any activity can be judged in terms of right and wrong if that activity can be brought under some kind of rational control, i.e., if it can be brought under some rule and if a judgment can be made concerning some value or goodness of the consequences of that action. Thoughts or beliefs, as mental activities, can only be characterized as right or wrong in conjunction with certain rules of right thinking or believing in relation to certain desirable ends or results. It is right to believe that $8 + 4 = 12$ or that water is composed of two parts hydrogen and one part oxygen because these ideas are governed by objective rules that can be tested. A belief or thought can only be shown wrong insofar as it contravenes an established rule or does not demonstrably lead to the desired results. "Right" and "wrong" are normative terms no less in logic and ethics than in the everyday practical affairs of people. There are right and wrong ways to build a house, to secure one's health or happiness, to reason toward a conclusion, or to behave in relation to other humans. Corresponding to each of these activities, Lewis claimed, are certain rational directives or imperatives which indicate (1) what is technically right or wrong, (2) what is prudentially right or wrong, (3) what is logically right or wrong, and (4) what is morally right or wrong. These four basic classes of rational imperatives, according to Lewis, presume that actions can be responsibly controlled and that intelligent criticism and judgment, in terms of right and wrong, apply.

Technical rightness is generally concerned with how we should proceed to achieve an already assumed or desired end. Technical rightness involves rightness of a subordinate kind, since the goal is some instrumental good—something good not in itself but for the sake of something else. To cleanse a wound and kill its infection by strong, even painful medicine, for example, may be technically right, simply because this technique has proven to be the most effective and thorough. If our desired end is to heal a certain wound effectively, certain medical techniques are objectively right or valid toward achieving this end, and other methods are objectively wrong. Thus judgments of technical rightness can be both normative and objective. According to Lewis, "To determine what is objectively right to do, we must not only utilize properly all the relevant evidence open to us in forecasting the probable consequences of the doing, but we must also utilize it *cogently*."[46] An action that is only subjectively right is one in which the agent thinks or believes that its results will be the ones desired but lacks the proper evidence or cogency for his belief.

Prudential rightness is concerned not with technical or instrumental ends or values, but with the attainment of happiness or well-being. Technical rightness implies imperatives or rules of action that are *hypothetical* in the sense that *if* we desire certain ends, then the use of certain means is right for the achievement of those ends. If one wants to build a two-story house, technically one should dig the foundation first. But it is not imperative that one should build a two-story house. In the matter of choosing methods for securing or achieving happiness or well-being, however, it is misleading, according to Lewis, for us to say that *if* we want to attain happiness it is prudent to adopt this or that means. What is misleading is the idea that the desire for happiness is purely hypothetical or episodic, when in fact this desire is "both perennial and universal to humankind. Any hypothetical imperative, 'If you want X, do A,' if valid in any sense at all, becomes an *unqualified* imperative when you *do* want X—and hence the unqualified imperative to prudence when you *do* want to be happy, which is always the case."[47] Always debatable and open to criticism, of course, are the choices of particular means or methods used to attain the end of happiness. But whether or not to attain or try to attain the end of happiness is really not a debatable question for mankind.

Logical rightness, in terms of thinking or believing, is already present or involved in any rational form of technical or prudential imperatives. We cannot decide what to do in any technical or prudential sense without assuming and using certain objective principles of thinking and believing that are subject to logical tests of validity or cogency. "There is logical rightness of conclusions validly related to their premises, and logical wrongness of fallacious inference. There is rightness or wrongness of belief by reference to evidence given or available."[48] The goal of logical thinking is arrival at objectively correct or sound conclusions on the basis of sufficient evidence. Although particular conclusions are always open to question and criticism in terms of their premises and the rules of inference by which they are obtained, logical rightness or correctness is such a fundamental ingredient of rationality that denying or contravening it is impossible without some kind of contradiction. Man can certainly fall into error and become subject to illogicality, but to suppose that illogicality or the desire to be illogical can be meaningfully or deliberately cultivated makes no sense. Consequently the general suggestion that the need or imperative to cultivate logical rightness or correctness in our thinking is merely a hypothetical or episodic imperative would be misleading. What does make sense, according to Lewis, is to say that we have a categorical need or obligation to make our thinking as logically sound as possible. While denial of any categorical imperative as logical is not logically inconsistent, to adopt a skeptical attitude toward being logical is pragmatically inconsistent. The person who asserts that he does not care whether his thoughts or beliefs are logical or not is simply undermining his own thinking. One who denies any need to be rational or logical in the way he forms his ideas must face or accept the irrational consequences of such a denial. To deny any need for consistency and objectivity in one's thinking entails thoughts which defeat their own purposes or which rebound in their own confusion or unintelligibility.

Moral rightness is related to technical, prudential, and logical rightness, but is not identical with them. Moral actions, insofar as they are subject to deliberation and claim to be rational, objective, and based on criticizable rules or norms, can certainly be characterized in terms of right and wrong. To say that one has a moral obligation to be honest, or that honesty as a general policy is morally right and dishonesty is wrong makes perfectly good sense. Conflicts can, of course, arise between what is technically or prudentially right and what is morally right, although one cannot easily see how any conflict between logical and moral rightness *per se* can exist. Technical, prudential, and moral imperatives or directives pertain directly to overt action in the physical world and toward other human beings. Logical imperatives concerned with how and what we should think or infer are only indirectly involved with action in either a physical or social setting. Technical rightness is just as much concerned with efficient ways to eliminate or destroy things as with making or building anything. In war, nations and armies are preoccupied with finding the most efficient ways of killing or destroying one another. Hence if one's goal is to destroy an entire city, certain methods can be demonstrated better than others, in a technical sense of accomplishing this particular aim. Just because they are technically right, however, certainly does not mean that any such methods of wholesale destruction are morally right. Moral rightness, according to Lewis, never simply reduces to efficiency, because moral aims are universal and overriding; they cannot be satisfied at the expense of some people for the benefit of others. Even prudential claims and interests, which more nearly coincide with moral aims or ends, can conflict with what is morally right or sound. It is prudent, for example, for one to be careful and guard one's own safety or security—but when one can offer help to people in trouble, denial of such help on the ground of interference with one's own safety or well-being would not be morally right. Thus "the aim of prudence can be and should be overruled by that of justice when the two dictates are incompatible."[49] This does not mean, according to Lewis, that all prudential imperatives are simply abandoned whenever justice or moral rightness takes precedence over prudence. Prudence does not always conflict with justice; in one sense, justice even requires or presupposes prudence. "Without individual interests there could be no group or social interests, and without the validity of self-interest, no validity of any social interest. . . . If justice requires giving weight to the interest of another equally as to one's own, that equation is also reversible and requires that one's own interest be weighed equally with that of any other."[50]

Lewis claimed that man's nature, specifically his rationality, involves the clear recognition and use of moral, prudential, technical, and logical imperatives. If man either could not recognize imperatives or use them in living his life, he would not, according to Lewis, be fully rational. Logicality and prudence involve more than the mere knowledge of what to think or do; they also require a commitment or willingness to draw cogent conclusions or perform worthwhile deeds. Similarly morality involves more than the simple knowledge of what justice requires; it requires a rational commitment to fulfill objective moral obligations to the best of our ability. Therefore it is empirically true that man does acknowledge and live by rational imperatives on some occasions. But it is equally true that man also occasionally fails to heed or practice imperatives which nevertheless are valid and objectively binding. This discrepancy between what man does and what he ought to do underscores the very need and meaning for having any imperatives at all. If man always did what he ought to do, imperatives would have no meaning. It makes no logical sense to say that one ought to be just or fair, if there is no chance for one to fail to do so.

We must, however, confront another question: how to explain or justify the validity of moral imperatives and the validity of the claim that they override or take precedence over all other imperatives. It would seem that the argument that man ought to follow moral imperatives because he is able to do so, takes an interest in doing so, or subjectively believes it right to do so is plainly a fallacy. If moral obligations are objectively valid, they cannot be grounded in any subjective manner. If such a thing exists as an objective obligation to keep promises, this obligation cannot be grounded in the fact that one is able to keep promises, takes an interest in keeping them, or believes it right to do so. It would seem, however, that establishing the validity of moral imperatives on the basis of objective facts or any empirical evidence is also impossible. The argument that it is morally obligatory or right for one to keep promises because such behavior will lead to good or satisfying consequences which can be objectively tested depends on the illicit leap or inference from "is" to "ought." No argument is valid that attempts to derive a conclusion about what "ought to be" from premises that contain no reference to "ought." For this reason, Lewis held that "what is right and what is just, can never be determined by empirical facts alone."[51] It is important to note that, while Lewis believed objectively determined facts to be relevant to the validity of any moral imperative, he pointed out that they are not in themselves sufficient. Two things needed to explain or validate the rightness of any moral action are (1) rules or directives of right conduct, and (2) objective value that can be found as a result of performing that action. If the keeping of promises is generally right or an obligation in a moral sense, a general rule or principle must exist for this, in addition to empirical evidence that some objective value can be found as a consequence of keeping promises in accordance with that moral rule.

Thus, in order to substantiate his view that moral obligations of any kind are right or have objective validity, Lewis must show (1) that objective rules or principles lie behind moral imperatives, and (2) that moral imperatives lead to or imply empirically verifiable judgments of value. He must, in other words, show that general moral rules or principles exist from which more specific imperatives can be said to follow; and that valid moral obligations have content to them in the achievement of factually verifiable good consequences, without which moral obligations would be purely formal and empty. Thus Lewis clearly departed from Kant, Royce, and any purely *a priori*, formal attempt to ground moral values or imperatives. In this sense his theory has an empirical side and is naturalistic. Moral rightness cannot be grounded simply in the formal sense of following the right rules; for if those rules have no tangible bearing on the production of empirically testable good consequences, they are empty of any real moral value. If promise keeping is morally right, the consequences of keeping promises must be observably good or worthwhile. The question is: Can it be shown that value judgments of what is said to be good are empirically testable?

Lewis attempted to show this by correlating what he identified as the three main types of value predication with the three main types of empirical statements. First are expressive statements of value qualities found in direct experience. To judge that a certain food tastes good or that some presented material looks or feels good would exemplify this point. Statements of immediate value correspond to empirical statements of apprehensions of colors, sounds, or textures. His point was that, just as we directly and empirically experience the qualities red, blue, hardness, or softness, so also we directly and empirically experience qualities of value—what is good, bad, nice, or unpleasant. Lewis claimed that "without the experience of felt value and disvalue, evaluations in general would have no meaning."[52] For Lewis expressive statements of immediately found or apparent value do not involve apprehensions which are really evaluations or judgments. They simply report what is given and do not make any critical judgment of appraisal, and are not classified by Lewis as forms of knowledge. Such expressive statements of immediate value are only verifiable in the senses that (1) they are self-verifying for the person who makes them, and (2) they are not subject to error except in the trivial sense of some misuse of language. But Lewis's claim that immediate values can be given as empirical facts and involve no judgments or knowledge is problematic. This is not to deny that no distinction between what is given and not given (but rather judged or interpreted) can be made in some sense, the question is whether this distinction can be made in precisely the way that Lewis sought to make it.

Besides expressive statements of value qualities as immediately experienced, there are value statements called "terminating judgments" and "nonterminating judgments." Both of these judgments involve possible knowledge. Evaluations in the form of terminating judgments signify predictions of actual value qualities under specified conditions. If I eat a certain food, for example, I will enjoy it. Such judgments are empirically verifiable and are comparable to ordinary empirical predictions or terminating judgments, e.g., if I turn on a radio, I will hear certain sounds. Nonterminating judgments assert that a certain object or situation has an objective property of goodness or value. Evaluations in this form are the most important and complex type of value judgment that we can make. To assert that a certain picture is good or that a hammer is good for driving nails is to make a claim about objective facts in the sense of attributing some extrinsic value to the object. Lewis held that no objectively existing thing has intrinsic value, but that *"all values in objects are extrinsic only.*"[53] Intrinsic value, that which is good in itself, can only be located in some directly apprehended experience; whereas the value of any object or objective situation is extrinsic in the sense that the object may lead toward or provide the occasion of some direct apprehension of value. Thus Lewis divided extrinsic or objective value judgments into those which claim inherent value and those which involve instrumental value. Inherent values of some object are those values disclosed by the experience of that object itself. To claim that a person has inherent value means that certain value qualities can be found in one's experience of, or acquaintance with, that person himself. Instrumental value attributed to some object signifies something beyond the object itself or some use to which that object can be put. A person may be said to have instrumental value, for example, in the sense that he may be a lawyer or doctor whose services can be utilized by other people. The claim that judgments of inherent or instrumental value are non-terminating judgments means that for testing or certifying these judgments, an indefinite series of terminating judgments is needed. To claim that a hammer is good for driving nails implies that if any number of people on any number of occasions seek to use a hammer for this purpose, they will find that a hammer indeed has this instrumental value. Such judgments are called nonterminating because there is no theoretical limit to the number of terminating judgments or predictions involved in the objective claim that a thing has inherent or instrumental value. In the moral sphere, to say that an individual is a good man or that honesty and justice are morally good is to make nonterminating judgments that can never be conclusively verified; such judgments can only be rendered more highly probable or better supported by factual evidence. In this sense Lewis agreed with naturalists or pragmatists such as Dewey and James that moral judgments can never be absolutely final or certain.

Where Lewis seems to depart from other naturalists and pragmatists, however, was in his insistence on the need for rational, even *a priori* rules or principles to serve as a ground for the moral rightness of any action or the imperative force of any valid moral directive. For Lewis, the statement that just actions are morally right and imperative—that they take precedence as morally obligatory actions over prudence or other values—cannot be explained or validated on empirical grounds alone. Stevenson, it will be remembered, had complained that Dewey's ethics and any naturalistic interest theory of values failed to account for the imperative force of moral judgments. Stevenson argued that this was the result of failure to consider seriously the emotive meaning in ethical discourse. Lewis was clearly opposed to any Emotive Theory of ethics concerning the analysis and cognitive status of the concepts "good" and "right." Lewis held that judgments of what is good or evaluations generally are definitely forms of empirical knowledge. The view that value judgments are not factual statements but merely expressions of emotion, thus neither true nor false, Lewis considered as "one of the strangest aberrations ever to visit the mind of man. The denial to value-apprehensions in general of the character of truth or falsity and of knowledge, would imply both moral and practical cynicism. It would invalidate all action; because action becomes pointless unless there can be some measure of assurance of a valuable result which it may realize."[54] Lewis insisted that human life "can prosper only if there are value-judgments which are true; judgments which predict the accrual of value-quality as a consequence of action, and which are positively verifiable by adoption of the mode of action in question. Only on this condition could any action have that kind of rightness or correctness which all sensible action aims to have."[55] To say that any object or situation is good is to claim a potentiality for the realization of value discoverable in experience. But Lewis claimed that the "goodness resident in the object as a potentiality for producing experience of a certain quality, is no more dependent upon the *actual* appreciation of it in some experience than the objective roundness of a round thing is dependent on its actually being measured with calipers."[56] Objective value or the value resident in any object or situation is not relative to, or dependent upon, any particular person who may appreciate or apprehend that value. To say that milk is good food or that honesty is a good policy certainly does not imply that these things are good only for some particular person. But at the same time, to say that something is objectively good does not mean or imply that every person who may view that object will invariably find or agree that it is good—no more than saying that an object is green or round implies that everyone will agree on these facts either. Lewis claimed that the attribution of objective value as a potentiality of an object or situation to produce certain experiences is objective "in the sense that any potentiality of a thing depends on what it would, could, might, lead to, but not necessarily on what it does effect in actual fact. An actual trial of it may happen to be inconclusive or misleading as to the objective potentiality tested . . . Furthermore, what potentiality is resident in a thing, is independent of the question whether in point of fact it is tested at all."[57] Of course a legitimate attribution of objective value, as of any objective property, must be testable, but no empirical test, it must be noted, is infallible or absolutely conclusive. Lewis admitted that legitimate disagreements about values exist as do disagreements about other factual matters. His point was that disagreements about whether something has inherent or instrumental value cannot be considered, in principle, as incapable of empirical resolution. It is pointless to argue about the claim that a certain direct experience discloses an intrinsic or positive feeling of value. Such direct experiences of value are indisputable, yet they are neither judgments nor knowledge in Lewis's sense of these terms. Value disagreements usually involve disputes about whether certain objects, situations, or states of affairs actually have the kind of value claimed for them. Disputes of this sort, whether on moral, aesthetic, economic, or political topics, are always capable in principle of empirical resolution, though no guarantee exists that they will actually be resolved or that their resolution is easy or simple.

On this point it is pertinent to ask whether Lewis has not in some way underestimated the real character of value disagreements, and whether he has not overplayed the similarities between judgments of a thing's roundness or hardness and judgments of a thing's goodness or value. No doubt Lewis was correct in saying that we do claim certain things as objectively good and that this claim has definite bearing upon our behavior. We act as though certain things do have objective value; but such action is far from proof that the things so judged actually have the kind of value we attribute to them. To provide adequate evidence for objective value claims in ethics is perhaps as difficult as it is rare. Such issues as euthanasia, abortion, or capital punishment raise complex and very serious moral questions that have not been adequately resolved; but what is worse, one cannot easily see how any or all of these issues *could* be settled in the context of the conditions under which they actually arise. To say that any of these issues is or must be capable in principle of objective settlement when we do not *know* the exact principles that could solve them—or how any principles could do justice to the seemingly legitimate and antagonistic claims or interests on either side—seems rather empty. Perhaps certain moral and other value problems will always be with us as reminders of what a serious or profound moral perplexity really is, or as simple reminders that individual differences must be respected and cannot be ignored or overridden. We shall return to this point of the problem of ethical disagreement in Lewis's theory after we have examined his attempt to formulate and defend three basic laws or principles that, he believed, stand behind our ethical conduct. These are the law of objectivity, the law of compassion, and the law of moral equality.

First, because of the essential generality of any ethical rule or principle, it is important for us to realize that no ethical rule or principle can automatically determine every detail or cover every concrete situation that may arise. With respect to the legitimate claims of prudence and justice, for example, Lewis observed that "no concrete act can be so dictated by justice as to leave no feature of it undetermined and no remaining alternative of detail to be governed by prudence. I ought to pay my bill and satisfy my creditor; but payment by check or cash, today or the first of next month, may satisfy his just claim."[58] Another point important for us to realize is that any truly basic principles of moral conduct, as with any basic principles including those of logic, are incapable in any direct sense of being proven. "How, for example, should we prove any principles of logic which are basic and comprehensive enough to stand as first? We cannot derive statements of the logical from premises which themselves say nothing about the logical."[59] So also must this be true of any comprehensive and most general principles of morals. The best way to show the reasonableness of any basic principles of logic or morals is by *reductio ad absurdum*. According to Lewis, we can show that, if we try to repudiate any basic principles of logic or morals, we inevitably end in pragmatic contradictions. This means that we essentially defeat our own purposes at every turn and simply abrogate any attempt to be rational or self-governing in our thoughts and actions. Thus Lewis held that since human beings are in fact rational, the basic principles of man's moral life cannot be rationally repudiated. They can only be repudiated from the standpoint of irrationality. To be rational without being objective is impossible. But objectivity is no less needed in morals than in science or logic. Objectivity is also a practical demand insofar as man must consider more than any present moment or mere feeling discloses to him. Man must consider possibilities, alternatives, that which is absent, and that which is future. "To weigh the absent but represented in the *full-size* of it, and not in the measure of any presentational or emotive feeling which serves to intimate it, is to be objective. And to weigh it only in the measure of its immediate intimation as a present feeling, is to be subjective."[60]

Thus Lewis argued that what he termed the Law of Objectivity lies at the foundation of all imperatives of thought and action. As formulated it reads, "So conduct and determine your activities of thinking and of doing, as to conform any decision of them to the objective actualities, as cognitively signified to you in your representational apprehension of them, and not according to any impulsion or solicitation exercised by the affective quality of your present experience as immediate feeling merely."[61] To this law Lewis added a corollary regarding the future: "Conduct yourself, with reference to those future eventualities which cognition advises that your activity may affect, as you would if these predictable effects of it were to be realized, at this moment of decision, with the poignancy of the here and now, instead of the less poignant feeling which representation of the future and possible may automatically arouse."[62] Since man is essentially a social creature, this Law of Objectivity implies an imperative for individuals in their relations to one another, i.e., "to govern one's activities affecting other persons, as one would if these effects of them were to be realized with the poignancy of the immediate—hence, in one's own person."[63] Lewis further suggested that this general principle of respect for others be divided into two additional principles, which he called the Law of Compassion and the Law of Moral Equality. The Law of Compassion includes or applies to all creatures who, like ourselves, are subject to suffering and enjoyment. The Law of Moral Equality "is relevant only in the case of other creatures who are like us also in their cognitive capacities and, in consequence, in the necessity of governing their own behavior by deliberation, and of acting under constraint of the imperatives of rationality."[64]

For Lewis, normative principles as rational imperatives are not peculiar to ethics but stand behind all of our science and knowledge, behind our most serious interests in, and beliefs about, matters of fact. We cannot validate any belief about any particular fact without assuming the rightness of the objective procedures needed to collect, certify, and weigh evidence. Thus if rational imperatives or directives would be eliminated or questioned in ethics, they would have to be eliminated or questioned as far as any objective knowledge or objective pursuit is concerned. We cannot classify moral rightness generally or any ethical decision as merely emotive without implying that all other kinds of rightness, whether logical, legal, prudential, technical, or scientific are merely emotive as well. Any decision or conclusion as to the rightness of a certain specific action requires two sorts of premises, according to Lewis. "First, it requires some presumption as to rightness itself or the specific kind of rightness which is in question. It is such a premise which introduces the norm. And second, it requires some further premise or premises which introduce particularities of the case to be decided and relate it to the norm or rule of right doing."[65] Formally considered, no fundamental difference exists between the validity or rightness of decision-making whether in logic and science or in ethics. Whether the decision is one regarding what to conclude or believe in science—or whether it concerns how to act morally—we are obligated to be as objective as possible in considering the facts or evidence upon which our decision will be based. From this it easily follows that science and logic are not value-free or ethically neutral. It was asserted (by Ayer and Stevenson, for example) that science *per se* makes no moral or value judgments at all; and this is true in the narrow sense that science does not attempt to show that honesty is good or that objectivity in making judgments is right or obligatory. But while science may not make specific moral or value judgments regarding how people should conduct their lives, it must nevertheless assume and implicitly use certain norms or imperatives to carry out its own aims. In this sense science is no less value-free or ethically neutral than any working system of legal or social justice. Moreover and specifically, science must use the same norm as any rational ethics: the principle or law of objectivity. For this reason, Lewis asserted that "the first imperative is the law of objectivity: recognize that your experience signifies a reality beyond your present feeling of it, and act appropriately to that reality you recognize and not merely in response to the immediately felt quality and the inclination or aversion with which you are affected."[66]

Lewis pointed out that, while norms or rules are necessary or apply to virtually all human activities, they are not all on the same level of importance, nor are they all categorical. The rules of playing chess are only imperative if one wants to play that game; chess playing itself is not imperative or obligatory. But "concern for consistency in supposition and belief, for validity in inference, and for cogent determination of beliefs according to the weight of the evidence is not avoidable for the animal that thinks deliberately— nor is determination of his physical doing according to the advice of cognitive prediction, or the end of attaining a good life, or justice in the social order in which he lives. These are not matters with which any human can concern himself or not, as he chooses."[67] Thus, according to Lewis, a categorical imperative exists; but unlike Kant's conception of this principle, it is neither metaphysical in referring to anything *noumenal* nor is it peculiar to ethics in excluding prudence, logical consistency, or factual cogency. Further, this categorical imperative does not afford "sufficient ground by itself for any specific and positive code of social conduct. We read into it our own, whatever it be; and that is exactly what the statement of it invites. What it says is only this: whatever code of conduct you think is the one to which you ought to adhere must also be that to which you think any fellow of yours ought to adhere."[68]

It is quite clear from this statement that Lewis represented a return to normative ethics by making use of metaethics or a critical analysis of the forms and uses of ethical concepts and discourse. Recent tendencies among American philosophers show that Lewis is not alone in this concern for substantive questions. Two concepts which played an important role in Lewis's theory—those of generalization and justice—have received extensive treatment and major emphasis in Marcus Singer's *Generalization in Ethics* (1961), and John Rawls's *A Theory of Justice* (1971). Marcus Singer explicitly stated that "what I hope to do is to lay the groundwork for a rational and normative system of ethics."[69] He distinguished between moral rules and moral principles: moral rules are more concrete or specific than moral principles; and moral rules do not hold in all circumstances, while moral principles do. Also, moral principles are always relevant, but moral rules are not. As Singer observed, "The rule against lying is not relevant to a situation in which lying is not involved, and the rule against killing is not relevant where killing is not involved."[70] Singer's approach to ethics is in accord with Lewis's in a number of respects.[71] On several important points, however (especially on the use of generalization in ethics), Singer's theory is more complete than that of Lewis, as Singer gave careful, elaborate attention to the problem of how moral principles function in ethical argumentation. Singer basically agreed with Lewis that moral judgments and rules can be justified and require justification. In other words, reflection on, or rational concern with, morality is essential to morality. Singer formulated a number of moral principles essential to the justification of any moral rules of action. Of prime importance is what he called the "generalization argument." While this principle can be formulated in several ways, it is always relevant as a principle to any moral situation. One formulation of the generalization argument is as follows: If everyone were to perform a certain action A, the consequences would be undesirable or disastrous; therefore no one ought to perform that action A. The generalization argument itself depends on what Singer called "the generalization principle." The generalization principle asserts that *"what is right (or wrong) for one person must be right (or wrong) for any similar person in similar circumstances."*[72] This principle is clearly paralleled in Lewis's theory (the formal criterion of the moral imperative), and Singer acknowledged that his generalization principle "has traditionally been known as the principle of fairness or justice or impartiality."[73] Another principle which Singer formulated as the "principle of consequences" asserts that "if the consequences of A's doing x would be undesirable, then A ought not to do x."[74] This principle has its counterpart in Lewis's ethics (any moral imperative must have content or no moral rule can be considered right apart from the question of whether its consequences are good or desirable for all those affected). Thus, although both Lewis and Singer agree with the Kantian ethics that one basic moral principle or categorical imperative is necessary and relevant to all moral decisions, they reject Kant's claim that the consequences of actions are irrelevant to the determination of the moral rightness of actions. Thus they reject Kant's strict claim that lying is always wrong, even for benevolent motives, or no matter what the consequences may be. Both Lewis and Singer insist that, although lying may be generally wrong, its wrongness cannot be construed purely in formal terms apart from the consequences it may have. Lying for purely selfish motives and personal gain is one thing, and clearly wrong; but lying to a man bent on murder or on bringing serious harm to other human beings is quite another kind of action. As Singer observed, "It does not at all follow that it is *always* wrong to lie or make a false promise. All that Kant has shown is that it is generally wrong (and surely this is enough)."[75] According to Singer, to hold that lying is always wrong is to confuse a moral rule with a moral principle. Singer's generalization principle, for example, merely asserts that what is right or wrong for one person must likewise be right or wrong for any similar person in similar circumstances. But obviously the person who lies for selfish gain and the person who lies to prevent a murder or serious harm are not similar. According to Singer, instead of asking whether lying could ever be willed as a universal principle, Kant should have asked whether the following could be willed as a universal law: that everyone should lie in the specific situation where it is known that telling the truth will be put to a morally bad use and where lying will effect the prevention of murder or serious harm. Singer and Lewis insist on distinguishing the abstract or general principle of conforming one's actions to a universal law from the various concrete situations where such a law may apply.

There are, however, points of disagreement between Lewis and Singer. An important one concerns the status of so-called moral principles. Singer held that "the principle of consequences is a necessary ethical or moral principle. It is necessary not only in the sense that its denial involves self-contradiction. It is necessary also in the sense that like the generalization principle, it is a necessary presupposition or precondition of moral reasoning. There can be sensible and fruitful disagreement about matters within the field delimited by it, but there can be no sensible or fruitful disagreement about the principle itself."[76] While Lewis would have agreed with Singer on this last point, he nevertheless held that any denial of fundamental moral principles is not self-contradictory but pragmatically contradictory. For Lewis, the difference between self-contradiction and pragmatic contradiction was no minor matter since the former is a purely formal notion, and formal principles are insufficient for the grounding of ethics or, indeed, of any rational imperatives. Formal or logical principles require a ground, to explain why it is imperative or obligatory for anyone to recognize or abide by them. Acceptance of any such principle as Singer's generalization principle (what is right or wrong for one person must also be right or wrong for any similar person in similar circumstances) must, for Lewis, be pragmatically grounded in order to explain why such a principle is imperative for any rational agent. To deny a rational imperative (such as treating what is right or wrong as identical for similar persons in similar circumstances) is to produce a contradiction—but neither a logical contradiction nor a self-contradiction. As Lewis asserted, "The contradiction is one between the attitude of assertion and what is so asserted, not a purely logical contradiction."[77]

Earlier we raised the question of whether Lewis had not underestimated the real character of value disagreements. Certainly a troublesome point about ethical disagreements is that moral disputes can occur on a number of levels. Usually a dispute over some specific issue (abortion or euthanasia, for example), is very likely to include some kind of disagreement about the principles which are considered to cover these specific matters. That Lewis carefully marked the difference between major and minor premises in ethical argumentation is certainly to his credit. Further to his credit was his admission that very general principles like the laws of objectivity, compassion, and moral equality do not automatically tell us how we should act in specific situations. If a weakness is present in Lewis's theory, it probably resides in what he failed to say or in the simple fact that his theory is incomplete. Lewis provided us with nothing like a complete social ethics or theory of justice. Yet his rationalistic and naturalistic approach implied that a system of social ethics including a theory of justice is possible. Clearly Lewis placed strong emphasis on the autonomy of individuals, as well as on the necessity of consulting general or universal principles and consequences in determining the morally right action in a social context. Yet autonomy, universality, and consequences are by no means easily coordinated or harmonized under any existing social conditions.

Attempts to Derive "Ought" from "Is": John Searle and James Feibleman

Recent Anglo-American ethical theory has displayed much interest in the Is-Ought question[78]; can judgments about what ought to be or what ought to be done be derived from judgments about what is in fact the case? Although this is not a new question in moral philosophy, it is fair to say that in recent years it has emerged as the central question of ethical theory and it has received more careful attention by philosophers than ever before. John Searle's article "How to Derive 'Ought' from 'Is,'" originally published in 1964, and later included with modifications in his book *Speech Acts*, 1969, has produced considerable comment from other philosophers. Searle disputes the often made claim that ought-statements cannot be derived from is-statements or that descriptive premises cannot entail an evaluative conclusion. He sets out to demonstrate a counter-example to this thesis. Searle takes as his example the connection between someone's making a promise and that person's being under an obligation to keep the promise made. Thus, if Jones promised to pay Smith five dollars, then in some sense Jones ought to pay Smith five dollars. If we can show from the fact that a promise has been made that the promise ought to be kept, we will have derived an ought-statement from an is-statement or several "is" statements. To demonstrate a counter-example to the view that no ought-statement can ever be derived from is-statements alone, it is not necessary to prove that any is-statement always implies some ought-statement. Nor is it necessary that any is-statement implies an ought-statement alone or in the absence of other is-statements. For example, in the case of Jones, who makes a promise to pay Smith five dollars, it may only follow that Jones ought to pay Smith five dollars–other things being equal—that is, that no reason to the contrary can be given. This *ceteris paribus* clause (other things being equal) is sometimes met and sometimes not met. But when it is met it becomes a purely factual premise or condition in the argument. However, because the inclusion of the *ceteris paribus* clause tended to produce certain misunderstandings of his argument, Searle modified his proof "excluding from consideration within the proof the various kinds of consideration that the *ceteris paribus* clause·is designed to deal with."[79] Thus, from a series of factual premises, starting with the premise that Jones asserts that he promises to pay Smith five dollars, we can eventually infer an ought-statement, in this case, that Jones ought to pay Smith five dollars. If Jones declares that he promises to pay Smith five dollars, then with the additional empirical premise that, under normal conditions, when a man declares that he is making a promise, he is in fact making a promise (assuming this normal condition is met here), it then follows that Jones has promised to pay Smith five dollars. Further, if Jones promised to pay Smith five dollars then it follows that Jones has placed himself under an obligation to pay Smith five dollars. Also, "If one has placed oneself under an obligation, then at the time of the obligating performance, one is under an obligation. That, I take it, also is a tautology or analytic truth, i.e., one cannot have succeeded in placing oneself under an obligation if there is no point at which one was under an obligation."[80] Finally, if Jones is actually under an obligation to pay Smith five dollars, then it follows that Jones ought to pay Smith five dollars. This conclusion follows, according to Searle, from the tautology that "If one is under an obligation to do something, then as regards that obligation one ought to do what one is under an obligation to do."[81] Here we have, according to Searle, a clear counter-example to the thesis that no "ought" can be derived from any "is" or that no evaluative statement can be derived from purely descriptive statements. Searle claims that many other counter-examples to this thesis can be generated. To understand this it is necessary to see the distinction which Searle makes between brute facts and institutional facts. It is a brute fact that someone uttered a sound but it is an institutional fact that someone made a promise. It is a brute fact that two individuals are moving small pieces of wood on a flat board containing sixty-four square spaces. But it is an institutional fact that these same two people are playing the game of chess. Institutional facts depend on the existence of constitutive rules which not only serve to regulate behavior but are absolutely necessary to define or identify the meaning of the behavior in question. Without the rules of chess it is not possible to play *that* game. In a similar fashion, without certain constitutive rules it is not possible for people to have obligations, rights, responsibilities or to make promises. Searle argues that his proof that "ought" can be derived from "is" rests on an appeal to the constitutive rule that to make a promise is to undertake an obligation, and that this rule is a meaning-rule of the descriptive word "promise". Whether someone uttered the words "I promise to pay you five dollars," is only a brute fact. For this to entail that a promise was actually made, we need to interpret this speech act as falling under certain rules which give meaning to what it is to actually make a promise. This requires us to assume that making a promise is not a bare fact or brute fact, but an institutional fact. Further, institutional facts are generated from this fact itself—namely, that if someone makes a promise then he places himself under a certain obligation, and if he places himself under an obligation, then he is in fact under an obligation in this case to pay a certain person five dollars. From this it follows that the person who is under an obligation to pay a certain person five dollars ought to pay that person five dollars.

What significance does this derivation of "ought" from "is" have specifically for ethics, we might ask? If the general statement that one cannot derive ought-statements from is-statements is false, then it cannot be used to refute ethical naturalism or particular arguments which claim to base ethical conclusions on statements of fact. Some further grounds will be needed to show that arguments used by naturalists in ethics are unsound. Further, Searle claims that his demonstration points up the important fact that the traditional view of the separation or logical independence of facts and values fails to account for institutional facts. From the brute fact that a man returned a certain object it does not follow that what he did was morally right or what he ought to have done. But from the institutional fact that a man, under certain circumstances, paid back the money he owed, it does follow in some sense that he did what was right or what he ought to have done. Paying back what is owed to someone is no less a fact than merely returning something or other, but as an institutional fact, like the institutional fact of promising, it is logically tied to certain constitutive rules and obligations. Because institutional facts are logically tied to certain rules and obligations, they can serve as premises in arguments from which evaluative or moral conclusions can be derived. Searle propounds the suggestive principle that "No set of brute fact statements can entail an institutional fact statement without the addition of at least one constitutive rule."[82] He does not claim to know for certain whether this principle is true, but at least it is consistent with his derivation of "ought" from "is." This seems to suggest that if moral conclusions are to be proved at all they require premises which include statements of institutional facts and constitutive rules.

Searle's attempted demonstration has called forth considerable comment and criticism. He has replied to a good number of objections which have been brought against his derivation. (See *Speech Acts*, Chapter 8, section 8.3). I will comment on three strategic points in his demonstration which I believe are interconnected: (1) whether Searle in effect assumes evaluative or even moral premises in his arguments, (2) whether he really draws evaluative or any morally significant conclusions from his premises, and (3) whether the alleged tautologies he uses in his arguments are bona fide tautologies.

In one clear sense of the notion of moral premise, Searle does not assume moral premises in his arguments. He even asserts that "the obligation to keep a promise probably has no necessary connection with morality."[83] Searle doubts whether the obligation to keep a promise always involves a moral obligation. He suggests that it is not always very important to keep a promise and when the obligation to keep a promise is not very important, then breaking the promise may make the person who breaks it remiss but not immoral. Therefore, from the premises that Jones is obligated to pay Smith five dollars, and when one is under an obligation to do something, then, with respect to that obligation, one ought to do what one is under an obligation to do, we cannot automatically infer that Jones ought to pay Smith five dollars in any specific moral sense of the term "ought." In other words, Searle's argument does not prove any moral "ought" nor does it appear to assume any specifically moral statements in its premises.

However, Searle uses a number of alleged tautologies in his arguments, and the question can be raised as to whether they are bona fide. One statement he uses as a tautology or analytic premise is "All promises are acts of placing oneself under (undertaking) an obligation to do the thing promised."[84] Now while one may admit that there is *some kind* of connection between promises and acts of placing oneself under an obligation, one can certainly question whether this connection is analytic or logical. For one thing, promises are easily made but obligations are often difficult to fulfill and burdensome. From a promise that is easily and even hastily made, it would seem inappropriate to automatically infer an act of placing oneself under a strict obligation to keep that promise. Another premise that Searle uses as a tautology or analytic truth is the following: "If one has placed oneself under an obligation, then at the time of the obligating performance, one is under an obligation."[85] Here again there seem to be good reasons for questioning whether this statement is analytic. Certainly, people can place themselves under all sorts of obligations—an overly zealous person, for example, can place himself under the obligation to personally feed all the hungry or cure all the sick. But how does it follow that one is actually under such obligations merely because one has placed oneself under them. It is certainly logically possible for a person to think or believe he is under certain obligations which he is not in fact under. For one thing, it is not rational or reasonable to say that someone is under an obligation to perform an action which that person cannot possibly perform. Yet it makes perfectly good sense to say that a person may think or believe that he has such an obligation or that he has placed himself under such an obligation.

Another alleged tautology that Searle uses in his argument is the statement, "If one is under an obligation to do something, then as regards that obligation one ought to do what one is under an obligation to do."[86] This is the most crucial step in Searle's argument since it is used to infer the particular ought-statement that Jones ought to pay Smith five dollars. His conclusion only follows deductively as the result of assuming that this premise is an analytic truth or tautology. But is it? Certainly if one is under an obligation to do something, then one is under an obligation to do that thing— but it still does not necessarily follow that one ought to do it in all cases, but rather only as a general or normal course of action. If this statement were a tautology, then it could never be right to override or locate an exception to a moral obligation. If one is under the obligation to tell the truth, then it would never be right to tell a lie (for example, to save someone's life) if this statement (that one ought to do what one is under an obligation to do) were a tautology. All we can reasonably say is that if one is under an obligation to do something, then normally or generally one ought to do what one is under an obligation to do. But this is not a tautology and will not serve the purposes of Searle's argument—to prove deductively that "ought" can be derived from "is." Consequently, it would seem that Searle has failed to derive "ought" deductively from "is."

Another way of putting this criticism of Searle is as follows. There can be no exception to a tautology or analytic truth. But clearly there can be exceptions to the assertion that "if one is under an obligation one ought to do what one is under an obligation to do." Hence, this assertion that "if one is under an obligation, then as regards that obligation one ought to do what one is under an obligation to do," is clearly not a tautology. We can also add that the possibility of entertaining exceptions to this statement is necessary to the idea of having any significant, i.e., nonmechanical moral choices. If it were analytically true that one always ought to do what one is under an obligation to do, then one would obviously never have to make a. moral decision to override a moral obligation. But surely we do have to make such decisions. Not only do we have to decide what obligations we should assume—but when one obligation conflicts with another we have to decide which is to take precedence.

The assertions "one ought to do what one ought to do" and "one ought to do what one is under an obligation to do" are not equivalent. The former is a tautology but it is also trivial. It makes no sense to say that one as a rule ought to do what one ought to do, but not necessarily always. But it does make sense to say that one as a rule ought to do what one is under an obligation to do, but not necessarily always. Thus, if we argue that X is under an obligation to do Y and when X is under an obligation to do Y, X ought generally but not necessarily always to do Y, we cannot infer that X ought to do Y. In order to draw the deductive conclusion that X ought to do Y from the premise that X is under an obligation to do Y, we have to assume the additional premise that whenever X is under an obligation to do Y, X ought to do Y. This is the premise Searle assumes, since it will not serve his purpose to assume merely the tautology that one ought to do what one ought to do. In his deduction of "ought" from "is" Searle has to assume that the statement "whenever X is under an obligation to do Y, X ought to do Y" is analytic. But we have argued that logic alone cannot determine whether one ought to fulfill an obligation.

There is, however, a simpler way to derive, in a purely deductive form, an "ought" from an "is," but I do not see how this can have any real relevance to ethics *per se*. It is well known that any statement follows from a contradiction. Therefore, from the contradiction that Jones owes Smith five dollars and Jones doesn't owe Smith five dollars, we can infer that Jones ought to pay Smith five dollars. Here we have derived an "ought" from an "is," but this turns out to be trivial or useless since we can equally infer that Jones ought not to pay Smith five dollars from the same premise. Also, it is well known that a tautology follows from any statement at all, hence from the premise that Jones promised to pay Smith five dollars we can infer that Smith ought to do what he ought to do. One may say that here again we have deductively derived an "ought" from an "is", but again this conclusion is trivial or useless. From this it seems to follow that there is no non-trivial way in which we can deductively derive an "ought" from an "is" and hence no significant way in which we can deductively derive a moral or evaluative conclusion from premises that only state facts or analytic truths.

If it is not possible to derive "ought" from "is" deductively, in any significant way, perhaps it is possible to derive "ought" from "is" inductively. This is, in fact, the claim of the contemporary American philosopher, James K. Feibleman. In the preface of his *Moral Strategy, An Introduction to the Ethics of Confrontation* (1967), Feibleman asserts that "what-ought-to-be is a natural development from what-is when what-is is sufficiently understood to enable inductions from it to guide the behavior of those responsible for change and direction."[87] Feibleman is a contemporary naturalist who not only challenges the separation of facts and values, but more important, he has actually constructed a rich ethical theory which seeks to integrate values and facts in a naturalistic and even in a cosmic framework.[88] He claims that the whole, cosmic universe is not only a set of facts, but every fact contains qualities or values. For Feibleman "there is no qualitative distinction between qualities and values. Values are only high qualities."[89] He observes that since the time of the Greeks, with very few exceptions, "ethical subject matter has been looked at exclusively in human terms. The good for instance has been defined as the human good. No doubt human good is good; but the good is not exclusively human, though human good is. The good as such is the quality of what is needed."[90] Values occur at many different empirical levels and not only at the level of the human individual. They are not created or brought into existence by judgments, preferences, or choices but by confrontations of material agents of all kinds. If the good is defined as the quality of what is needed then it exists as a natural bond between whole material things. Any "need itself is an empirical fact, and the good is an empirical quality which accompanies the need-reduction. From the point of view of a subject, that object which it needs is good for it."[91] Water is good for a tree no less than vitamin A or fresh air for man, or orbiting electrons for a hydrogen atom. The fact that what may be needed by one individual may not be needed by another or may actually be detrimental to another individual, does not imply that values are subjective in the sense of depending only on the subject. For Feibleman, what is bad or evil is just as objective and empirical as what is good. "Anything can suffer destruction and in so doing allow for the quality of destruction, which is evil."[92] Consequently, there is a general or cosmic evil which is the result of the inability of any material thing to act without disturbing its environment.[93] It is a mistake, according to Feibleman, to limit ethics to the human sphere and to confuse values with evaluations. "What a man knows that he needs or wants and what he feels, is ethical, no doubt; but the ethical is not confined to such cases. The viscera make their demands as much as society does, and what is needed may be termed the good in both instances. The emotive theory of ethics, like the instrumental or utilitarian, is hardly sufficient to include all known instances of the good. It confines ethics to the human and limits the human to the conscious."[94]

Clearly, Feibleman's whole approach to ethics is ontological. He holds that three fundamental ethical domains exist; the actual, the ideal, and the strategy for getting from the actual to the ideal.[95] These three domains correspond to the three universes of being— existence, essence and destiny—developed at length in Feibleman's *Ontology* (1951). Ontologically, qualities are the stuff of existence. "All else—the relations and their logic—only shows where the qualities are. The way in which everything in the world is bonded together with everything else is its ethical aspect."[96] If ethics is defined as the theory of the good and morality as the practice of the good, then morality exists at a number of important empirical levels. "It exists for the individual toward himself, through his conscience (his self-respect, personal integrity, dignity). It exists for the society through its establishments (its laws, customs, traditions). It exists for the human species through its commitment to other species of beings. And it exists for the cosmos through the relation of all species in the material order."[97] Ultimately an ethics is simply an ontological system viewed qualitatively as the organization of bonds between wholes.[98] For Feibleman the purpose of a theory of ethics is to offer an adequate description of moral behavior as well as sound proposals or strategies for improving all manner of moral encounters. But obviously, these purposes can only make sense through the acquisition of empirical knowledge. Any normative ethics must seek to understand the actual norms in use by any individual, society, or species of existence and relate these to the most ideal or complete set of values that would sustain and fulfill the existence of all things. That this is a tall order, Feibleman is quite willing to admit. "The goal of all actual things is to exist in a world where everything has the freshness and novelty of change together with the dependability of permanence."[99] As Feibleman sees it, the whole universe is in the process of putting itself back into essential order and man can only hasten or delay this process.

Nature comprises what Feibleman terms "moral integrative levels" or "the ethical integrative series" which is all-inclusive and enables us to understand all manner of moral encounters in reality. These levels comprise the individual, the social, the human, and the cosmic. Although Feibleman's theory emphasizes human ethics his approach insists that human individuals and their societies do not exhaust the field of ethics. He does claim that man is engaged with all these levels, however, "There are evidently no men without societies and no societies without moral orders of some sort. Therefore moral orders as much as men or societies are natural objects. What is called conventional is a subdivision of the natural just as much as what is human is."[100] What Feibleman calls the moral integrative series operates as a scale of values where it is possible for the individual to measure his own worth. For the moral integrative levels there is no opposition or separation between facts and values or between the empirical and the normative. Facts and values simply involve different directions of one and the same natural order. "The empirical looks down the levels, the normative looks up. Normative considerations always involve wider contexts, but there is no specifically empirical (as opposed to specifically normative) subject-matter."[101] The moral goodness of anything cannot be seen in isolation but depends upon that thing's inclusiveness in a wider system. Empirically, the moral position of man requires for its complete explanation everything else in the world. At the same time, what is good for man includes whatever is needed by man to sustain and fulfill his existence. Consequently, there is not only a natural effort on man's part to reduce his needs or realize what is good for him, but also an inevitable movement enhanced by enlightenment to widen one's area of interest and to take other things and levels of existence into consideration. "Self-interest leads inevitably to an interest in nature. An individual who is really concerned about himself would want above all to know where he fits into that wider scheme of things out of which he emerged and into which he must disappear."[102] While man naturally can be expected to feel what Feibleman calls a "type responsibility" in terms of his membership in a given group or class, the important thing is that through increased understanding, this responsibility can and should be widened to take in all orders of existence.

However, in an obvious sense man is also aggressive and excessive in the satisfaction of his needs. This inevitably results in consequences which are not only bad for other orders of existence, but which may also be bad for the whole human species in the long run. Feibleman insists that "the good life is life lived to the fullest and may be said to consist in the greatest enjoyment of the highest achievement."[103] However, Feibleman makes a distinction between all those unexceptional individuals who make up the bulk of the human species, or what he terms "demotic man", and those exceptional individuals termed "heroic man." "Demotic morality is founded on those actions of the individual which are aimed at reducing his primary needs and which thus take himself as his end. Heroic morality is founded on his actions aimed at reducing his secondary needs and which thus take his society or, beyond it, humanity or the cosmos, as his end."[104] Feibleman admits that cultural relativism is a fact and cannot be brushed aside. The individual cannot easily, if at all, surmount or step out of the perspective by which his culture furnishes the norms of all human behavior. There is, of course, the idea or ideal of a trans-cultural ethics. But the very effort to discover a trans-cultural ethics is itself culturally conditioned.[105]

It is to his credit that Feibleman acknowledges a problem here for the type of ethics he espouses. A more serious problem for Feibleman's ethics, and one also brought up by him, emerges with what are called "moral encounters with near-by species." "The life of one species is made possible by the murder and subsequent consumption of the members of another. Diet defeats all moral theory."[106] "The morally bad is inherent in the eating hierarchy for the eaten as certainly as the morally good is inherent in food for the hungry; it was what was needed. Man needs beef to eat. Yet those who have been to a slaughterhouse are hardly in a position to argue from the point of view of cattle that man is what is needed."[107] If diet really defeats all moral theory, then it should follow that the universe as a whole or nature as such, does not constitute a realizable moral order at all. Food is something that is needed by all living things, and, since Feibleman defines the good as that which is needed, we arrive at the paradoxical result that diet is good for all living things, but is also bad for those which are eaten, and hence diet defeats all moral theory. Feibleman claims that "We must answer for what we have done and continue to do to brother sheep and sister cow . . . to the species of higher animals on whom we subsist we are guilty of immorality."[108] It thus becomes hard to see how Feibleman can defend his claim that *the* good is what is needed when this good turns out to be inevitably bad for some other species. This seems to indicate that the normative and the factual are not as integrated as Feibleman wants to maintain. Feibleman does say that "just as evolution is an exception in a cosmic universe of entropy, so ethics is an exception in the cosmic domain of species aggression."[109] If we admit that anything good rarely occurs without being mixed with something bad, it is hard to see how Feibleman can claim that "Every entity and every process is naturally good, and every entity and process being naturally good is also morally good."[110] If every entity or process in nature were morally good, then ethics would not seem to be an exception but rather the rule. And if every entity or process in nature were morally good, then any distinction between fact and value or between "is" and "ought" would simply have collapsed or disappeared. Consequently, it is difficult to understand how Feibleman can reconcile his principle of cosmic evil—that no material thing can act without disturbing its environment—with his definition of the good as that which is needed and with his further claim that every entity and process being naturally good is morally good also. Surely, "natural good" and "moral good" are not synonymous terms. Surely, disturbing the environment, while necessary for moral evil, is not sufficient. It would seem that, if we assume that every entity and process is naturally good and also morally good, we have then begged the question of the moral worth of anything and at the same time collapsed any real distinction between "is" and "ought." Further, if diet by itself really defeats all moral theory, then there would seem to be no moral ground for distinguishing between the cruel and unnecessary killing of animals on the one hand and carefully controlled fishing and breeding animals for needed food on the other.

Certain aspects of life and the world, it would seem, can be regarded as neither morally good nor morally evil. The big fish naturally eats the smaller fish and man may in turn eat the larger fish. Why, we may ask, can these events and many others such as earthquakes and devastating storms not be regarded as nonmoral or amoral? It is well known that the human body must continuously kill countless germs in order to survive and maintain its health. Killing and death are quite normal processes inside nature and it is hard to see how they can be considered immoral or morally bad as such. Usually, we would want to say that it is the way or reason something is killed that raises moral questions. Moral questions or issues seem to require a moral point of view in order to have any meaning or take on any significance, and not every encounter or point of view can be counted as a moral one, let alone a morally good one. Feibleman is quite right to suggest that man must consider more than himself if he wants to develop a complete and adequate ethics. Other species and the quality of the environment are indeed real factors in any rational ethics that tries to be fair and comprehensive.[111] Feibleman declares that, "The goodness of anything, extrinsically considered, must depend upon its inclusion in a wider system."[112] He also asserts that, "For all encounters, human or other, there is a criterion of its moral effectiveness. We can ask, does a particular encounter increase order without loss of completeness? Then we know it was good. Does it increase disorder or increase order with loss of completeness? Then we know it was bad."[113] No doubt it is difficult to ascertain with precision what is to count as order and completeness on a cosmic scale. Nevertheless, Feibleman is certainly right that some endeavors are wasteful and disruptive while others have the effect of improving and harmonizing existing conditions.

Any form of ethical naturalism must squarely face the problem as to how any moral point of view can be maintained and justified in terms of nature or the natural world itself. Many naturalists have opted for some form of humanism as their moral point of view. Here I would argue that it is one of Feibleman's distinct contributions to have shown the incompleteness of human good for any naturalistic ethics and the need to look beyond the human species. Clearly, Feibleman is right in holding that humanity is not an absolutely valid ethical isolate. But I would also argue that if species other than man, as well as the whole cosmic environment, are to be taken into consideration in ethics, this cannot be done by reducing values to facts or by simply assimilating what is good to what is needed. Somewhere a distinction between fact and value or between "is" and "ought" still has to be maintained, so that we can always, in principle at least, discern a difference between what happens to be the case and what ought to be, or between the fact that any need exists and alternative ways of satifying that need. Not all ways of satisfying a need are equally good or morally desirable, and it certainly makes sense to question whether it is good to satisfy every need, especially since they cannot all be satisfied and since some needs, at least, are pathological and undesirable in the first place.

Feibleman is indeed to be applauded for developing a much richer ethical theory with far broader concerns than most of his contemporaries. He is also on the right track in insisting that ethical theory, to be complete, must include inquiries into what is ideal, what is actual, and strategies for getting from the actual to the ideal. We can agree with his efforts of trying always to see the normative and the empirical as intimately related rather than as separate and opposed. Surely, he is right in insisting that facts must have relevance in determining our values or what we ought to do and be. However, we have also questioned Feibleman's claim that the relation between fact and value is inductive. To admit that facts have relevance in determining our values, or what ought to be, does not mean that facts inductively determine or set the moral goals we ought to pursue. That facts are necessary to values or that inductions from past facts are necessary to any rational planning for the future only signifies that any meaningful link between what "is" and what "ought" has to include past facts and inferences therefrom. But any attempt to reduce the relation between "is" and "ought" in ethics to a purely empirical or inductive relation will either beg the question of the real moral worth of things or blur the real difference between the mere occurrence of some fact and the normative question of whether it ought to exist or whether it is good for it to be.

Situation Ethics: Joseph Fletcher

During the 1960's and into the present decade, a number of moral philosophers have addressed themselves to normative issues such as civil disobedience, conscientious objection to war, the death penalty, euthanasia, abortion, and others that have gained extensive public attention. So much recent work has been done on so many different moral issues that a short summary of all these efforts is impossible. Instead, we will consider a selection of representative ideas that have exerted some measure of influence.

Since World War II, many American religious thinkers have turned their attention to the problems of ethics. Such works as Reinhold Niebuhr's *Moral Man and Immoral Society: A Study in Ethics and Politics* (1948), Paul Tillich's *Love, Power and Justice* (1960), Jacques Maritain's *The Rights of Man and Natural Law* (1943), Will Herberg's *Judaism and Modern Man* (1951), and Paul Ramsey's *Deeds and Rules in Christian Ethics* (1967) are some of the more prominent works in this area. But the work of Joseph Fletcher, specifically his *Situation Ethics: The New Morality* (1966), has created the greatest impact, controversy, and debate. Fletcher, who served as Dean of St. Paul's Cathedral in Cincinnati and Professor of Social Ethics, Episcopal Theological School, Cambridge, Massachusetts, has written extensively on such topics as euthanasia, birth control, abortion, sexual morality, and genetic control.[114] His whole approach to ethics is to remove it from the abstract, general level on which philosophers ordinarily discuss it–to bring ethics face to face with specific problems in concrete situations. Although Fletcher gives attention to the views of James, Dewey, Kant, Mill, and other thinkers, he does not offer any elaborate metaethical analysis nor does he give extensive attention to the cognitive status of moral judgments. Fletcher agrees with those philosophers who hold that moral judgments cannot actually be verified and that statements about what "ought to be" cannot be derived or inferred from descriptive statements about any facts. But he claims that, even though moral judgments or decisions cannot be verified, they can be justified or vindicated. Moral judgments or decisions can be definitely supported by reasons, but those reasons must fit the particular circumstances of the moral situation in question. No mere general law or abstract principle can ever make

or justify a decision in a concrete ethical case. Like the existential-
ists, Fletcher prefers to consider ethics in terms of decision making.
What is unique about man is that he must daily face and decide
issues of vital concern to him and others; and in the moral sphere
these decisions are neither cut-and-dried nor decidable in terms of
preestablished rules or principles. To adopt or accept any form of
ethical legalism is a serious moral error, according to Fletcher, for
legalism implies neglect of the intricacies or intimate features
involved in specific moral situations. Fletcher has strongly criticized
the whole Western religious tradition as too legalistic in its conception of morality. "Judaism, Catholicism, Protestantism—all major
Western religious traditions have been legalistic. In morals as in
doctrine they have kept to a spelled-out 'systematic' orthodoxy."[115]
Fletcher does not think that rules as such should be discarded or
that they are entirely useless in moral situations. Like William
James, he is willing to accept the usefulness, even the necessity, of
rules as long as they are treated in a flexible, functional manner. To
take ethical rules as final or complete (since they are at best only
general, not specific, guides for deciding a course of action in a particular situation) is a mistake. Such rules as "lying is always wrong"
or "abortion is inherently sinful" fail to come to grips with the
situational variables that pertain to every ethical situation.

Religious ethics, especially Christian ethics, has traditionally
supposed that it is possible to establish absolute or rigid regulations
for man's conduct on a supernatural basis. This absolute or supernatural morality sought to identify moral virtue with perfection and
thus regarded any exceptions or deviations from its absolute
precepts as wrong and sinful. The American Puritans had an
excessively legalistic conception of morality in Fletcher's sense of
the term. What is particularly bad about a legalistic approach is that
it tends to depersonalize both man and his decision making so that
real love or concern for people and their welfare is subordinated to
the process of rule-keeping or rule-following. The worst thing in life,
according to Fletcher, is not evil or suffering, but plain indifference
to what happens. Thus "the true opposite of love is not hate but
indifference. Hate, bad as it is, at least treats the neighbor as a *thou*,
whereas indifference turns the neighbor into an *it*, a thing. This is
why we may say that there is actually one thing worse than evil
itself, and that is indifference to evil."[116] Absolutist or legalistic

ethics such as Puritanism is preoccupied with such matters as obedience, sin, punishments, and rewards. But in its rigid adherence to what is right and lawful, it neglects the purpose or good that ethical rules are supposed to serve. Heretics and unbelievers were executed simply because they were judged wrong according to certain rules. According to Fletcher, any ethical rules are, at best, only relatively good—i.e., good in relation to certain circumstances and purposes and not good in relation to other situations. The only thing which Fletcher allows as absolutely or unconditionally good is love, but he firmly insists that love is not really a thing or property but a predicate. What makes Fletcher's Situation Ethics specifically Christian is his insistence that love is the basis of all moral value and that God is love incarnate in the person of Jesus Christ. Love, therefore, is not an abstract principle or law that inheres in certain right deeds, but is a personal concern that is only truly revealed in specific living situations. Fletcher's position might also be called a situational love ethics—or better, a Christian situational love ethics—since the taking of situational variables into account in making a decision is not enough; the important consideration in any ethical choice is the element of *agape* or love in a deeply religious sense. Agape implies a concern or caring for persons as ends in themselves. It is not the same kind of love as that based merely on liking, preference, or desire. Agape or true Christian love, as Fletcher views it, is not simply based on approval or subjective feelings; it has or requires an intellectual or rational component and is perfectly consistent with calculation or measurement of the practical consequences of intended actions. Agape in this sense is neither erotic nor fanatical. True caring for other people is the very opposite of impulsiveness, dogmatism, or action based solely on feeling. To care about people is to care about all the particular variables that can affect or influence their personal lives. Thus, just as Fletcher opposed legalism as a depersonalizing, oversimplifying factor in moral situations, so also he opposed what he terms "antinomianism," which would dispense with any moral rules or general norms and simply rely on spontaneous judgments. Fletcher finds one form of antinomianism in the existentialism of the contemporary French philosopher Jean-Paul Sartre. Fletcher comments on Sartre, "In every moment of moral choice or decision 'we have no excuses behind us and no justification before us.' Sartre refuses to admit to any *generally* valid principles at all. Nothing even ordinarily valid, to say nothing of universal *laws*."[117] In opposition to this view, Fletcher asserts, "The situationist follows a moral law or violates it according to love's need. For example, 'Almsgiving is a good thing *if* . . .' The situationist never says, 'Almsgiving is a good thing. Period!' His decisions are hypothetical, not categorical. Only the commandment to love is categorically good."[118] Hence Fletcher's Situation Ethics distinguishes between the use of ethical principles which would throw light on situations and reliance on rigid rules which would claim or pretend to decide moral issues dogmatically or categorically. Ethical principles are acceptable so long as they are pragmatically, relatively used. Even agape must be used differently in different situations, since the principle of love and concern for individual persons does not tell anyone how to apply this principle automatically in particular contexts, especially in conflict situations. What does the principle of love tell one to do, for example, in specific cases of euthanasia, abortion, or conflicts in time of war? What is the most loving action in such situations where deep-seated conflict exists between people's interests? There is no *general* solution to these problems—no general rule of abortion, euthanasia, or anything else—that will apply to every case. Each situation must be examined on its own merits in relation to agape and on some estimate of the consequences resulting from one action rather than another.

Christian love, as Fletcher interprets it, is not opposed to prudence and justice. "Prudence, careful calculation, gives love the carefulness it needs; with proper care, love does more than take justice into account, it *becomes* justice."[119] Love divorced from prudence or justice can only be sentimental; it cannot be wise or fair. "If to love is to seek the neighbor's welfare, and justice is being fair as between neighbors, then how do we put these two things together in our *acts*, in the situation? The answer is that in the Christian ethic the twain become one. . . . For what *is* it that is due to our neighbors? It is love that is due—*only* love. . . . Love is justice, justice is love."[120] Fletcher gives the example of a doctor with the problem of deciding whether to give the hospital's last unit of blood plasma to a young mother of three or to an old skid-row drunk; he claims that "to prefer the mother *in that situation* is the most loving decision. And therefore it is the most just decision too."[121] But why is this the case? The problem arises specifically because there is not enough blood for both. But on what *moral* grounds can the doctor decide in such a situation that the young mother deserves the blood more than the old man? What do age, motherhood, and sobriety have to do with the moral question of whether to help a human being? Surely all moral agents are equal as moral agents, though they may be quite different in many other respects. Therefore how can justice or love distinguish in any moral sense between persons by weighing extramoral factors such as age, marital status, and the like? Any decision made by counting these things is clearly extramoral. One would like to say that, in extreme or conflict situations of this kind, one should do as much as is humanly possible for *all* parties involved. But how can a moral decision be made in preferring the life of one human to another by weighing the practical consequences? Fletcher calls attention to the resemblance of his Situation Ethics to pragmatism. Like the ethics of James and Dewey, Fletcher's Situation Ethics is clearly liberal in calling for change and more progressive attitudes toward man's social and moral problems. "Situationism, it appears, is the crystal precipitated in Christian ethics by our era's pragmatism and relativism. Historically, most men really have been situationists, more or less, but the difference today is that we are situationists as a matter of rational and professed method. . . . We are deliberately closing the gap between our overt professions and our covert practices. It is an age of honesty, this age of anxiety is."[122] One apparent difference between Fletcher's Situation Ethics and the pragmatism of James and Dewey, however, is that Fletcher finds and endorses rather simple solutions to complex moral issues, whereas James and Dewey did not. While Fletcher denies that any rigid rules or laws can be made to cover such matters as abortion, euthanasia, or any phase of sexual conduct, he does not hesitate to judge particular cases. In certain situations he favors direct mercy killing, abortion, artificial insemination, or sterilization. But he does not favor certain courses of action as morally right for no reason; he holds that situational decisions can be vindicated or justified on moral grounds. It will be noticed, however, that any justification or reason given to support a decision in favor of abortion or euthanasia must be general, at least in the sense that the same justification can apply to other similar situations. If abortion is morally right in a particular situation, it will presumably be right for essentially similar situations that arise. One cannot easily see how justice as fairness would apply at all if this were denied—and Fletcher clearly holds that moral decisions must be based on justice. But since he insists on giving the terms "love" and "justice" an exclusively utilitarian interpretation, there is a serious difficulty in his analysis. Fletcher asserts, "As the love ethic searches seriously for a social policy it must form a coalition with utilitarianism. It takes over from Bentham and Mill the strategic principle of 'the greatest good of the greatest number' . . . it reshapes the 'good' of the utilitarians, replacing their pleasure principle with *agape*. In the coalition the hedonistic calculus becomes the agapeic calculus, the greatest amount of neighbor welfare for the largest number of neighbors possible."[123] Not only are consequences to be calculated, but those consequences which represent a greater good for people also represent the correct ethical choice in a conflict situation. Acceptance of this reasoning, however, allows that if a greater good for people will be achieved by unfairness or injustice to some or a few, that is the correct ethical choice. The trouble with this is that Fletcher holds that only the end justifies the means, nothing else.[124] He asserts, "In the relativities of this world where conscience labors to do the right thing, we may always do what would be evil in some contexts if in *this* circumstance love gains the balance. It is love's business to calculate gains and losses, and to act for the sake of its success."[125] He cites an extreme example: if we can only carry one person from a burning building where the choice is between saving one's father or a scientist who has discovered a cure for a widespread, fatal disease, we should save the scientist—since, according to the agapeic calculus, this choice represents the greater good.[126] This situation and Fletcher's solution to this problem are highly questionable for a number of reasons. First, such an extreme situation only presents an opportunity for calculation or real deliberation in the abstract or in retrospect. That any individual actually confronted with such a problem would have the time, opportunity, or presence of mind to make such a calculation in terms of agape, as Fletcher supposes, is hardly to be expected. For extreme cases of this kind are not really genuine ethical problems at all, but are abstract, intellectual puzzles. When we puzzle over such extreme cases in the abstract or insofar as we view the actual situation from a considerable distance, we have in fact a different situation than the one presented in actuality. But secondly, in what sense does an extreme case such as this present an ethical choice or call for a specifically moral decision? Not all choices or situations are specifically ethical even though they may contain ethical implications of some kind. One required condition for an ethical choice is that such a choice is in fact rationally possible for the individual making it. It is not enough that an individual be able to react or respond in *some* way to a situation; he must be able to respond in a *responsible* way; i.e., the person making a moral choice must be able to bear the responsibility for whatever he does or chooses to do. But if one's choice is limited beforehand, so that some human being is lost or sacrificed no matter what one does, it is meaningless to speak of that choice as being ethically or morally correct. If one could save both persons but leaves one of them behind for reasons of dislike or indifference, we can say that this is a wrong action. Or if one is able to save both persons and does so, we can say that the right choice has been made. But to suggest that one has made the right choice by saving the scientist rather than one's father is perfectly arbitrary from an ethical viewpoint. To save any human being from fire while possibly endangering one's own life would normally be considered morally praiseworthy. But the very idea of attempting to calculate which human being is more deserving of salvation on moral grounds clearly violates the principle that persons should always be treated as ends, never merely as means—a principle, by the way, which Fletcher himself professes to accept.

In these cases and others, Fletcher's Situation Ethics seems to confuse moral judgments with efficiency ratings. Clearly there is a difference between rating the value of a person in terms of how useful or important he is to others and in judging a person morally. A person can receive a high rating in one category and a low rating in the other. A man can be very useful and important to many people even though he is dishonest and unvirtuous. But a person can also be judged as honest and morally good even though he contributes very little, as compared to others, to the well-being or advancement of mankind. Thus if we base a so-called moral decision simply on the social benefits of an action, we are in fact making an efficiency rating rather than a moral judgment. As C. I. Lewis and others pointed out, prudence and justice are not the same even though they are related. Honesty, for example, may generally be prudent, but it is not always so. Fairness in dealing with people entails justice, but not necessarily happiness or that which is expedient or prudent. Also, it seems inappropriate to identify love and justice as Fletcher does. Love may entail mercy or forgiveness, whereas justice does not actually entail these things. The concept of just or fair punishment does not mean no punishment at all or forgiveness of a wrong committed. Out of love or mercy one may decide not to punish, and in such an instance may override the demands of justice in favor of a higher principle of love.

In conclusion we may say that the positive contribution of Fletcher's Situation Ethics is that it has focused attention on the importance of examining particular cases in ethics. Fletcher's work also calls important attention to a whole series of questions in what might be termed "bioethics" and the ethics of medicine—the patient's right to know, the right to a dignified death, abortion, artificial insemination, genetic control, and so on. As Fletcher himself admits, however, the idea of bringing ethics face to face with its particular situations is not really new. And in examining his ethics, we have found a number of confusions pertaining to the question of how to identify what is morally relevant for deciding actions in particular situations.[127] No moral decision can be made in any situation unless we know what is relevant and what is irrelevant in the making of any moral decision. To conclude, as Fletcher does, that what is relevant simply varies from situation to situation and is based on love or agape is insufficient. Any ethical situation must include not only the people affected by any decision made, but also the person who makes the decision. Insofar as similar situations may have different decision making agents, we could arrive at the odd result that the morally right thing to do or decide depends upon the doer or decider. While Fletcher apparently seeks to avoid complete lawlessness and subjectivity in his ethics, his stated principles do not clearly reveal how he can avoid these consequences. This is undoubtedly because he has failed to work out a careful metaethics and has failed to provide a clear, satisfactory explanation of how we can know what is morally relevant to a moral decision no matter who makes the decision.

Morality and the Law: John Rawls and Others

One important characteristic of recent moral philosophy is the attempt to apply the rigorous methods of metaethics, the logical analysis of ethical concepts, to many substantive issues in current social ethics. Recent years have seen a greater interest than ever in problems that relate morality to law and justice. Definitely we may say that the interest of American philosophers in such matters as racial discrimination, civil disobedience, the morality of punishment, the morality of war, the concept of violence, as well as the meaning and justification of human rights and liberty parallels wide public concern with these same problems. The great interest in these issues indicates, in fact, that moral philosophy and careful thinking about social issues are very much alive. Careful thinking can have a positive influence in removing confusion and working toward settlement of these serious problems. On the other hand, the present concern with virtually all problems of morality and law signifies the clear imperfection of our present system of law and the definite need for improved understanding and techniques that would bring the concepts of morality and law into a more perfect harmony. Civil disobedience is a clear example of one serious conflict between legal and moral issues. Although many different kinds of civil disobedience can be identified, such actions basically involve a deliberate breaking of the law for the purpose of calling attention to what is believed to be an existing injustice.

One of the most significant illustrations of recent acts of civil disobedience involved the active protests of Dr. Martin Luther King, Jr., and others concerning segregation laws. In his now famous *Letter from Birmingham City Jail, April 16, 1963*,[128] Dr. King explained in vivid detail why the action of civil disobedience was necessary in the face of unjust laws that discriminated against the Negro. Dr. King argued that "all segregation statutes are unjust because segregation distorts the soul and damages the personality. . . . An unjust law is a code inflicted upon a minority which that minority had no part in enacting or creating because they did not have the unhampered right to vote."[129] He further insisted that an act of civil disobedience must be nonviolent and performed openly with one's clear willingness to accept the subsequent penalty for breaking the law. Acts of civil disobedience must, in other words, be based on clearly moral motives or a respect for law in the most universal sense. Against the charge that so-called peaceful and orderly acts of civil disobedience nevertheless precipitate violence and disorder, Dr. King argued that this is "like condemning the robbed man because his possession of money precipitated the evil act of robbery."[130] Nonviolent protests, sit-ins, or demonstrations are only used because other methods have failed to secure basic human rights. Dr. King listed four basic steps that any nonviolent attempt to seek justice should include: "(1) Collection of the facts to determine whether injustices are alive. (2) Negotiation. (3) Self-purification and (4) Direct Action."[131] Thus although acts of civil disobedience involve the breaking of existing laws and may disrupt the existing social order, they must nevertheless be distinguished from both criminal and revolutionary activities. Criminal acts are clearly illegal and are not based on moral motives. The purpose of a criminal act is not to call attention to, or correct, a prevailing social injustice. Also, criminal behavior *per se* is not nonviolent; it does not involve a willingness to accept any penalty or punishment for breaking the law. Revolutionary activities, on the other hand— unlike acts of civil disobedience—involve the possible violent overthrow of an entire system of government and are not simply limited to a protest against specific laws or policies held to be unjust.

An act of civil disobedience, it should be noted, is not or cannot always be direct—i.e., an actual violation of the particular law or policy considered unjust. An act of protest against the government's foreign policy or policy on nuclear weapons, for example, may take the form of breaking other laws (such as those against occupying public buildings) for the purpose of calling attention to the policy at issue. Such violations would be indirect acts of civil disobedience. Another type of action that closely resembles civil disobedience is conscientious objection or refusal. A pacifist or person with certain strong religious convictions may refuse to serve in the armed forces, to fight in time of war, or even to salute the flag. To distinguish clearly between acts of civil disobedience and acts of conscientious objection may, in certain contexts, be difficult or even impossible. Most acts of conscientious objection are, however, individual or personal actions based upon the individual's own moral or religious code; and as such, they are not political actions and do not obligate others to the same course of action. Because of his religious convictions, a person may conscientiously refuse to serve in the armed forces without implying that others who do not share the same religious convictions are obligated to do the same.

In recent years John Rawls has developed an elaborate theory of justice including an analysis and justification of civil disobedience and conscientious refusal. Rawls's book, *A Theory of Justice* (1971), has had wide impact and caused extensive comment.[132] Rawls has attempted to defend a social contract theory of justice, in the tradition of Kant and others, which he believes superior to any utilitarian account. Beginning with the assumption that justice is a primary but not sole virtue of any social institution, Rawls argues that "each person possesses an inviolability founded on justice that even the welfare of society as a whole cannot override. For this reason justice denies that the loss of freedom for some is made right by a greater good shared by others."[133] Consequently "the rights secured by justice are not subject to political bargaining or to the calculus of social interests . . . analogously, an injustice is tolerable only when it is necessary to avoid an even greater injustice."[134] From this it is apparent that Rawls's conception of justice is similar to that of C. I. Lewis—but Rawls's account is worked out in much greater detail with more extensive supporting argumentation. At the outset Rawls points out that one should not confuse the conception of justice with what he calls a "social ideal." Social institutions can be expected to possess other virtues than justice—for example, efficiency or liberality. "A complete conception defining principles for all the virtues of the basic structure, together with their respective weights when they conflict, is more than a conception of justice; it is a social ideal. The principles of justice are but a part, although perhaps the most important part, of such a conception."[135]

Rawls's social contract theory involves the idea that the principles of justice are to be regarded as the results of an agreement or contract that rational, free persons would make in an initial or original position of equality. "Thus we are to imagine that those who engage in social cooperation choose together, in one joint act, the principles which are to assign basic rights and duties and to determine the division of social benefits. Men are to decide in advance how they are to regulate their claims against one another and what is to be the foundation charter of their society."[136] Rawls remarks that this original condition of equality corresponds to the idea of a state of nature in traditional social contract theories. We must carefully note, however, that this state of nature or initial position of agreement is hypothetical and does not refer to any actual historical agreement made between people. Rawls even assumes that "the principles of justice are chosen behind a veil of ignorance. This ensures that no one is advantaged or disadvantaged in the choice of principles by the outcome of natural chance or the contingency of social circumstances."[137] Those engaged in making the original agreement are neither to know their social status or position in society nor any facts about their particular talents or fortunes. No one in the original position is to have any unfair advantage over anyone else. Since all are equal, Rawls calls this hypothetical position of agreement "justice as fairness." While this postulated agreement describes no actual society, a society so based would represent an ideal model since it is based on "principles which free and equal persons would assent to under circumstances that are fair. In this sense its members are autonomous and the obligations they recognize self-imposed."[138]

Rawls provisionally formulates two principles of justice that would, he argues, be chosen in the initial position: "First: each person is to have an equal right to the most extensive basic liberty compatible with a similar liberty for others. Second: social and economic inequalities are to be arranged so that they are both (a) reasonably expected to be to everyone's advantage, and (b) attached to positions and offices open to all."[139] Rawls claims that the first principle takes precedence over the second. Thus violations of, or departures from, the notion of equal liberty cannot be justified in terms of producing some kind of greater economic or social benefits. Clearly, Rawls's theory of justice is to be taken as an alternative to, or in basic disagreement with, the traditional utilitarian account of social justice as a "principle of rational prudence applied to an aggregative conception of the welfare of the group."[140] One important contrast between Rawls's theory of justice and utilitarianism is that the former is deontological while the latter is teleological. This does not mean, however, that utilitarianism considers consequences whereas the social contract theory does not. Rather it means that the concept of right in the contract theory takes precedence over the concept of good. A utilitarian theory generally measures or determines questions of moral rightness in terms of what produces the greatest good for the greatest number. The contract theory or Rawls's theory of "justice as fairness" insists that "the principles of right, and so of justice, put limits on which satisfactions have value; they impose restrictions on what are reasonable conceptions of one's good."[141] Theoretically at least, according to utilitarianism, it is possible or may be desirable to compromise or restrict some people's rights or freedoms in order to achieve a greater balance of good or satisfactions for all. According to Rawls, this would be impossible for the social contract theory, since it does not define the concept of equal liberty for all in terms of contingent, future circumstances; this concept is to be agreed upon in the original position as a principle having priority over other principles. Rawls claims that his concept of "justice as fairness" has the advantage that men publicly express their respect for one another. Thus Rawls's theory agrees with the moral position of Kantian ethics: that human beings should always be treated as ends in themselves, never merely as means. The utilitarian theory, on the other hand, may treat persons as means rather than ends if such treatment is necessary for achieving the greatest good for the greatest number.

Rawls elaborates his conception of justice in his treatment of such items as majority rule, equal liberty, the concept of justice in political economy, and so on. We shall not attempt to follow his theory in all its different dimensions but will briefly look at his treatment of two important items that concern the subject of morality and law—civil disobedience and conscientious refusal.

In his *Theory of Justice*, Rawls considers civil disobedience, a crucial question for any theory which claims to offer a moral foundation for a democratic society. Rawls asks, "At what point does the duty to comply with laws enacted by a legislative majority (or with executive acts supported by such a majority) cease to be binding in view of the right to defend one's liberties and the duty to oppose injustice?"[142] One has no problem in complying with just or fair laws, but what about unjust ones? It might seem from a moral point of view that we are never obligated to obey unjust laws. But this, according to Rawls, is not true. "The injustice of a law is not, in general, a sufficient reason for not adhering to it any more than the legal validity of legislation (as defined by the existing constitution) is a sufficient reason for going along with it. When the basic structure of society is reasonably just, as estimated by what the current state of things allows, we are to recognize unjust laws as binding provided that they do not exceed certain limits of injustice."[143] To determine when unjust laws exceed tolerable limits may not be a simple matter, but it is clear that acts of civil disobedience have traditionally occurred only when serious injustices are involved or when basic liberties have been violated—the Fugitive Slave Law is a case in point. With this in mind, we can see a strong similarity between Rawls's definition of civil disobedience and Martin Luther King's conception. Rawls defines civil disobedience as "a public, nonviolent, conscientious yet political act contrary to law usually done with the aim of bringing about a change in the law or policies of the government. By acting in this way one addresses the sense of justice of the majority of the community and declares that in one's considered opinion the principles of social cooperation among free and equal men are not being respected."[144] He maintains further that acts of civil disobedience may be direct or indirect. Although such acts must be political rather than merely personal or individual, he alleges that they cannot be based solely on the vested interests of a group. Acts of civil disobedience must somehow be addressed to a commonly held conception of justice in the society at large. Rawls admits that his conception of civil disobedience is more restrictive than traditional conceptions. For example, Thoreau's refusal to pay a tax on the grounds that payment would make him an agent of injustice would be classified by Rawls as conscientious refusal rather than civil disobedience. Conscientious refusal, according to Rawls, is not necessarily based on an appeal to the majority sense of justice nor is it necessarily a political act; it may be founded on religious or other principles at variance with constitutional order. Ultimately civil disobedience is justified in terms of one's right to oppose serious infractions of basic human liberties or rights. Social order is not equivalent to justice, and therefore no democratic state has a right to use force or coercive measures to uphold manifestly unjust laws or institutions. As Rawls declares, "To employ the coercive apparatus of the state in order to maintain manifestly unjust institutions is itself a form of illegitimate force that men in due course have a right to resist."[145]

Any attempted justification for acts of civil disobedience obviously depends upon how such acts are defined. Recent discussions of this issue by American philosophers reveal a number of important disagreements.[146] Serious debate has occurred over such issues as whether acts of civil disobedience must be nonviolent, performed in an open manner, or accomplished with a willingness to accept the penalty prescribed by law. Perhaps the most serious

disagreement concerns the first issue—whether acts of civil disobedience must, by definition, be nonviolent. Robert Hall, in his recent
book *The Morality of Civil Disobedience* (1971), argues that
restricting acts of civil disobedience to those actions which are
nonviolent is improper. Hall points out that the idea of civil
disobedience emerged in the United States "among men of rather
diverse political, religious, and philosophical views, and was embod-
ied in equally diverse actions."[147] An act of civil disobedience,
according to Hall, must be an illegal act for which a moral
justification of some sort is given; but it cannot be presumed that the
moral justification is the same for all cases or that it necessarily rules
out the use of force. To add further qualifications to any definition
of civil disobedience, Hall argues, would prejudice the whole
question of moral justification. "If we say that an act of civil
disobedience must be nonviolent, or that it must be public, or that
the agent must be willing to accept punishment, as others have
argued, we shall eliminate many acts from possible justification
before considering their moral implications."[148] Hall maintains that
not all acts undertaken as instances of civil disobedience can be
justified from everyone's moral perspective. But if some notion of
moral justification is built into the definition as a special requirement, this will have the result of undermining any rational consideration of the whole matter. It may be true that nonviolent acts of civil
disobedience have a greater respectability or that we should rationally always choose nonviolent action when a meaningful choice is
possible. But this does not automatically imply that any use of force
is destructive of the moral character of an act of civil disobedience.

Robert Paul Wolff, in a recent essay "On Violence" (1969),
correctly points out that the concepts of violence and nonviolence,
as used in contemporary discussions of civil disobedience and
politics, are often inherently confused and poorly defined. The
concepts "depend for their meaning in political discussions on the
fundamental notion of legitimate authority, which is also inherently
incoherent."[149] One usually thinks of violence as an illegitimate use
of force employed to gain some end against the will of another. But
clearly, as Wolff points out, the notion of violence cannot be restricted to bodily harm. "When you occupy the seats at a lunch
counter for hours on end, thereby depriving the proprietor of the
profits he would have made on ordinary sales during that time, you

are taking money out of his pocket quite as effectively as if you had robbed his till or smashed his stock."[150] Wolff arrives at the extreme conclusion that we cannot politically distinguish between legitimate and illegitimate uses of force since such a distinction must be based on a pure fiction—the idea of legitimate political authority. He declares, "I have come to the conclusion that philosophical anarchism is true. That is to say, I believe that there is not, and there could not be, a state that has a right to command and whose subjects have a binding obligation to obey."[151] Wolff uses the concept of autonomy to explain this view. Each person has a responsibility for authorship of his own actions. Thus, for Wolff, political obedience to the will of the state would be heteronomous, not self-determined. He argues that even in a democracy which operates in terms of majority rule or consent of the governed, heteronomy is necessarily involved insofar as there is absence of unanimity. Obedience to the will of the majority is not true autonomy. Wolff argues that there is "no valid *political* criterion for the justified use of force. Legality is, by itself, no justification."[152] Political arguments of whatever sort that are used to defend legitimacy of the use of force are, in other words, rhetorical rather than logical. Such arguments may be persuasive, but they cannot be proven correct. From this, Wolff argues that the belief in nonviolence as related to civil disobedience has no logical merit. Physical harm differs only in degree, not in kind, from the injuries inflicted by so-called nonviolent techniques of political action. Also, what is considered a matter of violence is intimately related to one's central interests, and since different people or groups have different central interests, conflicting conceptions of violence will inevitably occur. Wolff denies that one has any moral obligation to resist an unjust law openly rather than secretly, for nobody is obligated to accept or suffer unjust punishment. Civil disobedience thus requires no elaborate defense. "The choice is simple: if the law is right, follow it. If the law is wrong, evade it."[153]

Moral philosophy has recently shown great interest in the whole problem of the morality of punishment, including the issue of capital punishment.[154] Some of the questions considered include: whether punishment can be justified on moral grounds at all; whether punishment, if justifiable, should be defended on grounds of utility or deterrence of crime or in terms of retribution and justice; whether some treatment or some form of rehabilitation should be substituted for traditional forms of punishment; whether criminals are morally responsible for their actions or whether they are mentally sick or compulsive and thus not responsible for their misconduct; whether capital punishment is ever justified or whether it is an inhumane (cruel and unusual) form of retribution. In an important essay, "Two Concepts of Rules" (1955), Rawls distinguishes between what he terms "justifying a practice" and "justifying a particular action falling under the practice"; and applies this to the justification of punishment. Rawls argues that the two classical, competing views of punishment, the utilitarian and the retributive, can be reconciled if we see that the former applies to practices and the latter applies to particular actions falling under a practice. The retributive view essentially holds that the guilty should be punished as a matter of justice; one who commits a crime should be made to pay for his offense in fair proportion to the seriousness of the crime. This is only a simple matter of justice, not vengeance. The utilitarian view, on the other hand, essentially holds that punishment is justified in terms of its useful consequences in maintaining social order and deterring future criminal acts. So stated, these two views of punishment appear incompatible. But Rawls suggests that it is important for us to distinguish two different questions: (1) why it makes sense to punish a particular offender and (2) the more general question, why punish anyone at all? Rawls claims that a retributive answer to the first question makes sense; i.e., punishing a particular offender because he is guilty or has broken a particular law makes sense. But for the second question (why punish anyone at all?), a utilitarian answer makes sense—that punishment ultimately serves the best interests of society and deters crime. Rawls points out that "the judge and the legislator stand in different positions and look in different directions: one to the past, the other to the future. The justification of what the judge does, qua judge, sounds like the retributive view; the justification of what the (ideal) legislator does, qua legislator, sounds like the utilitarian view."[155] Although this way of reconciling the two views would not satisfy traditional retributivists such as Kant or utilitarians such as Bentham, it may help overcome some of the major defects in these traditional viewpoints. One major problem of the utilitarian view is that it may allow punishment of the innocent if such action deters crime or serves the interests of society. The retributive theory, on the other hand, seems unworkable in the sense that expecting a punishment to fit the crime in equal proportion (as, for example, mass murder) is not always possible or realistic.

In his recent essay "Why Punish the Guilty?" (1964), Richard Wasserstrom discusses whether some form of treatment or rehabilitation should not be substituted for punishment. Punishing someone for an action he could not help clearly makes no sense. For example, it makes no sense to punish a person because he is mentally ill. Thus if all criminal behavior is a form of sickness, criminals should be treated for their illness, not punished. Obviously all criminal behavior has not been established as a form of sickness or compulsive behavior that cannot be resisted. One of the most difficult determinations in particular cases is the degree or quality of control or responsibility that a person may have over his actions. This question clearly cannot be answered *a priori* or from mere definition of the terms involved in the question. Wasserstrom observes that "given all of our present knowledge, there is simply every reason to suppose that some of the people who do commit crimes are neither subject to irresistible impulses, incapable of knowing what they are doing, nor suffering from some other definite mental disease. And, if this is so, then it is a mistake to suppose that the treatment of criminals is on this ground always to be preferred to their punishment."[156] Wasserstrom further argues that if we make the desire to commit an illegal act the defining characteristic of mental illness—if we make psychopaths of all criminals—we have decided a matter of fact by the mere decision to use words in certain ways. "The illness which afflicts these criminals is simply the criminal behavior itself . . . At this point any attempt to substantiate or disprove the existence of a relationship between sickness and crime is ruled out of order."[157] Wasserstrom concludes by suggesting that the ultimate reason for punishing the guilty is that punishment is the only realistic method for deterring crime. As better methods of preventing or deterring crime are found, punishment can, of course, be reduced. But as long as punishment, or the threat of punishment serves as the best available deterrent, the contention that it is justifiable is only realistic.

A number of recent studies by both British and American philosophers have concerned the relation between morality and law—specifically regarding the topic of the enforcement of morals by the criminal law.[158] Should criminal law concern itself with the enforcement of morals and punish immorality as such? Can the immorality of a certain type of action ever form sufficient reason for making that kind of action illegal? Or is it possible to set theoretical limits on the power of any government to legislate against immorality? Should the state legislate morality in such areas as prostitution, homosexuality, adultery, and abortion? One obvious problem with the attempt to legislate morals, especially in the area of sexual conduct, is that often such laws cannot effectively be enforced. Lon Fuller, for example, argues that he would "have no difficulty in asserting that the law ought not to make it a crime for consenting adults to engage privately in homosexual acts. The reason for this conclusion would be that any such law simply cannot be enforced and its existence on the books would constitute an open invitation to blackmail, so that there would be a gaping discrepancy between the law as written and its enforcement in practice."[159] Another problem with the enforcement of morals by the criminal law is that such enforcement may involve a clear infringement upon individual liberty. Also persuasively argued, however, is that some kind of moral conformity is essential to the integrity and survival of any social order. The English jurist Lord Patrick Devlin has argued that "the suppression of vice is as much the law's business as the suppression of subversive activities; it is no more possible to define a sphere of private morality than it is to define one of private subversive activity."[160] Morality, Lord Devlin admits, involves both a public and private sphere of interest. The problem, however, is to balance or reconcile these interests. Most people would agree, he adds, that "there must be toleration of the maximum individual freedom that is consistent with the integrity of society."[161] Some forms of behavior clearly give rise to strong feelings of indignation, intolerance, or disgust in the majority of people. Deliberate cruelty to animals is a case in point; such behavior exceeds the bounds of tolerance. Similarly, according to Devlin, homosexual behavior or other sexual practices may arouse strong feelings of indignation and disgust—and may represent forms of behavior that society simply will not tolerate. But Devlin also holds that such matters are not decided by rational argument. "Every moral judgment, unless it claims a divine source, is simply a feeling that no right-minded man could behave in any other way without admitting that he was doing wrong."[162] Devlin's views have inspired a lively debate over the whole problem of the enforcement of morals by the criminal law. And while the issue of homosexuality is without doubt a very emotional one, one cannot easily see how its satisfactory resolution can be based on emotional grounds rather than on evidence and rational argument. It is not only that feelings of indignation, intolerance, and disgust are subject to fluctuation; it is also probable, perhaps inevitable, that any legislation or enforcement of morals based on such emotions will exhibit inconsistency, arbitrariness, and unfairness.

One of the most serious current problems confronting legislators, philosophers, and the general public is the issue of abortion—indeed, one could hardly find a more highly charged emotional issue. Does the unborn fetus have a right to life which should be protected by law? At what point in the development of a human life does performance of an abortion become morally impermissible? If abortion is permitted, on what grounds and in what situations? These and other questions raise serious, seemingly insurmountable difficulties. While recent discussion of this topic has by no means resolved these problems,[163] fundamental issues have been identified and key ideas clarified. A primary question in this whole dispute is the determination of when any living being has a right to life. When does a living organism have the status of a moral agent whose right to life should be respected? One recent answer to this question: "An organism possesses a serious right to life only if it possesses the concept of a self as a continuing subject of experiences and other mental states, and believes that it is itself such a continuing entity."[164] While this answer may be acceptable for identifying conditions sufficient for establishing a right to life, one cannot easily see how these conditions can count as necessary ones. Human fetuses or even infants obviously have no concept of a self as a continuing subject of experiences. It is nevertheless reasonable to suppose that they have the potentiality to develop a concept of self which can be realized under suitable conditions. If the potentiality of the developing human organism is not respected or protected, as having a right to develop, one cannot easily see how any mature organism could emerge to have its rights protected or respected. In other words, if one believes that a mature human being who possesses a concept of self as a continuing subject of experiences should be respected as having a moral right to life, then respect and protection of the developing human organism who will become the mature human being also seems necessary. This does not, of course, settle the troublesome problems of abortion—what to do when one life and its interests conflict with another or with other values. Should the fetus be aborted if evidence shows that it will be abnormal, deformed, or mentally retarded? Should it be aborted if its continued existence is a threat to the physical or psychological wellbeing of the mother? Should it be aborted if the birth is unwanted or will impose a hardship on the family or on society? There are no easy answers to these questions because they present us with serious conflicts between different lives and values. The problems of abortion, in their most basic dimensions, display a coming together of the most serious problems in ethical theory and practice. On the theoretical side, there are all the problems involved with the meaning and cognitive status of any normative or imperative judgments concerning the value of the human fetus or developing individual. On the one hand, it has been claimed that a fetus is not a person or human being any more than an acorn is an oak tree. On the other hand, it has been argued that a human fetus is certainly human and that the point of origin of the human being (and consequently the possession and needed protection of its rights) must be defined from the time of conception, since any later determination is only arbitrary. What sort of evidence is relevant to any claim that the human fetus has, or does not have, a moral right to its life which should be respected and protected? On the practical side, we have the problems of deciding and planning for the concrete cases which arise daily in our lives. Though it cannot be claimed that the developments within American Ethics have satisfactorily solved the problem of abortion or other pressing moral questions, what can be claimed is that the problems have been clearly faced, identified, and, in some measure, clarified. The real problems of ethics are always with us as constant reminders that the human condition needs perfecting. They stand as a persisting challenge to any person or any society that hopes to make itself truly civilized or humanized.

Notes

1 — Puritan Ethics

1. Perry Miller, *The New England Mind From Colony to Province,* (Cambridge: Harvard University Press, 1953), p. 40.
2. Gerald N. Grob and Robert N. Beck, eds., *American Ideas: Source Readings in the Intellectual History of the United States,* vol. 1 (New York: Collier-Macmillan, 1963), p. 51.
3. Ibid.
4. See Larzer Ziff, *Puritanism In America: New Culture in a New World,* (New York: Viking, 1973), p. 141.
5. Vernon Louis Parrington, "The Twilight of the Oligarchy," in *Puritanism in Early America: Problems in American Civilization,* ed. George M. Waller (Boston: Heath, 1950), p. 52.
6. Edmund S. Morgan, *The Puritan Family: Religion and Domestic Relations in Seventeenth-Century New England,* (New York: Harper & Row, 1966), p. 185.
7. Larzer Ziff, *Puritanism in America,* p. 218.
8. Perry Miller, *Jonathan Edwards,* (New York: Meridian, 1959), p. 194.
9. Jonathan Edwards, "Sinners in the Hands of an Angry God," in *Jonathan Edwards: Representative Selections,* eds. Clarence H. Faust and Thomas H. Johnson (New York: American Book Co., 1935), p. 161.
10. Ibid., p. 164.
11. Ibid., pp. 163-64.
12. Jonathan Edwards, "Notes on the Mind," in Faust and Johnson, *Jonathan Edwards: Representative Selections,* p. 28.
13. Ibid.
14. Ibid., p. 29.
15. Jonathan Edwards, *The Nature of True Virtue,* (Ann Arbor: University of Michigan Press, 1960), p. 69.
16. Ibid., p. 77.
17. Ibid., p. 2.

18. Guy W. Stroh, *American Philosophy from Edwards to Dewey*, (Princeton: Van Nostrand, 1968), p. 20.

19. Edwards, *The Nature of True Virtue*, p. 98.

20. Jonathan Edwards, "Of Being," in Faust and Johnson, *Jonathan Edwards: Representative Selections*, pp. 275-76.

21. Edwards, *The Nature of True Virtue*, p. 92.

22. Jonathan Edwards, "Freedom of the Will," in Faust and Johnson, *Jonathan Edwards: Representative Selections*, pp. 275-276.

23. Ibid., p. 276.

24. Perry Miller, "The Puritan State and Puritan Society," in *Puritanism and the American Experience*, ed. Michael McGiffert (Reading, Mass.: Addison-Wesley Co., 1969), p. 43.

25. Clyde A. Holbrook, ed., *Jonathan Edwards: Original Sin*, (New Haven: Yale University Press, 1970), p. 130.

26. Ibid., p. 134.

27. Paul Ramsey, ed., *Jonathan Edwards: Freedom of the Will*, (New Haven: Yale University Press, 1957), p. 133.

28. Stroh, *American Philosophy from Edwards to Dewey*, p. 7.

29. Ramsey, ed., *Jonathan Edwards: Freedom of the Will*, p. 277.

30. Ibid., p. 215.

31. Ibid., p. 213.

32. Ibid., p. 217.

33. Ibid., p. 402.

34. Samuel Eliot Morison, "The Puritan Pronaos," in Waller, *Puritanism in Early America*, p. 79.

35. Perry Miller, "The Puritan Way of Life," in Waller, *Puritanism In Early America*, p. 6.

36. Edwards, *The Nature of True Virtue*, p. 70.

37. Ramsey, ed., *Jonathan Edwards: Freedom of the Will*, p. 215.

38. Ibid.

39. Ibid., p. 217.

2 — Enlightenment Ethics

1. Nelson F. Adkins, ed., *Thomas Paine: Common Sense and Other Political Writings* (New York: Bobbs-Merrill Co., 1953), p. 84.

2. Thomas Jefferson, "Letter to Charles Yancey, Monticello, January 6, 1816," in *The Political Writings of Thomas Jefferson: Representative Selections*, ed. Edward Dumbauld (New York: Bobbs-Merrill Co., 1955), p. 93.

3. John Dewey, *The Living Thoughts of Thomas Jefferson* (New York: Fawcett Publications, 1957), p. 125.

4. Henry Steele Commager, *Jefferson, Nationalism and the Enlightenment* (New York: George Braziller, 1975), p. 74.

5. Thomas Jefferson, "Letter to Thomas Law, Esq., Poplar Forest, June 13, 1814," in *The Life and Selected Writings of Thomas Jefferson*, eds. Adrienne Koch and William Peden (New York: Modern Library, 1944), p. 637.

6. Ibid., p. 638.

7. Ibid.

8. Thomas Jefferson, "Notes on Virginia, Query XVII," in Dumbauld, *The Political Writings of Thomas Jefferson: Representative Selections*, p. 36.

9. Thomas Jefferson, "Statute of Virginia for Religious Freedom," in Dumbauld, *The Political Writings of Thomas Jefferson: Representative Selections*, p. 35.

10. Thomas Jefferson, "Letter to Doctor Benjamin Rush, Washington, April 21, 1803," in *The American Enlightenment, The Shaping of the American Experiment and a Free Society*, ed. Adrienne Koch (New York: George Braziller, 1965), p. 346.

11. Thomas Jefferson, "Cabinet Opinion, July 15, 1790," in Dumbauld, *The Political Writings of Thomas Jefferson: Representative Selections*, p. 83.

12. Thomas Jefferson, "Letter to James Madison, January 30, 1787," in Koch, *The American Enlightenment, The Shaping of the American Experiment and a Free Society*, pp. 314-15.

13. Thomas Jefferson, "First Inaugural Address, March 4, 1801," in Dumbauld, *The Political Writings of Thomas Jefferson: Representative Selections*, pp. 42-43.

14. Thomas Jefferson, "Letter to George Wythe, August 13, 1786," in Koch and Peden, *The Life and Selected Writings of Thomas Jefferson*, pp. 394-95.

15. Commager, *Jefferson, Nationalism and the Enlightenment*, p. 114.

16. Ibid., p. 66.

17. See Dumas Malone, *Jefferson and the Ordeal of Liberty: Jefferson and His Time*, vol. 3 (Boston: Little, Brown & Co., 1962), chapter 3.

18. "A Declaration by the Representatives of the United States of America in General Congress Assembled," in Koch, *The American Enlightenment, The Shaping of the American Experiment and a Free Society*, p. 380.

19. Commager, *Jefferson, Nationalism and the Enlightenment*, p. 60.

20. Thomas Jefferson, "Letter to Edward Coles, Monticello, August 25, 1814," in Koch, *The American Enlightenment, The Shaping of the American Experiment and a Free Society*, p. 361.

21. Thomas Jefferson, "Autobiography," in Koch, *The American Enlightenment, The Shaping of the American Experiment and a Free Society*, pp. 299-300.

22. Jeremy Bentham, "Anarchical Fallacies," in *Human Rights*, ed. A. I. Melden, (Belmont, Cal.: Wadsworth Publishing Co., 1970), p. 31.

23. Ibid., p. 30.

3 — Transcendentalist Ethics

1. Immanuel Kant, *Critique of Pure Reason* (New York: American Home Library Co., 1902), pp. 59-60.

2. Ralph Waldo Emerson, "The Transcendentalist," in *The Complete Essays and Other Writings of Ralph Waldo Emerson*, ed. Brooks Atkinson (New York: Modern Library, 1940), p. 93.

3. Henry David Thoreau, "Journal, March 5, 1853," in *The American Transcendentalists, Their Prose and Poetry*, ed. Perry Miller (New York: Doubleday, 1957), p. 2.

4. Ralph Waldo Emerson, "Self-Reliance," in Atkinson, *The Complete Essays and Other Writings of Ralph Waldo Emerson*, p. 148.

5.   Henry David Thoreau, *Walden; or, Life in the Woods and On the Duty of Civil Disobedience* (New York: Rinehart, 1948), p. 282.

6.   Edward H. Madden, *Civil Disobedience and Moral Law in Nineteenth-Century American Philosophy* (Seattle: University of Washington Press, 1968), p. 96.

7.   Margaret Fuller, "Woman in the Nineteenth Century," in Miller, *The American Transcendentalists, Their Prose and Poetry*, pp. 334-35.

8.   Ralph Waldo Emerson, "The Over-Soul," in Atkinson, *The Complete Essays and Other Writings of Ralph Waldo Emerson*, p. 275.

9.   Ralph Henry Gabriel, "Emerson and Thoreau," in *The Transcendentalist Revolt Against Materialism*, ed. George F. Whicher (Boston: Heath, 1949) p. 64.

10.   Ralph Waldo Emerson, "Compensation," in Atkinson, *The Complete Essays and Other Writings of Ralph Waldo Emerson*, p. 175.

11.   Thoreau, *Walden; or, Life in the Woods and On the Duty of Civil Disobedience*, p. 183.

12.   Carl Bode, ed., *The Best of Thoreau's Journals* (Carbondale: Southern Illinois University Press, 1967), p. 63.

13.   Joel Porte, *Emerson and Thoreau: Transcendentalists in Conflict* (Middletown, Conn.: Wesleyan University Press, 1965), p. 120.

14.   Henry David Thoreau, *A Week on the Concord and Merrimack Rivers* (Boston: Houghton Mifflin Co., 1961), p. 75.

15.   Ibid.

16.   Ibid., pp. 386-87.

17.   Ralph Waldo Emerson, "Divinity School Address," in Atkinson, *The Complete Essays and Other Writings of Ralph Waldo Emerson*, p. 73.

18.   Ralph Waldo Emerson, "Compensation," in Atkinson, *The Complete Essays and Other Writings of Ralph Waldo Emerson*, p. 174.

19.   Ibid., p. 180.

20.   Ralph Waldo Emerson, "Spiritual Laws," in Atkinson, *The Complete Essays and Other Writings of Ralph Waldo Emerson*, p. 190.

21.   Thoreau, *Walden; or, Life in the Woods and On the Duty of Civil Disobedience*, p. 11.

22.   Ibid., p. 74.

23.   Bode, *The Best of Thoreau's Journals*, p. 188.

24.   Porte, *Emerson and Thoreau: Transcendentalists in Conflict*, p. 122.

25.   Ibid., p. 154.

26.   Thoreau, *Walden; or, Life in the Woods and On the Duty of Civil Disobedience*, p. 111.

27.   Ibid., p. 285.

28.   See Henry David Thoreau, "Journal, October 1, 1851," in Bode, *The Best of Thoreau's Journals*, pp. 132-33.

29.   Thoreau, *Walden; or, Life in the Woods and On the Duty of Civil Disobedience*, p. 284.

30.   Henry David Thoreau, "Life Without Principle," in Miller, *The American Transcendentalists, Their Prose and Poetry*, p. 325.

31.   Thoreau, *Walden; or, Life in the Woods and On the Duty of Civil Disobedience*, p. 287.

32. Ralph Waldo Emerson, "Emancipation in the British West Indies," in Atkinson, *The Complete Essays and Other Writings of Ralph Waldo Emerson*, p. 843.

33. Ibid., p. 844.

34. Henry David Thoreau, "Life Without Principle," in Miller, *The American Transcendentalists, Their Prose and Poetry*, pp. 309-10.

35. Ralph Waldo Emerson, "The Transcendentalist," in Atkinson, *The Complete Essays and Other Writings of Ralph Waldo Emerson*, p. 101.

36. Thoreau, *Walden. or, Life in the Woods and On the Duty of Civil Disobedience*, p. 277.

37. See Atkinson, *The Complete Essays and Other Writings of Ralph Waldo Emerson*, p. 831.

38. Ibid., p. 861.

39. Ibid., p. 879.

40. Ibid., p. 885.

41. Ibid., p. 890.

42. Thoreau, *Walden; or, Life in the Woods and On the Duty of Civil Disobedience*, p. 286.

43. Ibid., p. 287.

44. Ibid., p. 289.

45. Ibid.

46. Ibid., p. 288.

47. Ralph Waldo Emerson, "Man the Reformer," in *Nature, Addresses and Lectures*, vol. 1 (Boston: Houghton Mifflin Co., 1903), p. 247.

48. Ibid., pp. 255-56.

49. Thoreau, *Walden; or, Life in the Woods and On the Duty of Civil Disobedience*, p. 290.

50. Emerson, "Man the Reformer," in *Nature, Addresses and Lectures*, p. 256.

51. Thoreau, *Walden; or, Life in the Woods and On the Duty of Civil Disobedience*, p. 290.

52. Ralph Waldo Emerson, *Miscellanies*, vol. 11 (Boston: Houghton Mifflin Co., 1904), p. 89.

53. I. H. Bartlett, ed., *William Ellery Channing: Unitarian Christianity and Other Essays* (New York: Bobbs-Merrill Co., 1957), p. 47.

54. D. H. Meyer, *The Instructed Conscience: The Shaping of the American National Ethic* (Philadelphia: University of Pennsylvania Press, 1972), p. 30.

55. Ralph Waldo Emerson, "The Transcendentalist," in Atkinson, *The Complete Essays and Other Writings of Ralph Waldo Emerson*, p. 93.

56. Bode, *The Best of Thoreau's Journals*, p. 64.

57. Ralph Waldo Emerson, "Spiritual Laws," in Atkinson, *The Complete Essays and Other Writings of Ralph Waldo Emerson*, p. 190.

58. Ralph Waldo Emerson, "Politics," in Atkinson, *The Complete Essays and Other Writings of Ralph Waldo Emerson*, p. 431.

4 — Pragmatist Ethics

1. See Philip P. Wiener, *Evolution and the Founders of Pragmatism* (Cambridge: Harvard University Press, 1949), chapter 2.

2. Edward H. Madden, *The Philosophical Writings of Chauncey Wright:*

Representative Selections (New York: Liberal Arts Press, 1958), pp. 20-21.

3.   Charles Sanders Peirce, "The Fixation of Belief," in *Collected Papers of Charles Sanders Peirce*, vol. 5, eds. Charles Hartshorne and Paul Weiss (Cambridge: Harvard University Press, 1934-35), p. 230.

4.   See Charles Sanders Peirce, "How to Make Our Ideas Clear," in Hartshorne and Weiss, *Collected Papers of Charles Sanders Peirce*, vol. 5, pp. 259-60.

5.   William James, *Pragmatism: A New Name for Some Old Ways of Thinking, Together With Four Related Essays Selected from The Meaning of Truth* (New York: Longmans, 1959), p. 46.

6.   Ibid., p. 47.

7.   Charles Sanders Peirce, "How to Make Our Ideas Clear," in Hartshorne and Weiss, *Collected Papers of Charles Sanders Peirce*, vol. 5, pp. 259-60.

8.   Charles Sanders Peirce, "A Survey of Pragmatism," in Hartshorne and Weiss, *Collected Papers of Charles Sanders Peirce*, vol. 5, p. 318.

9.   James, *Pragmatism . . . With Four Related Essays from the Meaning of Truth*, p. 310.

10.   Ibid.

11.   Ibid., pp. 310-11.

12.   Ibid., p. 304.

13.   John Dewey, *Philosophy and Civilization* (New York: Capricorn Books, 1963), p. 26.

14.   Ibid., p. 21.

15.   William James, *Psychology* (New York: Holt, 1910), p. 4.

16.   Ibid., p. 3.

17.   Ibid.

18.   Guy W. Stroh, *American Philosophy from Edwards to Dewey* (Princeton: Van Nostrand, 1968), p. 136.

19.   William James, "The Moral Philosopher and the Moral Life," in *The Will to Believe and Other Essays in Popular Philosophy and Human Immortality* (New York: Dover, 1956), p. 189.

20.   Ibid.

21.   Ibid.

22.   Ibid., p. 195.

23.   Ibid., p. 200.

24.   Ibid., p. 201.

25.   Ibid., p. 203.

26.   Ibid., p. 209.

27.   William James, *The Principles of Psychology*, vol. 2, (New York: Dover, 1950), p. 578.

28.   Ibid., p. 579.

29.   Ibid., p. 572.

30.   William James, "The Dilemma of Determinism," in *The Will to Believe*, p. 149.

31.   Ibid., p. 151.

32.   Ibid., p. 161-62.

33.   Ralph Barton Perry, *Characteristically American* (New York: Alfred A. Knopf, 1949), p. 70.

34. James, *Psychology*, pp. 152, 159.
35. Ibid., p. 152.
36. William James, *Essays in Radical Empiricism and A Pluralistic Universe* (New York: Longmans, 1958), p. 23.
37. James, *Pragmatism . . . With Four Related Essays from the Meaning of Truth*, p. 229.
38. James, *The Principles of Psychology*, vol. 2, p. 463.
39. Ibid., p. 450.
40. William James, "The Will to Believe," in *The Will to Believe*, p. 22.
41. John K. Roth, ed., *The Moral Equivalent of War and Other Essays, and Selections from Some Problems of Philosophy by William James* (New York: Harper Torchbooks, 1971), p. 7.
42. Ibid., p. 14.
43. Ibid., pp. 13-14.
44. Richard Hofstadter, *Social Darwinism in American Thought* (Boston: Beacon Press, 1944), p. 31.
45. William James, "Great Men and Their Environment," in *The Will to Believe*, pp. 232-33. Quoted from Herbert Spencer's "Study of Sociology."
46. Ibid., p. 233.
47. Ibid., pp. 225, 227.
48. Ibid., p. 245.
49. William James, "The Sentiment of Rationality," in *The Will to Believe*, p. 98.
50. Ibid., p. 99.
51. William James, "The Will to Believe," in *The Will to Believe*, p. 17.
52. Ibid., pp. 25-26.
53. James, *Pragmatism . . . With Four Related Essays from the Meaning of Truth*, p. 273.
54. Ibid., p. 58.
55. Gail Kennedy, ed., *Pragmatism and American Culture* (Boston: Heath, 1950), p. 57.
56. William James, *The Meaning of Truth: A Sequel to Pragmatism* (Ann Arbor: University of Michigan Press, 1970), p. 184.
57. William James, "Letter to H. G. Wells, September 11, 1906," in *The Letters of William James*, vol. 2, ed. Henry James (Boston: Atlantic Monthly Press, 1920), p. 260.
58. William James, "Letter to Mrs. Henry Whitman, June 7, 1899," in James, *The Letters of William James*, vol. 2, p. 90.
59. William James, "The Sentiment of Rationality," in *The Will to Believe*, pp. 70, 84, 95, 102.
60. John Wild, *The Radical Empiricism of William James* (Garden City: Anchor Books, 1970), p. 275.
61. William James, "The Moral Philosopher and the Moral Life," in *The Will to Believe*, p. 211.
62. Rollo May, "The Emergence of Existential Psychology," in *Existential Psychology*, ed. Rollo May (New York: Random House, 1961), p. 12.
63. William James, *The Varieties of Religious Experience: A Study in Human Nature* (New York: Modern Library Edition, 1929), p. 489.

64.   Charles Sanders Peirce, "Reviews, Correspondence and Bibliography," in Hartshorne and Weiss, *Collected Papers of Charles Sanders Peirce*, vol. 8, p. 18.

65.   Charles Sanders Peirce, "Exact Logic," in Hartshorne and Weiss, *Collected Papers of Charles Sanders Peirce*, vol. 3, p. 58.

66.   Stroh, *American Philosophy from Edwards to Dewey*, pp. 265-66.

67.   Dewey, *Philosophy and Civilization*, pp. 83, 92.

68.   James, *The Varieties of Religious Experience*, p. 489.

69.   Ibid., p. 507.

70.   Ibid., p. 513.

71.   William James, "The Sentiment of Rationality," in *The Will to Believe*, p. 109.

72.   William James, "The Moral Philosopher and the Moral Life," in *The Will to Believe*, p. 195.

5 — Idealist Ethics

1.   Guy W. Stroh, *American Philosophy from Edwards to Dewey* (Princeton: Van Nostrand, 1968), p. 74.

2.   J. H. Buckham and G. M. Stratton, *George Holmes Howison, Philosopher and Teacher* (Berkeley: University of California Press, 1934), p. 3.

·3.   Ibid., p. 127.

4.   Ibid., p. 149.

5.   Ibid.

6.   Ibid.

7.   Borden Parker Bowne, *Personalism* (Boston: Houghton Mifflin Co., 1908), p. 20.

8.   Ibid., p. 253.

9.   Ibid., pp. 253-56.

10.   Ibid., p. 266.

11.   James E. Creighton, "Two Types of Idealism," in *The Development of American Philosophy: A Book of Readings*, eds. W. G. Muelder and L. Sears (Boston: Houghton Mifflin Co., 1940), p. 294.

12.   Ibid., p. 295.

13.   Ibid., p. 296.

14.   Ibid., p. 300.

15.   See Josiah Royce, *Lectures on Modern Idealism* (New Haven: Yale University Press, 1964), p. 15.

16.   Ibid., p. 254.

17.   Josiah Royce, *The Religious Aspect of Philosophy: A Critique of the Bases of Conduct and of Faith* (New York: Harper Torchbooks, 1958), p. 376.

18.   Ibid., p. 433.

19.   Josiah Royce, *The Spirit of Modern Philosophy* (New York: Norton, 1967), pp. 207-08.

20.   Ibid., p. 208.

21.   Ibid., p. 206.

22.   Ibid., pp. 206-07.

23.   Royce, *The Religious Aspect of Philosophy: A Critique of the Bases of Conduct and of Faith*, p. 201.

24.   Ibid., p. 195.

25.   Ibid., p. 219.

26. Josiah Royce, *The Philosophy of Loyalty* (New York: Macmillan, 1908) p. 15.
27. Ibid., pp. 16-17.
28. Ibid., p. 108.
29. Ibid., p. 118.
30. Josiah Royce, *The Sources of Religious Insight* (New York: Scribner's, 1940), p. 203.
31. Ibid., p. 206.
32. Stroh, *American Philosophy from Edwards to Dewey*, p. 183.
33. Josiah Royce, *Race Questions, Provincialism and Other American Problems* (Freeport, N.Y.: Books for Libraries Press, 1967), p. 85.
34. Ibid., pp. 85-86.
35. Josiah Royce, *The Problem of Christianity: The Christian Doctrine of Life,* vol. 1 (Chicago: Henry Regnery, 1968), p. 67.
36. Ibid.
37. Josiah Royce, *The Problem of Christianity: The Real World and The Christian Ideas,* vol. 2 (Chicago: Henry Regnery, 1968), pp. 312-13.
38. Royce, *The Problem of Christianity*, vol. 1, p. xix.
39. Royce, *The Problem of Christianity*, vol. 2, p. 150.
40. Royce, *Lectures On Modern Idealism*, p. 255.
41. Ibid., p. 256.
42. Ibid.
43. Ibid., p. 237.
44. Josiah Royce, *The World and the Individual*, Gifford Lectures, Second Series: *Nature, Man, and the Moral Order* (New York: Macmillan, 1904), pp. 32-33.
45. Ibid., p. 430.
46. Ibid., p. 361.
47. Royce, *The Sources of Religious Insight*, p. 272.
48. Ibid., p. 85.
49. Ralph Waldo Emerson, "Spiritual Laws," in *The Complete Essays and Other Writings of Ralph Waldo Emerson*, ed. Brooks Atkinson (New York: Modern Library, 1940), p. 190.
50. Royce, *The Spirit of Modern Philosophy: An Essay in the Form of Lectures,* p. 448.
51. Ibid.
52. Josiah Royce, *Studies of Good and Evil: A Series of Essays Upon Problems of Philosophy and of Life* (New York: Appleton, 1898), p. 101.
53. Royce, *The Religious Aspect of Philosophy: A Critique of the Bases of Conduct and of Faith*, p. 168.
54. Ibid., pp. 180-181.
55. Royce, *The World and the Individual*, p. 359.
56. Royce, *The Religious Aspect of Philosophy: A Critique of the Bases of Conduct and of Faith*, p. 215.
57. Ibid., p. 216.
58. Royce, *The Problem of Christianity*, vol. 1, p. 327.
59. Ibid., p. 144.
60. Royce, *Race Questions, Provincialism and Other American Problems*, p. 62.
61. Ibid., p. 74.
62. Josiah Royce, *The Hope of the Great Community* (Freeport, N.Y.: Books for Libraries Press, 1967), p. 4.

63. Ibid., p. 1.

64. William James, "A Pluralistic Universe," in *Essays in Radical Empiricism, A Pluralistic Universe* (New York: Longmans, 1909), pp. 47-48.

65. John Dewey, *The Influence of Darwin On Philosophy and Other Essays in Contemporary Thought* (Bloomington, Ind.: Indiana University Press, 1965), pp. 17-18.

66. George Santayana, *Character and Opinion in the United States* (New York: Norton, 1967), pp. 106-107.

67. Charles Sanders Peirce, *Collected Papers of Charles Sanders Peirce, vol. 7, Science and Philosophy and vol. 8, Reviews, Correspondence, and Bibliography*, ed. Arthur W. Burks (Cambridge: Harvard University Press, 1958), p. 80 (vol. 8).

6 — Naturalistic Ethics

1. John Herman Randall, Jr., "Epilogue: The Nature of Naturalism" in *Naturalism and the Human Spirit*, ed. Yervant H. Krikorian (New York: Columbia University Press, 1944), p. 356.

2. John Dewey, *Experience and Nature* (New York: Dover, 1958), p. 4a.

3. George Santayana, *The Life of Reason; Or, The Phases of Human Progress, vol. 1, Introduction and Reason In Common Sense* (New York: Scribner's, 1905) pp. 38-39.

4. George Santayana, *The Sense of Beauty* (New York: Scribner's, 1896), pp. 38-39.

5. George Santayana, *Realms of Being* (New York: Scribner's, 1942), p. 8.

6. Guy W. Stroh, *American Philosophy from Edwards to Dewey*, (Princeton: Van Nostrand, 1968), p. 193.

7. Santayana, *Realms of Being*, p. xii.

8. Stroh, *American Philosophy from Edwards to Dewey*, p. 192.

9. George Santayana, *Interpretations of Poetry and Religion* (New York: Harper, 1957), p. 108.

10. Ibid., p. v.

11. Stroh, *American Philosophy from Edwards to Dewey*, p. 204.

12. George Santayana, *Winds of Doctrine, And Platonism and the Spiritual Life* (New York: Harper Torchbooks, 1957), p. 144.

13. John Dewey, *The Quest for Certainty: A Study of the Relation of Knowledge and Action* (New York: Capricorn Books, 1960), p. 255.

14. Dewey, *Experience and Nature*, p. 1a.

15. John Dewey, *Philosophy and Civilization* (New York: Capricorn Books, 1963), p. 26.

16. John Dewey, *Essays In Experimental Logic* (Chicago: University of Chicago Press, 1916), pp. 307-308.

17. Stroh, *American Philosophy from Edwards to Dewey*, p. 248.

18. John Dewey, *Theory of Valuation* in International Encyclopedia of Unified Science, vols. 1 and 2 (Chicago: University of Chicago Press, 1939), p. 58 (vol. 2, no. 4).

19. Dewey, *The Quest for Certainty: A Study of the Relation of Knowledge and Action*, p. 256.

20. Dewey, *Theory of Valuation*, p. 66.

21. Ralph Barton Perry, *Realms of Value: A Critique of Human Civilization* (Cambridge: Harvard University Press, 1954), pp. 2-3.

22. Morris R. Cohen, *A Preface to Logic* (Gloucester, Mass.: Peter Smith, 1973), pp. 168-169.

23. Sidney Hook, "Naturalism and Democracy," in Krikorian, *Naturalism and the Human Spirit*, p. 57.

24. Ernest Nagel, *Logic Without Metaphysics, and Other Essays In the Philosophy of Science* (Glencoe, Ill.: Free Press, 1956), pp. 50-51.

25. John Dewey, *Human Nature and Conduct: An Introduction to Social Psychology* (New York: Modern Library, 1930), p. v.

26. Santayana, *Realms of Being*, pp. 479, 483.

27. Stroh, *American Philosophy from Edwards to Dewey*, p. 191.

28. Ibid., p. 198.

29. George Santayana, *Dominations and Powers: Reflections on Liberty, Society and Government* (New York: Scribner's, 1951), p. 18.

30. Santayana, *Realms of Being*, p. xii.

31. Stroh, *American Philosophy from Edwards to Dewey*, p. 193.

32. George Santayana, *Soliloquies in England, and Later Soliloquies* (Ann Arbor: University of Michigan Press, 1967), pp. 258-59.

33. Paul Arthur Schilpp, ed., *The Philosophy of George Santayana* (New York: Tudor, 1951), p. 562.

34. Santayana, *Winds of Doctrine, And Platonism and the Spiritual Life*, p. 145.

35. Santayana, *Realms of Being*, p. 473.

36. Santayana, *Winds of Doctrine, And Platonism and the Spiritual Life*, p. 144.

37. Ibid.

38. Santayana, *Realms of Being*, p. 475.

39. George Santayana, *The Life of Reason, Or, The Phases of Human Progress*, One-Volume Édition (New York: Scribner's, 1955), p. 454.

40. Santayana, *Winds of Doctrine, And Platonism and the Spiritual Life*, p. 151.

41. Santayana, *Realms of Being*, p. 834.

42. Stroh, *American Philosophy from Edwards to Dewey*, p. 265.

43. Paul Arthur Schilpp, ed., *The Philosophy of John Dewey* (New York: Tudor, 1951), p. 251.

44. Ibid., p. 252.

45. John Dewey, "Half-Hearted Naturalism," *Journal of Philosophy* XXIV (1927):58.

46. Ibid., p. 62.

47. Schilpp, *The Philosophy of John Dewey*, p. 604.

48. John Dewey, *The Early Works, 1882-1898, vol. 3: 1889-1892, Early Essays and Outlines of a Critical Theory of Ethics* (Carbondale: Southern Illinois University Press, 1969), p. 366.

49. Ibid., p. 368.

50. Dewey, *The Quest for Certainty*, p. 258.

51. Dewey, *Theory of Valuation*, p. 17.

52. Santayana, *Winds of Doctrine, And Platonism and the Spiritual Life*, p. 144.

53. Dewey, *Theory of Valuation*, p. 24.

54. Ibid., p. 45.

55. John Dewey, *Reconstruction In Philosophy* (Boston: Beacon Press, 1960), p. 177.

56. G. E. Moore, *Principia Ethica* (Cambridge: Cambridge University Press, 1959), p. 7.
57. Ibid., p. 41.
58. Ibid.
59. Santayana, *Winds of Doctrine, And Platonism and the Spiritual Life*, pp. 140-41.
60. Ibid., pp. 146-47.
61. Ibid., p. 148.
62. Ibid., p. 147.
63. Moore, *Principia Ethica*, p. 108.
64. Dewey, *The Quest for Certainty*, p. 268.
65. Ibid., p. 260.
66. Ibid., p. 258.
67. John Dewey, *Logic: The Theory of Inquiry* (New York: Holt, Rinehart & Winston, 1938), p. 503.
68. Ibid., p. 161.
69. Stroh, *American Philosophy from Edwards to Dewey*, pp. 203-04.
70. Santayana, *The Life of Reason, Or, The Phases of Human Progess*, One-Volume Edition, pp. 456-57.
71. Ibid., p. 258.
72. Ibid.
73. Ibid., p. 264.
74. Santayana, *Realms of Being*, pp. 557, 549.
75. John and Shirley Lachs, eds., *Physical Order and Moral Liberty, Previously Unpublished Essays of George Santayana* (Charlotte, N.C.: Vanderbilt University Press, 1969), p. 213.
76. Ibid., p. 286.
77. George Santayana, *Character and Opinion in the United States* (New York: Norton, 1967), p. 31.
78. Schilpp, *The Philosophy of George Santayana*, p. 533.
79. Santayana, *Character and Opinion in the United States*, p. 166.
80. Santayana, *Dominations and Powers*, p. 351.
81. Ibid., p. 109.
82. Ibid., p. 110.
83. Ibid., p. 109.
84. Santayana, *Winds of Doctrine, And Platonism and the Spiritual Life*, p. 215.
85. John Dewey, *Art as Experience* (New York: Capricorn Books, 1934), p. 348.
86. Ibid.
87. John Dewey, *A Common Faith* (New Haven: Yale University Press, 1934), p. 27.
88. Ibid., p. 26.
89. Dewey, *Art as Experience*, p. 39.
90. Ibid., p. 46.
91. Ibid., p. 341.
92. Ibid., p. 343.
93. Stroh, *American Philosophy from Edwards to Dewey*, p. 261.
94. John Dewey, *Moral Principles in Education* (New York: Philosophical Library, 1959), p. 2.
95. Ibid., p. 15.

96. Dewey, *Art as Experience*, p. 348.
97. See C. L. Stevenson, "The Emotive Meaning of Ethical Terms," *Mind* 46 (1937); and C. L. Stevenson, *Ethics and Language* (New Haven: Yale University Press, 1944).
98. C. L. Stevenson, *Facts and Values: Studies in Ethical Analysis* (New Haven: Yale University Press, 1963), p. 25.
99. Ibid., p. 29.
100. Ibid.
101. Ibid.
102. John Dewey, "Ethical Subject-Matter and Language," *Journal of Philosophy* XLII (1945): 703.
103. Stevenson, *Ethics and Language*, p. 36.
104. John Dewey, *Freedom and Culture* (New York: Capricorn Books, 1939), p. 158.
105. Ibid., p. 162.
106. John Dewey, *Democracy and Education: An Introduction to the Philosophy of Education* (New York: Macmillan, 1961), pp. 87, 99.
107. See Stevenson, *Ethics and Language*, p. 258.
108. See Milton K. Munitz, *The Moral Philosophy of Santayana* (New York: Humanities Press, 1958), p. 109.
109. R. M. Hare, *The Language of Morals* (Oxford: Clarendon Press, 1952), p. 82.
110. Sidney Hook, *The Quest for Being, and Other Studies in Naturalism and Humanism* (New York: Dell Publishing Co., 1963), p. 58.
111. G. J. Warnock, *Contemporary Moral Philosophy* (London: Macmillan, 1967), p. 63.
112. See Stevenson, *Ethics and Language*, p. 263.
113. Ibid., p. 259.
114. John Dewey and James H. Tufts, *Ethics* (New York: Holt, 1936), p. 296.
115. Dewey, "Ethical Subject-Matter and Language," p. 709.
116. Schilpp, *The Philosophy of George Santayana*, p. 562.
117. We have already mentioned a possible criticism of Dewey's view that experimental or scientific methods should and can be used for the solution of moral problems. See this chapter, p. 375.
118. Schilpp, *The Philosophy of George Santayana*, p. 562.
119. Bertrand Russell, *Portraits from Memory, and Other Essays* (New York: Simon & Schuster, 1969), p. 96.
120. One notable contemporary American philosopher, Henry David Aiken, shows the influence of Santayana's detached naturalism in his *Reason and Conduct: New Bearings in Moral Philosophy* (New York: Alfred A. Knopf, 1962), p. xv. Aiken declares, "Perhaps the greatest value of Santayana's writings for me is the almost fanatical detachment with which he examined the various symbolic forms that compose not only the life of reason but also those supra-rational forms of life in which the life of reason itself is always incysted. And in that detachment I have found both a great wisdom and a method. I suppose that I have returned oftener to Santayana's writings than to those of any other single philosopher save Hume."
121. See James K. Feibleman, *The New Materialism* (The Hague: Martinus Nijhoff, 1970), chapter 11: "Spirit as a Property of Matter." See also James K. Feibleman, *Ontology* (Baltimore: Johns Hopkins Press, 1951).

122. See James K. Feibleman, *Moral Strategy* (The Hague: Martinus Nijhoff, 1967).

123. See Sidney Hook, *Political Power and Personal Freedom: Critical Studies in Democracy, Communism, and Civil Rights* (New York: Collier Books, 1962).

124. Santayana, *Dominations and Powers*, p. vii.

125. Morris Raphael Cohen, *American Thought: A Critical Sketch* (New York: Collier Books, 1962), p. 364.

126. John Dewey, *Individualism; Old and New* (New York: Capricorn Books, 1962), p. 169.

7 — Recent Directions In Ethical Analysis

1. Charles L. Stevenson, *Ethics and Language* (New Haven: Yale University Press, 1944), p. vii.

2. See A. J. Ayer, *Language, Truth and Logic*, 2d ed. (New York: Dover, 1946), pp. 5-16, and C. G. Hempel, "The Empiricist Criterion of Meaning," in *Logical Positivism*, ed. A. J. Ayer (Glencoe, Ill.: Free Press, 1959), pp. 108-129.

3. These and other articles are collected in C. L. Stevenson, *Facts and Values: Studies in Ethical Analysis* (New Haven: Yale University Press, 1963).

4. Stevenson, *Ethics and Language*, p. 1.

5. Stevenson, *Facts and Values: Studies in Ethical Analysis*, p. 13.

6. Ibid.

7. Ibid.

8. Ibid., p. 15.

9. Ibid., p. 16.

10. Ibid.

11. Ibid., p. 18.

12. Ibid., p. 21.

13. Ibid. p. 24.

14. Stevenson, *Ethics and Language*, p. 267.

15. Stevenson, *Facts and Values: Studies in Ethical Analysis*, p. 84.

16. Stevenson, *Ethics and Language*, p. 267.

17. Ibid., pp. 154, 169.

18. Ibid., pp. 155-56.

19. Stevenson, *Facts and Values: Studies in Ethical Analysis*, p. 4.

20. See Stevenson, *Ethics and Language*, p. 60.

21. Stevenson, *Facts and Values: Studies in Ethical Analysis*, pp. 84-85.

22. Ibid., p. 87.

23. Ibid., p. 67.

24. Stevenson, *Ethics and Language*, p. 307.

25. Joseph Margolis, *Values and Conduct*, (New York: Oxford University Press, 1971), p. 6.

26. Stevenson, *Facts and Values: Studies in Ethical Analysis*, p. 3.

27. See Paul Edwards, *The Logic of Moral Discourse* (Glencoe, Ill.: Free Press, 1955), p. 47.

28. Stevenson, *Ethics and Language*, p. 6.

29. Stevenson, *Facts and Values: Studies in Ethical Analysis*, p. 67.

30. Ibid., p. 4.
31. Margolis, *Values and Conduct,* p. 36.
32. J. O. Urmson, *The Emotive Theory of Ethics* (New York: Oxford University Press, 1968), p. 45.
33. Ibid., p. 64.
34. Ibid., p. 69.
35. Edwards, *The Logic of Moral Discourse,* p. 47.
36. Ibid., p. 148.
37. Ibid., p. 28.
38. Ibid., p. 194.
39. C. I. Lewis, *The Ground and Nature of the Right* (New York: Columbia University Press, 1955), pp. 78-79.
40. C. I. Lewis, *An Analysis of Knowledge and Valuation* (LaSalle, Ill.: Open Court Publishing Co., 1946), p. 3.
41. Ibid.
42. Paul Arthur Schilpp, ed., *The Philosophy of C. I. Lewis* (LaSalle, Ill.: Open Court Publishing Co., 1968), pp. 672-73.
43. Lewis, *An Analysis of Knowledge and Valuation,* p. 554.
44. Stevenson, *Ethics and Language,* p. 97.
45. Lewis, *The Ground and Nature of the Right,* p. 59.
46. John Lange, ed., *Clarence Irving Lewis, Values and Imperatives: Studies in Ethics,* (Stanford: Stanford University Press, 1969), p. 38.
47. Ibid., p. 184.
48. Lewis, *The Ground and Nature of the Right,* p. 14.
49. Ibid., p. 82.
50. Ibid., pp. 83-84.
51. Lewis, *An Analysis of Knowledge and Valuation,* p. 554.
52. Ibid., p. 375.
53. Ibid., p. 387.
54. Ibid., p. 366.
55. Ibid., p. 373.
56. Ibid., p. 389.
57. Ibid., p. 458.
58. Lewis, *The Ground and Nature of the Right,* p. 82.
59. Ibid., p. 85.
60. Ibid., p. 88.
61. Ibid., p. 89.
62. Ibid.
63. Ibid., p. 91.
64. Ibid.
65. Lange, *Clarence Irving Lewis, Values and Imperatives: Studies in Ethics,* p. 109.
66. Ibid., p. 135.
67. Ibid.
68. Ibid., pp. 199-200.
69. Marcus G. Singer, *Generalization in Ethics: An Essay in the Logic of Ethics, with the Rudiments of a System of Moral Philosophy* (New York: Alfred A. Knopf, 1961), p. 6.

70.   Ibid., p. 103.
71.   For a comparison of Singer and Lewis, see J. Roger Saydah, *The Ethical Theory of C. I. Lewis* (Athens: Ohio University Press, 1969), Chapter 5.
72.   Singer, *Generalization in Ethics*, p. 5.
73.   Ibid.
74.   Ibid., p. 105.
75.   Ibid., p. 231.
76.   Ibid., p. 64.
77.   Lange, *C. I. Lewis: Values and Imperatives, Studies in Ethics*, p. 168.
78.   See W. D. Hudson, ed., *The Is/Ought Question: A Collection of Papers on the Central Problem in Moral Philosophy* (London: Macmillan, 1969).
79.   John R. Searle, *Speech Acts: An Essay in the Philosophy of Language* (London: Cambridge University Press, 1969), p. 188.
80.   Ibid., p. 179.
81.   Ibid., p. 181.
82.   Ibid., p. 185.
83.   Ibid., p. 188.
84.   Ibid., p. 179.
85.   Ibid.
86.   Ibid., p. 181.
87.   James K. Feibleman, *Moral Strategy, An Introduction to the Ethics of Confrontation* (The Hague: Martinus Nijhoff, 1967), from Preface.
88.   The following is a modified account of my paper "Feibleman's Contribution to Ethical Naturalism," originally read at *Symposium: The Philosophy of James K. Feibleman*, Sixty-Ninth Annual Meeting of the Southern Society for Philosophy and Psychology, Nashville, Tennessee, April 8, 1977.
89.   James K. Feibleman, "A Theory of Values" *Studium Generale*, July 24 (1971), p. 638.
90.   Ibid., p. 636.
91.   James K. Feibleman, *Moral Strategy*, p. 34.
92.   Ibid., p. 185.
93.   Ibid., p. 184.
94.   James K. Feibleman, "A Theory of Values", p. 637.
95.   James K. Feibleman, *Moral Strategy*, p. 203.
96.   Ibid., p. 175.
97.   Ibid., pp. 20-21.
98.   Ibid., p. 5.
99.   James K. Feibleman, *Ontology* (Baltimore: Johns Hopkins University Press, 1951), p. 524.
100. James K. Feibleman, *Moral Strategy*, p. 106.
101. Ibid., pp. 195-96.
102. Ibid., p. 170.
103. Ibid., p. 12.
104. Ibid., p. 212.
105. Ibid., p. 139.
106. Ibid., p. 162.
107. Ibid.
108. Ibid., p. 164.
109. Ibid., pp. 184-85.

110. Ibid., p. 176.
111. For recent work on this topic, see William T. Blackstone, ed., *Philosophy and Environmental Crisis* (Athens: University of Georgia Press, 1974).
112. James K. Feibleman, *Moral Strategy*, p. 223.
113. Ibid., p. 190.
114. See Joseph Fletcher, *Moral Responsibility: Situation Ethics at Work* (Philadelphia: Westminster Press, 1967); Joseph Fletcher, *Morals and Medicine* (Boston: Beacon Press, 1954); and Joseph Fletcher, *The Ethics of Genetic Control: Ending Reproductive Roulette* (New York: Anchor Books, 1974).
115. Joseph Fletcher, *Situation Ethics, The New Morality* (Philadelphia: Westminster Press, 1975), p. 18.
116. Ibid., p. 63.
117. Ibid., p. 25.
118. Ibid., p. 26.
119. Ibid., p. 88.
120. Ibid., pp. 88-89.
121. Ibid., p. 98.
122. Ibid., p. 147.
123. Ibid., p. 95.
124. Ibid., p. 120.
125. Ibid., p. 132.
126. Ibid., p. 115.
127. For an analysis of Fletcher's ethics, see Paul Ramsey, *Deeds and Rules in Christian Ethics* (New York: Scribner's, 1967) Chapter 7.
128. Reprinted in Edward Kent ed., *Revolution and the Rule of Law* (Englewood Cliffs, N. J.: Prentice-Hall, 1971).
129. Ibid., pp. 17-18.
130. Ibid., p. 20.
131. Ibid., p. 13.
132. See Norman Daniels, ed., *Reading Rawls: Critical Studies of a Theory of Justice* (New York: Basic Books, 1974); and Brian Barry, *The Liberal Theory of Justice: A Critical Examination of the Principal Doctrines in A Theory of Justice by John Rawls* (London: Oxford University Press, 1973).
133. John Rawls, *A Theory of Justice* (Cambridge: Harvard University Press, 1971), pp. 3-4.
134. Ibid., p. 4.
135. Ibid., p. 9.
136. Ibid., p. 11.
137. Ibid., p. 12.
138. Ibid., p. 13.
139. Ibid., p. 60.
140. Ibid., p. 24.
141. Ibid., p. 31.
142. Ibid., p. 363.
143. Ibid., pp. 350-351.
144. Ibid., p. 364.
145. Ibid., p. 391.
146. See Jeffrie Murphy, ed., *Civil Disobedience and Violence* (Belmont, Cal.: Wadsworth Publishing Co., 1971).

147.   Robert T. Hall, *The Morality of Civil Disobedience* (New York: Harper & Row, 1971), p. 14.
148.   Ibid., p. 15.
149.   Edward Kent, ed., *Revolution and the Rule of Law*, p. 61.
150.   Ibid., p. 70.
151.   Ibid., p. 66.
152.   Ibid., p. 67.
153.   Ibid., p. 71.
154.   See G. Ezorsky, ed., *Philosophical Perspectives on Punishment* (Albany: State University of New York Press, 1972); and Hugo Bedau, ed., *The Death Penalty in America: An Anthology* (Garden City, N.Y.: Anchor Books, 1967).
155.   G. Ezorsky, ed., *Philosophical Perspectives on Punishment*, p. 85.
156.   Ibid., p. 332.
157.   Ibid., p. 333.
158.   See Richard A. Wasserstrom, ed., *Morality and the Law* (Belmont, Cal.: Wadsworth Publishing Co., 1971).
159.   Lon L. Fuller, *The Morality of Law* (New Haven: Yale University Press, 1964), p. 133.
160.   Patrick Devlin, *The Enforcement of Morals* (London: Oxford University Press, 1972), pp. 13-14.
161.   Ibid., p. 16.
162.   Ibid., p. 17.
163.   See M. Cohen, T. Nagel and T. Scanlon, eds., *The Rights and Wrongs of Abortion* (Princeton: Princeton University Press, 1974); and John T. Noonan, Jr., ed., *The Morality of Abortion, Legal and Historical Perspectives* (Cambridge: Harvard University Press, 1970).
164.   Cohen, Nagel and Scanlon, eds., "Michael Tooley: Abortion and Infanticide" in *The Rights and Wrongs of Abortion*, p. 59.

Selected Bibliography

1 — Puritan Ethics

Aldridge, Alfred. *Jonathan Edwards*. New York: Washington Square Press, 1964.

Beck, Robert N., and Grob, Gerald N., eds. *American Ideas: Source Readings in the Intellectual History of the United States*. Vol. 1 (1629-1865). New York: Collier-Macmillan, 1963.

Edwards, Jonathan. *The Nature of True Virtue*. Ann Arbor: University of Michigan Press, 1960.

Faust, Clarence H., and Johnson, Thomas H., eds. *Jonathan Edwards: Representative Selections*. New York: American Book Co., 1935.

Hall, David, ed. *Puritanism in Seventeenth-Century Massachusetts*. New York: Holt, Rinehart & Winston, 1968.

Holbrook, Clyde A. *The Ethics of Jonathan Edwards: Morality and Aesthetics*. Ann Arbor: University of Michigan Press, 1973.

————, ed. *Jonathan Edwards: Original Sin*. New Haven: Yale University Press, 1970.

McGiffert, Michael, ed. *Puritanism and the American Experience*. Reading, Mass.: Addison-Wesley, 1969.

Miller, Perry, ed. *The American Puritans: Their Prose and Poetry*. New York: Doubleday, 1956.

Miller, Perry. *Jonathan Edwards*. New York: Meridian, 1959.

————. *The New England Mind: From Colony to Province*. Boston: Beacon Press, 1961.

————. *The New England Mind: The Seventeenth Century*. Boston: Beacon Press, 1961.

Morgan, Edmund S. *The Puritan Family: Religion and Domestic Relations in Seventeenth-Century New England*. New York: Harper & Row, 1966.

Ramsey, Paul, ed. *Jonathan Edwards: Freedom of Will*. New Haven: Yale University Press, 1957.

Schneider, Herbert W. *The Puritan Mind*. New York: Holt, 1930.

Simpson, Alan. *Puritanism in Old and New England*. Chicago: University of Chicago Press, 1955.

300 *American Ethical Thought*

Smith, John E., ed. *Jonathan Edwards: Religious Affections.* New Haven: Yale University Press, 1959.

Stroh, Guy W. *American Philosophy from Edwards to Dewey: An Introduction.* Princeton: Van Nostrand, 1968.

Ziff, Larzer. *Puritanism in America: New Culture in a New World.* New York: Viking, 1973.

2 — Enlightenment Ethics

Adkins, Nelson F., ed. *Thomas Paine: Common Sense and Other Political Writings.* New York: Bobbs-Merrill, 1953.

Cohen, William. "Thomas Jefferson and the Problem of Slavery." *Journal of American History* 56, 1969.

Commager, Henry Steele. *Jefferson, Nationalism and the Enlightenment.* New York: George Braziller, 1975.

Davis, David B. *The Problem of Slavery in the Age of Revolution 1770-1823.* Ithaca, N.Y.: Cornell University Press, 1975.

Dewey, John. *The Living Thoughts of Thomas Jefferson.* New York: Fawcett, 1957.

Dumbauld, Edward, ed. *The Political Writings of Thomas Jefferson: Representative Selections.* New York: Bobbs-Merrill, 1955.

Jurgenson, C. E., and Mott, F. L., eds. *Benjamin Franklin: Representative Selections.* New York: Hill and Wang, 1962.

Koch, Adrienne, and Peden, William, eds. *The Life and Selected Writings of Thomas Jefferson.* New York: Modern Library, 1944.

Koch, Adrienne, ed. *The American Enlightenment.* New York: George Braziller, 1975.

Koch, Adrienne. *The Philosophy of Thomas Jefferson.* Gloucester, Mass.: Peter Smith, 1957.

Malone, Dumas. *Jefferson and the Ordeal of Liberty.* Boston: Little Brown, 1962.

Melden, A. I., ed. *Human Rights.* Belmont, Cal.: Wadsworth, 1970.

Stroh, Guy W. *American Philosophy from Edwards to Dewey: An Introduction.* Princeton: Van Nostrand, 1968.

3 — Transcendentalist Ethics

Atkinson, Brooks, ed. *The Complete Essays & Other Writings of Ralph Waldo Emerson.* New York: Modern Library, 1940.

Bartlett, I. H., ed. *William Ellery Channing: Unitarian Christianity and Other Essays.* New York: Bobbs-Merrill, 1957.

Bode, Carl, ed. *The Best of Thoreau's Journals.* Carbondale, Southern Illinois University Press, 1967.

Emerson, Ralph Waldo. *Nature, Addresses and Lectures*, Vol. 1, Boston: Houghton Mifflin, 1903.

———. *Miscellanies, Vol. 2.* Boston: Houghton Mifflin, 1960.

———. *The Conduct of Life.* New York: Dolphin Books, n.d.

Frothingham, O. B. *Transcendentalism in New England: A History.* New York: Harper, 1959.

Kant, Immanuel. *Critique of Pure Reason.* New York: American Home Library Co., 1902.

Konvitz, Milton and Whicher, Stephen, eds. *Emerson: A Collection of Critical Essays.* Englewood Cliffs, N.J.: Prentice-Hall, 1962.

Linscott, R. N., ed. *The Journals of Ralph Waldo Emerson.* New York: Modern Library, 1960.

Madden, Edward H. *Civil Disobedience and Moral Law in Nineteenth-Century American Philosophy.* Seattle: University of Washington Press, 1968.

Meyer, D. H. *The Instructed Conscience: The Shaping of the American National Ethic.* Philadelphia: University of Pennsylvania Press, 1972.

Miller, Perry, ed. *The American Transcendentalists: Their Poetry and Prose.* New York: Doubleday, 1957.

Murray, James G. *Henry David Thoreau.* New York: Washington Square Press, 1968.

Porte, Joel. *Emerson and Thoreau: Transcendentalists in Conflict.* Middletown, Conn.: Wesleyan University Press, 1965.

Sherman, Paul, ed. *Thoreau: A Collection of Critical Essays.* Englewood Cliffs, N.J.: Prentice-Hall, 1962.

Simon, Myron, Parson, and Thornton, eds. *Transcendentalism and Its Legacy.* Ann Arbor: University of Michigan Press, 1966.

Staebler, Warren. *Ralph Waldo Emerson.* New York: Washington Square Press, n.d.

Stroh, Guy W. *American Philosophy from Edwards to Dewey.* Princeton: Van Nostrand, 1968.

Thoreau, Henry David. *A Week on the Concord and Merrimack Rivers.* Cambridge: Houghton Mifflin, 1961.

———. *Walden and Civil Disobedience.* New York: Rinehart, 1948.

Whicher, George, ed. *The Transcendentalist Revolt Against Materialism.* Boston: Heath, 1949.

Whicher, Stephen. *Freedom and Fate: An Inner Life of Ralph Waldo Emerson.* Philadelphia: University of Pennsylvania Press, 1953.

4 — Pragmatist Ethics

Brennan, Bernard. *The Ethics of William James.* New Haven: College and University Press, 1961.

Hofstadter, Richard. *Social Darwinism in American Thought.* Boston: Beacon Press, 1944.

James Henry, ed. *The Letters of William James.* 2 vols. Boston: Atlantic Monthly Press, 1920.

James, William. *Essays on Faith and Morals.* New York: Meridian Books, 1962.

———. *The Will to Believe and Other Essays in Popular Philosophy and Human Immortality.* New York: Dover, 1956.

———. *Pragmatism, A New Name for Some Old Ways of Thinking, Together with Four Related Essays Selected from the Meaning of Truth.* New York: Longmans, 1959.

———. *The Varieties of Religious Experience.* New York: Modern Library, 1929.

———. *The Principles of Psychology.* 2 vols. New York: Dover, 1950.

———. *Essays in Radical Empiricism and a Pluralistic Universe.* New York: Longmans, 1958.

———. *The Meaning of Truth: A Sequel to Pragmatism.* Ann Arbor: University of Michigan Press, 1970.

Kennedy, Gail, ed. *Pragmatism and American Culture.* Boston: Heath, 1950.

Marcell, David W. *Progress and Pragmatism: James, Dewey, Beard, and the American Idea of Progress.* Westport, Conn.: Greenwood Press, 1974.

May, Rollo, ed. *Existential Psychology.* New York: Random House, 1961.

Moore, Edward. *William James.* New York: Washington Square Press, 1965.

Perry, Ralph Barton. *The Thought and Character of William James.* New York: Harper, 1964.

_____ *In the Spirit of William James.* Bloomington, Ind.: Indiana University Press, 1958.

_____ *Characteristically American.* New York: Alfred A. Knopf, 1949.

Roth, John K. *Freedom and the Moral Life: The Ethics of William James.* Philadelphia: Westminster Press, 1969.

_____ ed. *The Moral Philosophy of William James.* New York: Crowell, 1969.

_____ ed. *The Moral Equivalent of War and Other Essays.* New York: Harper, 1971.

Stroh, Guy W. *American Philosophy from Edwards to Dewey.* Princeton: Van Nostrand, 1968.

Wiener, Philip P. *Evolution and the Founders of Pragmatism.* Cambridge, Mass.: Harvard University Press, 1949.

Wild, John. *The Radical Empiricism of William James.* Garden City: Anchor Books, 1970.

5 — Idealist Ethics

Barrett, Clifford, ed. *Contemporary Idealism in America.* New York: Russell & Russell, 1964.

Browne, Bordon Parker, *Personalism.* New York: Houghton Mifflin, 1908.

Buckham, J. W., and Stratton, G. M. *George Holmes Howison, Philosopher and Teacher: A Selection from His Writings with a Biographical Sketch.* Berkeley: University of California Press, 1934.

Cotton, James H. *Royce on the Human Self.* Cambridge, Mass.: Harvard University Press, 1954.

Fuss, Peter. *The Moral Philosophy of Josiah Royce.* Cambridge, Mass.: Harvard University Press, 1965.

Marcel, Gabriel. *Royce's Metaphysics.* Chicago: Regnery, 1956.

Powell, Thomas, *Josiah Royce.* New York: Washington Square Press, 1967.

Robinson, Daniel. *Royce and Hocking — American Idealists: An Introduction to Their Philosophy, with Selected Letters.* Boston: Christopher, 1968.

Royce, Josiah. *Lectures on Modern Idealism.* New Haven: Yale University Press, 1964.

_____ *The Religious Aspect of Philosophy.* New York: Harper, 1958.

_____ *The Spirit of Modern Philosophy.* Boston and New York: Houghton Mifflin, 1892.

_____ *Studies of Good and Evil.* New York: Appleton, 1898.

_____ *The World and the Individual.* 2 vols. New York: Dover, 1959.

_____ *The Philosophy of Loyalty.* New York: Macmillan, 1908.

_____ *Race Questions, Provincialism and Other American Problems.* New York: Books for Libraries Press, 1967.

———— *The Sources of Religious Insight.* New York: Charles Scribner's Sons, 1940.

———— *The Problem of Christianity.* 2 vols. New York: Macmillan, 1913.

———— *The Hope of the Great Community.* Freeport, N.Y.: Macmillan, 1967.

Santayana, George. *Character and Opinion in the United States.* New York:·Charles Scribner's Sons, 1924.

Smith, John. *Royce's Social Infinite: The Community of Interpretation.* New York: Liberal Arts Press, 1950.

Smith, John E. *Themes in American Philosophy: Purpose, Experience, and Community.* New York: Harper and Row, 1970.

Stroh, Guy W. *American Philosophy from Edwards to Dewey.* Princeton: Van Nostrand, 1968.

6 — Naturalistic Ethics

Arnett, Willard E. *George Santayana.* New York: Washington Square Press, 1968.

Bernstein, Richard J. *John Dewey.* New York: Washington Square Press, 1967.

Cahn, Steven, ed. *New Studies in the Philosophy of John Dewey.* Hanover, N.H.: University Press of New England, 1977.

Chisholm, R.; Feigl, H.; Frankena, W.; Passmore, J.; and Thompson, M. *Philosophy: Humanistic Scholarship in America.* Englewood Cliffs, N.J.: Prentice-Hall, 1964.

Dewey, John. *Reconstruction in Philosophy.* Boston: Beacon Press, 1960.

———— *The Quest for Certainty: A Study of the Relation of Knowledge and Action,* New York: Capricorn, 1960.

———— *Theory of Valuation.* Vols. 1 and 2. Chicago: University of Chicago Press, 1939:

———— *Theory of the Moral Life.* New York: Holt, Rinehart and Winston, 1960.

———— *Human Nature and Conduct: An Introduction to Social Psychology.* New York: Holt, 1922.

———— *Freedom and Culture.* New York: Putnam, 1939.

———— *The Public and Its Problems.* New York: Holt, 1927.

———— *On Experience, Nature, and Freedom: Representative Selections.* New York: Liberal Arts Press, 1960.

———— *Philosophy and Civilization.* New York: Capricorn Books, 1963.

———— *Democracy and Education: An Introduction to the Philosophy of Education.* New York: Macmillan, 1961.

———— *Liberalism and Social Action.* New York: Capricorn Books, 1963.

———— *Outlines of a Critical Theory of Ethics.* New York: Hillary House, 1967.

———— and, Tufts, James H. *Ethics.* New York: Holt, 1932.

———— *Moral Principles in Education.* New York: Philosophical Library, 1959.

Gouinlock, James. *John Dewey's Philosophy of Value.* New York: Humanities Press, 1972.

Hendel, Charles W., ed. *John Dewey and the Experimental Spirit in Philosophy.* New York: Liberal Arts Press, 1959.

Krikorian, Yervant H., ed. *Naturalism and the Human Spirit.* New York: Columbia University Press, 1944.

Lachs, John., ed. *Animal Faith and Spiritual Life, Previously Unpublished and Uncollected Writings by George Santayana with Critical Essays on His Thought.* New York: Appleton-Century-Crofts, 1967.

Lachs, John, and Lachs, Shirley, eds. *Physical Order and Moral Liberty, Previously Unpublished Essays of George Santayana.* Charlotte, N. C.: Vanderbilt University Press, 1969.

Moore, G. E. *Principia Ethica.* Cambridge: Cambridge University Press, 1959.

Munitz, Milton K. *The Moral Philosophy of Santayana.* New York: Humanities Press, 1958.

Santayana, George. *Winds of Doctrine, and Platonism and the Spiritual Life.* New York: Harper, 1957.

_____ *The Life of Reason: The Phases of Human Progress.* New York: Collier Books, 1962.

_____ *Realms of Being.* New York: Charles Scribner's Sons, 1942.

_____ "Apologia Pro Mente Sua." In *The Philosophy of George Santayana,* ed. Paul Arthur Schilpp. New York: Tudor, 1940.

_____ *Dominations and Powers: Reflections on Liberty, Society and Government.* New York: Charles Scribner's Sons, 1951.

_____ *The Sense of Beauty: Being the Outlines of Aesthetic Theory.* New York: Charles Scribner's Sons, 1896.

_____ *Character and Opinion in the United States.* New York: Norton, 1967.

Schilpp, Paul Arthur, ed. *The Philosophy of George Santayana.* New York: Tudor, 1951.

_____ ed. *The Philosophy of John Dewey.* New York: Tudor, 1951,

Sprigge, Timothy L. S. *Santayana: An Examination of his Philosophy.* London: Routledge and Kegan Paul, 1974.

Stroh, Guy W. *American Philosophy from Edwards to Dewey.* Princeton: Van Nostrand, 1968.

Warnock, G. J. *Contemporary Moral Philosophy.* London: Macmillan, 1967.

Wilson, Douglas L., ed. *The Genteel Tradition, Nine Essays by George Santayana.* Cambridge, Mass. Harvard University Press, 1967.

7 — Recent Directions in Ethical Analysis

Aiken, Henry D. *Reason and Conduct: New Bearings in Moral Philosophy.* New York: Alfred A. Knopf, 1962.

Barry, Brian. *The Liberal Theory of Justice: A Critical Examination of the Principal Doctrines in a Theory of Justice by John Rawls.* London: Oxford University Press, 1973.

Bedau, Hugo A, ed. *The Death Penalty in America: An Anthology.* New York: Doubleday, 1967.

Blanchard, Brand. *Reason and Goodness.* London: George Allen and Unwin, 1961.

Brandt, R. B. *Ethical Theory.* Englewood Cliffs, N.J.: Prentice-Hall, 1959.

Chisholm, R.; Feigl, H.; Frankena, W.; Passmore, J.; and Thompson, M., eds. *Philosophy: Humanistic Scholarship in America.* The Princeton Studies. Englewood Cliffs, N.J.: Prentice-Hall, 1964.

Cohen, M.; Nagel, T.; and Scanlan, T., eds. *The Rights and Wrongs of Abortion.* Princeton: Princeton University Press, 1974.

_____ *War and Moral Responsibility.* Princeton: Princeton University Press, 1974.

Cox, Harvey, ed. *The Situation Ethics Debate.* Philadelphia: Westminster Press, 1968.

Edwards, Paul. *The Logic of Moral Discourse.* Glencoe, Ill.: Free Press, 1955.

Ezorsky, G., ed. *Philosophical Perspectives on Punishment.* Albany: State University of New York Press, 1972.

Feibleman, James K. *Moral Strategy.* The Hague: Martinus Nijhoff, 1967.

Feinberg, Joel, ed. *Moral Concepts.* London: Oxford University Press, 1969.

———. *Doing and Deserving, Essays in the Theory of Responsibility.* Princeton: Princeton University Press, 1970.

Fletcher, Joseph. *Moral Responsibility: Situation Ethics at Work.* Philadelphia: Westminster Press, 1967.

———. *Moral Medicine; The Moral Problems of the Patient's Right to Know the Truth, Contraception, Artificial Insemination, Sterilization, Euthanasia.* ——— Beacon Press, 1960.

———. *The Ethics of Genetic Control: Ending Reproductive Roulette.* New York: Anchor Press, 1974.

———. *Situation Ethics: The New Morality.* Philadelphia: Westminster Press, 1966.

Frankena, William K. *Ethics.* Englewood Cliffs, N.J.: Prentice-Hall, 1963.

Fuller, Lon L. *The Morality of Law.* New Haven: Yale University Press, 1964.

Goodpaster, K. E., ed. *Perspectives on Morality: Essays by William K. Frankena.* Notre Dame, Ind.: University of Notre Dame Press, 1976.

Goheen, John D., and Mothershead, John L., eds. *Collected Papers of Clarence Irving Lewis.* Stanford: Stanford University Press, 1970.

Hall, Robert T. *The Morality of Civil Disobedience.* New York: Harper and Row, 1971.

Hancock, Roger N. *Twentieth-Century Ethics.* New York: Columbia University Press, 1974.

Hook, Sidney. *The Paradoxes of Freedom.* Berkeley and Los Angeles: University of California Press, 1967.

———. ed. *Determinism and Freedom in the Age of Modern Science.* New York: Collier Books, 1961.

Hudson, W. D., ed. *The Is-Ought Question, A Collection of Papers on the Central Problem in Moral Philosophy.* London: Macmillan, 1969.

Kaplan, Abraham. *American Ethics and Public Policy.* New York: Oxford University Press, 1961.

Kent, Edward, ed. *Revolution and the Rule of Law.* Englewood Cliffs, N.J.: Prentice-Hall, 1971.

Kerner, George C. *The Revolution in Ethical Theory.* New York: Oxford University Press, 1966.

Lange, John, ed. *Clarence Irving Lewis, Values and Imperatives: Studies in Ethics.* Stanford: Stanford University Press, 1969.

Lewis, C. I. *Mind and the World Order: Outline of a Theory of Knowledge.* New York: Charles Scribner's Sons, 1929.

———. *An Analysis of Knowledge and Valuation.* LaSalle, Ill.: Open Court Publishing Co., 1946.

———. *The Ground and Nature of the Right.* New York: Columbia University Press, 1955.

———. *Our Social Inheritance.* Bloomington, Ind.: Indiana University Press, 1957.

Margolis, Joseph. *Values and Conduct.* New York: Oxford University Press, 1971.

———. *Psychotheraphy and Morality, A Study of Two Concepts.* New York: Random House, 1966.

———. *Negativities: The Limits of Life.* Columbus: Charles Merrill Co., 1975.

Melden, A. I. *Rights and Persons.* Berkeley: University of California Press, 1977.

Melden, A. I., ed. *Essays in Moral Philosophy.* Seattle: University of Washington Press, 1958.

Murphy, Jeffrie G., ed. *Civil Disobedience and Violence*. Belmont, Cal.: Wadsworth, 1971.

Noonan, John T. Jr., ed. *The Morality of Abortion, Legal and Historical Perspectives*. Cambridge, Mass.: Harvard University Press, 1970.

Northrop, F. S. C. *The Complexity of Legal and Ethical Experience: Studies in the Method of Normative Subjects*. Boston: Little, Brown, 1959.

Olafson, Frederick A. *Ethics and Twentieth-Century Thought*. Englewood Cliffs, N.J.: Prentice-Hall, 1973.

Pepper, Stephen C. *Ethics*. New York: Appleton-Century Crofts, 1960.

Rawls, John. *A Theory of Justice*. Cambridge, Mass.: Harvard University Press, 1971.

Ramsey, Paul. *Deeds and Rules in Christian Ethics*. New York: Charles Scribner's Sons, 1967.

_____ *Fabricated Man: The Ethics of Genetic Control*. New Haven: Yale University Press, 1970.

Saydah, S. Roger. *The Ethical Theory of Clarence Irving Lewis*. Athens: Ohio University Press, 1969.

Searle, John R. *Speech Acts: An Essay in the Philosophy of Language*. London: Cambridge University Press, 1969.

Sellars, W. S., and Hospers, J., eds. *Readings in Ethical Theory*. New York: Appleton-Century-Crofts, 1952.

Singer, Marcus. *Generalization in Ethics, An Essay in the Logic of Ethics, with Rudiments of a System of Moral Philosophy*. New York: Alfred A. Knopf, 1961.

Stace, W. T. *The Concept of Morals*. New York: Macmillan, 1937.

Stevenson, Charles L. *Ethics and Language*. New Haven: Yale University Press, 1944.

_____ *Facts and Values: Studies in Ethical Analysis*. New Haven: Yale University Press, 1963.

Urmson, J. O. *The Emotive Theory of Ethics*. New York: Oxford University Press, 1968.

Warnock, G. J. *Contemporary Moral Philosophy*. London: Macmillan, 1967.

Author
Index

Subject
Index